THE MOTHER IN PSYC
AND BEYOND

The question of what it means to be a mother is a very contentious topic in psychoanalysis and in wider society. *The Mother in Psychoanalysis and Beyond* explores our relationship to the maternal through psychoanalysis, philosophy, art, and political and gender studies.

Over two years, a group of psychotherapists and members of the public met at the Philadelphia Association for a series of seminars on the Maternal. In the discussions that followed, a chasm opened up slowly and painfully between the idealised longings and fantasies we all share and the realities of maternal experiences: here were met the great silences of love, loss, longing, memories, desire, hatred and ambivalence. This book is the result of this bringing together in conversation and reflections of what so often seems unsayable about the Mother. It examines how issues of personal and gender identity are shaped by the ideals of separation from the mother, the fears and anxiety of merging with the mother, and how this has often led, in psychoanalysis and society, to holding mothers responsible for a variety of personal and social ills, and problems in which maternal vulnerability is denied and silenced.

There are two main themes running throughout the book: Matricide and Maternal Subjectivity. On the theme of matricide, several contributors discuss the ways in which the discourse and narratives of the Mother have been silenced on a sociocultural level and within psychoanalysis and philosophy in favour of discourses that promote independence, autonomy, power, and the avoidance and denial of our fundamental helplessness and vulnerability. On the theme of maternal subjectivity, several chapters look at the actual experience of mothering and/or our relationship to our mother, to highlight the ways in which the maternal is intimately connected with human subjectivity.

The Mother in Psychoanalysis and Beyond provides new and provocative thinking on the maternal and its place in various contemporary discourses. It will appeal to psychoanalysts, psychotherapists and psychologists of different schools, scholars and advanced students of art, gender studies, politics and philosophy as well as anyone interested in maternity studies and the relationship between the maternal and human subjectivity.

Rosalind Mayo and **Christina Moutsou** are senior psychoanalytic psychotherapists and writers working in private practice in the UK. Christina is a visiting lecturer of psychoanalytic psychotherapy at Regent's University.

'The mothering that, one way and another, informs psychoanalytic treatment – and the mothers that haunt psychoanalytic theory – have been, perhaps unsurprisingly, difficult to write well about. In these remarkably illuminating and various essays, that are unusually both evocative and informative, we begin to get a new sense of what it might be to write about the so-called maternal without sentimentality or the rigours of abstraction. This is a more than useful and telling collection of writings.'

– Adam Phillips, psychoanalyst and writer

'This is where psychoanalysis meets existential reality, when mothers describe their deeply felt experience allowing us to move from mythology and theory to the everyday reality of the rawness of the mothering experience.'

**– Professor Emmy van Deurzen, Principal,
New School of Psychotherapy and Counselling**

'This is an extraordinary book. The editors, highly respected thinkers and psychoanalysts, have generated a remarkable collection of contributions by a diverse and impressive group of contributors who address one of the most central questions that therapists of all persuasions must ponder: what does it really mean to be a mother, and how have the relationships all of us experienced with our own mothers affected who we are as human beings? This book should be required reading for every therapist, whatever their orientation. A stunning achievement!'

**– Professor M. Guy Thompson, author of *The Death
of Desire: An existential study in sanity and madness,
Second edition* (Routledge)**

'This is a brilliant book of enormous value to anyone with an interest in the origins and outcomes of our most complex, ambivalent and enriching relationship. My mother died at Easter and I have found here a handbook to understand the contradictions of mothering. How to reconcile the intimacy of growing inside another human being, to the stranger that she and maybe we all become to our daughters and sons. It is a courageous, intellectually prescient, and unhesitating look at the schism between the truth and dreams of motherhood. There are passages of great beauty and emotion. Read it.'

**– Belona Greenwood, journalist, scriptwriter,
and founder and co-organiser
of Words and Women**

THE MOTHER IN PSYCHOANALYSIS AND BEYOND

Matricide and maternal subjectivity

Edited by Rosalind Mayo and Christina Moutsou

Routledge
Taylor & Francis Group

LONDON AND NEW YORK

First published 2017
by Routledge
2 Park Square, Milton Park, Abingdon, Oxon OX14 4RN

and by Routledge
711 Third Avenue, New York, NY 10017

Routledge is an imprint of the Taylor & Francis Group, an informa business

© 2017 selection and editorial matter, Rosalind Mayo and Christina Moutsou; individual chapters, the contributors

British Library Cataloguing-in-Publication Data
A catalogue record for this book is available from the British Library

Library of Congress Cataloging-in-Publication Data
A catalog record for this book has been requested

ISBN: 978-1-138-88504-2 (hbk)
ISBN: 978-1-138-88505-9 (pbk)
ISBN: 978-1-315-71530-8 (ebk)

Typeset in BemboStd
by codeMantra

CONTENTS

LIST OF CONTRIBUTORS

The Editors

Rosalind Mayo is a senior psychoanalytical psychotherapist who trained at the Philadelphia Association (PA), London where she was a member of the teaching faculty, and also held several positions over the years, including Chair of Ethics and Chair of the PA. Her academic background is theology and philosophy from King's College London and Heythrop. She is an Associate of King's College. Prior to training as a therapist, her working background was in teaching, working with the long-term unemployed with 'mental health' issues; and group development work, particularly for women. She is still involved in various types of groups for women. She works and lives in King's Lynn, Norfolk. She has co-edited with Paul Gordon and contributed in *Between Psychotherapy and Philosophy* (Whurr 2004). Current projects include a book on the mystic Margery Kempe of Lynn, and her relation to the dominance of particular images and narratives of female subjectivity in Christianity in the twenty-first century. Email: Rosalindmayo@aol.com

Christina Moutsou was born in London in 1972 and grew up in Thessaloniki, Greece. From 1996–1998 she was an EU TMR doctoral fellow doing research on ethnic representation and cosmopolitanism in Brussels towards her Ph.D. in social anthropology at the University of Cambridge (obtained in 1999). Subsequently, she trained with the PA and upon qualification in 2002, she was involved in reopening and setting up the Freegrove therapeutic community with Paul Gordon, which she ran with him for five years. Christina has taught psychotherapy at various training and university courses including the PA introductory course and training, CHT, NSPC, teaching Freudian psychoanalysis at Birkbeck and teaching and running a supervision group at the University of Hertfordshire. She has a number of publications on the cusp of anthropology and psychotherapy and is one of the co-editors and a contributor in another two books, *Crossing European Boundaries* with Jaro Stacul and Helen Kopnina (Berghahn 2006) and *Rethinking Audit Cultures* with Lucy King (PCCS 2010). For the last three years, she has been working on a novel in which the maternal, the erotic, the intertwining of the past and the present and the importance of our unconscious connections with others are central themes. She juggles being a full-time mother with her private practice, her writing and supervising phenomenological research in psychotherapy, mainly for NSPC. Christina is a member of the Relational School. She lives and practises in Queen's Park, NW London. Christina is a visiting lecturer at Regent's University. Email: cmoutsou@gmail.com, Website: www.space-for-thinking.co.uk

Contributors

Melissa Benn is a writer, journalist and campaigner. As a freelance writer, her essays and journalism have appeared in a wide range of publications, including *The Independent*, *The Times*, *The London Review of Books*, *Cosmopolitan* and *Public Finance*. She is a regular contributor to *The Guardian* and *New Statesman*. Melissa has written, or edited, seven books, including two novels. Her non-fiction works include *Madonna and Child: Towards a New Politics of Motherhood* (1998). Melissa is a regular speaker and broadcaster. She has written and presented several Radio Four programmes and has spoken at the Hay, Edinburgh, Bath and Cheltenham literary festivals, among many others. In September 2013, she published *What Should We Tell Our Daughters? The Pleasures and Pressures of Growing Up Female,* an exploration of young women's lives from the perspective of a feminist in midlife and mother of teenagers. She is an active campaigner for comprehensive education. In 2011 her book *School Wars: The Battle for Britain's Education* provoked widespread debate, and in late 2015 Routledge published *The Truth About Our Schools: Exploding the Myths, Exploring the Evidence,* which Melissa co-authored with Janet Downs. Melissa lives in London with her husband, a psychotherapist and writer, and has two daughters, now in higher education. Email: mbenn@dircon.co.uk, Website: www.melissabenn.com

Pat Blackett was born in Libya in 1958. She grew up on the coast in Kent. Her parents met in France during the Second World War, her father was English and her mother French. She is the youngest of four children. She graduated from Reading University with a degree in typography and graphic communication in 1981. She then worked in publishing and worked for *The Guardian* and *The Observer* until 2005 when she became a freelance administrator working for psychoanalytic organisations. She has been studying and teaching astrology for over 30 years and is a member of the Company of Astrologers. She is also involved in animal welfare and is a volunteer for Pets as Therapy.

Alison Davies is a psychotherapist and supervisor who trained with the Philadelphia Association. She is also a trained music therapist. Based in Cambridge, she has experience working in the NHS and in private practice. Her particular interest has been group work. A recent co-edited book, *Group Music Therapy: A Group Analytic Approach*, published by Routledge (2014) illustrates her interest in communication in therapy groups both verbally and non-verbally through music. She is both a musician (LRAM and ARCM) and an artist (Masters in Fine Art). Website: www.alisonbronwendavies.uk

Lakis K. Georghiou is relatively new to psychotherapy having finished his UKCP recognised training at the Philadelphia Association in 2013. He is also a member of the dental profession and teaches undergraduates. He is currently studying for an MA in clinical education. He is very interested in how contemporary psychoanalysis can both inform the phenomenological and existential underpinning of his training and contribute to gender relations. He hopes to continue to incorporate his psychotherapy to assist in both the welfare of his students and the dental profession at large. He lives in London and is married with a family. Email: lg.hygeia@virgin.net

Kate Gilbert was born in 1952 and educated by the sisters of Notre Dame, Northampton (1964–1971). She graduated in modern languages from London University in 1974, completed the post-graduate Certificate in Education in 1975 and taught French and Spanish at the secondary level. She married in 1975 and gave birth to two children in 1979 and 1981. In the early 1980s, while doing an MA in romance studies at London University, she became interested in Lacan's *Ecrits*, his rereading of Freud, and the writings of Foucault, Kristeva and Barthes. In the mid-1980s, she completed an Infant Observation course at the Tavistock, trained in humanistic psychotherapy at the Gestalt Centre and developed a private practice in Hove. Having become increasingly interested in the effects of the unconscious, she decided to train in psychoanalytic psychotherapy with the PA. She graduated in 2002 and developed a full psychoanalytic practice in North London. She has taught on various psychotherapy trainings and is a governor on the board of The College of Psychoanalysts. Her current interests involve research into the effects of psychotherapy on the symptoms of multiple sclerosis, and the possibility of psychotherapy treatments of post-war trauma in the Balkans. Kate has been married for 40 years and has 5 grandchildren. Email: gilbertkate@hotmail.com

Jane Haynes trained as a Jungian psychoanalyst, but she now works primarily as a relational psychotherapist through 'dialogue'. She is a founding member of a new multidisciplinary private clinic: www.thebluedoorpractice.com along with her daughter Tanya in Marylebone. She is also a consultant to the Eastern European Institute for Psychoanalytic Studies in St. Petersburg. She is the author of several journal publications and books including a co-edited book (with Juliet Miller) on psychological aspects of infertility and assisted reproduction: *Inconceivable Conceptions* (Routledge 2003). A memoir *Who Is It That Can Tell Me Who I Am?* with a foreword by Hilary Mantel was shortlisted for the PEN J.R. Ackerley literary autobiography prize. Her latest book, *Doctors Dissected* with Martin Scurr (Quartet Books Ltd. 2015) is concerned with the inner lives and emotional health of GPs (paperback due in January 2016 with a new foreword by Professor Mike Pringle, President of the Royal College of General Practitioners).

Amber Jacobs is a feminist theorist and writer and teaches in the department of psychosocial studies, Birkbeck College. Her work is concerned with the question of postpatriarchal futures in the fields of feminist philosophy, psychoanalysis, visual culture and social theory. Her book *On Matricide: Myth, Psychoanalysis, and the Law of the Mother* (Columbia University Press 2006) has become a key text in feminist theory. She lives in London with her family. http://www.bbk.ac.uk/psychosocial/our-staff/full-time-academic-staff/amber-jacobs

Melike Kayhan was raised in Istanbul and moved to England in 1992, where she lived and worked in Oxford and London for 21 years. She has a Master's degree in gender, culture and politics from Birkbeck College, London University. Her dissertation included a field study of a group of men from an ethnic community drawing on psychoanalysis. She trained in psychoanalytic psychotherapy with the Philadelphia Association. In January 2013, she returned to Istanbul and started working at the Marital Therapy Institute as a couple and family therapist, before setting up the Face to Face Therapia-Psychoanalysis, Psychotherapy and Marital Therapy Centre at Levent in Istanbul. She is influenced by phenomenological and philosophical thinking, but her practice is largely based on psychoanalytic psychotherapy and psychoanalysis. Email: facetofaceterapi@gmail.com, Website: www.facetofaceterapi.com

Lucy King has trained at the Philadelphia Association and is the current chair of the PA. She is a senior psychotherapist working in Cambridge where she has previously studied and done research as a biologist. She is the author of several publications and co-edited books including more recently *Rethinking Audit Cultures* with Christina Moutsou questioning the current NHS audit culture for talking therapies. She co-edited with Rosemary Randal *The Future of Psychoanalytic Psychotherapy* (Whurr 2003) and edited and contributed to *Committed Uncertainty in Psychotherapy* (Whurr 1999). Email: lk10000@cam.ac.uk

Barbara Latham grew up in New Zealand. From 1972, she began training at the Philadelphia Association in London, with R.D. Laing and others, to become a psychotherapist. She works in London as a therapist and supervisor and continues to enjoy teaching at the PA. Barbara is also a writer, and these two activities, psychotherapy and writing fiction, have informed each other. Her website at www.barbaralatham.co.uk has many of her short stories as well as other papers. A memoir is currently being completed.

Eti Wade is a visual and conceptual artist identifying as a mother artist. She has three sons and has been making work about motherhood since the birth of her middle son in 2000. Her work is included in the Brooklyn Museum Feminist Artist Database and the Birthrites Collection at Salford University. Wade has recently exhibited her first solo show *On a (m)other's watch* at Goldsmith's University, London (curated by Samantha Lippett) and was recently included in the Afterbirth Project exhibition at Whitemoose Gallery Barnstaple, *The Egg, the Womb, the Head and the Moon* exhibition at ArtsMill, Hebden Bridge (2014), and the 'identity and the self' exhibition at the Garis and Hahn Gallery in New York (2013). Eti regularly publishes and lectures about the new maternalist aesthetics and contemporary maternal art practices, recently giving papers at the Museum of Motherhood conference in New York, the MIRCI conference in Rome, Italy and the Motherhood and Creative Practice at London South Bank University. She is a photography and arts educator and has run the photography MA at the University of West London. Wade is currently working on her doctoral thesis: *The Mother as Subject and Author in Contemporary Visual Art*. Website: http://www.etiwade.com/

Lynda Woodroffe started her working career as a science teacher in London schools before becoming an advisory teacher to science teachers in 1987. In 1992, Lynda gained a Master's degree in science education from the Institute of Education, London University. She later worked in London University (the Institute of Education and University College London) as an administrative officer while studying for a Ph.D. and as a researcher working on systematic reviews of research studies in education. In 2006 she left research work to train to be an integrative psychotherapist/counsellor at the Minster Centre, London. After qualifying with the Diploma in Counselling in 2008, Lynda then practised in NW London. At the same time, she attended the last part of the course in integrative psychotherapy and counselling at the Master's degree level, gaining the MA in 2011. She has continued to work as an integrative psychotherapist to date. She is also on the editorial board of the online journal *Contemporary Psychotherapy* (www.contemporarypsychotherapy.org) and has published several articles and reviews on this journal. Website: www.lyndawoodroffe.co.uk

FOREWORD

Françoise Barbira Freedman[1]

This edited volume, gestated in seminars of the Philadelphia Association, carries the gentle rebel genes of local ancestors. As an encompassing polysemic concept, 'the maternal' both explodes and implodes a perceived central dissociation in Freud's group that R.D. Laing was reluctant to engage with: what lies in the shadow of Oedipus? As one of the authors puts it, following Winnicott's apt avoidance of reifications, 'there is no such thing as "the maternal": there is a birth mother and someone who has to care for an infant'.[2] The editors set out to retrieve the complex layers of theory, experience and representation that allow us to access our relation to the 'mother' without predicating the necessity of matricide for the emergence of self, feminine or masculine. Metis – whose rape and ingestion by Zeus created Athena, subsequently born from Zeus' forehead – is called upon to rethink the cultural sources of our current patriarchal ideal of performative womanhood.

The Greek goddesses that provide an Ariadne's thread through the maze of questions raised by the dominant Oedipus model are still dominated by the leadership of Athena. We may be drawn to Aphrodite but can she pull her weight in the board room? The contours of Metis's personality are blurred; Hestia is so domestic we cannot side with her if we rally with the historical Euroamerican feminist movement, even in the most tenuous way; Artemis and Demeter are more complex but less explored figures. The Oresteia herald this book: the revenge murder of Clytemnestra by her son, which Luce Irigaray saw as the matricide fundamental to the patriarchal imaginary, provides a backdrop for the scenes unveiled in the book.

Without meandering too far along a phenomenological path, the editors interweave the multifarious authors' contributions around themes that allow for the reclaiming of subjectivity and agency. Each of the contributions takes to task the sociocultural Pandora's box of our Judeo-Christian tradition and its critiques about matters related to 'the maternal', from Marianism to contradictions inherent in gender roles for migrants in multi-ethnic Britain. Some authors offer keys, others provide metaphors, stories, references or cross-cultural quandaries. Others write about their artistic creativity. The tensions and contradictions inherent in maternity and the experience of motherhood, as first exposed by Adrienne Rich, are presented not so much as painfully incarcerating women in bodies silenced and alienated by patriarchy than as foundations of self-expression. There is an inspiring and salutary atmosphere of exploration. At times the reader feels the deep draw that must have brought the seminar groups together to produce this book. While visual arts and writing offer means to heal deep wounds caused by abandonment and neglect, this book stands out in its compassionate, open-ended outlook.

How much are we mourning and longing for the Mother, a seemingly ever elusive, imaginary figure we must separate from to grow into ourselves as males and perhaps even more so as females? Is this our human heritage, the price paid for the long period of dependency caused by our immature large brains at birth? Does 'the Maternal' take different forms across cultures in space and time? It is pertinent that the dawn of anthropology as an academic subject, at the time when Freud was forming his thinking, revolved around the precedence of matriarchy and the evolutionary superiority of patriarchy. The complexity of gender relations in matrilineal societies – in which the mother's brother enjoys greater authority than paternal figures – did not filter through general discussions to the extent of questioning the earlier theories of mother-right and father-right. Yet, here we find a clear rejoinder, located between current approaches to kinship as 'relatedness' and 'nurture.' The questioning of muted maternal subjectivity is informed by the disciplines of social anthropology and divinity studies as well as by psychoanalysis and psychotherapy.

Can 'the Maternal' be best approached through narratives? Given the plethora of books and articles on issues related to matricide, a major contribution of this volume may be the use of enlightened narratives by psychotherapists from different backgrounds, writing about their resolutions as both experiential and professional. At the time of reading I was assisting my daughter with the birth of her first baby, a girl, also my first grandchild. The experience of a relatively easy home birth, with a birth pool set in our garden studio and a team consisting of my daughter's loving partner and his mother, besides two midwives from the NHS home birth team in Cambridge, was both elating and anomalous. If more than 1% of women experienced this transition to motherhood in the United Kingdom (where gratefully this is an officially open option in maternity care), can we dare imagine the implications for facilitating the foundations of early attachment and also for healing and consolidating maternal bonds? Of course my question is a rhetorical one because I fiercely believe this to be the case and work to support women in achieving more fulfilling experiences of maternity through body-based practices. Yet my daughter's experience, coupled with reading the narratives in this book, caused me to revisit many aspects of relationships in our female lineage to the ascending third generation in a way that I had not anticipated.

My first birth took place in the Cambridge maternity hospital in the midst of a long-term anthropological fieldwork in the Peruvian Upper Amazon where I subsequently returned with my baby. I was not just proficient in the language but also in the local culture of maternity within an animistic gendered cosmos where complementarity rules are supreme. My legacy is one of sharing the lives of a people whose everyday preoccupation is to maintain the precarious balance between male and female through generations and in the cosmos as a whole. This they do in small local groups in which three or four generations of women are involved in the raising of babies, and many, if not all, men are closely involved. The gentle lessons of acceptance and self-acceptance that some of the authors of the book convey through their narratives take me back to the equanimity of my indigenous mothers and sisters that I was socialized to embody. Amazonian forest people have their myths of matricide and, as with Daphne, the bodies of the mutilated mothers give rise to wondrous plants, including tobacco. But these myths are firmly in the time of the ancestors, long ago. Rather, it is the daily celebration and grind of life together that provide a grid to question, interpret, understand, heal and accept the wonders of maternal intimacy and its transformations through the lifecycle.

This book carries a longing to bridge and reconcile archetypes and the current plurality of voices and experiences. The preservation of tensions throughout the book, with no attempt to tie the knots either of the warp or the weave at the end, is a strength. In an Amazonian scenario fuelled by people's familiarity with the use of the psychotropic substances that R.D. Laing was known to use, one could imagine Metis being regurgitated or perhaps retrieved from Zeus's entrails surgically. There could then follow a dialogue between her and Athena. Mother and daughter would find each other again or anew, like Persephone who visits her mother Demeter periodically out of the underworld.

Besides our individual, ever unquenched quest for the mother we never completely know but long to be close to at this conjuncture in sociocultural world history, there may also be a longing for cross-generational female groups now rare on the margins of world society. Perhaps 'the maternal' is best conceived in the plural, inclusive of the women we call grandmothers, sisters and daughters in our respective human groups of affiliation.

Notes

1 Medical Anthropologist, University of Cambridge and Founder/Director, Birthlight Trust.
2 Latham, Chapter 9.

PREFACE

Like all of us, this book has been born of a mother. Unlike with humans though, the maternal origin of a book is not always such a straightforward question. We first came together in April 2010 to explore our common interest in the Mother, from a personal, theoretical and psychotherapy point of view; and a social, political and ethical perspective. We were vaguely aware of the affinity of our own sensibilities on the maternal. We met repeatedly discussing ideas, experience, thinking of possible wider forums for our conversations, and also, having fun in the process! We were both senior members of the Philadelphia Association (PA), nearly contemporaries in our training, although Ros was there earlier in the history of the PA, when the organisation was shaken by a bitter split and Christina joined just at the aftermath of that. Our conversations eventually took the form of the 'Maternal Seminars', a name we gave them, which we hoped would invite questions as well as a creative response and a wish to become engaged.

The seminars were held at the PA from January 2011 to July 2013. The title was also somewhat ironic and perhaps provocative, as the PA was known to harbour more of a 'paternal' spirit through its history of being founded by R.D. Laing in the 1960s. Although, as one of the contributors recalls, Laing also had questions about 'the mother' both personal and clinical (see Jane Haynes, Chapter 3). It was also not a secret in such a small organisation that a striking number of members had histories of having felt painfully unmothered, but also some were feeling so within the organisation. Although of course in reality, feeling unmothered may have more generic links with being a psychotherapist.[1] To begin to acknowledge the hard to conceptualise wounds around the maternal that draw many to the world of psychotherapy, the seminars and our book project aimed to address the importance of our relation to the Mother, as connected with the inherent vulnerability of being human.

It had long been recognised in the PA that many people wishing to train there were looking for a place to be — a 'home'. Indeed the PA does have a long and respected tradition and practice of community homes-houses; another strand in the maternal matrix. But the PA is also well known for its critical stance and questioning of mental illness as pathology, and within this framework it offers a radical critique of psychoanalytic theory and practice from an existential and phenomenological perspective. Such a critical tradition we hoped to sustain and revive in the seminars and to harbour as part of the present book and our psychotherapy *origins* from the PA.

And yet, ironically, given this radical stance, when it came to questions on the maternal-mother, in the PA, as throughout almost all psychotherapy organisations and trainings, the texts on the matter were almost all psychoanalytically informed, Bion, Winnicott, Freud, Stern, Klein, Green, Kristeva, mostly 'male narratives' on the maternal-mother, which almost all without exception pathologise and/or idealise. And yet from as far back as the 1970s, and coming predominantly from feminists and female philosophers who had been 'allowed' entry into the male sanctuary, there have been many incisive, provocative, and detailed analyses and critiques of the 'Canon of Male Philosophy', from the ancient philosophy of the Stoics, Plato, Socrates and Aristotle through to Rousseau, Kant, the Enlightenment (sic), Heidegger, Lacan, Derrida and Levinas. For example, Marion Iris Young's critique of the Phenomenology of Merleau–Ponty and more recently, the work of Stone Butler, Cavarero and Oliver.[2]

We were lucky to foster a space of lively debate and to cover a range of fascinating topics during the maternal seminars. Some of the speakers were PA members and students nearing qualification, but many were external with an impressive record of publications on the topic. Most of the chapters constituting this book are a written version of the original papers given in the PA during the maternal seminars. We would like to thank all the contributors to this book, but also the speakers who were not able to give us a written version of their paper: Daniela Bruni and Pamela Stewart for joining with us, and creating a lively and thought-provoking debate. We would also like to thank the Philadelphia Association for hosting the seminars, including funding any costs involved, and allowing some space for 'the maternal'. A special thank you goes to Pat Blackett and Lakis Georghiou who both provided a lot of support throughout the project. We would also like to thank wholeheartedly Kate Hawes, the editor of the psychoanalysis section at Routledge for her encouraging response to our proposal and giving us the opportunity to turn it into a book and, finally, Charles Bath and all other staff at Routledge who have further assisted us in the process.

Notes

1 There has been much speculation recently (such as in psychotherapy research) and less so about the reasons for which somebody may choose to train as a psychotherapist. Therapists have been called 'the wounded healer' adopting Jung's now infamous term and psychotherapy has been referred to as 'the impossible

profession'. It is not the place here to expand and think critically about such arguments, but certainly the link alluded to is between psychotherapy and difficulties around giving and/or receiving mothering.

2 For an analysis and citation of the recent philosophical critique by feminist philosophers of the lack of representation of female experience in male-centred writing, see Introduction. However, as long ago as the eleventh and twelfth century women like Hildergaard of Bingen and Heloise apropos Abelard were writing philosophy on being a woman in a man's world. Also, see Hannah Arendt and her concept of *natality*.

ACKNOWLEDGEMENTS

Introduction: We wish to thank the University of Minnesota Press for its very kind permission to use the quotation from Helen Cixous featured at the start of the Introduction ("I look for myself throughout the centuries and I don't see myself anywhere.") From Helen Cixous and Catherine Clement *Sorties: Out and Out: Attacks/Ways Out/Forays*.

From *The Newly Born Woman*, Translated by Betsy Wing, pp. 63–132.
Minneapolis, MN: University of Minnesota Press, 1986.
Original French language edition, copyright 1975 by Union Generale d'Editions, Paris.
English translation, copyright 1986 by the University of Minnesota.
111 Third Avenue South, Suite 290
Minneapolis, MN 55401

Chapter 3: A previous version of Jane Haynes' chapter appeared in the *Kings College Cambridge Review* in December 2014. We wish to acknowledge the kind permission of KCR in granting us their permission for its republication here, which is an extended and rewritten version.

Chapter 10: A previous version of Melissa Benn's chapter appeared in the Breakpoint chapter in *What Should We Tell Our Daughters? The Pleasures and Pressures of Growing Up Female* (John Murray/Hodder & Stoughton, 2013). We wish to acknowledge the kind permission of John Murray for granting us their permission for its republication here, as a thoroughly extended and rewritten version.

THE MATERNAL

An introduction

Rosalind Mayo & Christina Moutsou

Adrienne Rich wrote:

> The woman's body, with its potential for gestating, bringing forth and nour-
> ishing new life, has been through the ages a field of contradictions: a space
> invested with power, and an acute vulnerability; a numinous figure and the
> incarnation of evil; a hoard of ambivalences.
>
> *(Rich 1976: 102)*

Earlier this year (2015), as the arrival of a new royal baby drew nearer, the media
turned its attention to encouraging public speculation and guessing games, as to
what the new baby would be called, especially if it was a girl. Bookmakers took
bets on the favourite names, whilst interviews with members of the public revealed
for the most part the usual 'royal names'. Occasionally, and usually by women, who
appeared to show much more interest in the matter, the name Diana was hoped
for, with the accompanying wish that she would not be forgotten. Diana, deceased
mother of the father to be, and another son, Harry. Few of us needed any reminder
of this beautiful and tragic woman. Perhaps many of us held our breath wondering
if it was a girl, would 'they', or not, tempt fate and call up her name again. After all,
she had been more or less quietly put away, with as much ceremony and grief as
could be given, or permitted, to soothe and appease her troubled spirit, and that of
the common people who wanted to hold onto this tragic soul, for numerous and
complex reasons. But whatever the ambiguities and ambivalence the woman and
her name may summon up, she had not been forgotten by her sons, but remembered as only they, her children could do, as their beloved mother. And when eventually the newly born grandchild of this woman made its appearance, and it was a
girl, fourth in line to the throne, she was to be given the name, among others, of
Diana, in remembrance of her grandmother.[1]

I looked everywhere for grandmothers and found none.
(Elisabeth Barret Browning, in Nikolchina 2004: 2)

It is early November as we are writing this, and many of the shops have already announced the preparation for Christmas. And although in the United Kingdom, currently, only 17% of the population are calling themselves Christian,[2] Christmas cards will carry the usual images, including the iconic, instantly recognisable image of the mother of Christ, the Virgin Mary or Holy Mother of God, an image sold on cards and icons throughout the Western world. It seems that living in a neoliberalist world[3] (Verhaeghe 2014; Sennet 2005), the wishes, longings and fantasies for, and of an image of a holy mother, who is seen as always accessible, and present and who understands everything, however far removed from the realities and facts of most people's lives, is still for some a belief. But for others, what does this image represent, what desires and fantasies does this image of a mother convey? Is the image about the person we all secretly long for, the wish to return perhaps to some likely nonexistent childhood, a pre-oedipal, pre-lapsarian state, into the enveloping arms of our childhood mothers, where forgetfulness of the world and all its harsh realities and its pain can be soothed and taken away and forgotten?[4] Is it perhaps a wish for oblivion, or the longing we all share at some level for an ideal mother, and if so, why? What does an ideal mother mean, and psychically represent for any of us?

Whilst the Virgin Mary has in the past been presented as the ideal mother, particularly during the middle ages, and as a woman that all women should seek to follow and emulate, in the twenty-first century, and given so few people are professing Christians or religious, what else is at stake here? Whatever this image represents, and it obviously holds and carries more than one projection, is that powerful desires and longings are awakened by this mother maternal imago that are not similarly kindled by images of either Jesus or the Christian saints, and so there is perhaps something very profound in this image that touches the human psyche (Atkinson 1991; Warner 1976).

I look for myself throughout the centuries and don't see myself anywhere.
(Helene Cixious in Nikolchina 2004: 2)

According to Jacques Derrida, a preface or a beginning is another lie, it is written with hindsight. An introduction is much the same thing, it is written after the body of the work has been completed, and sometimes it requires several attempts to get it right, each attempt a way to get us going, to set us off. Many women, and many mothers, have set us off and got us going on this work, particularly and specifically, our own birth mothers, grandmothers, and great-grandmothers. And then there have been those people (women and men) who have re-mothered us through their intellectual, creative, inspiring and healing relationships, that have nudged us in the right places to move on in our own life journeys and to believe in our own stories and experiences, and so it is in part to all of these that this introduction is also addressed.

One of the criticisms of Freud from an existential perspective, and there have been many, is his invention of the unconscious. Such criticism is phrased not so much in the sense of disputing that we may not be aware of the reasons for which we act or think in a certain way, but more so because he turned the concept into a noun, an entity, 'the unconscious' (Heaton 2010: pp. 20–21). The maternal presents us with a similar predicament. It raises the question of what it is we mean when we are turning a reference to the Mother into a noun. Is it about our relationship to our mothers? Being born of and from a woman–mother is probably the most universal experience of being human. Or is it a female preoccupation with becoming a mother? And if yes, to what extent is this preoccupation important to think about and defining of female, and also indirectly, of male identity and subjectivity. Or is 'the maternal', like the unconscious turned into noun, a recognition of a wider issue, one that is potentially defining of the human condition?

What we aim to argue throughout this book, but mainly demonstrate through the setting out of experience, narrative, prose, theory, and representation through art, is that the maternal is the foundation of the human condition, influencing how we live our lives, how we situate ourselves culturally, politically, and in our intimate relationships. However, it is often overlooked and silenced as that which we need to grow out of and leave behind. The Mother brings us into the world though pain and making herself vulnerable, but it is the newborn's prolonged helplessness that shapes the human condition as one of interdependence and relationship, being paramount to survival. Of course, anthropologists would point out that child rearing practices vary widely cross-culturally and frame how kinship is conceived of and mentalised in different societies.[5] Cross-cultural variation, however, including community sharing of babies and adoption practices, does not significantly vary the immense need for close attachment that marks the beginning of life.

In a series of striking images of mothers and babies in an African country in a conference entitled 'Womb to World' (Birthlight conference, 19th September 2015) where we were invited to give a talk, Antonella Sansone remarked on the observed lack of eye contact between mothers and breastfeeding babies in African societies. She said that eye contact seems necessary for bonding when separation has already occurred, but as she demonstrated in a visually striking way, babies in such societies, as well as mothers of course, were integrated from day one to the everyday community life. The mother's and the baby's inherent vulnerability and interconnection were not only being catered for, therefore, but being endorsed on a sociocultural level. Different generations of women were involved in the raising of children through the communal sharing of the carrying, feeding and providing of continuous close intimate physical contact for young babies (Sansone 2004).

It is almost 40 years since the publication of Adrienne Rich's book, *Of Woman Born: Motherhood as Experience and Institution*. It is still well-regarded and influential, often cited in texts on motherhood, maternity, and the mother-daughter relationship, and it has never been out of print. The tensions and contradictions inherent in maternity and maternal experience (motherhood) form the basis of Rich's analysis. She examines the contradictory meanings of motherhood in contemporary Western societies, and argues that the potential experience of a woman to her body, and her children, are at odds with the patriarchal expressions and representation of that experience. The institution of motherhood, Rich claims, has 'a history, it has an ideology' (Rich 1976: p. 33). Rich looks at the actual everyday experiences of maternity and mothering, and reveals the various and usually very subtle ways that it operates as a patriarchal institution to constrain, regulate, control and delineate women-mothers self-expectations, perceptions, experiences, and daily realties of being a mother, which lead to harsh judgements of their selves as women and mothers. The consequence of this is the silencing of the female-maternal voice and actual lived experience. This, she says, is most obvious in a woman's relation to her silenced body.[6]

> In the most fundamental and bewildering of contradictions, it has alienated women from our bodies, by incarcerating us in them.
>
> *(Rich 1979: 13)*[7]

Rich's text is a careful analysis and critique of the political, cultural and psychological contexts of maternity and the mother, threaded through this is her own, at times anguished experience, of her daily realities and experience as a mother, and as a woman, poet and writer.

> Once in a while someone used to ask me, 'Don't you ever write poems about your children?' The male poets of my generation did write poems about their children—especially their daughters. For me poetry was where I lived as no one's mother, where I existed as myself.
>
> *(Rich 1979: 31)*

Rich's text reveals its own dilemmas and contradictions: the difficulties in writing a maternal-mother text that is both regarded as 'scholarly and academic', and combining it with other textual forms and styles. Her personal experience and reflections are written in a poetical form, with a lyrical intensity, suggesting much is held back, but these are parenthetically marginalised from the main 'body' of the text, which whilst pointing to the distorting and disabling patriarchal representations of the maternal, also highlights the stark silences and cost of being a woman, writer, and a mother[8] (Kristeva 1977).

This different form of narrative and style signifies the painful contradictions for her, and for most women-mothers; the struggles between the ideals of motherhood and the daily realities. And like the maternal body that she describes with intensity and eloquence, she inhabits the ambivalence and the contradictions of being woman, mother, poet, writer and trying to hold onto some sense of self.[9]

Rich associates her poetic text with the unconscious; that is, that which consciousness represses, in its relentless search for order, meaning and truth. Patriarchy, Rich claims, has been unable to situate the woman's body because it defies a stable representation and coherence, and so a woman's body remains an enigma for men, an undecidable space that lacks a coherent identity and is always subject to flux (Walker 1998; Irigaray 1995; Le Doeuff 1991). Following Rich's work, other texts have critiqued the place of women in Freudian psychoanalysis. Especially pertinent is the repression and misunderstanding of female sexuality through Freud's invention of the universalising and male focussed model of the Oedipus complex.[10]

Adrienne Rich's text stands as a testament to the intensity, the undecidability, the uncertainty, ambiguity and vulnerability of maternal experience. And as a woman -mother- poet (*intentional breakup of words*) once again presents the maternal body as the site of extraordinary struggle. In this regard, we believe that her text stands, with its mingled narratives of the analytic, critical, autobiographical, lyrical and poetic, as a metaphor, for the struggles of all women to articulate the intense, diverse and contradictory experiences of maternity and mothering, and still believe in a sense of self and identity, however discontinuous, uncertain, vulnerable, and ambiguous. And in this we suggest she brings us into the twenty-first century in relation to rethinking our Western ideas and theories of human subjectivity.

Of Woman Born set many of the questions that followed in the next three decades, which continued to explore the relationship between maternity and mothering as experience and practice, and its connections and relation to female subjectivity and identity, within its historical, social, political and cultural context. We now have a rich and complex body of maternal studies from across many disciplines and perspectives, and in a variety of textual forms and styles[11] (Doane and Hodges 1992; Lazzare 1976; Bassin et al. 1994; Malin 2000; Cusk 2001; Irigaray 1991). Maternity and mothering is no longer seen or thought of as a fixed static state of biological essentialism where the mother is seen as passive, and maternal care is seen as a biological given for women, an instinctive part of the feminine psyche (De Beauvoir 1949). It is now recognised that maternal care and practices and maternal subjectivities vary across cultures, and change across generations of women (Mariotti 2012; Malin 2000) influenced by the political, social, religious, cultural and economic (Rubin 1975; Steedman 1986). And that the concepts and cultural conceptions of childhood and infancy, as well as adolescence have also changed.[12] Maternal care is recognised now as a set of ideas, behaviours, beliefs, and practices, which vary across time, cultures and communities, and contexts. And where 'skills' learnt on the job, and where getting it wrong, may be as important as what getting it right might sometimes mean, and where personal feelings, intuitions, emotional and psychological confidence interact with actions and activities that change over time, reflecting the differences and impacts with different children, and the families and communities these are a part of (Baraitser 2009).[13]

Nonetheless, for the majority of women who mother, their own feelings and self-perceptions as a mother, and self-judgements, can be experienced as negating, full of doubt, and pervaded with fears and anxiety of getting it wrong, whatever the age of the children might be. Mothers, much more than fathers, are the ones in society who if all goes well may receive some recognition, but if it goes wrong, or ill with a child, no matter what that might be, the mother is the one who will be censored and blamed (Parker 2005).[14]

In a striking and evocative case study, entitled 'Rita's Grief', Emmy van Deurzen (2011) portrays maternal ambivalence from an existential perspective, freeing it from the unbearable guilt and conflict that accompanies the experience in the psychoanalytic understanding of the term. Rita goes to therapy in the midst of severe depression and grief and a number of suicide attempts after having lost her husband and five-year-old son in a tragic car accident. In the course of therapy, she describes the repeated conflicts that her husband and Rita had around motherhood. Rita resented the isolation that motherhood imposed on her which was compounded further by the fact that she was foreign and that marrying in Britain meant losing touch with her family of origin. Her husband wanted a second child while she craved going back to work and creating a life for herself. As the therapy progressed, van Deurzen describes the deep, unresolved guilt that she sensed in her patient. Eventually, Rita discloses that on the day of the fatal accident, she has had a bitter argument with her husband over his wish to pay a family visit to his parents. Rita resented these visits as they reminded her of her isolation from her own family of origin, and she used the foggy and icy weather as a pretext for postponing it. When her husband decided to make the visit without her and take their son with him, Rita shouted angrily: 'Go then, and I hope you slip on the ice,' which is exactly what happened that day. The car slipped on the ice and both her husband and son were killed instantly.

With much tenderness, but also determination, Van Deurzen unravels the complex web of guilt and self-deprecation that so often becomes entangled with the relentless helplessness the experience of motherhood brings along with it, even under more ordinary circumstances. Rita's grief is now fully expressed as well as the complexities of her relationship with her late husband and the deep connection with her lost son.

> There is a wistfulness and devotion in her when she speaks of her little boy that carries her forward in spite of herself ... She comes to accept that those years she had with Ralph are still hers to keep and to cherish and I encourage her

to claim them and make the most of them…. She also enlists Ralph's school in the process of remembrance, when she realises how important it is to find support in one's bereavement and to let the dead reconnect with their own lives, rather than keep them isolated and tied into one's own wretchedness…

(2011: 326–328)

Van Deurzen demonstrates convincingly the ordinary expression of maternal ambivalence in contrast with the complexities of grief when it is driven by idealisation and denigration. When she tackles the irrationality of Rita's thought processes, guilt and reproach transform to mourning for the loss and, eventually, to building a life for herself in which she retains a place for the connection with her lost husband and son.

In Western culture the mother is the 'impossible subject', caught in an ever-increasing split between her idealisation and her denigration. 'Rita's Grief' highlights through her lived experience this split. The Mother is part object and part subject, who stands as the gateway to sanity and becoming a mature adult, according to Western philosophical theory and psychoanalysis, or as the cause, the harbinger of her children's madness and even criminality (Plaza 1982; Walker 1998; Kristeva 1987; Ettinger 2006). The Mother is everywhere and nowhere (Baraitser 2009), saturated in our culture as we are with idealised images on the one hand, and yet theoretically she is a shadowy figure, a container and receptacle (Plato to Augustine, to the church Fathers) (Lloyd 1984; Walker 1998; Jantzen 2004: pp. 167–192), a bits person, hated, feared, envied, the one who must bear destruction, abjection and abandonment, and still remain intact without retaliation, and yet the one who must know just what the right amount of presence and attention and care is, and what too much is, at the right time, at the right moment, with each of her different individual children (Rose 1996). This was summed up very well by the psychoanalyst Alice Balint, who claimed:

> The ideal mother has no interests of her own … For it remains self-evident that the interests of the mother and the child are identical, and it is the generally acknowledged measure of the goodness or badness of the mother how far she feels this identity of interests.
>
> *(Balint 1952: 111)*

The conscious starting point for this collection of papers was the recognition that as psychotherapists working in the psychoanalytic tradition, albeit one that took a critical position and stance towards that theory and practice,[15] that the 'subject' (sic) of the maternal-mother was more usually taught from the traditional psychoanalytic texts, with the very occasional interruption of Kristeva and Irigaray. Psychoanalytic theories of the maternal-mother have been, and are very influential, perhaps more so now than ever before, despite the prevalence of CBT and other cognitive theories promoted in the NHS. Theories of attachment and object relations theory of child development are also very influential in relation to judgements about children's and adolescents' mental health and development (Urwin 1985).

One of the surprising things about Adrienne Rich's text is that it appeared during what was then called the second wave feminist movement, a time that many women were arguing for more power in all areas of their lives (Heilbrun 1997): greater control of their bodies, reproduction, contraception, abortion rights, child-care as well as legal and social changes (all documented in some of the papers in the book). However, when it came to the mother and maternity, there was at this time some very powerful arguments and anger, and turn against maternity, and especially one's own mother; who was seen as repressed, and possibly depressed as well, and as someone who was the 'carrier' for patriarchy, the one who taught her daughter submission and compliance, and who bred inferiority and abjection (McCrindle and Rowbotham 1977; Steedman 1986; Heilbrun 1997; Appignanesi 2008).

The 1980s and early 1990s saw a flowering of mother-daughter texts full of the tensions, passions, fears and ambivalence that would come to characterise this relationship for years to come, mother blaming or a more reparative tone seemed to be the only things on offer (Steedman 1986; Woodward 1983 [1928]). However, what is surprising is that the aims of the feminist project at this time to uncover buried female histories, stories and images of other women's lives, and to push sexuality to the front of the political agenda, rather ironically shared some of the intentions and scope of psychoanalysis. However, they also both shared the same images and narratives of the mother, trapped between idealisation and denigration, fearing the Mother's powerfulness, and what was not often said, then, and now, fearing her vulnerability. She was the woman to be left behind, forcefully, violently if necessary, abjected in order that 'adult maturity' could be achieved. Longing and need for one's mother, as Adrienne Rich had spoken so movingly about, was denied and repressed, such feelings and emotions belonged to babies and small infants, and definitely not adults. The powerful belief that the failure to do this resulted in psychosis has proved still to be enormously persuasive that few actually question it.

In *Writing a Woman's Life*, Carolyn Heilbrun observes:

> Lives do not serve as models, only stories do that.
> And it is a hard thing to make up stories to live by.
> We can only retell and live by stories we have heard.
> Stories have formed us all.

> *(Helbrun 1997: 37)*

The backbone to these papers forms the intentional decision and ethical commitment of the editors to present the multiple and diverse meanings, experiences and subjectivities of women-mothers, in their differences, complexity, messiness, vulnerability, ambiguity and ambivalence. Our reasons for this was, and remains, the desire and the plea to rethink and to question existing and dominant conceptions of human subjectivity as informed through the Western philosophical tradition, and psychoanalytic theory, and in particular maternal subjectivities.

Each of the papers presented here are profoundly and inherently personal, ethical, political and philosophical in just the sense that Adrienne Rich spoke of forty years ago. The papers draw on the current social, cultural, political, economic and symbolic contexts, always seeking to move from a theoretical discourse to personal experience, impact and influence of culture, and its constructions on human lives and experiences.

The form of the narratives set out here are a part of this intention and commitment. Whilst some are written in a more analytical style, others are written in a poetic, lyrical and personal reflective form, sometimes illustrated by the way in which they have been set down, using memory, performance, story, and poetry. Once again, this is the intention of the editors, that a weaving of different texts and styles of writing should, and may, better represent the diversity and multiplicity of human experience and voices, writing against the grain of presenting a unified, totalising narrative of academic mastery and closure, another form of matricide. And so our methodology is a reflection of the philosophy and ethics and value in bringing together different ways and styles, methods and approaches, with none put forward as the 'right way' or 'right interpretation'.

We live at a time when difference and complexity, uncertainty, messiness and difficulty, helplessness and vulnerability are seen as weaknesses, and as failures of individual and private responsibility, which are frequently socially and politically spoken of, and perceived, as the person's fault. This is particularly true in mental health. We hope that in presenting narratives that attempt to articulate human subjectivities, especially in relation to the maternal, as infinitely and undecidably vulnerable, unknowable and interconnected, this collection may contribute in a small way to representing a more complex, diverse, and so inclusive and compassionate understanding of our human condition.

As this book began to take shape, some significant themes emerged repeatedly, discussed by many of the contributors completely independently of each other. As such, they revealed a sense of the connecting threads that bind this work and bring it together, while at the same time allowing for diversity and a pluralism of different, deeply unique and personal voices and experiences that can be heard throughout the book. We would like to identify here some of these emergent themes:

1. **The story of Athena**

    The birth of Athena is discussed in several papers in this book as the archetypical representation of matricide. Not only is Athena the motherless daughter of her father, Zeus, but she is also the prototype of the invulnerable woman, who rejects motherhood and close relationships that imply vulnerability (see Blackett, Chapter 7 on the invulnerable Goddesses). One could say that symbolically and on many levels, we increasingly live in a world that promotes and endorses the model of Athena for all of us, and especially so for women. This is a model prioritising rationality and defensiveness against strong feelings, and being in power and control, as well as being suspicious and critical of any form of helplessness and vulnerability.[16] One only needs to have a brief look at the government's policies regarding mental health provisions in the NHS (and this is not only the current government, but a buildup over several years) to see the model of Athena encapsulated and endorsed through the suspicion and abolishment of any long-term therapy which recognises attachment and vulnerability, the need for connection, and the outright pathologising of dependency needs (Sennet 2005; Taylor 2014).[17]

2. **Madonna and Child**

In Chapter 5, Kate Gilbert argues that the Madonna and Child image underlies our perceptions of motherhood, even in completely secular milieus: a very similar concept of the Virgin Mother constitutes the predominant socio-cultural model of motherhood in many Middle Eastern societies (see Kayhan, Chapter 6). Athena was not born helpless through the pain and mess of childbirth (a male concept of childbirth according to Augustine) but instead she was born fully adult and armoured from her father's head: The Virgin Mary is a different idealised model of a woman who conceives a child outside of sexual intercourse and, therefore, remains pure and virginal (intact was the qualification given by the church Fathers in order to declare Jesus as Son of God) but the Madonna is also selfless, faultless and altruistic and largely silent. She is the essence of the perfect mother. To the degree that women unknowingly aspire to this model, but also to the degree that men expect their wives and partners to be a Madonna, there is an inevitable repression and denial of the diverse and real daily experiences of motherhood and female subjectivity, which do not conform to this image. The danger also is that of creating a binary opposition, and thus a splitting between the idealised Madonna and the denigrated Whore, the woman who is abusive and destructive in relation to her sexuality and, therefore, dangerous to her children and to society as a whole (see Haynes, Chapter 3 on mother denigration).

3. **Demeter and Persephone**

The myth of Demeter and Persephone has been used by psychoanalysis and in cultural discourses as a symbolic narrative of the necessity for mother-daughter separation, and maternal pathology.[18] Persephone is abducted and raped by Hades and her grieving mother brings about death and destruction, before she agrees with Hades to see her daughter for half of the year. Persephone though can never be fully released from the underworld. One possible interpretation of the myth is that the emergence of female desire and sexuality requires the violent separation between mother and daughter, which constitutes the basis of emotional health and maturity. However, as Jacobs (2007) points out, looking at the structural and emotional significance of the myth, it becomes apparent that this is a myth about the emergence of patriarchy and the sterility and destruction that the subordination of the Mother brings about. It is also a myth about the importance of the close relationship between mothers and daughters that one could say forms the basis for a society where attachment, vulnerability and bonds are not perceived as threats and where loss does not come about through intrusion and violence, but through the awareness of our finality (see Moutsou, Chapter 13).

4.   **The existential ground of the maternal**

The central premise of this book is that the maternal is the ground of our being (see Latham, Chapter 9). Most chapters in this book have a strong affinity to prioritising personal experience and narrative, to academic discourse (see Woodroffe, Chapter 11). Through layers of various forms of prose including poetry, storytelling, memoir writing and, sometimes, humorous self-reflection, many of the contributors highlight in different ways how their personal and intricate relationship with the Mother has been paramount to their life trajectories. The argument here is that accepting the importance and centrality of the maternal in our lives is integral to self-acceptance and the enrichment of our lives. This also takes the form of accepting a diversity of means through which this connection is experienced, such as art, music, embodiment which go beyond and transcend the sociocultural assumption of the semantic superiority of language (Davies, Chapter 12).

5.   **Storytelling and the intergenerational transmission of the maternal**

> I mean, they say you die twice. One time when you stop breathing and a second time, a bit later on, when somebody says your name for the last time.
> *(Banksy, Wikiquotes)*

In 'One Thousand and One Nights' (Al-Shaykh 2013 [1706]), Scheherazade tells the Sultan stories, not only as a way of saving her own life, but also that of other women. One could say that the telling of stories is an alternative model to Freud's binary pair of Eros and Thanatos, the understanding that the falling in love with another can only be eventually taken over by the so-called 'death instinct', the ultimate destruction (Freud 1920).

Stories provide a different understanding of our connection with one another, across time and generation, and through memory and images (see Mayo, Chapter 14). In the powerful writings of black women authors like Toni Morrison, Alice Walker and others, we are reminded at what cost Western societies have overlooked the importance of our historical roots, connections and memories. This is especially so in relation to the Mother, as the stories of our mothers, as well as stories about our mothers and ourselves become inevitably interwoven with our choices and identities and how we live our lives. As much as maternal inheritance may at times feel like a burden, it is also inevitably 'the ground of our being' (see King, Chapter 2).

6.   **The representation of maternal subjectivities**

Many of the contributors ask the question, in what ways can we try to give voice to the experience of female-maternal subjectivities: In Chapter 10, Melissa Benn considers the effects of the sociocultural and political representations of the maternal on our daughters. Maternal representations through images, such as advertising and the media, art, music, poetry and films play a pivotal role in how we collectively and individually relate to the concept (see Wade, Chapter 8, Georghiou, Chapter 4, and Blackett, Chapter 7). Not only are these images often constructs based on inflexible idealised or denigrated models of the maternal, they also create a powerful universalising of the experience, which excludes and forecloses diversity, divergence, and the reality of mothers' everyday lives. The question remains, as Jacobs asks (Chapter 1) whether we can individually and as a society find ways to represent maternal subjectivities that offer an alternative to a universal and universalising Oedipal model, which silences and excludes the reality not only of female embodiment and sexuality, but also of any adult identity not complying with the acceptance of imposed separation between mother and child.

Having now identified some of the themes interconnecting many of the chapters in this book, we would like to conclude with a brief summary of each chapter. The book is divided in two parts, named 'matricide' and 'maternal subjectivities'. The division is to a large extent artificial, as most chapters touch upon both subjects. Matricide, as the symbolic silencing and obliteration of the mother's discourse, however, is more predominant as a subject in the first seven chapters of the book. The following seven chapters focus more strongly, but not exclusively, on the articulation of various forms of maternal subjectivities, as a creative response to matricide. Consistently, with the emphasis on pluralism which underlines the book, each chapter presents with a different mix of theory, prose and personal narrative from a multitude of perspectives. In this sense, the book is eclectic at core, drawing from psychoanalysis, phenomenology, socio-political and cultural discourse, storytelling and the arts.

Amber Jacobs (Chapter 1) revisits the notion of matricide, as spelt out in her homonymous book (2007). Even though this is the only purely theoretical chapter in the book, it is interestingly written in the first person, as the author's reflection on why the structural analysis of myth can provide a creative and generative response to the silencing of the Mother.

In Chapter 2, Lucy King looks at maternal inheritance, through the concepts and images of the mother from the very sceptical perspective of second wave feminism, and then psychoanalytic theory. In addressing Julia Kristeva's often-recited assertion that 'matricide is our vital necessity', she looks at the mother–daughter relationship, and female identity, and asks the question of whether the maternal could pose less of a threat to the formation of female identity, and if so how.

Jane Haynes (Chapter 3) observes that mothers have been accused of caus-ing 'universal ills' and through her free associative exploration of Shakespearean mothers, the hero Peter Pan, R.D. Laing's difficulties with his own mother as well as extracts from her patients talking about their mothers during a psycho-therapy session, she highlights the centrality of the Mother in and throughout our lives.

Lakis Georghiou (Chapter 4) examines the patriarchal representations of the maternal in American film and mainly in the pivotal *Kramer versus Kramer*. He discusses how gender stereotypes constructed to fit the patriarchal and cap-italist discourse not only disempower women, but also impoverish the forma-tion of male subjectivity and identity and impact on the lives of men, women and children.

Kate Gilbert (Chapter 5) looks at the stereotype of the Madonna that, she argues, underlies predominant cultural discourses about the Mother. She distinguishes between earlier and more humane representations of Madonna through biblical texts, and then considers the impact of the construction of the idealised perfect version of the virgin mother, by the established Church, in creating a Mariology. In the latter, the Madonna is rigidly presented as the image of the perfect mother who is defined as selfless, without desire and subservient.

Melike Kayhan (Chapter 6) discusses the mother–son relationship in the context of Kurdish society, which is based on her research on the construction of male identity among Kurdish men living in contemporary Britain. Kayhan concludes that the construction of mothers as deprived of sexual identity and desire within the marital bond, eroticises the mother–son relationship, and con-tributes to a problematic notion of male identity and female identity and desire, one that is highly conflicted and is split between sexual and relational intimacy.

Why does a woman have a child, or not? The replies to this will be as varied and different as the women themselves, and subject to culture, race, religion, class, economics, education, psychology and health, as well as differ-ent forms of intergenerational transmission. In Chapter 7, Pat Blackett gives a personal account of her decision to remain childless. Although her decision comes as an assertion of her free will and choice, she reflects that it has also perhaps been the outcome of her experience of her own mother as a reject-ing mother who did not want to have children. Through recounting Bollen's fascinating work on the female archetypes of the Ancient Greek goddesses, Blackett draws out some of the connections and desires involved in the choice to become a mother, and its connection to intimate and close relationships, female autonomy and power, and female vulnerability and risk.

In the second part of the book on maternal subjectivities, Eti Wade (Chapter 8) discusses the emergence of her art practice through her personal experience of motherhood. She reflects on how postnatal depression following the birth of her first son left her feeling deviant and isolated and how managing to represent her subjective experience through her art work allowed her to find an acceptable, healing and creative individual maternal response.

In Chapter 9, Barbara Latham names 'the maternal' as the ground of our being, and describes our beginnings as humans in inarticulacy, as that which we both forget, and which we are often tempted, as adults, especially psychotherapists, to move away from, and disavow. Through extracts of memoir writing about her mother who died suddenly when the author was seventeen years old, she demonstrates the inextricable, enduring and lifelong connections between the mother and the daughter's life that time does not erase.

Melissa Benn (Chapter 10) discusses the idealistic expectations of young women in the twenty-first century in relation to maternity, childcare and work and careers, and the politics and economics of the female division of labour that render such expectations unrealistic. She contrasts the everyday subjective experiences of motherhood and the gender divides that underlie it with the modern middle class myth that 'women can have it all'. She argues for a new concept of work that creates less division between motherhood and a working life, as well as between men and women.

In Chapter 11, Lynda Woodroffe looks at her maternal history, and its difficulties and pain, and considers its connection to her own experience of becoming a single mother twice, once very early in her life, and once in her forties. She also relates this to the early loss of her father. From these experiences of loss and disappointment, she reflects on how eventually she was able to make something creative and enabling for herself, enough to be *her own* kind of mother to her two sons.

Drawing upon her experience as a music therapist as well as a psychotherapist, Alison Davies (Chapter 12) proposes music as an alternative to language. From her early childhood, she experienced a growing love and affinity with music, rather than words. Her mother, on the other hand, was a very capable woman with language, and Alison discusses the, at times, tense and difficult situations and connections this caused them both. She draws upon the work of Christopher Bollas on the early bodily connection between mother and child as an antidote to hysteria. Recalling 'the music of [her] mother's voice', she is not only referring to music as ordinarily understood, but to all forms of nonverbal communication between mothers and their children that once again provide nurturing examples of the enduring and life enriching bond between mother and child.

The subject of breasts and breastfeeding can be guaranteed to provide controversy, even outrage and conflict. It is a subject as much to do with political, cultural and social and economic control and censure, as it is to do with the health and choice of a mother and a baby and a woman's body. Christina Moutsou's contribution (Chapter 13) begins with a poem recounting her experience of breastfeeding her two children. In it, she makes the connection between the maternal and the erotic, as both she claims entail transcendence, as well as an acceptance of vulnerability and loss. However, she goes on to argue that the collective suspicion and wish to control the mother and her breastfeeding is due to its potentially erotic and pleasurable experience for women in motherhood. The dread of the woman's/mother's erotic subjectivity is embedded in our inability and refusal to endorse the creative potential of both the maternal and the erotic, and the collective tendency to control women's bodies and desires.

To conclude, Rosalind Mayo (Chapter 14) in the final chapter of the book gives voice to her mother's story. Using an embedded narrative within the text, she goes on to raise questions about maternal stories and narratives, history and memory and their connections to human subjectivities. Caroline Steedman's 'Landscape for a Good Woman' has proved a pivotal piece of work on the social construction of female maternal identity. In revisiting this text, Rosalind raises questions about the class construction of motherhood and its representation, and the silencing not only of the Mother, but of the representation of working class experience, which she claims is more likely to be pathologised culturally and by psychological theories. Finally, she goes on to ask what happens to women as they age, when they become Demeter. What is our relationship to and representation of the ageing Mother. At the end of her chapter, she begins to unravel the silencing and fear of the Mother's ageing within feminist theory and narrative and its collusion with a youth culture, revealing its fear of vulnerability and death, as another form of matricide.

Notes

1 Princess Charlotte Elizabeth Diana: Born May 2, 2015.
2 A YouGov poll (2014) found 77% of the British population were 'not very' or 'not at all' religious. And 66% of the population said they had no connections at all with any religion.
3 See Paul Verhaeghe's article in the Guardian (September 24, 2014) for an excellent essay on neo-liberalism and its effects on the lives of 'ordinary people', and on our sense of ourselves and where the market and its forces leaves the majority of people feeling powerless. He also draws out very well, and pertinent to a maternal context, the factors that shape people's sense of agency and powerlessness, those who are the winners, and those who are the losers, and the judgements applied in both. This is also pertinent to conceptions of mothers and the social class economic context: For example, choosing not to have children is regarded in a middle class context as the right of a woman over her reproduction, and her body, and her choice about her life.

For a woman from a working class background expectations that she will have babies and likely not have a professional working life are what informs the judgments that she is abnormal, uncaring or selfish, if she makes the same decision not to have children. The maternal, motherhood, maternity and women's bodies are still the site of politics, economics and social and cultural forces and pressures.

4 For some time now in the literature and also coming as a criticism from the psychoanalytic context, Kristeva or Irigaray, for example, it has been argued that the emphasis on maternal experience denotes a backward glance, a return to a kind of biologism that rests on an intimate and idealised perception of mothering and the maternal connection and relationship. Brenda O' Daly and Maureen T. Reddy (1991) in *Narrating Mothers: Theorizing Maternal Subjectivities* among others argue that in these accounts we learn less about what it is like to mother than about what it is like to be mothered. Countering this claim, see Baraitser (2009) *Maternal Encounters* and see Malin (2000) *The Voice of the Mother: Embedded Maternal Narratives in Twentieth-Century Women's Autobiographies.* It is worth noting here the radical difference between the majority of Western thinking and theory of female and male subjectivity and its connections to the maternal with some African American thinking. For example, Toni Morrison's powerful and searing novel, *Beloved* (1987) among others represents one strand of this thinking, in which the loss of the *Motherline,* (as in *Beloved* and *Sethe*) results in the loss of the characters' roots, their authenticity and their sense of self. All of which Morrison claims, has happened under Western capitalism. See also Alice Walker (1983).

5 Renowned anthropologist Marilyn Strathern's work on the influence of new reproductive technologies on how we conceptualise kinship was pioneer in thinking about kinship in broader terms than biology. Her books *After Nature: English Kinship in the Late Twentieth Century* (1992a) and *Reproducing the Future: Essays on Anthropology, Kinship and the New Reproductive Technologies* (1992b) explore the links between biology, social relations and kinship. Strathern argues that the social is not opposed to biology, but that the two are intertwined in the representation and reconceptualization of modern families.

6 More recently, Naomi Stadlen's work on giving mothers and their experience voice has crossed the threshold between academia and popular discourse. Her bestselling book *What Mothers Do Especially When It Looks Like Nothing* (2004) and on *How Mothers Love* (2012) have actually been read by mothers. She has also for many years been running groups for mothers at the Active Birth Centre creating a space where mothers of young babies are encouraged to talk freely about the everyday experience of motherhood.

7 Indeed, Luce Irigaray (later than Adrienne Rich) contends that the entire edifice of Western culture is erected on this silencing of the maternal body. She argues that matricide is the founding instance of a patriarchal imaginary, and cites Clytemnestra as the mythical inscription of this. See the bodily encounter with the mother in *The Irigaray Reader* (Whitford 1991; Walker 1998; Irigaray 1985).

8 In Stabat Mater, Julia Kristeva sets out in two columns a scholarly investigation of the Virgin Mary and of the maternal as symbolised by her, with her personal reflections on her own maternity and birth of her son: Here, her writing takes up a more lyrical-emotional form. This is very much the same as what Rich had done 10 years earlier. Kristeva said that as a child she was 'bathed' in the liturgy of the Orthodox church. The Stabat Mater is a thirteenth-century hymn to the Virgin Mother (see *The Kristeva Reader,* Moi 1986).

9 See online article (2013) *All Things Maternal,* where the novelist Zadie Smith comments on an article by Laura Sandler, in which she had said that motherhood is a threat to creativity as a writer. Sandler asks whether in order to write a woman should have only one child. Replying to this Jane Smiley comments, the key is not having only one

child, but excellent day care and a social world that allows fathers to have time and motivation to be present in the care of children. These conversations show two things, the class and economic context from which they arise, and just how much many of the questions and issues that Rich's text raised, almost 40 years ago now, are still as relevant, and are still key questions in this context, whatever changes in terminology or shifts in thinking have gone on. Of course, Rich was also from a privileged background, white, Western educated and middle class.

10 In *Jocasta's Children* (1989) Christiane Olivier argues that Freud's Oedipus model has created a patriarchal expectation that sexual pleasure is bound with reproduction for women. She argues for a reintegration of female sexuality and the maternal. Similarly, *Descent to the Goddess* (Brinton Perera 1981) proposes an alternative model of femininity through the myth of Inanna's visit to her dark sister in the underworld which bears similarities with the Demeter and Persephone myth.

11 Particularly significant works are these of Chodorow (1978), Dinnerstein (1987), Hirsh (1989), Gilligan (1982), and Ruddick (1989).

12 Emily Jeremiah identifies a shift in terminology from Motherhood to Mothering, which she claims signifies a move from previous conceptions of motherhood as essentialist to current poststructuralist influences. In this context, she cites Judith Butler's notion of Maternal Performativity, which we are unconvinced by (see Jeremiah 2015 *Motherhood To Mothering and Beyond: Maternity in Recent Feminist Thought*).

13 For an excellent discussion of these experiences on a daily, almost minute by minute basis in the relationship with one's child or children, and its shaping of maternal subjectivity and reality and its significance to thinking about human subjectivity, see Lisa Baraitser (2009) *Maternal Encounters: The Ethics of Interruption*.

14 Mother blaming is very prevalent in the psychoanalytic context in both theory and practice. Mothers are blamed for everything from anorexia, depression, being unemployed, ADHD and bipolar disorder.

15 We are referring here to the Philadelphia Association's training that engages philosophy, particularly phenomenology and existential thinking (among others) in a critique of psychoanalytic theory and practice. Space does not allow us to elaborate on philosophy's 'engagement' (sic) with the Maternal. However, in the last 20 years, there are numerous texts by feminist philosophers that do this very well such as the work of Cavarero (2000) and Walker (1998). For an excellent discussion of the pregnant body from a phenomenological perspective, see Iris Marion Young (1990a,b).

16 See Adam Phillips (2010: pp. 123–142) on the importance of endorsing our helplessness as a way of staying true to what it is that makes us human and the intrinsic nature of close relationships.

17 Barbara Taylor's memoir *The Last Asylum* (2014) is a very important and eloquent account of the increasingly strong pathologisation of adult vulnerability and dependency needs and the closing down in this country of mental health establishments that could foster such needs to an extent. Sennet (2003, 2005) also raises the question of vulnerability and how it is seen in the workplace, under capitalism.

18 Susie Orbach's work has brought to the fore the centrality of the mother-daughter relationship for the developing identity of the daughter. In *Fat is a Feminist Issue,* she points out that a woman's relationship with her body is a reflection of the mother-daughter relationship and the intergenerational transmission of poor self-image and self-doubting. In the more recent, *Understanding Women: A Feminist Psychoanalytic Approach* (2012), Eichenbaum and Orbach, the founders of the Women's Therapy Centre, argue for a reconceptualization of female sexuality in which embodiment and the issue of mother-daughter differentiation are at core.

References

Al-Shaykh, H. (2013 [1706]) *One Thousand and One Nights*. London, England: Bloomsbury.

Appignanesi, L. (2008) *Mad, Bad, and Sad: A History of Women and the Mind Doctors From 1800 to the Present*. London, England: Virago.

Atkinson, W.C. (1991) *The Oldest Vocation: Christian Motherhood in the Middle Ages*. Ithaca, NY: Cornell University Press.

Balint, A. (1952) Love for Mother and Mother Love. In Balint M. (ed). *Primary Love and Psychoanalytic Technique*. London, England: Hogarth Press.

Banksy (accessed on 26/11/2015) *Wikiquotes*. https://en.wikiquote.org/wiki/Banksy.

Baraitser, L. (2009) *Maternal Encounters: The Ethics of Interruption*. London, England: Routledge.

Bassin, D., Honey, M. and Kaplan, M. M. (1994) *Representations of Motherhood*. New Haven, CT: Yale University Press.

Brinton Perera, S. (1981) *Descent to the Goddess: A Way of Initiation for Women*. Toronto, Ontario, Canada: Inner City Books.

Butler, J. (1994) Bodies That Matter, in C. Burke, N. Schor and M. Whitford (eds.). *Engaging with Irigaray*. New York, NY: Columbia University Press.

Butler, J. (2000) 'Longing For Recognition: Commentary on the Work of Jessica Benjamin.' Roundtable on the Work of Jessica Benjamin. In *Studies in Gender and Sexuality* 1(3): 271–290.

Cavarero, A. (2000) *Relating Narratives: Story Telling and Selfhood*. London, England: Routledge.

Chodorow, N. (1978) *The Reproduction of Mothering. Psychoanalysis and the Sociology of Gender*. San Francisco, CA: University of California Press.

Cusk, R. (2001) *A Life's Work: On Becoming a Mother*. London, England: Fourth Estate.

De Beauvoir, S. (1984 [1949–1974]) *The Second Sex* (trans. H.M. Parsley). Harmondsworth, England: Penguin.

Dinnerstein, D. (1987) *The Rocking of The Cradle and The Ruling of The World*. United Kingdom: Souvenir Press, The Women's Press.

Doane, J. and Hodges, D. (1992) *From Klein To Kristeva: Psychoanalytic Feminism and the Search for the 'Good Enough' Mother'*. Ann Arbor, MI: University of Michigan Press.

Ettinger, B.L. (2006) From proto-ethical compassion to responsibility: Besideness and the three primal mother-phantasies of not- enoughness, devouring and abandonment. *Athena Philosophical Studies*, 2:100–135.

Eichenbaum, L. and Orbach, S. (2012 [1982]) *Understanding Women: A Feminist Psychoanalytic Approach*. London, England: Outside In … Inside Out.

Freud, S. (1991 [1920]) Beyond the pleasure principle. In *Sigmund Freud: 11. On Metapsychology*. London, England: Penguin Books.

Gilligan, C. (1982) *In a Different Voice: Psychological Theory and Women's Development*. Cambridge, MA: Harvard University Press.

Heaton, J. (2010) *The Talking Cure: Wittgenstein's Therapeutic Method for Psychotherapy*. London, England: Palgrave MacMillan.

Heilbrun, C. (1997) *Writing A Woman's Life*. United Kingdom: Women's Press.

Irigaray, L. (1991) The bodily encounter with the mother, (trans. D. Macey), in M. Whitford (ed.). *The Irigaray Reader*. Oxford, England: Basil Blackwell.

Irigaray, L. (1995) *Speculum of the Other Woman* (trans. G. C. Gill). Ithaca, NY: Cornell University Press.

Jantzen, G. (2004) How to give birth like a man. In *Volume One: Foundations of Violence*. London, England: Routledge.

Kristeva, J. (1977) Stabat Mater, in T. Moi (ed.). *The Kristeva Reader*. Oxford, England: Blackwell.

Kristeva, J. (1987) *Black Sun: Depression and Melancholia*, (trans. L.S. Roudiez). New York, NY: Columbia University Press.

Lazzare, J. (1976) *The Mother Knot*. New York, NY: McGraw-Hill.

Le Doeuff, M. (1991) *Hiparchia's Choice. An Essay Concerning Women, Philosophy, Etc.* Oxford, England: Basil Blackwell.

Lloyd, G. (1984) *The Man Of Reason: "Male" and "Female" in Western Philosophy*. London, England: Methuen.

Malin, J. (2000) *The Voice of the Mother: Embedded Maternal Narratives in Twentieth-Century Women's Autobiographies*. Carbondale, IL: Southern Illinois University Press.

Mariotti, P. (ed.) (2012) *The Maternal Lineage. Identification, Desire and Transgenerational Issues*. London, England: Routledge in Association with the Institute of Psychoanalysis.

McCrindle, J. and Rowbotham, S. (ed) (1977) *Dutiful Daughters. Women Talk about Their Lives*. United Kingdom: Pelican.

Morrison, T. (1987) *Beloved*. New York, NY: Alfred Knopf.

Nikolchina, M. (2004) *Matricide in Language: Writing Theory in Kristeva and Woolf*. New York, NY: Other Press.

Olivier, C. (1989) *Jocasta's Children: The Imprint of the Mother* (trans. G. Craig). London, England: Routledge.

Orbach, S. (2006 [1978]) *Fat is a Feminist Issue*. London, England: Arrow Books.

Parker, R. (2005) *Torn in Two: The Experience of Maternal Ambivalence*. London, England: Virago.

Plaza, M. (1982) The mother/the same: The hatred of the mother in psychoanalysis. *Feminist Issues* 2(3): 75–89.

Rich, A. (1976) *Of Woman Born: Motherhood as Experience and Institution*. New York, NY: Norton.

Rose, J. (1996) Of knowledge and mothers: On the work of Christopher Bollas. *Gender and Psychoanalysis*, 1(4):411–428.

Rubin, G. (1975) The traffic In women: Notes on the political economy of sex. In R.R. Reiter (ed.). *Towards An Anthropology Of Women*. New York, NY: Monthly Review Press.

Ruddick, S. (1989) *Maternal Thinking: Towards a Politics of Peace*. London, England: Women's Press.

Sansone, A. (2004) *Mothers, Babies and their Body Language*. London, England: Karnac Books.

Sennet, R. (2005) *The Culture of The New Capitalism*. New Haven, CT: Yale University Press.

Stadlen, N. (2004) *What Mothers Do Especially When It Looks Like Nothing*. London, England: Judy Piatkus Ltd.

Stadlen, N. (2012) *How Mothers Love: And How Relationships are Born*. London, England: Judy Piatkus Ltd.

Steedman, C. (1986) *Landscape for a Good Woman*. London, England: Virago.

Strathern, M. (1992a) *After Nature: English Kinship in the Late 20th Century*. Lewis Henry Morgan Lectures. Cambridge, England: Cambridge University Press.

Strathern, M. (1992b) *Reproducing the Future: Essays on Anthropology, Kinship and the New Reproductive Technologies*. Manchester, England: Manchester University Press.

Taylor, B. (2014) *The Last Asylum: A Memoir of Madness in Our Times*. London, England: Penguin Books Ltd.

Urwin, C. (1985) Constructing motherhood: The persuasion of normal development. In C. Steedman, C. Urwin and V. Walkerdine (eds.). *Language, Gender and Childhood*. London, England: Routledge & Kegan Paul.

Van Deurzen, E. (2011) *Everyday Mysteries: A Handbook of Existential Psychotherapy.* 2nd ed. London, England: Routledge.

Verhaeghe, P. (2014) *What About Me? The Struggle for Identity in a Market-Based Society.* Melbourne, Australia: Scribe Publications.

Walker, A. (1983) *In Search of Our Mothers Gardens. Womanist Prose.* San Diego, CA: Harcourt Brace Jovanovich.

Walker, M. B. (1998) *Philosophy and the Maternal Body: Reading Silence.* London, England: Routledge.

Warner, M. (1976)(2013) *Alone Of All Of Her Sex: The Myth & The Cult of the Virgin Mary.* Oxford, England: Oxford University Press.

Woodward, K. (1983 [1928]) *Jipping Street.* London, England: Virago.

Young, I.M. (1990a) Throwing like a girl. In *Throwing Like a Girl and Other Essays in Feminist Philosophy and Social Theory.* Bloomington, IN: Indiana University Press.

Young, I.M. (1990b) Pregnant embodiment: Subjectivity and alienation. In *Throwing Like a Girl and Other Essays in Feminist Philosophy and Social Theory.* Bloomington, IN: Indiana University Press.

PART I

On matricide

1

RETHINKING MATRICIDE

Amber Jacobs

Working on the maternal in the context of psychoanalytic feminism is, for me, motivated by a strong political commitment to working towards what I have termed elsewhere 'post patriarchal futures' (Jacobs 2007: 3).

First I want to ask, can the practice of theory making – and in this instance, theorising matricide – have any productive and potentially usable links with the actual practices of mothering, with being a mother, with having a mother, with thinking about being and/or having a mother and representing the vicissitudes of the maternal realm in the sociosymbolic, material, cultural and clinical dimensions? Theorising matricide in the context of feminism and psychoanalysis is one way I have found, to understand, give an account of, if not transform the complex relation between the psychosexual and the social rather than being thought by it.

I must confess that when writing my book *On Matricide*[1] (Jacobs 2007), I did not give much conscious direct attention in my research to the figure of the actual living so-called 'real' mothers and the vicissitudes of their practices. The experiential aspect of the maternal realm was obviously present somewhere in my work – how could it not be? I will return to this later but what I initially focused on was the meaning of matricide in contemporary theory and culture and the implications of Irigaray's contention that matricide underlies Western culture and epistemologies – but is not acknowledged or theorised (Irigaray 1991: 38). Working on matricide was for me a direct way of responding to Irigaray's call for the necessity to transform and expand psychoanalytic theoretical paradigms so that psychoanalysis's indispensable insights into the workings of unconscious desire could be used to theorise a maternal sexual subject position.

I was determined to get beyond the impasse that psychoanalytic feminism found itself in when it could not get beyond Lacan's theory of the symbolic – a theory in which femininity could only function as the limit of representation, as other, and as lack. I was writing and thinking with a force of frustration with the psychoanalytic theories whose potential I could not abandon yet whose models of femininity and the maternal systematically reproduced the terms of a patriarchal phallic binary model of culture and subjectivity that I sought to transform and/or move beyond.

It was then, through turning to the question of matricide via psychoanalysis, structural anthropology and Greek myth that I tried to go some way to rectify this situation and force feminism into a new stage of engagement with psychoanalysis with a view to hypothesising a different model of the symbolic order that did not depend upon Oedipus and castration as its one and only organising centre.

I wanted to construct a theoretical model where femininities and the maternal could function as active agents of meaning that could generate fantasies and underlying cultural laws that could lead to modes of thinking, speaking, remembering, mourning, desiring, knowing and representing that were not reducible to or organised around the Oedipal structure of classical psychoanalysis. My desire was to theorise a structure that could allow for previously foreclosed ontological and epistemological manifestations to have access to the symbolic order/representation and theory *without* resorting to essentialism or any sense of a pre-given pre-symbolic unmediated notion of the feminine.

Works by theorists and philosophers such as Luce Irigaray (1991), Adriana Cavarero (1995), Jean Laplanche (1989), Juliet Mitchell (2000), Bracha Ettinger (2006), Judith Butler (2000), Alison Stone (2014) and my own work, are, among others, key contributors to the building of a strong contemporary tradition of psychoanalytic feminist theorising beyond Oedipus. The approaches of the theorists just listed are diverse and rooted in different intellectual agendas, but their work with psychoanalysis is linked by a shared commitment to thinking about the unconscious as a genuinely plural and mutable force which is, by definition, resistant to being fixed and reduced to one univocal framework of meaning. Rather than adhering to the phallic binarism that characterises the classical psychoanalytic model of the unconscious, these theorists (via different strategies and intellectual contexts) stay close to the spirit of the unconscious – namely, its core of ineffable unknowability and the fundamental multiplicity of its manifestations, its contents and its structures.

The Oedipal/castration model – with patricide as its organizing centre – can describe only *one* aspect of the relation between the psychosexual and the social under Western patriarchies. The fierce attachment to this model as the one and only master model/theory in psychoanalysis comprises what I see as an often rigid, heterosexist normative hegemonic monopoly on sanity, on subjectivity, representation and on meaning. This monotheism in contemporary psychoanalysis with regard to Oedipus as the one and only model needs to be contested and rejected if we are going to be able to use psychoanalysis in the service of theorising femininity and the maternal in relation to a specificity rather than as mirror or other to the masculine subject.

I am not suggesting that Oedipus and its organising underlying Law-of-the-Father no longer holds and needs to be *replaced* – but I *am* saying that it is only *one* part of the story and should be able to coexist with other models. Thus, my question is not Why Oedipus? But, why *only* Oedipus?

The 'law-of-the-father' remains the dominant model of psyche and culture in psychoanalysis and underpins the organisation of Western societies.[2] The law(s) of the mother, however, is an underdeveloped and marginal concept. The occlusion of the laws of the mother points to the entrenched status of patriarchal structures underlying our contemporary social and psychic realities. My theorisation of the laws of the mother via the matricidal myth of the Oresteia (dramatized by the ancient tragedian Aeschylus) attempts to rectify the marginalisation of the mother and locate her as an active agent for the transmission of symbolic laws that determine our cultural organisation.

The issues then that I try to tackle turn around the question of theorising alternative underlying cultural laws and prohibitions, which inaugurate different passages into symbolic subjectivity, which are not reducible to Oedipus. In this way, we can begin to posit the possibilities of theorising (rather than pathologising) other fields of desire, sexualities and meanings, different kinship arrangements and their concomitant generated unconscious processes and their symbolic representation.

What is in question then is firstly, a symbolic economy that does not solely refer, in the first instance, to the paternal symbolic function but instead resurrects the mother out of the so-called 'imaginary' presymbolic primitive realm and places her within the social arena of language, representation and history. And secondly, what is in question is a nonmonolithic model of the symbolic order – a heterogeneous model comprised of more than one process, more than one structure, more than one law that organizes sexed subjectivities. Whilst, in my reading, Lacan theorised a static and historical symbolic order – organized around an immovable one and only law-of-the-father to which we must all submit or negotiate – I am proposing a model with more than one structural process/more than one law that can produce subjectivities whose relation to the social symbolic world can no longer be systematically reduced to the phallic function of Oedipalisation.

Matricide is a term that has hitherto been used (in psychoanalysis and feminism) descriptively in a somewhat vague and loose way. It has been used to point to the subordination, the denigration, the marginalisation of and the silencing of the mother in Western discourses, or it is used to describe a conscious or unconscious fantasy of wanting to kill the mother. However, all these things: killing, marginalizing, silencing, subordinating, and denigrating are not the same – they are not reducible to one another.

What I found then was that matricide had not yet been theorised as an underlying cultural law functioning to determine aspects of our cultural and psychic organization. It had merely been used to *describe* a culture where the mother *as subject* did not yet exist.

I want to take a moment to clarify what I mean when I refer to the maternal subject *not* existing. I am thinking of the large amount of psychoanalytic feminist scholarship that has convincingly deconstructed the many discourses about the mother in the Western tradition and has found that the mother only exists as object – object of need, blame, fantasy, love, hate and ambivalence – a fantasised figure either relentlessly idealised or relentlessly denigrated, or turned into a monstrous abject other to be feared – a phallic controlling castrating mother who threatens to swallow up identity. She is nowhere theorized in terms of her own subjectivity, sexuality and unconscious and nowhere posited as instrumental in the transmission of culture and society on the symbolic level. She only exists in the many projections and fantasies generated from the male imaginary that the dominant symbolic order confirms and reproduces (Irigaray 1995: 34–46).

The centrality of the role of the mother in post-Kleinain and Object Relation traditions of contemporary psychoanalysis provides a paradox for psychoanalytic feminism. That is, despite the relation to the mother being positioned centre stage in the Object Relations psychoanalytic tradition, she is nevertheless rendered as object (of desire and fantasy) with no theorised sexual subjectivity. She is either a monstrous gothic fantasy of the Kleinian infant, or the Winnicottian 'good enough' environment destined to determine her infant's future mental health in her containing function – thus susceptible to blame and/or idealisation. The mother in psychoanalysis is at once ever present in her determining psychic function for the infant and yet all absent in terms of her sexed subjectivity and her symbolic and cultural currency. In addition to this, the different traditions within psychoanalysis all seem to converge around a consensus that 'matricide is our vital necessity' (Kristeva 1989: 27).

Whilst the concept of patricide in psychoanalysis theorises a prohibition/law leading to a set of generative organizing fantasies that Lacan termed The-Name-of-the-Father, matricide has not been translated into such clear conceptual terms.

The dead father generates a creative loss that leads to a process of genealogical transmission of cultural bonds between father and son and between sons forming the bedrock or cornerstone of Western cultures and kinship systems, as we know it. Matricide however does not seem to be able to produce that same kind of generative loss and instead functions only to *describe* the symptoms of the ontological dereliction that Irigaray has persistently diagnosed resulting from women living in a culture where femininity only exists as a fantasy or product of the male imaginary (Irigaray 1995:118–133).

Whilst it is important to continue fleshing out Irigaray's deconstructive diagnosis of Western cultural production and continue to articulate the damaging symptomology produced by the radical exclusion of the maternal and matricidal fantasies in dominant Western cultures, it is also important to take the project one step further than this powerful deconstructive diagnosis.

In my work, I wanted to go further than describing the *symptom* and get on to theorizing the latent law of matricide that could hypothesize a different kind of loss pertaining to a different fantasy structure that was organized around a different structural center to that of the name-of-the-father. That is to say, I wanted to do more than use psychoanalysis as a tool to describe and analyze the structures of oppression – which I think can run the risk of the initial politicized description of the symptom becoming ossified and fixed as an immutable and inevitable truth or prescription.

I wanted psychoanalysis to function in a different way for feminism – a way that would move on from a focus on identifying the symptoms surrounding the mother and the daughter and their exclusion from the symbolic order – a way that would move on from repeatedly producing litanies of symptoms associated with needing the mother, fearing her, blaming her, desiring her, loving her, hating her, and all the complex narcissistic borderline neurotic and psychotic processes and fantasies associated to her highly cathected, idealized and denigrated body. The voluminous rich material, clinical, sociological, literary, visual and other that describes the complex symptoms pertaining to the mother and the daughter (Jacobs 2007: 129–148) in a culture that can only theorise the paternal genealogy and sequesters the mother and the daughter to a no-place outside symbolic agency needs to be thought about in relation to an absent or yet-to-be-theorized structural maternal law.

That is to say, psychoanalysis needs to stop settling for mirroring and unwittingly confirming the inevitability of the descriptions of the pathologies pertaining to the mother and needs instead to start building a theory that could help rectify the situation.

Matricide then, is no longer associated (in my work) with pathology and description – that is to say – no longer used to describe the manifest symptoms of the marginalisation of the mother in cultures and discourses – but instead functions as a generative structural organising concept to be utilized by a psychoanalytic feminism committed to post-patriarchal futures and committed to a model of the symbolic and the unconscious that can accommodate a plurality of unconscious structures allowing for the expression of a heterogeneous palimpsest of structural psychosexual processes – not reducible to Oedipal phallic heteronormativity.

The questions now turned around the hypothesis of matricide as producing a generative loss functioning to transmit a maternal genealogy – a transgenerational unconscious structure or law that could work to mediate the mother-daughter and/or between women relations allowing for the specificities of femininities as active participants in the symbolic process and the transmission of a different cultural inheritance or bond.

Now before I try to explain what my theory of a matricidal underlying law/prohibition consists of – and how I arrived at its definition (via working with myth and structural anthropology), I want to quickly address what could be construed as a potentially utopian thrust in all this – together with a hint of wish fulfilment – the wish or belief that if we theorise matricide we will not only cure all the ills of patriarchy but psychoanalysis will become an empowering politicized tool subverting dominant normative theories, the symbolic will be able to accommodate a multitude of subjectivities organised around different laws other than Oedipus, the mother-daughter relation could be given structural mediation and would thus cease to fall into the destructive dynamics concerning too close proximities, destructive envy, collapsed identifications and separation problems and the matricidal law or law of the mother would produce the possibility of a different model of culture – a yet-to-be-future beyond phallic binarism that could finally be pronounced as post-patriarchal.

This is obviously not only a tall order but also reproduces an underlying teleological fantasy of a 'happily ever after' resolution. I want to stress now that these are *not* my hopes or fantasies for a feminist psychoanalytic model of matricide in its theorised form. To my mind – change happens very slowly – the extent to which the dominant structures are internalised and entrenched in the unconscious means that positing any kind of voluntarism whether it be performing gendered identities or theorising a maternal law is only viable if we are rigorous in addressing the complex relation between the psychic (i.e., the unconscious) and the social symbolic structures that it produces *or* is produced by.

To theorise a structural maternal law organised around a matricidal prohibition will at best create new spaces, new dialogues, and new possibilities with regard to the massive amount of work that is to be done in theorising, representing and symbolising the irreducible maternal in all its diverse meanings, processes and specificities *outside* the projections of the patriarchal imaginary.

A crucial point to add here is that the matricidal laws or laws of the mother that I have attempted to theorise is a law *in lower case*. That is to say, it is not THE Law of the Mother in capital letters mirroring THE Law of the Father as in the Lacanian schema. My notion of a matricidal law belongs to a model of the symbolic also with no capital S (that is to say, it does not pertain to some kind of systematic totalising master theory like Lacan's theory). It is not a matter of just adding matricide to patricide, the law of the mother to the law of the father – this would be problematic because it would be complicit with the positing of a hetero-normative binary model of complementarity, an idealized parental couple functioning to organise a master theory or laws determining culture and subjectivity. What I want to stress is that the matricidal law – or law of the mother that I am proposing – is *not the one and only* maternal law with a capital M; it is actually just one aspect of the *laws* of the mother which are yet to be theorised and will contribute to the creation of what Irigaray terms the 'yet to be female imaginaries'. The use of the plural is crucial. The Laws of the mother cannot then be reduced to or made symmetrical to the current dominant model of the singular Law of the Father (in capital letters). They function in very different ways.

However, we need, I think, to be tentative in announcing the heterogeneous mutable plural model of the symbolic as the new theoretical aspiration of the new

'good object', if you like, because we then risk elevating and idealising these concepts to the status of magic words which will create a 'better' world. We need to produce a more complex idea of what we mean when we actually use these words. In the current climate of the flourishing critical theories which have had a profound influence on the humanities (my work obviously included) terms like 'becoming', 'mutability', 'difference', 'heterogeneous', and 'plurality' form a kind of new 'good' orthodoxy. It is crucial – in my project – to be highly specific in relation to these terms and to avoid an overinvestment in them as easy ways to posit a model of an all-inclusive totality – a model of the symbolic or culture where nothing is excluded and hierarchy and binarism are a thing of the past. The very conditions of becoming a subject by definition necessitate profound losses and melancholic identifications and exclusions where there are always remainders, always excluded remnants that are foreclosed from symbolic mediation. What I want to work towards though is the gradual building up of a field of work or a paradigm that theorises different losses (from that of the castration/patricidal loss) – different ways of negotiating loss leading to different organisations of what can and cannot be structured/included/seen/heard/thought/said and represented.

So now I hope I have given some sense of my context, of the frame of my work and what is at stake in the debate. Now, I want to give you a brief sense of the *how* in my project – the instrument of intervention – the strategy or method. And so, we turn to myth.

Irigaray's call for scholars to turn to myth and tragedy because they comprise the root of our symbolic order as we know it has inspired much important work undertaken from different approaches in both feminism and philosophy. Feminist theorists have returned to myths and tried to foster them for the creation of positive identifications and representations for women. The Demeter-Persephone myth, for example, was adopted as a so-called 'feminist myth' that could give value and explain the dynamics of the mother-daughter relation (Foley 1994) – and more recently the Antigone, Medusa, Cassandra, Medea and Penelope myths have returned to contemporary culture in new rewritten and retheorised forms (Irigaray 1995; Butler 2000; Cavarero 1995; Atwood 2005; Wolf 1998; Zajko and Leonard 2006). In much of this contemporary feminist work on ancient Greek myth, the work that is being done aims to transform the thinking process itself rather than to just foster positive identifications.

Myth here will be approached like a symptom, the delirium of the patriarchal imaginaries that need to be analysed as if dream thoughts. I will show how the move from the manifest level of the myth to the latent content allows myth to be used as a politicized instrument of change. If we can uncover the latent hidden repressed content of the myth we can, I suggest, move towards deconstructing the patriarchal imaginary to discover what has been radically excluded. And in this case it is maternal laws which I found to be the radically excluded latent content of the specific myth I worked with – that is, the Oresteian myth.

Turning to Aeschylus's *Oresteia* (Aeschylus 1977) as my object of study whilst trying to think about the meaning of matricide in Western culture and discourses was in some senses an obvious move. It is a foundational ancient myth that tells of a son (Orestes) who murders his mother as a revenge murder for her murder of his father. Clytemnestra (his mother) had killed Agamemnon (Orestes father) as revenge for his murder of their eldest daughter who he had sacrificed in order to win a war. Father kills daughter, mother kills father, son kills mother. The Oresteia attempts to resolve itself around the question of Orestes' crime in the first court of democratic justice set up by Athena. Orestes, the matricidal son, is put on trial. The jury is split down the middle – half side with the mother's cause and half with the father. It is up to the goddess Athena to cast the determining vote. Athena votes for Orestes and, in so doing, condones matricide and implicitly condones the violence against the daughter by the father. Her reason for siding with Orestes is as follows:

> No mother gave me birth. Never bred in the darkness of the womb. In all my heart I am my father's child.

Orestes walks free and the father is pronounced prime author of identity by virtue of Athena's miraculous so-called 'motherless' birth. (Obviously that was a totally condensed potted version.)

No myth can be definitively understood as an isolated narrative or sequence. Myths, according to Levi Strauss, need to be read as an 'orchestral score' (Levi Strauss 1978: 44). Myths can only be analysed as fragments that overlap and mutate into and with other mythical fragments. Isolating a myth as Freud did with Oedipus and not analysing it in the context of the mythical orchestral score leads to an incomplete interpretation of the myth that can only function on a manifest level.

Via the methodology of studying the Orestian myth in the context of voluminous associated myths, I came across the myth of Metis, Athena's mother who, according to Hesiod, was raped by Zeus and subsequently became pregnant. During her pregnancy Zeus swallowed her whole and kept her inside of him where she gave him advice and council. Some months later Zeus was overcome with a headache and then out sprung Athena from his head. After Athena's birth, there is no trace of Metis – we will never hear of her again. But what we will persistently hear in the myths and tragedies, in poems, opera, philosophy and psychoanalysis is that Athena had no mother. In the Oresteia, Athena's apparent motherless status functions as a crucial justification for the institution of patriarchal law and the absolving of Orestes' matricidal crime.

In my rereading of the Oresteia (Jacobs 2007: 55–83), I uncover this related matricidal myth – the myth of Metis, Athena's raped and murdered mother – and show that it exists in cryptic forms in Aeschylus's text. In uncovering what I term the 'latent content of the Oresteian myth' I point to the systematic repression of the figure of Athena's mother in all receptions, reworkings and critiques of the myth.

The crux of my argument is that the denial of Athena's mother has resulted in the prevention of the myth from being effectively used in psychoanalytic theory as a model or structure that can account for fantasies and unconscious processes that are not reducible to the Oedipus/patricidal structure.

By uncovering the traces of Metis in the Oresteian myth we can suggest and restore a vital link between these two matricidal myths, whose severance hitherto has resulted in the incomplete theorisation of matricide in contemporary critical theories. Psychoanalytic theorists who have addressed the myth and have unwittingly reproduced the denial of Metis – Athena's mother. These range from Freud and Klein to more contemporary theorists such as Andre Green and Luce Irigaray (Jacobs 2007: 55–72).

So what is Metis's law? What is this law of the mother that the Oresteia had for so long censored or repressed in its latent cryptic substratum?

Metis's law, which I want to suggest forms just one aspect of the yet to be theorised *laws* of the mother, functions as a prohibition on the male parthenogenetic fantasy – that is to say, the fantasy that the father can procreate alone. This parthenogenetic fantasy underlies the Oresteian logic. Zeus's giving birth to Athena forms the belief or fantasy that is elevated to the status of law and in fact the patriarchal order – as represented in the Oresteia – depends upon it. As soon as Metis is introduced into the Oresteian constellation, the whole of its logic is fractured.

We can see how crucial the resistance to knowing Metis had to be to keep the logic of patriarchy standing. Every statement claiming that Athena had no mother is the manifest lie, the symptom of resistance or blind-spot that points to the desire to repress the maternal law, to repress and transgress the prohibition that dictates to the male child/subject you cannot generate/procreate alone. Instead, this maternal prohibition represented in the figure of the swallowed pregnant woman is incorporated in Zeus and in the myth and in discourse and theory.

Rather than representing the loss that this maternal prohibition should mobilise – the maternal generative function is incorporated, denied and appropriated reducing the mother to a container to nurse the seed (Apollo's words) and giving generative sovereignty to the father. The mechanism of the incorporation of the matricidal law (of Metis) that the Oresteia represents finally results in rendering matricide sterile in its capacity to deliver this maternal law.

Irigaray said 'what the Oresteia describes still takes place' (Irigaray 1991: 36). I would change that slightly to say what is latent, hidden or encrypted in the Orestiean text is still acted out in culture, that is to say, the systematic occlusion of the laws of the mother that prohibits the male parthenogenetic fantasy.

Undoing the repression of Metis and bringing to light the law of the mother that she represents means that in future transmissions and receptions of the Oresteian myth a new understanding of matricide, the mother and her law is facilitated and can hopefully be used in psychoanalysis for the purpose of constructing a maternal structuring symbolic function.

I want now to pause to pick up a thread that I left quite near the beginning – that is, the question of the so-called real mother, the practices, the experiential, and where this sits with my engagement with the mother in theory, with matricide, with Metis and my hypothesis of the maternal laws.

It is a crucial question that I continually resist confronting face on. In fact, in all honesty I think I am ever so slightly resistant to addressing the so-called real mother (despite being one and having one) and would rather talk about Metis any day. It is as if addressing the real mother represents an impasse to me linked to the fear and inevitability of making generalizations, appropriations and homogenizing the massive diversity and difference of the maternal subjects. From fear of colonizing difference I would always already prefer to avoid addressing the so-called real mother.

Perhaps too there is a primitive fear about being pulled into a kind of collapse into the detail and materiality of mother/mothering process and experience rather than being able to think about and theorise/represent it. I thus become subject to the exact potentially destructive mechanism or fantasy that my book describes, critiques and tries to rectify – that is, the ubiquitous fear and dread of engulfment into a mother or into mothering that threatens identity itself, turns thought to mush, forces one into an immediacy which can suggest a kind of borderline state of both madness and the sublime.

When asked, for instance, how my work on matricide contributes to debates on mothering practices, postnatal depression, social arrangements for combining mothering and work, child rearing, breast feeding, etc. I become somewhat pessimistic and conflicted. It is important to keep in check and subvert the desire to totally refuse to engage with (in my intellectual work) the realm of lived experience. I want to resist the seduction of locating research on the maternal safely in the esoteric abstracted intricacies of post-Lacanian psychoanalytic theory and philosophy as though theorizing is a haven – a psychic retreat or defence against the intense proximities, intimacies, passions, dependencies, and ambivalences, the chaos, despair and euphoria of doing and receiving processes of mothering.

Yet, ironically, killing off the so-called 'real mother' was necessary in my attempt to theorise matricide and a maternal subject position. The blind-spot in my own work, my own Metis – if you like – is this resistance or reticence about addressing the real mother. To my mind, there is no real mother; there are just a multitude of diverse processes and experiences that cannot be reduced or homogenized into any viable category. In this way, the maternal, for me, can only be approached via the sociosymbolic structures, representations, fantasies, and discourses that have to be negotiated and/or circumvented when living one's life as a 'mother'.

However, the question of 'real mothers' and lived experiences probably lies at the root of my desire to work on creating a theory of a generative matricide. The crushing sense of having no way in the current culture to know oneself as 'mother' outside the projections of the patriarchal discourses and projections, no way of symbolising, of thinking about what it means to occupy the position of mother in relation to another, no way other than to submit to the immediacy of the materiality of maternal experience, or to act out on the level of the symptom or the level of banal speech, or internalized misogyny.

The question for me now becomes: How will Metis and her law – and all the other laws pertaining to a maternal structural function that will hopefully continue to be theorised – help us give to the next generation a different structural inheritance so that we are not destined to unwittingly reproduce the terms of the dominant patriarchal matricidal imaginary transgenerationally?

How will Metis and the future yet-to-be-theorised laws of the mother help alter the very parameters of what can and cannot be said and thought, understood and practiced? Can Metis inspire or facilitate a mode of action as well as presenting prohibitions and cultural laws?

In conclusion: Theory into practice – Metis the goddess and metis as cunning intelligence

Thus far, I have tried to describe how in my work with the Oresteian myth, Metis the ancient goddess – raped, impregnated and swallowed by Zeus – can be traced as the radically marginalised and hidden matricide that the murder of Clytemnestra masks. Metis is conspicuous by her absence and this absence is both sustained and subverted by a myriad of reversals, inversions, and ellipses in the ancient Greek texts and psychoanalytic receptions of these texts.

Via this rereading of the *Oresteia* that seeks to bring Metis out of the darkness of Zeus's stomach, I have proposed a matricidal law organised around a set of parthenogenetic fantasies. Metis's law and her associated prohibitions could, I have suggested, contribute to what contemporary feminists and philosophers influenced by Irigaray have described as alternative symbolic systems existing according to different laws, structures and fantasies not reducible to the phallic Oedipal model.

In this way, Metis was used as a figure to theorize a maternal law; a law-of-the-mother that could function on at least two levels/registers. Firstly, in direct relation to Irigaray's call for symbolic change that would allow for forms of representation, fantasy and modes of subjectivity and sociality that the current dominant phallic symbolic forecloses. Secondly, Metis's law could be one way of limiting or holding in check the strikingly prevalent male parthenogenetic fantasies that permeate our culture – and thus could potentially act as a check/limit on an aspect of male psychic and physical violence towards women – and more specifically pregnant women. In this way, Metis's law is one contribution in the attempt to counter the destructive fantasies projected onto and acted out on the maternal body that feminist theorists and clinicians have so compellingly revealed (and cultures seems to reproduce and condone). The maternal laws underpinned by the Metis model could be used as a tool of analysis and a structure of representation that could allow for the recognition of the male parthenogenetic fantasy and its destructive effects as well as rendering a structural maternal genealogy visible and with symbolic status.

However, there is also a concomitant use of Metis that I want to sketch out here. As well as being the Goddess Metis that I have described, there is also in ancient Greek thought the *'concept'* metis; a specific form of Greek 'cunning intelligence' as it is evoked so vividly in Detienne and Vernant's astonishing book *Cunning Intelligence in Greek Culture and Society*. In their words:

> Metis is a type of intelligence and thought, a way of knowing; it implies a complex but very coherent body of mental attitudes and intellectual behavior which combine flair, wisdom, forethought, subtlety of mind, deception, resourcefulness, vigilance, opportunism, various skills and experience acquired over the years. It applies to situations which are shifting, disconcerting and ambiguous, which do not lend themselves to precise measurement, exact calculation or rigorous logic.
>
> *(Detienne and Vernant 1991: 3)*

Detienne and Vernant's book demonstrates that this form of cunning intelligence was very much alive and an important aspect of Greek culture and society – but has been systematically marginalized and overlooked by modern Greek/Classics scholars and philosophers because of the dominant legacy of the Platonic metaphysical tradition that condemned and banished metis as an unreliable corrupter of the Truth.

Modern Greek scholars who have neglected the importance of its role, its impact or even its existence have remained faithful to a particular image Greek thought created of itself, in which metis is conspicuous by its absence (Detienne and Vernant 1991: 42–48).

Through their analyses, Vernant and Detienne present us with the essential features of metis, its mode of operation, its terminology and its associations. They do this by tracing the concept back to its origins in the fields of hunting and fishing. Metis, the 'many faceted' intelligence, belongs to the duplicitous world of traps and devices: the knot, the net, the weave, the rope, the mesch, the bait, the noose and the snare. Metis functions through inversion and reversal; it pertains to all that is pliable, slippery and twisted, oblique, elusive and ambiguous, and it moves in more than one direction simultaneously.

One of the salient properties of metis that Vernant and Detienne are clear to convey is its radical resistance to being fixed or being made to be/do one thing. It is a movement rather than a position, and thus it can never be claimed for any cause or projected idea. It cannot be made to represent anything nor can it be identified with since it is never itself but always already shifting and reversing. It can neither be claimed as a stable concept and it can have no affiliations – any such move to claim metis as a shoring up of a position, argument or identity betrays the very specificity of its logic.

On several occasions in Vernant and Detienne's book, they will explicitly declare that metis is inextricably bound up with power relations and are consistent in their understanding of metis as a force of intelligence or way of knowing that functions on the side of the 'weaker', the 'frail' and the subordinate – operating to 'reverse the rules accepted in a trial of strength' with stratagem that are like 'spells to oppose brute force' (Detienne and Vernant 1991: 44).

Seemingly then, the interventions of metis are always in the service of the subordinate, subjected or oppressed, and the cunning of metis will forever disrupt and undo consolidations of power and domination.

Vernant and Detienne are clear that *'whatever Metis wins it does not keep'* (my italics) (Detienne and Vernant 1991: 28). Metis may reverse power relations, reverse binaries, turn the hunter into hunted, turn rational certainty inside out – but by its nature it will never shore up, consolidate, develop or sustain. Its movement will only ever shift ground and will never take root.

Metis, as it is described, most crucially *does not seek power*; what it wins it does not keep. On the one hand then, metis reverses or destabilizes power relations in the service of the subordinate; and on the other hand, it does not keep what it wins.

Metis, in its transformative action that undermines power relations and does not keep what it wins, cannot be used in the service of notions of possession, ownership, legitimacy and sovereignty. It is an action without origin – no single subject is its cause or reason – rather its movement emerges from the multiple and the heterogeneous. Metis transforms the constellation of power but crucially never comes from or acts from one place. In this way, metis produces an action or an intervention that does not depend upon a unitary subject or intent. Its transforming capacity is precisely in its multiplicity and simultaneous movement in divergent directions. Without this crucial characteristic of not keeping what it wins, it would inevitably become another potential form of domination and/or mastery.

Metis is a form of cunning intelligence that functions from and in 'a world of becoming, in circumstances of conflict' (Detienne and Vernant 1991: 46). It has no desire or idea of stability, mastery or resolution, and defies every tendency towards winning, keeping or controlling. If it has a trajectory that can be defined, then it is a circular one. Vernant and Detienne use the circle to describe the ultimate expression of metis:

> The ultimate expression of these qualities is the circle, the bond that is perfect because it completely turns back on itself, with neither beginning nor end, nor front or rear, and which rotation becomes both mobile and immobile, moving in both directions at once.
>
> *(Detienne and Vernant 1991: 42–48)*

In the same mechanism of exclusion as we saw in receptions and readings of the Oresteian myth towards Metis the Goddess, the concept metis – cunning intelligence – is similarly relegated to invisibility, written out of the accounts of Greek philosophy and epistemology until it was consolidated and presented as a lost form of thinking, acting and knowing by Vernant and Detienne. We can now see the relation between the myth Metis and the concept metis – both incorporated/swallowed and violently marginalized. We cannot also ignore the fact that this connection between the myth Metis and the concept metis brings the maternal into the terrain of this specificity of cunning intelligence.

For the most part, the references to Metis in feminist theory refer to the mythical figure Metis, the goddess, raped and incorporated by Zeus. Metis appears more generally in contemporary discourses as a metaphor to describe this violent action of raping, swallowing, appropriating and foreclosing, which characterizes a major aspect of the phallogocentric relation to the 'feminine' and maternal.

The philosophical or epistemological concept 'metis' – as cunning intelligence – is mentioned briefly by Adriana Cavarero in her discussion of Penelope's *'metic'* cunning in the doing and undoing of her weave (Cavarero 1995: 30). Yet, despite its explicit connection (via the thread that links the myth Metis and concept metis) to the 'maternal feminine', and also to an alternative epistemology or practice 'beyond ordinary logic', it has not been taken up substantially in feminist thought. It is as if the excavation of the myth and the mythical maternal goddess tallied more with the dominant strain of feminism linked to ideas of a maternal subject and to theories that claimed for the maternal something specific that would further ground ideas of female subjectivities and female sociosymbolic power. The decrypting of Metis as Athena's swallowed mother in the Orestean myth also releases and connects to the philosophical concept metis (cunning intelligence) and thus the metic mode of being and the figure of pregnant Metis are brought together. Metis and her law, her prohibition against the male appropriative and violent parthenogenetic fantasy, also releases and represents a different form or mode of knowing and being – a psychic and material praxis – an intelligence not reducible to either platonic binarism or linear teleological rationality. A metic mode of functioning that has been so actively denigrated and hidden into the margins of philosophy.

There are exciting possibilities regarding the connection between the swallowed pregnant Metis banished to Zeus's stomach and the concept metis – as cunning intelligence – also banished from the legacy of philosophy. Together, my hope is that they can be developed and used for the creation of cunning maternal interventions and transformations into psychoanalysis, culture and representation and, of course, living.

Notes

1 The main arguments presented in this chapter are based on my monograph: *On Matricide: Myth, Psychoanalysis and the Law of the Mother.* (New York, NY: Columbia University Press, 2007). However, this chapter charts further developments of my thoughts concerning matricide.
2 For a discussion of 'the-Law-of-the Father' and its status in psyche and culture, see Jacobs 2007, pp. 45–55).

References

Aeschylus. (1979) *The Oresteia* (trans. Robert Fagles). London, England: Penguin Classics.

Atwood, M. (2005) *The Penelopiad*. Edinburgh, Scotland: Canongate Press.

Butler, J. (2000) *Antigone's Claim: Kinship between Life and Death*. New York, NY: Columbia University Press.

Cavarero, A. (1995) *In Spite of Plato: A Feminist Rewriting of Ancient Philosophy*. London, England: Routledge.

Detienne, M. and Vernant, J. P. (1991) *Cunning Intelligence in Greek Culture and Society*. Chicago, IL: University of Chicago Press.

Ettinger, B. (2006) *The Matrixial Borderspace*. Minneapolis, MN: University of Minnesota Press.

Foley, H. (ed.). (1984) *The Homeric Hymn to Demeter*. Princeton, NJ: Princeton University Press.

Jacobs, A. (2007) *On Matricide: Myth, Psychoanalysis and the Law of the Mother*. New York, NY: Columbia University Press.

Jacobs, A. (2010) The life of Metis: Cunning maternal interventions. In *Studies in the Maternal*, Vol. 2 (1). London, England: The Open Journal of Humanities.

Kristeva, J. (1989) *The Black Sun: Depression and Melancholia* (trans. Leon S. Roudiez). New York, NY: Columbia University Press.

Laplanche, J. (1989). *New Foundations for Psychoanalysis* (trans. David Macey). Oxford, England: Blackwell.

Levi Strauss, C. (1978) *Myth and Meaning: The Massey Lectures*. London, England: Routledge.

Mitchell, J. (2000) *Mad Men and Medusas: Reclaiming Hysteria and the Effect of Sibling Relations on the Human Condition*. London, England: Penguin.

Stone, A. (2014) *Feminism, Psychoanalysis and Maternal Subjectivity*. London, England: Routledge.

Whitford, M. (ed.). (1991) *The Irigaray Reader*. Oxford, England: Blackwell.

Wolf, C. (1984) *Cassandra: A Novel and Four Essays* (trans. Jan Van Heurck). London, England: Virago.

Wolf, C. (1998) *Medea: A Novel* (trans. John Cullen). London, England: Virago.

Zajko, V. and Leonard, M. (eds.). (2006) *Laughing with Medusa: Classical Myth and Feminist Thought*. Oxford, England: Oxford University Press.

2

MATERNAL INHERITANCE

Lucy King

The maternal inheritance referred to in the title of this chapter is that of mother to daughter. We live in a patrilineal culture in which a son's link to his father and his paternal line is marked by the sharing of their name; a patriarchal culture which valorises the phallus and all that that symbolises, at the expense of the symbolic power and creative potential of the womb. If we are to take seriously the inequalities that still bedevil our society, then this is something that needs to be remedied. For as the philosopher and psychoanalyst Luce Irigaray trenchantly puts it, 'If we are not to be accomplices in the murder of the mother we also need to assert that there is a genealogy of women' (Irigaray 1993: 19).

In this chapter I look at the attitudes towards mothers that prevailed within the Women's Liberation Movement (or 2nd wave feminism as it came to be called), and within much psychoanalytic writing, well aware how these both reflect and are reflected in, wider culture. I start with a more personal narrative drawn from my own experience as a woman, a mother, a feminist and a psychotherapist; an attempt perhaps to insert something of a mother as a subject rather than merely an object for others, I have done this also in the final section, entitled just 'Motherhood'. The structure of the chapter is an attempt to consider each of these themes in turn, although they form threads that intertwine and intersect in a way that undermines this separation.

At the time I delivered the original seminar version of the chapter, I had just had an operation to correct a bunion and was very aware, sitting there with my foot in a 'post-surgical boot', that this was an affliction from which I had watched my mother become more and more crippled. Certainly a maternal inheritance I could have done without!

Earlier when I had started thinking, somewhat desperately, about what I might want to contribute to this series of discussions about 'The Maternal', I remembered that the conveners had suggested that I could if I chose, speak from a personal viewpoint. My title, 'Maternal Inheritance', certainly has echoes of some of my old interests as a biologist as well as later more political ones. While the research I did for my PhD involved showing how changing the environment in terms of temperature and light radically affected the patterns of cell division and growth in a particular species of fern, this reflected much wider interests in the complex interactions between genes and their environment. The recurrent, generally rather simplistic, and sometimes spurious, nature/nurture debate with all its political ramifications arising from the supposed implications for such things as intelligence, gender and race was, at the time, raising a great deal of heat, although rather less light.

I was also fascinated by the controversies surrounding the idea that the cytoplasm, and not just the genes in the cell nucleus, might play some important role in inheritance. This cytoplasmic inheritance is often referred to as 'Maternal Inheritance' since, generally speaking, sexual reproduction involves the fertilisation of a large female gamete/ovum by the nucleus of a much smaller male gamete/sperm; this meaning that most or all of the cytoplasm is maternal in origin. This at the time had political associations with the derided and supposedly completely discredited claims made by Lamarck for the inheritance of acquired characteristics that was said to have been responsible for the terrible failures of Soviet agriculture. This was considered a consequence of political ideology taking precedence over scientific endeavour. Times have changed over this, as in so many other ways, with the discovery of the significance of maternally inherited mitochondrial DNA.[1]

At the time I gave this seminar, I was in the middle of conducting a series of seminars with the Philadelphia Association's psychotherapy training group, under the title 'Mothers, Daughters, Sisters'. The seminars were based around the way that these relationships have been thought about (or, too often, largely ignored) by psychoanalysis. My starting point was Freud's claim that a young girl's relationship to her mother is inevitably mired in irresolvable ambivalence and her only escape from this is to turn away from mother and replace her with her father as her principle love-object. Boys, Freud says, have equally strong feelings of both love and hate towards their mother but, he suggests, are better able to divert hostility from their mother onto their father and thus preserve feelings towards mother that are predominantly loving (Freud 1931: 235). Important also in what I had to say was the overwhelming extent to which the focus of psychoanalytic writing about women is on them as daughters. More often than not, siblings are only mentioned in passing, as rivals or as in some way standing in for a parent; and mothers are generally seen only in the role of 'object'.

The Women's Movement views mothers

What I want to do here is to consider first of all the theme of 'Mother, Daughter and Sisters' as played out in the Women's Movement that gathered momentum immediately post-1968, the year in which there was a crescendo of radical student and workers' protests most famously in France.

It was an exciting time. The feminist Women's Liberation Movement arose partly out of and partly in reaction to the 1960s radical social and sexual revolutions; the thrust of these being to shed old conformities and conventional modes of living, and to 'get out from under' authoritarian social systems.

When I became involved with the Women's Movement in the early 1970s, it was characterised by an adherence to fluid, unstructured, nonhierarchical groups. There were no leaders, no spokeswomen. At first at least, it was very exhilarating. Small, rather intimate groups; political campaigning groups but also consciousness-raising groups in which people shared their experiences of home, of work, of intimate life. One of the abiding slogans of the time was: 'The Personal is Political'. There was a lot of warmth, a lot of emotion, an exciting sense of freedom and newness. In 1969 the first National Conference of the UK Women's Movement had been held in Ruskin College, Oxford. The next year's conference drew up a series of 'demands':

1.   Equal pay
2.   Free contraception
3.   Abortion on demand
4.   24-hour nurseries

Clear in these demands is that economic independence and parity (shockingly still far from being achieved) was fundamental. And that, also central to the Movement, was the conviction that the only way that women could gain greater control of their lives was through gaining greater control of their bodies and, in particular, control and choice over their part in pregnancy and reproduction. Embodied here was recognition of the source of their dependency and vulnerability, and a resistance to being labelled and confined by these. Vulnerability has strong associations with pregnancy and maternity, as well as infancy, all these involving dependency: on the medical profession, on partners and, for the child, on mothers. Being able, however, to take back some control; to choose whether or when to bear a child; to have choices over one's role in the nurturance and raising of a child; and real choices over work and family that includes both, and not, effectively, just either/or; then women's fertility can potentially become a source of real strength rather than of weakness.

The Women's Movement in the early 1970s idealised relationships between women at the peer level – "Sisterhood is Powerful" was proclaimed and, indeed it did, most of the time, feel that this was so. It was not, however, without its darker, more problematic side. When disagreements arose, as they inevitably did, the lack of structure made it very difficult to negotiate such conflicts in ways that avoided them becoming rather hostile, personal attacks. Overt personal rivalries, however, were taboo, and because, therefore, they could not be admitted, they could not be satisfactorily mediated. The determinedly nonhierarchical structure, seen at first as liberating, became a tyranny and, like in Animal Farm where 'everyone was equal but some were more equal than others', powerful 'behind-the-scenes' cliques formed. I never went to a National Conference but some of the tales from them sounded quite horrendous.

The battle was with patriarchy but it was not just men who were seen as the 'problem'; mothers were equally seen as the agents of patriarchy, exemplifying all that this new generation of women wanted to escape. Mothers were regarded as having submitted to patriarchy and then having coerced their daughters into conformity, all the while passing on to them all their latent impotent fury, resentments and incapacitating sense of inferiority.

There was plenty of support for this view around. Simone De Beauvoir, writer of the most classic of feminist texts "The Second Sex" (originally published in 1949) wrote:

> Most women simultaneously demand and detest their feminine condition; they live through it in a state of resentment. The disgust they have for their sex might well lead them to give their daughters a man's education, but they are rarely large-minded enough. Vexed at having produced a woman, the mother greets her with this ambiguous curse: 'You shall be a woman'.
>
> *(De Beauvoir 1972: 533)*

De Beauvoir goes on to claim that things get worse as the child grows and wants some independence:

> 'This seems to the mother a mark of hateful ingratitude; she tries to checkmate the girl's will to escape; she cannot bear to have her double become an other'. On the other hand, 'she cannot bear to have her daughter become really her double – to substitute for herself' (that is, for mother to be no longer unique and indispensable). (Ibid: 545)
>
> Whether a loving or a hostile mother, the independence of her daughter dashes her hopes. She is doubly jealous; of the world that takes her daughter away from her, and of her daughter who in conquering a part of the world robs her of it. (Ibid: 534)

This is a very bleak view. It was very far from mine but it clearly resonated with many people. The problem is that it seems to universalise what was her *own* experience, growing up and living in a specific cultural context. It chimes, however, with prevalent psychoanalytic (and implicitly patriarchal) views that maturity, the fulfilling of potential and even 'freedom' can be achieved only through a process of separation from mother with all that implies for women.

Adrienne Rich in *Of Woman Born* – another influential text at the time – offers an equally bleak view when she says:

> Few women growing up in patriarchal society can feel mothered enough; the power of our mothers, whatever their love for us and their struggles on our behalf, is too restricted. And it is the mother through whom patriarchy early teaches the small female her proper expectations. The anxious pressure

of one female on another to conform to a degrading and dispiriting role can hardly be called 'mothering' even if she does believe it will help her daughter to survive.

(Rich 1977: 243)

And she goes on to say:

Many daughters live in rage at their mothers for having accepted, too readily and passively 'whatever comes'. A mother's victimisation does not merely humiliate her, it mutilates the daughter who watches her for clues about what it means to be a woman. (Ibid: 243)

Martha Quest, the pregnant protagonist in Doris Lessing's novel *A Proper Marriage*, sees maternal power as the enemy of freedom. She, Martha the *free spirit*, vows to protect her unborn child from the *maternal* Martha (Lessing 1966: 127).

This view, although extremely negative, can at least be read in the context of the novel as culturally specific. It still speaks to many women today but it does not claim so much that 'this is how it is and ever will be'. Mothers are, as are fathers and children, the product of an infinity of factors of enormous diversity and complexity. Psychoanalysts for their part undoubtedly work with great sensitivity and specificity with individual people, but all too often they speak and write as if they are the possessors (even sole possessors) of great universal truths about the nature of human beings.

Struggling with this paper, I reread an account that my mother wrote about her family – my own maternal inheritance. She quoted a great aunt of mine, as having reported that: 'She and my grandmother were inseparable as children, forming an alliance against their mother, "the enemy"'. My grandmother grew up to become a relatively early student at Cambridge, becoming a scholar there in 1891 – although only being awarded a proper degree, posthumously, in 1948! She loved the great sense of sisterhood in college. She later became very actively involved with the fight for women's rights and suffrage and, although had no career as such (which she regretted), she lectured to the Women's Cooperative Guild in Bradford and was involved with all sorts of groups trying to improve the lot of women. My mother admitted that she herself by contrast had felt no such pleasure in the exclusively female atmosphere when she went to the same college after a coeducational schooling. In fact, her rebellion was to join the first mixed acting group at Cambridge, something that was very much disapproved of by her women tutors. She wrote somewhat regretfully in her account: 'In what was, I suppose, a natural reaction from our mother's enthusiasm, my generation of women seemed less concerned with these things. It has been left to our daughters to take up again the cause of women, unjustly treated in our society'.

She was a strong and feisty woman, my mother, and my difficulty with her was not that she submitted passively to patriarchy so much as that she could be forthright and provocative in a way that to me as a child witness could be embarrassing although perhaps it is always the lot of children to be rather embarrassed by their parents at certain times. As a child I felt rather intimidated by her power, not her weakness, although I later came to appreciate it much, much more.

In the feminist movement in the 1970s there were profound divisions between those who wanted an end to any gendered division of labour (including childcare), and those who wanted the revaluing of female roles such as improved status for motherhood, wages for housewives and so on. Even more acrimonious were the seemingly irreconcilable disagreements between those who believed that women should fight for equality with men – in workplace and home –'anything you can do I can do as well' as well as the other way round:'anything I am supposed to do, you could do also', and, on the opposite side, the 'radical feminists' who thought that men were the problem and advocated separatism and 'political lesbianism'.

Even though I never encountered the bitterness such disputes were said to elicit at National Conferences, I did find myself the target of considerable hostility when I had the temerity to go, heavily pregnant, to a meeting of my local women's group about child care. I think the feeling from some people there was that I was somehow submitting to the patriarchal status quo by choosing to become a mother. Again, a bit later, at the Women's Therapy Centre in London, I was criticised robustly by the group I was in for choosing to breastfeed – thereby fixing me in the traditional maternal role of primary carer.

Despite such incidents of disapproval, I really enjoyed the strength and warmth of the relationships between women within the women's groups although I was never in any degree a separatist. Exclusively female groups were a novelty for me after a coeducational schooling and experience in science that was always of mixed and often predominantly male groups. I had also recently become a member of a formerly exclusively male Cambridge college that was taking its first steps towards 'co-residence'. I became part of a pregnancy advisory group offering pregnancy tests, contraceptive advice and support for those unwillingly or problematically pregnant. For years we met in the local Women's Centre but were eventually expelled because we allowed couples to come together for help and we even had a few male members in the group.

This '2nd wave Feminism' sought increased power and control for women and it was men who were seen as those who had the power and who sought to control and possess their women. There is some force, however, to Luisa Murraro's claim in her paper on 'Female Genealogies' that part of the virulence of the anger against men and male power felt by women is a displacement of:

> Unresolved aversion toward the mother that is latent and ever ready to be directed against themselves or other women, especially against those who embody some aspect of the mother image.

> *(Murraro 1994: 327)*

If this is so, then maybe for all of us in this culture, 'mother' and the idea of the maternal are fraught with deep unease. This being especially problematic for women since, if she attempts to repudiate her mother, she repudiates herself in some sense since it is through her early identification with her mother as a woman that she gains her own sense of being a woman.

The mother in psychoanalytic literature and beyond

On the whole, feminists in the late 1960s, early 1970s were extremely wary of psychoanalysis, sometimes because, in the United States especially, many of these women had had close and wounding encounters (directly or indirectly) with psychoanalytic convictions about penis envy, masculinity-complexes, female masochism and women's general inferiority. At this time, such orthodox psychoanalytic views were very current and influential (again, especially in the United States). And within psychoanalytic literature (as in society more generally), mother blaming was pretty prevalent as unfortunately, it still is.

Eric Erikson in *Childhood and Society* writes that in case history after case history mothers are decried as pathogenic 'moms' and even as a "generation of vipers" (Erikson 1965: 282). He goes on to describes this 'mom' as being, 'a woman in whose life cycle remnants of infantility join advanced senility to crowd out the middle range of mature womanhood, who has thus become self-absorbed and stagnant' (Ibid 1965: 282).

Erikson even blamed mother blaming on mothers: 'No doubt both patients and psychiatric workers were blamed too much when they were children; now they blame all mothers because all causality has become linked to blame' (Ibid: 281).

Susan Contratto rather later, commented on this trend:

> Many professionals attribute delinquency, drug abuse, school failure, schizophrenia, depression, neurosis as well as physical ailments such as asthma, allergies, colitis etc. etc. and virtually all anti-social manifestations have been attributed to 'bad mothering' despite no clear evidence of links with any particular maternal pattern. Only gross neglect and abuse is clearly linked with psychological difficulties.
>
> *(Contratto 1984: 249)*

My shelves are stacked with feminist/psychoanalytic books about matricide, about 'bad mothers' or mothers who are narcissistically attached to their children and who won't let go (won't in essence let their offspring spring off). Both feminism and psychoanalysis in these books are concerned with women more or less exclusively as daughters. Mothers, whether seen as submissive agents of patriarchy or as having monstrous power over their children (or both), are figures that their daughters most definitely do not want to emulate. Maternal inheritance here is viewed as fundamentally problematic, perhaps because of the current role mothers play under patriarchy, perhaps by its very nature.

In *The Rocking of the Cradle and the Ruling the World* Dorothy Dinnerstein used psychoanalysis as the basis for her thesis that there is a need for women to stop being the sole or even chief carer of their infants and young children. She suggested that the predominantly female responsibility for the nurturing and education of the young results in a lifelong emotional crippling of both men and women. She called up fearsome images of *The Mermaid and the Minotaur*:

> The treacherous mermaid, seductive and impenetrable female representa-tive of the dark and magic underwater world from which our life comes and in which we cannot live, lures voyagers to their doom. The fearsome minotaur, gigantic and eternally infantile offspring of a mother's unnatural lust, male representative of mindless, greedy power, insatiably devours live human flesh.
>
> *(Dinnerstein 1978: 5)*

> To mother-raised humans, male authority is bound to look like a reasonable refuge from female authority. ... On the whole, our attitudes towards the second parent – the parent who ordinarily orbit, at the beginning, outside the enchanted mother-infant pair, and who then enters it so gradually that it remains for a long time a very lopsided triangle indeed – are far less infantile, far less inchoate, than our attitudes towards the first. ... Thus father can be seen as a more *human* being than the mother, more like an adult version of oneself, less engulfing, less nebulously overwhelming. (Ibid: 175)

In some ways, of course, society has changed in the direction advocated by Dinnerstein. In many families at least, childcare is now more evenly spread (although even today survey evidence shows that the bulk of both housework and the caring for both children and the elderly is still done by women). Furthermore, I think many women would agree that even when they are still somehow primarily responsible in that, even when there is apparent equality regarding specific tasks or hours spent with the child, many men still see themselves as virtuously 'helping their wives'. From a psychoanalytic perspective, any such changes at a practical level are probably not sufficient to alter what has been seen as the inevitable ambiva-lences in the child–maternal relationship.

So for Dinnerstein and a raft of other feminist writers of this period, Nancy Chodorow, Adrienne Rich, Jean Baker Miller amongst others, it is motherhood (i.e., that women mother rather than that they just give birth) that is primarily responsible for women's oppression as well as the sexual malaise of both sexes.

Judging from these views, it is hardly surprising if maternal inheritance has become something we may shrink from and fear. I am not in any way suggesting that all mothers are in reality 'good' and it is just the biased recollections of children who malign them. As a psychotherapist I am well aware that some mothers for all sorts of reasons and in all sorts of ways do not manage to provide adequate emotional care for their children, and that this leads to enduring, and sometimes dire, consequences, especially perhaps, for their daughters.

Not uncommonly, distressed women speak of needing to keep their mothers out, or at bay; of needing to find ways to feel that they themselves rather than their mothers are in control. Some young women, especially in adolescence, speak of how they experience their bodies as a possession of their mothers rather than as their own being. As a consequence they may act out this sense by restricting their eating or hurting their bodies. In extreme cases they may attempt to rid themselves of their bodies as if only then would they be able to be truly and purely themselves.

Christian Oliver in *Jocasta's Children* writes of how the emphasis in psychoanalysis (and wider culture influenced by it) places complete emphasis on the boy's Oedipal desire for his mother, but ignores entirely the mother's desire. She points out that Freud did not just live in a patriarchal society but all his mythological stories that he drew on are profoundly patriarchal. And she remarks 'God made Eve from Adam's rib and Freud made feminine sexuality from male libido' (Olivier 1989: 4).

The trouble for women is that while Freud may indeed have been accurately describing the limitations of women's lives, he used these descriptions to develop theories that implied that such limitations were part of women's essential nature. Thus, anatomy becomes destiny, and rebellion and failure are seen as the inability to achieve mature femininity. Not only that, but for Freud the sine qua non of mature femininity is a shift from clitoral to vaginal orgasm (Freud 1905: 220–221). A shift symbolising the leaving behind of active sexual pleasure in favour of the grateful receipt of a penetrating penis.

Olivier quotes Benoite Groult: 'Women were perhaps just about to take off on their own when a catastrophe befell them: Freud' (Groult 1977: 58).

For Freud:

> Our insight into this early, pre-Oedipus, phase in girls comes to us as a surprise, like the discovery, in another field, of the Minoan-Mycenaean civilisation behind the civilisation of Greece. Everything in the area of this first attachment to the mother seemed to me so difficult to grasp in analysis – so grey with age and shadowy and almost impossible to revivify…

Although he acknowledged that some of his female analytic colleagues had found this easier (Freud 1931: 226).

Far more crucial to him is the little girl's turning from her initial attachment to her mother towards her father as her object of desire, and consequent fierce rivalry with her mother. As later, Lacan saw this breaking of the exclusive, dyadic bond with mother, in obedience to 'the law of the father', as the essential move into the world of the symbolic.

Luce Irigaray sees the consequence of this patriarchal dominance:

> One of the lost crossroads of our becoming women is situated in the blurring and erasure of the relation with our mother, and the obligation to submit to the laws of the world of men – among themselves.
>
> *(Irigaray 1994: 99)*

And even more fundamentally:

> One thing is plain, not only in everyday events but in the whole social scene: our society and our culture operate on the basis of an original matricide (the primal mother of the primal horde).
>
> *(Irigaray 1993: 11)*

Kristeva puts it slightly differently but no less starkly:

> For men and women the loss of the mother is a biological and psychic necessity, the first step on our becoming autonomous. Matricide is our vital necessity the sine qua non of individuation, provided it takes place under optimal conditions and can be eroticised.
>
> *(Kristeva 1989: 27–28)*

One way in which the mother is symbolically murdered is that she is wiped out of the story, is 'disappeared'; shoved into the cracks in our world and only allowed out if she behaves herself – like the Furies at the end of Aescules' Orestia. Indeed the Orestia trilogy can be seen as a tale portraying a primitive and barbarous maternal power brought to book and tamed by enlightened patriarchal rationality. And of course, Athena, the goddess who passed judgment on the Furies, was said to have been born not of woman but out of the head of her father, Zeus; although it should be noted that Zeus for his part had swallowed up her mother for fear of the reproductive power of her womb; a womb that might nurture a rival male that would displace and kill him.

For Aeschylus, as for Plato, the mother wasn't really even an active parent; the womb was believed to be only a receptacle – the matrix out of which we grow.

> Apollo: "Here is the truth, I tell you – see how right I am. The woman you call the mother of the child is not the parent, just nurse to the seed, the new-sown seed that grows and swells inside her. The *man* is the source of life – the one who mounts. She, like a stranger for a stranger, keeps the shoots alive unless god hurts the roots."
>
> *(Aeschylus 1979: lines 665–671: 260)*

Furthermore, in certain classical Greek myths (as in other, later societies), the bond to the mother and to the family has to be renounced in favour of allegiance to the law of the state. Thus, Antigone is sentenced to death because she defies the state edict that the body of her brother, Polyneices must be left unburied and unmourned. And the leaving of mother and family in favour of allegiance to God (the Father) is part of other familiar religious narratives.

So if not actually murdered, the mother must it seems, according to classic versions of psychoanalysis, be buried, or left behind, abandoned. For maturity and indeed sanity are judged in terms of our having achieved separation from mother (and her allowing us to do this).

Of course, the development of any normal, healthy child involves a lessening of their initially total dependence on the (m)other and an inevitable and indeed necessary degree of separation. In Winnicott's view, the 'Good Enough Mother'[2] must, at first, be perfectly adapted to the baby's omnipotent demands. When the baby lies in her arms and looks into her eyes they must see themselves as the gleam in mother's eye. Gradually, however, there must develop some degree of 'de-adaptation' – allowing gaps in the mother's perfect attunement to her baby's desires. Only then can the child begin to experience the mother as having a separate existence and, perhaps even more crucially, begin to experience their own separateness, their own individual existence.

The ability to see the mother as a person in her own right and not just as mother is, however, a long and often tortuous process that is unlikely ever to be complete. For instance, Nancy Friday in *My Mother Myself* (Friday 1979) writes of how, having seen her mother and her mode of life as a terrible model and one she was determined to repudiate, it took many years before she could come to see and understand that her mother had had a vitality and sexual vibrancy that had been completely invisible to her as she grew up. Only then could she appreciate that she came from a line of strong, sexually adventurous women, pushing in their own manner against the constraints of the society in which they lived.

Another example of our reluctance or inability to change our perspective from which we view our parents is how difficult we find it as our parents age and begin to be the ones needing care. How hard it is to fully accept that they can no longer fulfill their parental role and be there for you. And surprisingly perhaps, this may be especially hard if you feel that they never have truly been there for you, and now there is no chance that they ever will be. You will never have the parent you longed for but didn't have.

This painful realisation is particularly acute given that, while our patriarchal culture may subscribe to a devaluing of motherhood, this paradoxically goes along with the maintenance of an ideal of expected maternal care. For while, as it is said, there are more ways of killing the cat than choking it with cream, 'choking her with cream' is another way that 'mother' is 'dealt with'. Idealised out of any real existence, so that she becomes the all nourishing, comforting, self-sacrificing 'good-object' with a consequent lack of subjectivity – more a fantasy of the Virgin Mary than of ordinary humanness. But of course, this trails behind it, the heavy undertow of a much darker fantasy of the mother, both denigrated and feared. Again we can look to the end of the Orestia, where the once powerful and much feared Furies, having been banished to the fringes, were renamed the Eumenides or kindly ones and presumably expected to behave accordingly.

In the twentieth-century world of psychoanalysis, this idealised image has been baldly stated by, for example, Alice Balint who claimed:

> The ideal mother has no interests of her own ... For it remains self-evident that the interests of the mother and the child are identical, and it is the generally acknowledged measure of the goodness or badness of the mother how far she feels this identity of interests.
>
> *(Balint: 111)*

So here, if not openly murdered, she is mutilated, split asunder into 'good' and 'bad'. Thus, when she is good, she is very, very good; and when she is bad, she is awful – even deadly.

Motherhood

All this makes the prospect of becoming a mother pretty daunting and it is perhaps hardly surprising that so many new mothers fall into depression or are overwhelmed by anxieties. It's all very well to dearly want a child, the experience of having that child and facing the responsibilities of being its mother may not feel quite the same. I remember a piece of research about the birth of a first child that concluded that conscious ambivalence during pregnancy towards having a child may actually decrease the chances of post-natal depression. One disconcerting aspect of becoming a new mother is how it apparently completely changes how the world sees you. For some women this may be the first time they feel they have a valued place in the world. For others, becoming a mother can seem to signal a disconcerting loss of her former identity. She can seem now *just* a mother. For example, suddenly by being called 'mum' in a maternity ward, rather than by one's name. Or even earlier through the way that a pregnant woman can feel her body has been invaded; taken over by the baby. Doctors may seem only interested in the baby's welfare. Furthermore, I recall a man of relatively limited acquaintance asking if he could put his hand on my bulging tummy. I suppose he at least asked, but it made me feel that my pregnant body was no longer regarded as my own intimate, private space. That I was just a receptacle, a *matrix*.

If so much of a woman's identity can become, in the eyes of society, swallowed up by her becoming a mother and if any perceived failure to merge her own interests with that of her child can lead to censure, it may become difficult for her not to feel potentially judged as a mother, by how her children 'turn out' – although the criteria for this may vary from family to family, social context to social context, that is, whether it is academic, behavioural or other accomplishments that are most valued. In this way it may be difficult for mothers to be entirely free of what might be described as 'narcissistic' involvement with their children. Mothers may now have 'other lives' by way of continuing to pursue their careers, but it is parents and still primarily mothers who are so often held responsible for anything judged to have gone wrong with their children (e.g., schools as well as governments seem increasingly prone to blaming parents for any problems they experience with their students).

One source of maternal guilt and anxiety that besets new mothers because of the pressure to be judged 'good' or 'good enough' is whether they have the expected 'maternal instincts'. Have they been able to 'bond' with their baby in the way the books tell them they should? Are they bad because they do not always feel unalloyed love and pleasure towards their infant as it fusses, yells, grizzles or is rejecting of their care? What will happen if they even hate their baby at times?

In *Hate and the Countertransference*, Winnicott (1947) made the seemingly shocking statement that 'mothers hate their babies from the word go' (with the implication that hate came before love), although he somehow managed to domesticate this hate in reassuring, comfortable ways (the equivalent of charging fees and keeping strict time boundaries in therapy sessions) – so mothers sing nursery rhymes such as Rock a Bye Baby, and institute bed times (the common phrase 'putting the baby down' might be considered a clue!) Winnicott suggests that mother's hate may allow babies to own their own hatred and so be important in a positive way – as long as it is expressed in such manageable ways.

Others such as Rheingold (1964), however, suggest that maternal ambivalence is a serious 'risk factor' and he seems to blame all the ills of the world onto 'noxious mothering' and 'maternal destructiveness'. Furthermore, he saw this as the norm, with overprotectiveness just the other side of it.

Rozika Parker in her book *Torn in Two* (Parker 1995) puts forward a refreshingly different view. She suggests not only that maternal ambivalence is universal but that it should be regarded as having potentially positive rather than just negative functions in development. Furthermore, development not just of the child (as with Winnicott) but also of the mother's maternal role. To have such positive effects, however, it must be acknowledged rather than acted out in damaging ways. Unfortunately, we tend to be so horrified by the idea of mothers having hateful feelings or thoughts towards their child that it can be difficult to own up to having any such feelings. It is striking how reports of maternal violence, abuse or neglect arouse even greater horror and outrage than that by fathers or others.

Winnicott has written of the idea that the child's ambivalence can lead to the development of concern for the loved person. Parker wants to extend this from the child's to the mother's ambivalence, believing that it too can stimulate the development of reflective identification with the child, and thus to a restoration of love. The mother's hatred can lead to persecutory anxiety (a bad baby) or to depressive anxiety (bad mother) but Parker suggests that depression (in the sense of Melanie Klein's 'depressive position') may be as much an achievement for the mother as for the child. It needs the recognition and acknowledgement of her ambivalence, of her hostile aggressive feelings and not their repression through fear of being judged (by herself as much as by others). This might seem more palatable if 'depression' here was replaced by 'concern' as in Winnicott's 'Stage of Concern,' his replacement of the 'Depressive Position' (Winnicott 1950–1955).

The fear of ambivalence, of course, is that the hatred will prove stronger than the love, or at least will nullify it. Also, because it is 'not allowed' it may seem especially yours – whereas, loving your baby is just what you are supposed to feel – a general, taken for granted attribute of all mothers.

Unmanaged ambivalence can lead to an increase in guilt and hence resentment towards the child. Managed ambivalence can, Parker suggests, increase creativity. Bion (1962) claims that there is not just the conflict between love and hate but also between the desire to know and understand versus the fear of knowing and understanding. The awareness and anguish over ambivalence may release the ability to think and understand what is going on between mother and child.

Parker points to Ferenzi's (1926) belief that the frustration in ambivalence can – if we can tolerate it and bear its pain – lead to an increased consciousness. He noted that the most significant people are not those we always love or are always hostile to, but are those we love for some things and hate for others. The struggle through conflict, intra- and inter-psychic, is how we grow and develop.

And so, even if it is true that ambivalence between mothers and daughters has greater intensity and is more difficult to bear because of the need both to identify and differentiate from each other – to see them as an 'other woman', then maybe we should strive to cherish the complexity of this relationship as enabling something of great value in the path towards maturity and wisdom. Admittedly this may involve a great struggle at least for some.

Adrienne Rich again in *Of Woman Born*:

> 'Matrophobia' as the poet Lynn Sukenick has termed it is the fear not of one's mother but of becoming one's mother. Thousands of daughters see their mother as having taught the compromise and self-hatred, they are struggling to win free of, the person through whom the restrictions and degradations of a female existence were perforce transmitted. Easier by far to hate and reject a mother outright, than to see beyond her to the forces acting on her. But where a mother is hated to the point of matrophobia there may also be a deep underlying pull towards her, a dread that if one relaxes one's guard one will identify with her completely.

And: "Matrophobia can be seen as a womanly splitting of the self, in the desire to become purged once and for all of our mother's bondage, to become individuated and free" (Rich 1986: 235–236).

Sylvia Plath's mother Aurelia wrote in her preface to the published selection of her daughter's *Letters Home*:

> Between Sylvia and me existed – as between my own mother and me – a kind of psychic osmosis which at times, was very wonderful and comforting; at other times an unwelcome invasion of privacy.
>
> *(Plath 1999: 32)*

For my part, I remember that although most of my fantasies about having a child were about having a daughter, when I gave birth to a son I found myself relieved as it seemed to make it easier to see him as separate from me – as an *other*.

A fear of merging may indeed be common within our culture but it gets inscribed into the psychoanalytic conviction that the gaining of 'freedom' and 'maturity' and the ability to 'take one's place in the world of the symbolic' is dependent on turning away from one's mother. A turning away that is more violently rejecting than might be the inevitable consequence of the lessening of dependency as the child grows into adulthood and out into the world. To me this conviction signals an ahistorical, acultural assumption of the premises of patriarchy.

But for all this, stuck between the cracks of such negativity about mothers and the maternal is something acknowledged to be precious so that, just a few pages earlier than her discussion of 'matrophobia' Adrienne Rich writes:

> Whatever the individual mother's love and strength, the child in us, the small female who grew up in a male-controlled world, still feels, at moments wildly unmothered. When we can confront and unravel this paradox, this contradiction, face to the utmost in ourselves the groping passion of that little girl lost, we can begin to transmute it, and the blind anger and bitterness that have repetitiously erupted among women trying to build a movement together can be alchemized. Before sisterhood there was the knowledge – transitory, fragmented, perhaps, but original and crucial – of motherhood and daughterhood.
>
> *(Rich 1986: 225)*

Murraro, following Irigaray, sees at the heart of political feminism, the need for a change in women's relation to the figure of the mother and, consequently, with the meaning of sexual difference. She goes on to say, 'Knowing how to love the mother is the basis of our liberation' (Murraro 1994: 331).

And Kristeva points to Winnicott's idea of a child's development of a 'capacity to be alone' (Winnicott 1958) that can happen initially only in the presence of another. This capacity is a precondition of a sense of a personal life – an 'interiority to be recreated in relation to an external world.' The key to what Kristeva claims Winnicott considers 'the most precious and mysterious freedom inherent in human being'… A freedom only achievable if the 'outside (to begin with the mother) allows for play, and let's itself be played with' (Kristeva 1999).

Julia Kristeva may most famously and memorably have claimed that matricide is our vital necessity, but she is one of the very few psychoanalysts who have written from the place of the mother as, for example, in her paper "Stabat Mater", (even though her picture of motherhood is a very orthodoxly psychoanalytic and hardly a feminist one) (Kristeva 1987) and she has also stated:

> Outside motherhood, no situations exist in human experience that so radically and so simply bring us face to face with that emergence of the other, I like to think that in our human adventure, we can encounter 'the other' – sometimes, rarely – if, and only if, we, men and women, are capable of that maternal experience, which defers eroticism into tenderness and makes an 'object' an 'other me'.
>
> *(Clement and Kristeva 2001: 57)*

Notes

1 Most genes are contained in a cell's nucleus. An egg once fertilised will contain equal amounts of such genetic material from each of the parents. Mitochondria are organelles that are the site of energy production in cells. They exist outside the cell's nucleus in the cytoplasm. It is now known that they contain genetic material (DNA) and that this divides and reproduces entirely independently of cell division and is passed down from the female parent to her offspring in the cytoplasm of the egg.

2 This famous (or maybe infamous) phrase is intended it seems, to be 'mother friendly' since it implies that being less than perfect is fine. But it is more complicated than that. Winnicott's description of the 'good enough mother' actually represents an ideal/ idealised image of care (see King 1994). Furthermore, this picture of ideal maternal care pays no account of the fact to which most mothers of more than one child can testify, that babies are born very different from one another 'from the word go' (to use Winnicott's own phrase). Any mother, however loving, may struggle to adapt to a baby whose temperament is very different from her own.

References

Aeschylus. (1979) *The Eumenides.* Part 3 of *The Orestia.* (Trans. Fagles, R.) Harmondsworth, England: Penguin Press.

Balint, A. (1952) Love for mother and mother love. In Balint M. (ed.). *Primary Love and Psychoanalytic Technique.* London, England: Hogarth Press.

Bion, W.R. (1962) *Learning from Experience.* London, England: Heinnemann.

Clement, C. and Kristeva, J. (1996) *The Feminine and the Sacred.* (Trans. Todd, J.M.) New York, NY: Columbia University Press.

Contratto, S. (1984) Mother. Sculptor and trustee of the faith. In Lewin, M. (ed.). *In the Shadow of the Past: Psychology Portrays the Sexes.* New York, NY: Columbia University Press.

De Beauvoir, S. (1972) *The Second Sex.* (Trans. Parshley, H.M.) Harmondsworth, England: Penguin Books.

Dinnerstein, D. (1978) *The Rocking of the Cradle and the Ruling of the World.* London, England: Souvenir Press.

Erikson, E. (1965) *Childhood and Society.* Revised ed. Harmondsworth, England: Penguin Books.

Ferenzi, S. (1926) The problem of acceptance of unpleasant ideas – advances in knowledge of the sense of reality. In *Further Contributions to the Theory and Technique of Psycho-Analysis.* London, England: Karnac.

Freud, S. (1905) *Three Essays on the Theory of Sexuality* Standard Edition 7 (Trans. Strachey, J.) London, England: Vintage and Hogarth Press.

Freud, S. (1931) *Female Sexuality.* Standard Edition 21. (Trans. Strachey, J.) London, England: Vintage and Hogarth Press.

Friday, N. (1979) *My Mother Myself.* London, England: Fontana.

Groult, B. (1977) *Ainsie soit-elle.* Paris, France: Grasset.

Irigaray, L. (1993) *Sexes and Genealogies.* (Trans. Gill, G.) New York, NY: Columbia University Press.

Irigaray, L. (1994) *Thinking the Difference for a Peaceful Revolution.* (Trans. Martin, K.) London, England: Athlone Press.

King, L. (1994) *There is No Such Thing as a Mother.* Winnicott Studies No 9 London, England: Karnac.

Kristeva, J. (1987) Stabat Mater. In *Tales of Love.* (Trans. Roudiez, L.) New York, NY: Columbia University Press.

Kristeva, J. (1989) *Black Sun.* (Trans. Roudiez, L.) New York, NY: Columbia University Press.

Kristeva, J. (1999) Psychoanalysis and freedom. *Canadian Journal of Psychoanalysis* 7.

Lessing, D. (1966) *A Proper Marriage.* Hertfordshire, England: St Albans Panther.

Murraro, L. (1994) Female genealogies. In *Engaging with Irigaray.* Burke, C. Schur, N. and Whitford, M. (eds.). New York, NY: Columbia University Press.

Olivier, C. (1989) *Jocasta's Children: The Imprint of the Mother.* (Trans. Craig, G.) London, England: Routledge.

Parker, R. (1995) *Torn in Two.* London, England: Virago.

Plath, A. (1999) Introduction to Silvia Plath's *Letters Home.* London, England: Faber and Faber.

Rheingold, J. (1964) *The Fear of Being a Woman: A Theory of Maternal Destructiveness.* New York, NY: Grune and Stratton.

Rich, A. (1986) *Of Woman Born.* 2nd ed. London, England: Virago.

Winnicott, D.W. (1947) Hate and the countertransference. In *Through Paediatrics to Psycho-analysis.* London, England: Hogarth Press.

Winnicott, D.W. (1950–1955) Aggression in relation to emotional development. In *Through Paediatrics to Psycho-analysis.* London, England: Hogarth Press.

Winnicott, D.W. (1958) The capacity to be alone. In *The Maturational Process and the Facilitating Environment.* London, England: Hogarth Press.

3

'O MOTHER, MOTHER WHAT HAVE YOU DONE?' (WILLIAM SHAKESPEARE: *CORIOLANUS*)

Jane Haynes

R.D. Laing and his wife Jutta were friends of mine. I was his PA during the preparation and execution of the 'Dialectics of Liberation' conference at the Round House in July 1967, and shortly after we became linked in sharing the experiences of parenthood. Jutta gave birth to her first son Adam several months before my first child Tanya was born and inevitably questions and philosophies of parenthood were frequent sources of our conversations. It is no secret that Laing felt a grudge towards his own mother for constantly impinging on his space and growing autonomy. One small example of where he seemed to maintain a lifelong resentment towards her was because he held her behaviour with regard to the withholding of any 'sweet treats' when he was little as a source of his subsequent addiction to eating sweets illicitly, and later on irresponsibly until he had ruined his adult teeth.

Laing never tired of sitting cross-legged on the floor and gazing around a room of 'disciples' and friends and asking, or provoking, by this question: 'Whose womb would you like to have been born from?' By which I understood him to be reflecting on the responsibilities of maternity and regretting the fact that we cannot choose our parents, and what a lottery the business of maternity is. As such it mirrors the random aspects, if not the entirely random nature of our lives. Inevitably, it also provoked us to gaze around the room – on those occasions when the question was addressed to a gathering – and to reflect about the endless varieties of motherhood 'on offer' and whether there could ever be an 'ideal' of motherhood.

Startling as his question is, it is by no means a novel one as God challenges the suffering Job:

> 'Out of whose womb came the ice? And the hoary frost of heaven, who hath gendered it?'

Outside of my consulting room I am not so much a people watcher as an obsessive observer of parents and their children and never more so than when I am, as it were, invisible. Last summer I was returning to London on the Eurostar and during the journey became aware of a grandmother, mother and small daughter sitting in contentment at the opposite table engrossed in a game of cards, which I identified to be the French version of *Happy Woodland Families* which I both loved and found consoling as a child and which I still love to play. By their gangway seat an almost newborn baby lay in its carrier. From time to time the repetitions of this game would be interrupted while the mother breastfed her baby and the grandmother soothed the sibling's frustrations by entertaining her on her knee with stories about the changing scenery. My nostalgia was aroused for that containing and uncomplicated experience of childhood, which was being reconstructed before my eyes and then through memory, although such containment had rarely existed within my own dysfunctional family context. It also provoked a conscious realisation that I had never forgiven my sibling for coming into the world and – as it had seemed to me as a powerless and confused child – changing my already fractured life forever. Nostalgia may relate not only to the Proustian memory of what has been lost to memory and yet, tucked away in the obscurities of our brain, can sometimes involuntarily be returned to consciousness, but also to what has never been, which in my case was the presence of a happy family of origin. A home.

Inevitably, such an absence will, or in my own case did, make the desire to achieve a stable and loving family of creation, in contrast to my family of origin, an imperative in my life. The sense of being a mother, despite my own children now being adults and parents themselves has never left me; both its exquisite burdens of responsibility and its unsurpassed joys, and it still provides me with my most constant and stable status as I travel through my life and watch our family flow into the universe. It is not without irony that as I write I am recalling that the only time when I have briefly stopped experiencing myself as 'Mother' is the substance of another indelible Langian memory.

When I gave birth to my first child, I had no desire for a status other than to be a mother and a wife. I had run away from school at the age of fifteen and by seventeen I had left home never to return. My experience of the first year of motherhood was spent feeling as though Heaven now existed on earth and in parenthesis this meant that I was utterly ill prepared for the acute postnatal depression that hit me with the birth – seven years later and four miscarriages on – of my second child. If the first birth was to bring Heaven to earth my second experience of maternity might well be likened to God's description of the hoary frost and ice cold conditions that conjure up the freeze of maternity in a postnatal depression.

In this context the information of postnatal depression will not be expanded on but is only to contextualise how happy and contented I was with full time motherhood. Although my attachment to my daughter and my determination not to be like my mother did lead to a sleep disturbance and attachment anxiety in her that was the eventual cause of finding myself with my baby at the 'Anna Freud Well Baby Clinic' which in those days was still run by Anna's close friend Dr. Josefine Stross who had accompanied the ailing Freud on his challenging journey to England when he left Vienna and his own doctor Dr. Max Schur was delayed by an appendicitis. Imagine then the one occasion in my life when I ceased to be a vigilant and consistent mother but allowed myself to be carried away into another kind of 'Heaven' by my desire to experience LSD which Laing at that time was regularly using to gain access into both his own and some of his patients' unconscious processes.

My daughter was almost five and along with her father and the Laing family we had taken off to our country cottage for a weekend of music, nature and song – Jutta had a wonderful voice – and Laing never travelled if he could help it without his small and thus portable clavichord. Hitherto my relationship to the idea of a drug-induced transcendent experience had not felt sympathetic to my role of motherhood and I had only listened with great interest to the reportage of other people's journeys and always with an awareness that for some it was not to find a 'Huxley' heaven but a hell and the anxiety that there was to be no deciding which way the drug would take effect until it was too late to arrest it. On this occasion my curiosity got the better of me and an invitation to take it under Ronnie's wing and with the knowledge that the substance was pure lysergic acid got the better of me; the time seemed propitious.

Accompanied by Laing's playing I swallowed the nectar from an exquisitely blown glass vial, which I still remember Ronnie licking out the remains. I could write at length about what happened, and the 'fabulous' experience can also be summed up by a Blakean metaphor that 'One thought filled immensity' but for the purpose of this essay I want to report that it was then and still is the only time in my life when I abdicated being a mother and entered another identity and reality in which my maternal status had disappeared. Had the Pied Piper appeared and piped my daughter away and across the fields I know that I should not have intervened or moved away from my rapturous meditations on nature!

As it happens a few weeks ago I was sitting with my family and older grandchildren – who are now past university age and experienced in the world of recreational drugs – and I told them this story. They listened in fascination but my daughter listened in horror. 'What, you mean you took LSD when I was a little girl, in front of me, and you didn't feel guilty?' No, strangely for someone who tends to be over-burdened with responsibility I didn't feel guilty; her father was there, and I had an experience of another transcendent reality that has continued to feed my imagination ever since. I also had one brief absence in an entire life-hood of being a mother from maternal responsibility and the anguish and joys that motherhood thrusts upon us forever.

This essay began and was presented as an almost spontaneous riff rather than a formalised written presentation and the ad hoc quotations that follow all reflect, in different ways, the conflicts of maternity and which were all collected quite randomly from men and women during the month when I was preparing an outline. They have not primarily been gathered from my patients but include spontaneous and often involuntary responses from acquaintances and even strangers to my own question: 'What images or thoughts first come into your head or mind when you hear the word 'Mother'?'

> My mother was a good mother. Intelligent, generous, not especially tender, devoted. She always looked good, not much money but a real sense of quality. She read (awful books but she read them). She arranged flowers and cooked.

> I walk into the room and she is sleeping. I go to her side and she is sleeping. I lie down beside her and do not want to wake up.

> I remember my Mum as being dizzy and confused and then suddenly she'd turn and be sadistic and tantalize me and then I couldn't decide if her dizziness was just a front to draw me in.

> I tried to think about my mother, but I turned into a puddle.

> I think of a blood battlefield, she was the champagne drinking conqueror and my father wandered behind her like the Stasi.

> When I came home for the holidays sometimes my mother would come in when I was sleeping in the night and sit at the end of my bed with a glass of wine and cry. I think she is probably an intelligent woman but I also think she has wasted her life and I have no idea who she is.

> Love, respect. I don't see her often enough. She's Jamaican. She was there when I came into the world and I need to be beside her when she dies.

> Feeling blue today after talking to my mother yesterday. I try not to take on her negative energy but it is hard. And she is already claiming time from me when I get back, which is of course understandable, but she doesn't make the prospect of a visit at all enticing. She is lonely, ill and my mother, which are all problematical.

> Why did you leave me?

> Their divorce overshadows everything. [Gulps] Just remembered my mother gave me a copy of David Hockney's book when I was about seventeen and said 'I hope you will be as famous as he was', but she died too quickly to know.

> My mother obsesses that I don't think she's good enough. She can only comfort me when I am on the edge of emotional collapse. I don't want her judgment I just want her to hug me and say, 'It's OK. I love you.'

I wanted to remember my mother warm and alive. In the middle of the night the undertakers came and covered her body with a white sheet. Only then I dissolved. After the body had gone I became fixated on the fact that I hadn't brushed her hair before she left. When I came down the next morning I found her glasses on the table by her bed. Her death was a huge event for me, and now I realize that I hadn't separated from her before she died, although I had been so independent but then I discovered that I hadn't ever emotionally separated from her.

A few weeks after anthologising these responses to my own question, I watched a brilliant and extraordinary documentary, *The Condemned* (first shown on BBC 4 in 2013) about 'Lifers' in a Russian high-security prison, where incarceration was based on having committed at least two murders, or multiple rapes and murder. Its director, Nick Read, writes:

My intention was to make a film about a community living on the very edge of the known, civilized world – to point a torch into their dark corner – and explore the concept of evil.

What did these seasoned criminals frequently allude to, to express nostalgia for? Their mothers.

Since collecting these responses, I have also published a book about the inner worlds – what goes on behind the white mask of professionalism in the minds and bodies of doctors – those professionals who are often the messengers of our mortality (Haynes 2015). What prevails in these interviews again and again, despite the fact that the contributors are often dealing with the dying on a daily professional basis, is the profound effects upon several of them of the physical death of a parent. For one contributor who had not, as most of them had not, experienced therapy, our interviews turned out to be the equivalent of an intense and miniature experience of psychotherapy. He entered my consulting room as a stranger and immediately reflected on the quality of light coming from the windows, it was a late August afternoon. He became silent and then suddenly lachrymose before he remarked that it was almost this date last year that his mother had died. At once I knew that he was carrying an untold story of maternal mourning and loss, which I needed to help him to turn into words, into a coherent narrative of his own maternal loss as he bore witness to the excruciating pain of his mother's death and his inability, despite being a doctor, to relieve her suffering except through his constant presence at her side:

The funny thing is I that I am not a weepy person and I only ever cried as a small boy but there are some moments where you are just taken back to being that small child who has hurt their knee and needs their mum and then the only way you can express the current emotion is by crying. Yes, I remember when Mum was effectively lying on her deathbed and unbeknown to me Dad had gone up to the cathedral to find a priest to administer the Last Rites.

He went round to the Bishop's secretary's office and one of the nuns – I went to a Catholic school – who taught me, went to call Father Grant.

Father Grant used to be the Parish priest when I was still involved in the church, singing in the choir and serving at the altar and all that sort of stuff. The doorbell went and I left Mum's bedside to open the door and there was Father Grant and Sister Eleanor, who taught me when I was seven or eight. As soon as I saw Sister Eleanor standing there I knew why they had come and I became that seven-year-old boy again who needs his mum. I started crying and I couldn't stop. I wouldn't normally do that and it certainly wouldn't ever happen to me at work but it was just something involuntary that happened. My dad didn't shed a tear when she died and neither did my brothers. I knew I would be fine but my father and brothers didn't know what to say to me. The thing is that when you start crying there is the awful fear that you will never stop, but the tears have to come.

(Haynes 2015)

I have written elsewhere how Laing, despite his visible maternal wounds and his addictive personality, has continued to inform my practice and to act as an internal supervisor, how often too I hear his clipped Glaswegian accent saying, 'It cuts no ice with me', when someone or other has been propounding some exclusive devotion to dogma. Along with Laing my clinical work has been deeply informed by the contribution of poets, writers and above all Shakespeare who was a specialist in describing wounds of the body and soul. It is not only Laing and the sprite Peter Pan who blamed mothers for universal ills. In an emotional crescendo, Shakespeare's hero Coriolanus howls, 'O mother, mother what have you done?'

A form of revengeful narcissism causes Coriolanus' fall from hero to exile that Shakespeare leaves us in little doubt is related to his overbearing and narcissistic mother, Volumnia. It is this familial flaw, which is responsible for his 'Fall' when the triumphant Coriolanus refuses to expose his bloody wounds in the public forum as Roman custom demanded. (You will find descriptions of these wounds in *Plutarch's Lives* (1579), but there is no equivalent account documented of his relationship with his impinging mother.) Shakespeare was not keen on mothers: often they are most present by their absence. He doesn't manage 'a good enough one', let alone a loving mother, anywhere. Hermione almost succeeds, but perhaps it is Queen Constance in *King John* who, driven to the edge of sanity by the murder of her child, who is the exception:

Young Arthur is my son, and he is lost: I am not mad: I would to heaven I were! For then, 'tis like I should forget myself: O, if I could, what grief should I forget! Preach some philosophy to make me mad, And thou shalt be canonized, cardinal; for being not mad but sensible of grief, My reasonable part produces reason. How I may be deliver'd of these woes, And teaches me to kill or hang myself: If I were mad, I should forget my son, Or madly think a babe of clouts were he: I am not mad; too well, too well I feel The different plague of each calamity.

(King John, 3.4., ln: 47–60)

Queen Constance reminds me of the myth of Persephone and Demeter and perhaps Shakespeare even had such a grief in his mind as he imagined these demented lines of such maternal verisimilitude or perhaps he was thinking of Niobe, the daughter of Tantalus who wept eternally for the loss of her children. We cannot know. For me the myth of Persephone and Demeter and that critical interloper Pluto, King of the Underworld, or the 'third' who disturbs the pubescent's relations, or rather her dependence upon her mother is one of the most perspicacious metaphors of the mother-daughter trajectory, which must inevitably be interrupted by the 'third', and who is the messenger of independent sexual desire. It is essential that the daughter, either through her Oedipal love, or the later sexualised love of an interloper to the family triangle, abandons her primary attachment to her mother. It is even more difficult for a daughter to experience the developmentally healthy separation from the mother as they are moving between puberty and sexual maturity, between dependence and independence if they cannot feel comfortable in their evolving sexuality in front of their mother. Persephone's tragedy is that she has to disappear into the darkness of the Underworld to sever the maternal bonds and thus her emotional life is compromised between her love for her grieving mother and her desire for the dark handsome stranger who has carried her away on his 'charger'.

Throughout the vicissitudes of the female adolescent quest for separate identity and individuation from the family of origin – so beautifully revealed in the myth of Persephone – it is critical that the adolescent does not feel maternal retaliation or envy. That she is forced neither into compliancy nor hyperbolic rebellion. There may be conflict but ideally it is conflict without the fear of maternal retaliation or abandonment which can be devastating to the daughter's self-worth and may lead to a permanent rift with the mother who is grieving too for the absence or waning of her own fertility.

When I was editing a book on the death of Princess Diana – *When a Princess Dies* – I literally had to produce the *Panorama* interview with her from the BBC archives to convince my co-editor that I had not imagined Diana's sensational public disclosure that she was in the habit of self-harming and because her thighs were invariably concealed they were the chosen limbs. Quite possibly, these wounds, which she, unlike Coriolanus did choose to disclose in the media 'forum', were associated with her abandonment by her mother, who left Diana sobbing on the staircase and trying to console her small brother, when her mother disappeared from their lives without warning. Diana probably went on invisibly crying for her mother all her life. Diana's mother, Frances Shand Kydd, did file for the custody of her children but then her own mother, Lady Fermoy, testified against her daughter and in favour of her son-in-law and an enforced reign of terror and childhood trauma began. To begin with, and perhaps later on in her marriage too, Diana was crying because she was abandoned and didn't understand why. Coriolanus was driven to despair and the betrayal of his country when his mother compromised his integrity – both as a man and a hero. The consequences were that both of these iconic victims were publicly traumatized and then exiled forever.

This cycle of maternal tragedy took on another poignant layer when I read Diana's will, on the Internet of all places, and in which her last will and testament reinvests her mother's authority: 'Should any child of mine be under age at the date of the death of the survivor of myself and my husband, I appoint *my mother* [my italics] and my brother Earl Spencer to be the guardians of that child and I express the wish that should I predecease my husband he will consult my mother with regard to the upbringing … of our children'. Diana, like so many abused 'children' never abandoned the longing for unconditional love and the idea of a happy family of origin, which was subsequently to elude and persecute her in her family of creation. It is possible to speculate that perhaps there might have been additional reasons of revenge or even self-empowerment that led her to issue an instruction that would be so controversial.

Flesh wounds can heal in a way that psychic wounds, although invisible, often do not. They have the capacity to eat their way into the self throughout their victims' lives and to erode self-esteem. I am amazed how often – in my consulting room – seemingly innocuous words from childhood, like 'stupid', 'idiot' and 'clumsy' continue their bite even into old age. There should be a recipe book for cooking, bottling and pickling the elusive essences of self-esteem. Absent mothers, wronged mothers, impinging mothers, blind mothers, obsessively vain mothers all suffocate their young. It is a more sophisticated form of what other animals are sometimes provoked to do. But who doesn't, at times of heightened vulnerability, long for the mother of their dreams, and a few of us may even have one. After all, even Peter Pan never stopped wanting one. As Peter said to Wendy, if only she could teach his lost boys to tell stories, they too might return home. Tolstoy as well as J.M. Barrie knew the importance of maternal soothing:

> With sleep drugged eyes I look intently at her face and suddenly she becomes tiny and small. Her face no bigger than a button, but I can still see it all quite clearly – I see her glance at me and smile. I like to see her so tiny. I screw up my eyes and she becomes no bigger than the little me I sometimes see in somebody else's pupils. But I move and the spell is broken.
>
> *(Tolstoy 1964)*

Yes, the psychologists may create theories but it is the poets and writers who pin down those immortal and universal moments when we at least have the sensation, if not the lasting experience of safe attachment, when the story has been told, the curtains arranged, a distant light burns and as Nabakov described in *Speak Memory*, the child feels as if everything is once more as it should be and that nobody will ever die, nothing will ever change.

Nobody can deny that being a mother is an impossible task. Yet, Laing's question has remained indelibly with me. In my work as a psychotherapist it continues to be free-floating in the back of my mind although I have extended it to include the parental couple. The poignancy of his question returns most particularly when I am working with patients whose narratives feature early dysfunctions of attachment, emotional impingement or repeated inconsistences of care, which have gone on to distort or to fill their lives with emotional obstacles. Sometimes, although I no longer practice as a classical Jungian psychoanalyst myself, patients will arrive in my consulting room who have had previous long analyses and they will sometimes say to me: 'Ah yes, I understand all the reasons very well why I have had emotional disturbance, it has all become clear and coherent to me but I still feel the same, I still feel as though I have never had the parent I wanted or needed and I still don't know how to feel better'. On those occasions I will recall and paraphrase some of Jung's words from his introduction to *The Secret of the Golden Flower* (1929) and suggest that there are no insoluble problems but that sometimes one just has to be able to *let go* of the problem, or the persecutory thought that one was not blessed to have the relationship with the mother of one's dreams and to turn this unanswered longing to a higher goal or horizon and to find a symbolic experience of forgiving maternity.

I was recently attending a yoga lesson and understood the first symbolic meaning of the lotus flower, which of course is an exotic and rarefied version of our more common water lily. I have always been struck by the symbiosis between the water lily's ugly, sprawled roots with muck, or the water equivalent of dung and its blossom. Now, I resonate to the idea that the symbolic elevation of the lotus flower is linked to the fact that while the flower's roots exist in muddy (primal) waters it is this compromised environment that gives birth to and sustains the beautiful adult maturity and vessel-like containment of its blossom. The image also works for me as a symbolic model of the containing mother, the idealised mother (and father!) of our yearnings and the optimum development of the self/child to grow beyond the primal and to realise individuation (Jung 1929). Once again, I want to emphasize that such a trajectory is an ideal and in the physicality of our lives it is a constant struggle not to be swamped by those perplexing and primal roots of our origins.

References

Barrie, J. M. (2015 [originally published 1902]) *Peter Pan*. Great Britain: Collins Classics.
Jung, C. G. (1929) Commentary on the 'Secret of the Golden Flower.' In *The Collected Works of C. G. Jung*: Volume 13. New York, NY: Bollingen Series, Princeton University Press.
Haynes, J. (2015) *Doctors Dissected*. London, England: Quartet Books.

Larkin, P. (1979) This be the verse, In *High Windows*. London, England: Faber & Faber.

Nabokov, V. (2000) *Speak, Memory: An Autobiography Revisited*. Penguin Modern Classics. London, England: Penguin Books.

Shakespeare, W. (1579) *Plutarch's Lives of the Noble Grecians and Romans*. England: Shakespeare Classic Library.

Shakespeare, W. (1623a) *Coriolanus*. England: Shakespeare Classic Library.

Shakespeare, W. (1623b) *King John*. England: Shakespeare Classic Library.

Tolstoy, L. N. (1964) *Childhood, Boyhood, Youth*. London, England: Penguin Books.

4

PATRIARCHY AND ITS ROLE AS SABOTEUR TO THE MATERNAL AND PATERNAL METAPHORS

Personal reflections

Lakis K. Georghiou

Introduction

One could say that we are often faced with binary opposites. Polarities that are often useful if only to awaken and frustrate our thinking on the identifications we take up in our lives and the positions we anchor ourselves to. Love-Hate, Good-Bad, Happy-Sad, Straight-Gay, Masculine-Feminine. When considering the 'Maternal', I cannot help but be drawn to the 'Paternal'. Perhaps this is a calling from my own gendered position as a man or a reaction to a set of seminars that sadly found men very much in a minority attendance. This certainly was not due to a lack of welcome. The invitation extended to me to contribute to this book is testament to this. Nevertheless, I wonder how many men might feel alienated or unable to connect enough to the 'stranger in themselves' to participate in this maternal/paternal discourse. Perhaps as I will explore, some men might not want to come so 'up close and personal' to the fact that they were born from a woman and were so dependent on their mother. The rich experience of attending the maternal seminars has certainly awakened me to aspects of motherly love, mother's ambivalence, matriarchy and matricide. We reflected on the importance of feminism, being a woman, daughter and sisterhood. It feels appropriate then in this one chapter to try to give some voice and recognition to the paternal in relation to maternal.

What can be said of the paternal? Could it be the 'third' angle of a metaphoric triangle that might challenge and frustrate the dyadic mother/baby experience? Is the maternal the domain of the woman and the paternal that of the man? How might we view these metaphors as different but distinct cogs that might 'shift the gears' in the optimal psychic development of a child? Is there an uneasy alliance or duel-like struggle between men and women in parenthood, tainted by patriarchy?

I will endeavour to examine these questions; drawing from film and my own uniquely cultured male experience. I also hope to muse on boy- and manhood using both psychoanalytic and sociopolitical references and conclude with some views on contemporary parenthood. Finally, I invite the reader to question with me the normative use of masculinity or femininity as I consider my own and possibly other men's gendered identity. I believe these terms to be problematic in the context of this chapter, due to their performative inferences.

I will begin by exploring the power yet absurdity of patriarchy; its historical context and what it has come to mean for both sexes, but particularly for some men who might come to often feel spurned in today's society. Although speaking most likely in a generic way and subverting the idea of normality, R.D. Laing wrote:

> Society highly values its normal man. It educates children to lose themselves and to become absurd, and thus be normal.
>
> *(Laing 196: p. 24)*

I hope to show how this 'normality' has backfired on male subjectivity, causing men to be paradoxically powerless and impotent despite a historic patriarchal backing. This experience might cause some men at times to feel spurned and alienated from themselves, their partners and their family.

Origins of patriarchy

One could describe patriarchy as a dominant social influence whereby male authority and voice is prioritised over women and children with an inequitable distribution of benefits and wealth. It defends male privilege by ordaining female subordination both explicitly and otherwise.

> Despite advances in feminism, the 'Law of the Father' remains the dominant model of Western psychological and cultural analysis, and the law of the mother continues to exist as an undeveloped and marginal concept.
>
> *(Jacobs 2012: inside cover)*

The origins of this patriarchy cannot be precisely traced but there is no doubt that men have generally held more power than women for thousands of years. Even to this day men are held on a higher pedestal, statistically earning more than women for doing the same job and more or less dominating the financial and political systems of most modern societies. This was not always the case.

> In Minoan society (2000–1500 BC) patriarchy was perhaps not so apparent. Women were equally represented as skilled craftswomen, entrepreneurs, priestesses and were found among the highest echelons of political life.

Evidence suggests that the priesthood was dominated by women. At some point in their cultural development, the Myceneans adopted the Minoan goddesses and associated these goddesses with their sky-god that the Greeks later called Zeus. The Greeks believed that the female chthonic gods were older than their Olympian gods and many speculate that the Greek god-system evolved from the Minoan Earth goddess.

(Castleden 1992: 175)

Somewhere along a timeline, the major gods shifted from being female to male.

According to Greek Myth, Metis, Athena's mother, was Zeus's first wife. Zeus swallowed Metis to prevent her from bearing children who would overthrow him. Nevertheless, Metis bore Zeus a child – Athena – who sprang forth fully formed from his head. In Aeschylus's Oresteia, Athena's motherless status functions as a crucial justification for absolving Orestes of the crime of matricide (killing of his own mother Clytemnestra). In his defense of Orestes, Zeus argues that the father is more important than the mother, using Athena's motherless birth as an example.

(Jacobs 2012: inside cover)

An example of misogyny in these times was the story of Pandora. She was the female Frankenstein of Greek mythology, a woman constructed by gifts from different gods who would wreak havoc by her untrustworthiness and by her ability to manipulate and seduce. Myths and tales as above, laws, philosophy and religion were created by men who favoured men. Men had the physical strength to enforce them, ultimately forcing women into a lower social class.

The formation of Christianity only confirmed patriarchy. All the prophets were male, as were God and Jesus, and the only dominant female figure, Mary, was only noted due to her relationship of being the virgin mother of Jesus. Even the hugely significant Mary Magdalene was eradicated from the scriptures after Jesus' death.

For women, being part of a patriarchal society means being defaulted to a sub-ordinated position. When De Beauvoir said: 'One is not born, but rather becomes, a woman' (1953: 301) she was saying that 'woman' is not born fully formed, she is gradually shaped at each stage by her upbringing to become conditioned. Biology does not determine what makes her a woman. She learns her role from man and others in society. Woman is not born passive, dependent and an 'object' to man's 'subject', but all the forces in the external world have conspired to make her so.

Patriarchy has been somewhat disguised by advances in sexual equality legislation and political correctness. It is, however, still very much embedded in our Western society, although this might not seem as obvious today, due to the positive impact of feminism. Foucault wrote of how pervasive power is everywhere in our daily lives acting on our bodies like 'quiet coercions' shaping how we behave (1975: 138).

Patriarchy and film

The Philadelphia Association's Film Club and Maternal Seminars jointly presented the film *Kramer versus Kramer* (1979) in order to stimulate a discussion on the way patriarchal constructions can still subtly find their way into many facets of human experience and particularly within co-parenting.

Cinema plays an integral part in cultural identity and should, I believe, be subject to critical examination. Since celluloid art was introduced at the turn of the last century, it has played a huge part in the socialisation of individuals; influencing both values and beliefs. One might say that at best it entertains and educates, but at its worst it has been able to manipulate, sedate and through hegemonic means reinforce patriarchy. Hollywood movies make a very interesting example towards reinforcing the argument of quiet coercion.

Kramer versus Kramer (1979) was one of many films made in the United States within a context, where the government in power during that time felt there was a 'crisis of liberalism'. The Reagan administration in reaction to the increase in women at work, changes in family configurations and the resultant threat to male power 'developed a covert antifeminist politic'. This sought to reconstruct patriarchal privilege by, for example, undermining the welfare state and reducing social services to those reliant on these, such as poor and middle-class black and white women (Eisenstein 1984: 330).

The film initially focuses on the challenges faced by a family during its breakdown. The mother is shown as chaotic, weak and under huge strain. The film's opening scene sees her walking out of the home leaving the father to pick up the pieces and attend to their young son. Berger (1972: 45) observed that 'according to usage and conventions which are at last being questioned but have by no means been overcome – men act and women appear. Men look at women. Women watch themselves being looked at'.

> ...Mainstream films do not propagate an image of emancipated women ... In spite of more than three decades of feminist film criticism, the male gaze continues to dominate the image of women in Hollywood film well in the 21st Century.
>
> *(Fol 2004: 2, 4)*

I chose this film amongst many of its time because it is both a complex and rewarding portrayal of how a man and woman meet as parents. In examining its patriarchal underpinnings, however, critics had mixed views. Some suggested that the film positively celebrated fatherhood while others said it achieved this at the expense of motherhood showing that:

> Fathers can eventually do the job of mothering even better than mothers can.
>
> *(Blaisdell 2007: 70)*

The viewer is allowed to journey alongside a hard-working, yet self-absorbed man as he experiences previously unknown domesticity. With comic incompetence, drama and reflection, he ultimately emerges into a more intuitive, sensitive and self-sacrificing father.

Subtle scriptwriting, however, shows him at the beginning of the film trivialising his wife's concerns and reinforcing stereotypes by reasoning his lateness home with:

> I'm sorry … but I was making a living.
>
> *(Benton 1979, IntR 10: 8)*

Later we see him and his boss jokingly deriding 'women's lib' as the reason for his wife's leaving. Emotional manipulation and a nail into any residual feminist strength comes when after one of their female neighbours remarks on the courage that was exhibited by the wife/mother leaving to 'find herself', the father remarks:

> I'd like to know what the hell kind of courage it takes to walk out on your husband and child.
>
> *(Benton 1979, IntR 10: 16)*

Thus, implying a lack of bravery instead and not taking on her designated social role seriously.

Skillful camera direction throughout the film shows scenes with him physically higher up in his offices with powerful scenic views or in dominant higher stair level positions such as in a courtroom scene with him looking down at his wife. When we witness his joy at his son's emerging bike riding skills in Central Park, we see her hidden behind the glass doors of a café seemingly being punished, a spectator from afar.

Introduction to my own cultural perspective as a contributor to this chapter

I have always been drawn to the cinema ever since my parents took my sister and I as young children on what seemed like eternally long tube rides on a Sunday from west London to the West End to see all the Disney Classics. These were the days before even video cassettes. I still have vivid memories of wicked stepmothers turning into dragons and princes thrashing through forests of thorns to save their damsels in distress; patriarchal fairy tales that placed women as either fearless aggressors or timid victims waiting to be rescued. Looking back at my childhood, my cultural inductions which I suspect are shared by many immigrant families of that day were both a comical mix of insecure projections from my parents to not lose the Greekness of the homeland and a desire to 'fit in' and embrace what life in England had to offer. These initially playful dimensions underwent a subtle shift in my adolescence, playing out as very dominant cultural discourses that would penetrate my fledging subjectivity in ways that I still continually ruminate over.

Culture is a complex phenomenon and is difficult to define. It cannot easily be defaulted from or avoided. For example, as gendered selves, we all need to broadly identify ourselves as either male or female. Cultural 'branding' begins therefore from birth. At this point I believe that layers of culture are 'painted' on us as if on a blank canvas. From the desires and disappointments of our nurturing carers, to our broader family and communities, all might influence any sense of a nationality, political or religious belief or indeed sexuality that we might come to embrace. We are in some ways therefore inducted inter-culturally with little free will or choice initially. I am drawn to Heidegger here when he spoke of how we are 'thrown' into a world that is already there before us; within say our own historical moment.

Individual and contextual experiences, however, affiliate us also within our own cultural uniqueness, for example, our profession, relationship and familial status or a disability. However which way we present, and with whatever cultural attachments we might come to identify ourselves with, we are richly embodied through the experience of our five senses and our resultant perception of the world. Not so much as a 'consciousness' but more a body that 'embraces and constitutes the world' (Merleau-Ponty 1948: 9).

Part of 'being' in the world for me in relation to myself and others around me relies not only on spoken words, therefore, but on a constant attention to the non-verbal language of the body. One could call this an intuitive, nonreductive approach towards myself and others, informed and filtered through the layers that culturally define me. Using the image of an iceberg as a useful model for my own cultural awareness, I see myself as uniquely shaped in my identifications as a: Man, Heterosexual, Husband, Father, Clinical Teacher, Psychotherapist, Dentist, British Citizen, Internationalist, 2nd Generation Greek Cypriot, Orthodox Christian.

As a young Greek adolescent, my parents unwittingly reinforced a patriarchal and sexist ideology. On the one hand purporting to encourage sexual conquests with non-Greek girls to 'gain experience' but on the other controlling who I might choose to go out with. There was an explicit rule not to stray, in case I ended up 'falling for' anyone who was not part of my ethnic community. The complete opposite ruling was given to many young Greek women whose virginity was prized until their wed 'lock' to a young man who would seek 'purity' in his bride to be. This resulted in subordination and ignorance for a wife where her husband's prowess could not be challenged.

When I found myself in a traditionally English boarding school, another layer of a dominant discourse took root on my cultural identifications. Here sensitivity and gentleness within a young boy were clearly discouraged and literally bullied out of me with what I felt was an overviewed collusion from those in authority, who may well have seen it as 'doing me good'.

All these cultural identifications and experiences have imparted an immeasurable subjectivity on me that clearly informs my way of being in the world. I see it as fluid, constantly challenged and undergoing metamorphosis by my interactions with the physical world and those others living alongside me. I take the poetic analogy of a 'stranger in ourselves' as a useful and welcome companion to my existential drama, where both free will and the 'historical' are majors players.

Psychoanalytic considerations

It could be said that my own experience of patriarchy forced me into perhaps a 'false self' position, where my relationship to what I now understand as the maternal and paternal metaphors was somewhat sabotaged. Psychoanalysis can be an interesting resource in introducing these metaphors. I invite a reflection here to try to give a context to my own relation to them and possibly also other males.

Despite huge advances in embryonic research and development, where fertilisation can be either in vivo or in vitro, the physical ability to carry a growing foetus is still an exclusive experience for women. It is with this reference that I initially introduce my interpretation of the maternal metaphor but later extend it to primary care givers.

Some theories of psychoanalysis such as from Bion (1979: 125) claim that a foetus will experience a sense of lack from the very moment of a traumatic, frightening birth and onwards into its adulthood. The resultant child will then strive for a return to the safety and warmth of the place of its origin; the mother, a place where embodiment begins. Heartbeats and body rhythms experienced in harmony with the mother; the initial point of reference.

An exit into the world and the experience of lack that follows, a necessary and inevitable educative life, might be claimed to be one successive compromise after another from that original womb fusion. Infants will then be transferred into the arms of a primary care giver. In Lacan's model, this would be mainly a biological mother. Optimally (although not universally) this mother will be enriched with enough of her own desire towards love, to form the requisite intimacy with a child. Kristeva (1981, 14) describes this experience for the mother as 'the slow, difficult and delightful apprenticeship in attentiveness, gentleness, forgetting oneself'.

Lacan claims that this desire is enthused or passed into infants with a resulting wish/joy for them to somehow stay safely basked and fused to the mother in an incestuous way, imagining they can remain her 'object of desire' or play thing.

One of the many insights I gained from the maternal seminars is that the experience of motherhood can vary hugely for new mothers and is unquantifiable. However, if we are to believe that a special dyadic relationship is indeed present between a newborn and its biological mother, can this be replicated if or indeed when the primary care giver is not the biological mother? Drawing from my own experience as a parent, I believe a 'good enough' experience as Winnicott (2007: 49) suggests of holding, feeding, transmission of love and security through mirroring can all be provided by a surrogate co-parent. I do, however, recognise the significance and potentiality of the unique connection between biological mother and child.

It is important at this stage to differentiate between biological parents and care givers.

In contemporary families today, infants are raised within the context of not only traditional biological woman/male models but also all male, all woman and single parent configurations with variations of biological influence in their care giving.

In a reinterpretation of Freud's thinking, Lacan introduced a paternal metaphor symbolised by the Phallus. This imaginary, elusive, perfect symbol of potency comes to signify in fantasy only what the child lacks in its offering to the mother and acts like a disruptive force challenging the dyadic bond. The infant recognises that 'it is impotent and unable to oppose the mother in the pursuit of her desire' (Bailly 2009: 146). She comes and goes, preoccupied by other desiring interests; the world.

Through a timely interception, the paternal metaphor makes separation possible. It comes to symbolise language, law and broader culture and can therefore introduce difference; rescuing the infant from the reality of its predicament. This being its inability on its own to become a subject. By helping to build a separate psychic structure, the paternal metaphor provides a rock to cling to or kick against symbolically, and thus, helps the infant to become grounded in a life of psychic separation.

Ideally, any resultant guilt or fear in a child for any incestuous fantasy can be safely accommodated. Although argued by many, it is also claimed that only this will help drive the infant into emotional stability, preventing psychosis, collapse and depression. With optimal acceptance of this by a child, it accomplishes and secures its place in the world and its laws; one of which prohibits incest by an integration of and kneeling to phallic law. The paternal metaphor therefore is not necessarily a father but *otherness*. Otherness meaning, at times for example, a single mother herself having to impart both the maternal and paternal metaphors or a female partner to a mother. It is perhaps therefore a different perspective, a challenger, a gentle disrupter, a reality checker, a village, a community or members of a family tree. So I postulate that perhaps the maternal could be seen as the metaphor that embodies 'sameness' as the crucial formative part of infant experience, that brings security through unconditional love and mirroring, and the paternal is that which allows 'otherness', through facilitation of subjective growth and free expression, that is not so easily attained until separation is made possible.

It is important to differentiate here between the phallic references of today in psychoanalytic theory, with previous biological determining historic references from Freud. What these references try to represent now is a theory of how men and women ultimately come to position themselves in relation to the paternal metaphor. Neither sex (infant or indeed parent) ever comes to possess the elusive Phallus, as it is purely a construct in fantasy, although men within a supportive patriarchal context have both enjoyed and, I postulate, suffered trying to pretend that they have it at the expense of women. When/if psychic separation occurs, both girls and boys will try to go on a quest for either identification or transfer of their love towards another object. What happens though if experiences do not go optimally?

However one sees inherent gender differentiation in biological terms, it could be said that boys are made aware very early on that they cannot ever be biological mothers themselves. In theory, however, although boys have the physical capability to consummate a sexual relationship with their mothers, this is clearly prohibited. Faced with these stark psychic realities placed on fledgling male identities, it is not difficult to see that shame, embarrassment and a future tricky identification with mother is clearly not straightforward. With inadequate *otherness* or when pre- and postnatal experiences of intimacy and love which were symbolised by the maternal influence are not so easily reachable because of what could be evoked in accessing them, survival could be seen as a precarious state of affairs, not easily negotiated and often leaving boys isolated in their experience.

Robert Bly in his book *Iron John* speaks of 'the tremendous pain that's involved in a boy's separation from his mother'. He feels this is persistent and long enduring. He recognises that daughters will experience this too but says that when looking up at their mothers they may say:

> 'That's what I'm going to be', meaning a woman. The son says, 'That's not what I'm going to be'.
>
> *(Bly 2013: 1)*

Bly raises an important point that to a degree resonates with my own experience of boyhood. However, when I consider, for example, my forced separation from my own mother when I attended a boarding school, I have come to realise that although this was indeed a major challenge, it was more that I had remained far too long under her influence. This caused much confusion and impacted significantly more on me I feel over the years than the actual separation did.

Kristeva echoes this when she says that there is a deep humiliation in the loss of the mother for a boy, as an object of love (to their father) and loss of their identification to her physical and emotional closeness, creativity and expressiveness (Minsky 1996: 190). The impact of this is heightened in my opinion if alternative, affirming and compensatory identifications are not forged/facilitated from then on.

Under the simultaneous insidious influence of patriarchal, macho conditioning that calls to 'Come on be a man, grow up and be strong, boys don't cry' some boys may sense they have to repress feelings of fear and ignore pain. I remember myself on the sports field at school having to repeat cross country runs time and time again on the same day, as I couldn't achieve the qualifying times.

Although patriarchy contributed greatly to me relinquishing for a long time a gentle nature and repressing my sensitivity, I came to realise that it played more of an aggravating role in a pre-existing drama. Coming to terms with what I was really caught up in offered me the voice and potency that now forms a huge part of what I am able to bring of myself to the psychotherapeutic encounter.

I often reflect on how useful to the phenomenological and existential underpin-nings of my psychotherapy training psychoanalytic theory can be. Many of the men and women I work with are held captive to the complex influence of the maternal and paternal metaphors in their own life experiences.

Sociopolitical references

> Men make up just one-in-eight teachers working in primary schools and only 48 are currently employed in state-run nurseries.
> The disclosure comes amid concerns that a lack of positive male role models may be putting boys off school at a young age and fuelling the gender gap in education.
>
> *(The Telegraph 2011, IntR 2)*

My understanding is that stereotypes exist of girls being superior intellectually than boys and that this can have an impact on children reaching their full potential in early primary school years.

> Official figures have shown that boys begin to lag behind girls by the age of five, with past research blaming the 'gender gap' on biological differences, dif-ferent learning styles, teachers' attitudes, a lack of male role models and even the 'feminisation of the classroom'.
>
> *(The Telegraph 2013: IntR 1)*

However we might conceive the term 'masculinity', its colouring of male sub-jectivity can become conditioned by the absence of good male role models and constructed at the level of fantasy towards women. Isolation and lack of recogni-tion during the growth from boy to man has in my opinion been heightened by the seductive allure of social media, the Internet and aggressive games on consoles. These lead to problems that can range from a difficulty in open expression and embodied face-to-face feelings, to at worst, a massively projected silent or explicit rage focused onto women, who then come to represent their lack and disorder.

Without wanting to defend it, I wonder if perhaps patriarchy paradoxically gave and continues to give a structure to masculinity; a crutch for men to grasp in this chaos, one that proves ultimately to be a poisoned chalice in its resultant subordination of women.

An example of this would be the 1950s man in America, perhaps the father of the generation of parents represented in *Kramer versus Kramer* (1979).

> He got up early, laboured responsibly, supported his wife and children and admired discipline. Reagan is a sort of mummified version of this dogged type. This sort of man didn't see women's souls well, but he appreci-ated their bodies; and his view of culture and America's part in it was boyish

and optimistic. Many of his qualities were strong and positive, but underneath the charm and bluff there was, and there remains much isolation, deprivation and passivity. Unless he has an enemy, he isn't sure that he is alive.

(Bly 2013: 1)

This might be testament to the amount of real fratricidal wars in the world.

Despite the apparent open derision of Patriarchy, especially with today's advances in equality legislation, there is still a paradox at play. The film *Fatal Attraction* (1987) is a good example of the continued manipulations at play for men and highlights the many serious issues that almost exclusively affect women. These might be their representation or treatment in corporate and political life as well as their 'choices' in balancing family life with work. The film firstly toys and conspires to reinforce the psychoanalytic double bind of how a man might come to negotiate a minefield of fantasies to renegotiate back into the arms of a woman who is not his mother; choosing either the idealised loving yet sexually unappealing wife or the femme fatale with whom he can debase as a whore in his fantasy; yet not love. The film is devious in that it portrays a single-minded, high powered career woman as the destroyer of families and their wholesome, innocent values. The overriding message reinforces patriarchy by claiming that although men can have it all – sex, power at work, family and love – women must choose.

Thankfully, in recent years there has been a significant shift in the cinematic representation of the experience for both sexes in fiction. For instance, *Revolutionary Road* (2008) depicts in a much more realistic way the experiences of a young and possibly naive married couple in 1950s America. Their dream-like hope for a more creative and 'free' union becomes tainted by patriarchal stereotypes and ultimately leads to tragedy. Whether these more balanced depictions of human experience are being led by the industry itself or from audience demands or both is uncertain, but thankfully even Disney's *The Lion King* (1994) could now be said to have introduced a more rounded view of family.

I wonder though if a great deal has actually changed for real men in the last 60 years from the 1950s male, aside from perhaps some men carrying a sort of reparatory apologetic guilt, one that stems from the inheritance of a previously strong, powerful yet demeaning patriarchal system. Certainly the feminist movement rightly forced men to wake up to the experience of women, and many men as a consequence have found a *compassion and clemency* that has resulted thankfully in a more thoughtful, reflective approach towards themselves and women.

Inner turmoil and violence

When one looks closely, however, at some important UK statistics about men, they bring to the surface some disturbing phenomena about some men's difficulties.

Suicide

In 1981, 4129 men and 2466 women in the United Kingdom committed suicide. When these figures were re-evaluated 30 years later the numbers had reduced for women by nearly 50% to 1391 but had risen in men to 4590 (Office of National Statistics 2012: IntR 3).

> The latest suicide statistics from the ONS show the greatest gender gulf since records began. The suicide rate for men is now three and a half times that of women. Breaking down the statistics, the most worrying trend is a rise in the rate among men aged 40–44. ... That suicide is a gendered phenomenon is a looming, inescapable, self-evident truth.
>
> *(The Guardian 2014: IntR 4)*

Domestic violence

Domestic violence affects both genders but there is dramatic slant towards women. Currently two women a week in the United Kingdom are killed by a current or former partner. This constitutes nearly 40% of all female homicide victims (IntR 8).

Over half (52%) of female victims aged 16 or over had been killed by their partner, ex-partner or lover (93 offences). In contrast, only five per cent of male victims aged sixteen or over were killed by their partner, ex-partner or lover in 2010/11 (21 offences) (IntR 9).

Aggressive objectification and misogyny through internet pornography and social media

In July 2013, a woman who had lobbied for the female image of Jane Austen to be included on the Bank of England £10 banknote received unbelievably violent and personally abusive insults online after a successful campaign. She said threat messages from 86 Twitter accounts to her had spoken of mutilating her genitalia, stalking her outside her house, beating and gang-raping her (IntR 7).

The relationship that some men have to 'straight' pornography is important to consider also. The role of the woman in pornography is controversial, whether enjoyed as victim or victor, degraded or dominant.

> ...Across every pornographic incarnation, women are commodified and defined according to how they will bring pleasure to the man ... The categorisation of the woman gives the masturbating man a sense of control by eliminating the natural unpredictability of human relations. Instead of representing women as fully formed, diverse and complex individuals, unique in needs and desires, pornography defines them into two basic categories: acts and attributes.
>
> *(Strager 2003: 53)*

In the 1960s, most pornographic material was depictions of nonviolent, consensual sex. Scientific evidence supported the view at that time that it was not harmful to read or watch. However, with this relaxed attitude came a gradual increase of sexually violent imagery. To examine the effects of this change on those who viewed this type of pornography, studies were undertaken to show whether aggressive behaviour towards men and women increased after men viewed neutral, erotic or aggressive-erotic films.

Results indicated that the aggressive-erotic film was effective in increasing aggression overall, and it produced the highest increase in aggression against the female (Donnerstein 1980: 269–277).

Much of the aggressive pornography out there perpetuates the rape myth – the view that women say *no* but don't mean it, and that they enjoy sexual coercion (Wallace 2001: 164).

In a study of sampled HIV positive gay men,

> 43% of the men reported recent bareback sex with a partner of unknown serostatus ... Worryingly, a significant correlation was observed between defining masculinity as sexual prowess and intentional unprotected anal sex.
>
> *(Halkitis and Parsons 2003: 367–378)*

Concluding with paternity and maternity

I have tried thus far to present examples of challenges faced by boys and men using some psychoanalytic ideas within the context of an ever-evolving yet manipulating Western society. Some of these involve men's struggle to adapt to varying expectations of them. Are men as fathers really important or necessary? Are men just sperm donors? Scanning the psychoanalytic literature ones finds slightly dated ideas from Winnicott about how fathers should adopt more of a supportive role towards mothers, implying mothers are of primary importance to a child.

> ...mother finds it a little difficult to know when to make use of her husband, and when to wish him out of the way.
>
> *(Winnicott 1991: 113)*

Other papers might talk of the usefulness of father's play and how it has a *vitality and boisterous quality* (Harris 2009: 201).

Much as though I agree with plenty of what Winnicott and Harris have written, I find references to what fathers might or might not be good at or capable of rather patronising. Aside from the optimal biological female/maternal capabilities previously explored, men and women should not be pitched up against each other to show what gender defining qualities, if any, they are able to offer a child. Issues around parenting are complex because by the time men and women occupy the life of a child they bring with them varying cultural identities, as well as varying capacities for love and engagement. These are based on their own subjective histories, current and previous connections with others, including significantly, relationships with their own parents. But rather than defining or stereotyping, why can we not merely wonder what each and every parent can uniquely offer their child?

Drawing from my own experiences when my children were infants, on both occasions, I felt my role was to some degree influenced by patriarchal stereotypes. Although I was profoundly enriched by my experience as a father, I at times felt an outward struggle in the community around me. I felt that my wife's role was in some way socially sanctioned and laid out. Mine was harder to grasp. I often sensed I was being somehow intrusive when I attempted to communicate my own perspective as a parent. Although I had a deep respect and honoured my wife's unique relationship to our children during the first few weeks after their birth, I also remember feeling at times implicitly conditioned as the peripheral supporter in parenthood; the back-up feeder, nappy changer or 'tea and biscuit' provider. When, for example, I wanted to cut my daughter's umbilical cord and hand her to her mother, something which we both wanted, I remember feeling awkward, as the no doubt tired midwife rolled her eyes at me; 'another one of those "new age" men'. Reflecting back, I felt that the 'maternal' and 'paternal' roles seemed quite clear and distinct, as long my wife and I stayed members of the club of Patriarchy and abided by the rules.

Are men as fathers sometimes pushing themselves into a position of playing out a role then, implicitly imposed on them, because they lack the sufficient road mapping of what being a father is for them? A paradoxical reversal perhaps of the patriarchal film *Stepford Wives* (1975) scenario, where instead of having subordinated women in a ready and willing subservient wife role, we might now have men; reprogrammed as soulless agreeable robots or angry deviant antifeminists, desperately unreflective, trying to reassert a lost identity through fatherhood. If some boys, young or older men are indeed in turmoil, awareness and support is needed for them to become more emotionally available to themselves and others.

The White Ribbon Campaign, a global charity that works towards ending violence against women (IntR 6), talks of:

1. Challenging and dismantling the structures of men's power and privilege, and ending the cultural and social permission for acts of violence.
2. Organising and involving men to work in cooperation with women in reshaping the gender organisation of society, in particular, our institutions and relations through which we raise children.

Robert Bly (2013) talks of a something 'fierce' that is needed once in a while in every relationship between a man and a woman. He gives the example of how in *The Odyssey*, Odysseus approaches Circe, who stands for a certain kind of matriarchal energy to whom he lifts up his sword to. To me this is certainly not another sub-ordinating re-enactment of patriarchy but a potent call to a true emancipation for both sexes. Wieland writes that:

> The absence of a parental couple in our founding myths and its substitution by male omnipotence – spiritual or technological – is ultimately based on an attack on mother and on life as the source of life. When life as the source of life is denied the death instinct reigns unabated. (1996: 313)

She is trying to say, I believe, that both sexes have been subject to a patriarchy, albeit now diminishing and that it continues to challenge the very essence of how we see ourselves and how we relate to each other, whether as women or men.

> Both men and women participate in this tortured value system. Psycho-logical patriarchy is a 'dance of contempt,' a perverse form of connection that replaces true intimacy with complex, covert layers of dominance and submission, collusion and manipulation. It is the unacknowledged paradigm of relationships that has suffused Western civilisation generation after gene-ration, deforming both sexes, and destroying the passionate bond between them. (IntR 5)

If patriarchy remains unchallenged, it will continue to act as a buttress, driving and influencing detrimentally the psyche of children. A cycle which will then be repeated as these children grow up to become parents themselves. Parents need to be able to find a way to survive their own psychic destruction by their children as Winnicott describes:

> Hello, object! I destroyed you, I love you. You have value for me because of your survival of my destruction of you. While I am loving you I am all the time destroying you in fantasy. (1980: 105)

This can only be done if both parents have a capacity to tolerate the strangeness in themselves and manage a level of integration or to hold a sense of love and respect for themselves and others around them. This is an intergenerational cycli-cal dilemma and challenge for the future. The ability to tolerate the frustrating onslaught of ambivalent projections as well as the recognition of a background of love and developing fellowship can allow both parents and child to move out of the arena of omnipotence and control. Ultimately, I sense this could facilitate a move-ment for a growing adult into a different arena of anxiety.

For Kierkegaard (1980: 61), this anxiety is 'the dizziness of freedom'. That which makes *choice* part of our own individual moral judgment. To transcend into this we need to take a 'leap of faith' which calls us towards risk taking.

This in itself embodies a sense of personal responsibility and ultimate fearlessness in all our abilities, whether men or women, to reach a sense of purpose and meaning in our lives.

This is not wish fulfilment on my part but a hopeful optimism.

> If I were to wish for anything, I should not wish for wealth and power, but for the passionate sense of the potential, for the eye which, ever young and ardent, sees the possible. Pleasure disappoints, possibility never. And what wine is so sparkling, what so fragrant, what so intoxicating, as possibility!
>
> *(O'Hara 2007: 26)*

References

Bailly, L. (2009) *Lacan*. Oxford, England: Oneworld Publications.

Berger, J. (1972) *Ways of Seeing*. London, England: BBC/Harmondsworth: Penguin.

Bion, W.R. (1979). *A Memoir of the Future, Book 3 The Dawn of Oblivion*. Perthshire: Clunie Press. [Reprinted in one volume with Books 1 and 2 and 'The Key', Karnac, London.]

Blaisdell, T. (2007) Frantic Fathers and Misplaced Mothers: Hegemonic Patriarchal Reinforcement of the Traditional Family in American Film. PhD Thesis, The University of Texas at Arlington.

Bly, R. (2013) *Iron John: Men and Masculinity*. London, England: Penguin, Random House.

Castleden, R. (1990) *Minoan Life in Bronze Age Crete*. London, England: Routledge.

De Beauvoir, S. (1973) *The Second Sex*. London, England: Vintage Books.

Donnerstein, E. (1980) Aggressive erotica and violence against women. *Journal of Personality and Social Psychology.* Aug; 39(2): 269–77.

Eisenstein, Z.R. (1984) The patriarchal relations of the Reagan state, signs, *Women and Poverty*, 10(2). Chicago, IL: The University of Chicago Press.

Fol, I. (2004) *The Dominance of the Male Gaze in Hollywood Films: Patriarchal Hollywood Images of Women at the Turn of the Millenium*. Norderstedt, Germany: Diplomarbeiten Agentur diplom.de.

Foucault, M. (1975) *Discipline and Punish: The Birth of the Prison*. New York, NY: Random.

Halkitis, P. N. and Parsons, J.T. (2003). Intentional unsafe sex (barebacking) among HIV-positive gay men who seek sexual partners on the Internet. *AIDS CARE*, 15(3).

Harris, A. (2009) *Fathers and Daughters: Heterosexual Masculinities. Contemporary Perspectives from Psychoanalytic Gender Theory.* London, England: Routledge.

Jacob, A. (2012) *On Matricide. Myth, Psychoanalysis, and the Law of the Mother*. New York, NY: Columbia University Press.

Kierkegaard, S. (1980) *The Concept of Anxiety*. Princeton, NJ: Princeton University Press.

Kristeva, J. (1981) Women's time (trans. A. Jardine and H. Blake). *Signs* 7(1): 13–35.

Laing, R.D. (1990) *The Politics of Experience*. London, England: Penguin.

Merleau-Ponty, M. (2008): *The World of Perception*. London, England: Routledge.

O'Hara, S. (2007) *Kierkegaard Within Your Grasp*. New York, NY: Houghton Mifflin Harcourt.

Strager, S. (2003) What men watch when they watch pornography, *Sexuality and Culture,* 7(1).

Wallace, P. (2001) *The Psychology of the Internet*. Cambridge, England: Cambridge University Press.

Wieland, C. (1996) Matricide and destructiveness: Infantile anxieties and technological culture. *British Journal of Psychotherapy* 12(3): 199.

Winnicott, D.W. (1964) *The Child, the Family and the Outside World*. London, England: Penguin.

Winnicott D.W. (1965) *The Maturational Processes and Facilitating Environment*. London, England: Karnac.

Winnicott, D.W. (1971) *Playing and Reality*. London, England: Routledge.

Electronic (Internet References: IntR)

1. The Telegraph (2013) Boys 'worse at school due to stereotypes', available at http://www.telegraph.co.uk/education/educationnews/9862473/Boys-worse-at-school-due-to-stereotypes.html. Accessed 11/10/2015.

2. The Telegraph (2011) No male teachers at 4500 primary schools, available at http://www.telegraph.co.uk/education/primaryeducation/8734967/No-male-teachers-at-4500-primary-schools-figures-show.html. Accessed 11/10/2015.

3. Office for National Statistics (2012) Suicides in the United Kingdom, available at http://www.ons.gov.uk/ons/rel/subnational-health4/suicides-in-the-united-kingdom/2012/stb-uk-suicides-2012.html#tab-Suicides-in-the-United-Kingdom-1981-to-2012-Registrations. Accessed 11/10/2015.

4. The Guardian (2014) Britain's male suicide rate is a national tragedy, available at http://www.theguardian.com/commentisfree/2014/feb/20/britain-male-suicide-rate-tragedy-failure. Accessed 11/10/2015.

5. imaginenoborders.org (no year available) Understanding Patriarchy, bell hooks, available at http://imaginenoborders.org/pdf/zines/UnderstandingPatriarchy.pdf. Accessed 11/10/2015.

6. Kaufman, M. (1999) The 7 P's of Men's Violence, available at http://www.michaelkaufman.com/1999/the-7-ps-of-mens-violence/#1. Accessed 11/10/2015.

7. The Guardian (2014) Jane Austen Twitter row: two plead guilty to abusive tweets, available at http://www.theguardian.com/society/2014/jan/07/jane-austen-banknote-abusive-tweets-criado-perez. Accessed 11/10/2015.

8. wewillspeakout.org (2007) Incidence and prevalence of domestic violence, available at http://www.wewillspeakout.org/wp-content/uploads/2013/03/domestic-violence-statistics-2009.pdf. Accessed 11/10/2015.

9. Home Office Statistical Bulletin (2010/11) Homicides, Firearm Offences and Intimate Violence, available at https://www.gov.uk/government/uploads/system/uploads/attachment_data/file/116483/hosb0212.pdf, p. 21. Accessed 11/10/2015.

10. Benton, R. (1979) Original Screenplay of *Kramer versus Kramer* p. 8 and p. 16. Available at http://www.thescriptsource.net/Scripts/KramerVsKramer.pdf. Accessed 11/10/2015.

5

THE MATERNAL

An immaculate concept

Kate Gilbert

It is one minute after 9am on Wednesday the 13th July 1955, and the young Catholic mother of five small children is weeping quietly over the sink as she washes up after the family breakfast. She lives in a Northamptonshire village located some seventy miles north of Holloway prison in Islington where Ruth Ellis, also a young mother, is now being hanged to death for the murder of her lover.

The local community, teachers, priest as well as her husband and family all agree that the weeping mother is a model of maternal virtue. Ruth Ellis is a mother judged by her society as unfit to live. Her daughter, three years old at the time her mother hangs, will die prematurely of cancer at the age of fifty.

This moment constitutes my first memory. The weeping mother is my own and on the day in question, I am her three-year-old daughter. I am the same age as the daughter of Ruth Ellis.

There is no doubt that what we are dealing with in the hanging of Ruth Ellis, the last woman to be executed in Britain, is both tragic and complex for all concerned. From my own point of view as a bewildered child in 1955 while watching my good mother cry for a putatively bad one, and in the years following when I would work as a psychotherapist, I have wondered a great deal about mothers. I would bear witness to and be complicit in the over-simplification of the most complex ethical problems faced by the task of mothering, mine as well as those of others. I would come to wonder about the myths that underpin our interpretation of 'the maternal' and it is to one of these myths that I shall turn to today, the myth of the Virgin Mary, Mother of God.

At three, unbeknown to me, I was bearing witness to the annihilation of more than one woman; obviously, there was the hanging of Ruth Ellis who murdered a man. But there was also my own mother who was being threatened with annihilation by the demands placed on her by her Church, her culture and herself. She lived the early years of her motherhood in self-sacrificing emulation of the Blessed Virgin Mary just as her mother before her had done. She would try to teach her four daughters to do the same in the years to come.

Mothers, I was taught, should be willing to die for their children. They should sacrifice themselves and their own needs, and certainly desires, to fulfil the needs and wants of their families. It is this annihilation of the mother as a subject that would render her 'good' and daughters were being encouraged to do likewise.

While Ruth Ellis was hanged for the murder of a man, who will be called to account for the annihilation of the many women down the ages who have sacrificed their own lives and unwittingly sometimes those of their children in the name of a myth that they played no part in creating? What are the effects on the children of these mothers, both boys and girls, as they witness and unconsciously join their mothers (and fathers) as they succumb to the power of this myth? Myths are made by men. The mythology of the Virgin Mary as developed by the Catholic Church has been the product of an exclusively male mind.

Now I want to look at the aetiology of the myth that underpins such practice.

The Mary of the Gospels and the Mary of Mariology

There is the Mary of the accepted Gospels (recognising that these are not the only Gospels, merely the most widely disseminated). There comes next the version of Mary that is the product of Catholic doctrine beginning in the early centuries of the Church. I shall suggest that the post-Jesus creation of the archetypal Mother, far from offering an image that is helpful, actually presents us with a dynamic, in her position in relation to her son that is potentially emotionally stunting for both mother and child.

I do not believe that it is only Catholics who suffer unconsciously from this idealised version of the relationship between Mother and Son. James D. Tabor points out in his online article 'Mary – Mother of God or Jewish mother of Seven?' (posted 5/31/13, updated 7/31/13) that those researching the origins and development of early Christianity draw a distinction between what they refer to as the 'historical' Jesus and the 'Christ' venerated by Christians. The study of the transformation of the Jesus perceived as travelling, messianic Jewish teacher and healer, into the eternal, divine Son of God – is called Christology.

What receives much less attention, Tabor points out, is a similar, perhaps even greater transfiguration – that of Mary, the Jewish mother of Jesus, and probably six other children, into the Blessed Ever-Virgin, the Mother of God, Star of the Sea and the Queen of Heaven. This evolution is known in the Catholic tradition as Mariology. It is the image produced by Mariological dogma that interests me most for the purposes of this discussion. To see whence she derives, I shall turn now to the Mary of the Gospels, a different kind of mother from the one who would later be idealised.

We see Mary, the young Jewish girl, drawn sketchily and variably through the four Gospels that form the original Christian canon. There are, notably, very few references in the Gospels to Mary's feelings as she lives out what is undoubtedly an often anguishing human life.

Luke's account of the Annunciation (New International Version Luke 1: 26–28) states:

> In the sixth month of Elizabeth's pregnancy, God sent the angel Gabriel to Nazareth, a town in Galilee, to a virgin pledged to be married to a man named Joseph, a descendent of David. The virgin's name was Mary. The angel went to her and said, Greetings, you who are highly favoured! The Lord is with you!

We now see one of the rare references to the young Jewish girl's frame of mind and feelings (V 29):

> Mary was greatly troubled at his words, and wondered what kind of greeting this might be.

This is a very natural response from the young girl, however religious. To be unmarried and become pregnant at this time was scandalous and potentially dangerous. Matthew (1: 18–20) shows that Joseph had suspicious thoughts of his own about the news:

> This is how the birth of Jesus the Messiah came about: His mother Mary was pledged to be married to Joseph, but before they came together she was found to be pregnant through the Holy Spirit. Because Joseph her husband was faithful to the law, and yet did not want to expose her to public disgrace, he had in mind to divorce her quietly. But after he had considered this, an angel of the Lord appeared to him in a dream and said: Joseph son of David, do not be afraid to take Mary home as your wife, because what is conceived in her is from the Holy Spirit.

There is an ordinariness to both Mary's and Joseph's responses to what must have been alarming news for each of them. Another moment where we receive a glimpse of Mary's state of mind through the account of Luke is when she and Joseph lose their son (Luke 2: 41–51):

> Every year his parents went to Jerusalem for the Feast of the Passover. When he was twelve years old, they went up to the Feast, according to the custom. After the Feast was over, while his parents were returning home, the boy Jesus stayed behind in Jerusalem, but they were unaware of it. Thinking he

was in their company, they travelled on for a day. Then they began looking for him among their relatives and friends. When they did not find him, they went back to Jerusalem to look for him. After three days they found him in the temple courts, sitting among the teachers, listening to them and asking them questions. Everyone who heard him was amazed at his understanding and his answers.

When his parents saw him, they were astonished. His mother said to him, 'Son why have you treated us like this? Your father and I have been anxiously searching for you.' 'Why were you searching for me?' he asked, 'Didn't you know I had to be in my Father's house?' But they did not understand what he was saying to them. Then he went down to Nazareth with them and was obedient to them. But his mother treasured all these things in her heart.

It is not difficult for any parent, indeed for any person, to imagine the various feelings conjured up by losing a twelve-year-old child in this way for three long days and nights only to find him safe and well and unaware of the anxiety he was causing them. We also have a sense in the following verses of Jesus being admonished by his mother, then realising that he may not behave like that towards them and returning to his obedient ways. This is a down-to-earth scene where there is misunderstanding between parents and child. We see the two generations at a time of transition struggling with what has just happened. They cannot fully understand one another.

The first reference to Mary in John's Gospel shows Mary as a mother with authority over Jesus as he does what she asks of him at the wedding at Cana (NIV John 2: 1–11):

On the third day a wedding took place at Cana in Galilee. Jesus' mother was there, and Jesus and his disciples had also been invited to the wedding. When the wine was gone, Jesus' mother said to him: 'They have no more wine.'

'Woman, why do you involve me?' Jesus replied. 'My hour has not yet come.'

His mother said to the servants: 'Do whatever he tells you.'

Nearby stood six stone water jars, the kind used by the Jews for ceremonial washing, each holding from twenty to thirty gallons.

Jesus said to the servants: 'Fill the jars with water', so they filled them to the brim. Then he told them; 'Now draw some out and take it to the master of the banquet.'

They did so, and the master of the banquet tasted the water that had been turned into wine. He did not realise where it had come from, though the servants who had drawn the water knew. Then he called the bridegroom aside and said: 'Everyone brings out the choice wine first and then the cheaper wine after the guests have had too much to drink; but you have saved the best till now.'

In this scene, Mary is portrayed as an initiating force in the start of her son's ministry and shows that she believes in what he has to do. She does not appear to be meek and retiring, attributes often associated with the later maternal version, and here is a Jesus who appears to listen to her with regard to timing in spite of his own view about the right moment to begin. There exists a dialogue between mother and son, man and woman.

In a later scene, one can witness the ongoing process of separation from the family of origin when Jesus uses familial terms in the spiritual rather than the biological sense (Matthew 12: 46–50):

> While Jesus was still talking to the crowd, his mother and brothers stood outside, waiting to speak to him. Someone told him, 'Your mother and brothers are standing outside, wanting to speak to you.'
>
> He replied to him, 'Who is my mother, and who are my brothers?' Pointing to his disciples, he said, 'Here are my mother and my brothers. For whoever does the will of my Father in heaven is my brother and sister and mother.'

I think what the reader witnesses here is a stage that Freud refers to nearly 2000 years later as one of the most painful psychic moments for any parent and child. The once exclusive love for the family is challenged by the desire to move outside and into the world so that new things can come into being. What we see in the apparently historical account of Jesus as well as Mary are portraits of human beings who struggle with experiences with which human beings from time immemorial have suffered and are continuing to suffer now. The psychic pain associated with separation from infantile bonds enhances the human being's capacity to achieve emotional maturity.

Having looked briefly at the 'historical' Mary of the Gospels, let us now look at the doctrinally developed figure of Mariology. Within the Marian tradition there are four doctrines concerning Mary that have evolved over time in the history of the Catholic Church and have established themselves as dogma. This means that they are taken to be divinely revealed.

The first doctrine of Mariology concerns *The Divine Motherhood*.

This was first proclaimed at the Third Ecumenical Council at Ephesus in 431. Mary was understood here not to be merely the mother of Jesus, *Christotokos*, but also to be the Mother of God, *Theotokos*. This doctrine had wide implications for the further teaching about Mary. If she was the Mother of God, her status was of a different order from that of any ordinary mother and a great deal of thinking about the nature of this mother needed to be done.

The second dogma refers to the *Perpetual Virginity of Mary*.

There are references in the Gospels to the brothers and sisters of Jesus (see NIV Mark 6: 3):

> 'Isn't this the carpenter? Isn't this Mary's son and the brother of James, Joseph, Judas and Simon? Aren't his sisters here with us?'

But the Church denied any actual biological claims on the body of Mary following the birth of Jesus. It was asserted as divinely revealed truth that she neither had intercourse with Joseph nor did she bear children from sexual intercourse.

The third Marian dogma concerns the question of the *Immaculate Conception*.

In 1854, with the Bull Ineffabilis, Pope Pius 1X solemnly proclaimed this dogma:

> The most Blessed Virgin Mary, from the first moment of her conception, by a singular grace and privilege from Almighty God and in view of the merits of Jesus Christ, was kept free from every stain of original sin.

The problem of original sin which is taken to be inherited from the disobedient behaviour of Adam and Eve is that it results, according to St Augustine, in concupiscence or sexual desire. Mary did not, according to divinely revealed truth, know this feeling.

The fourth dogma concerns the *Assumption of Mary*.

The Catechism of the Catholic Faith (item 966) states:

> The Immaculate Virgin, preserved free from all stain of original sin, when the course of her early life was finished, was taken up body and soul into heavenly glory, and exalted by The Lord as Queen over all things. (Catechism of the Catholic Church, item 966 at the Vatican website.)

So Mary, who long after her life on Earth has, according to doctrine, become the Immaculate Virgin, is not subject as are other humans to the putrefaction of the flesh. Her purity of soul protects her from the wages of sin. She is not buried but assumed into Heaven.

It is my own belief that this distinction between the 'historical' Mary and the doctrinally developed Holy Virgin Mother is not well understood by the general population in the largely secularised twenty-first century. Yet, we are undoubtedly all familiar with the art, sculpture, architecture, poetry, literature, and popular references to the Madonna. The figure who is the subject of art in its various forms has tended to be the Mary of Mariology.

The myth of Mary from a secular point of view

Through the myth, we see a mother wholly absorbed in her son. He is central to her throughout his life and hers. There is no earthly father with whom he has to compete. There is no sexual desire for a man in this mother. He has no brothers and sisters for whom he might suffer feelings of rivalry. At the passion and death of the thirty-three-year-old Jesus, the mother of Mariology is fully engaged with his suffering. His suffering is hers. There is no evidence in the myth of competing claims. The Mother is totally devoted from birth to death and beyond to her son and after life on Earth is over she joins him in heaven for all eternity.

The blissful state of the newborn held by the loving embrace and gaze of the mother is prolonged ad aeternum. He is God. She is the mother of God. She is invulnerable in a certain sense. There is a version of her in which she does not die, but merely goes to sleep. This is referred to as *The Dormition*. Her body will not ever be corrupted by death. Jesus will never have to face the loss of his beloved mother. In the myth, Jesus is spared the experience we all most dread apart perhaps from our own death. Peculiarly this mother of Mariology functions as a protection against the most demanding moments of emotional growth.

There is a fundamental, infantile desire in all of us to be the centre of our parent's lives and love. Within the dogma of the Church the desire for centrality tessellates well with the Marian figure who places herself forever around the son, sublimating all her own needs and desires to his. This mythical woman annihilates herself so that he might live.

The woman in our world (and not just the woman, but the one who takes up the place of the mythical mother) unconsciously learns to place herself or himself around the self of the other in a complementarity characteristic of codependency. It is surely problematic to promote this as a dynamic to which to aspire.

The fictional work of Colm Toibin, *The Testament of Mary* gives humanity to Mary as mother of the crucified Christ that we never see through the idealising iconography arising out of Mariology. He shows a woman in the most profound struggle with her grief and torment, he portrays her daily annoyances and dislikes, a rounded creature who at the terrible time of watching her son being executed, also cares about her own safety (Toibin 1996: 84).

The paradox in the story of Jesus being man while also being God is surely to be understood through the constant struggle that exists in becoming human. The moving portrait of a suffering and riven mother struggling to face the truth of what she has done and not done as depicted by Toibin is edifying and uplifting in a very particular way. Jesus in her story is not her only concern though he matters to her very much indeed. Here is the rub. For this Mary, she matters too. She cares about her own survival at the same time as being utterly distraught at the murder of her son. She is alive in her own right. She has a life separate from his. Such a rendering of Mary is shocking.

The potency of the myth of Mary is in evidence in the iconography of the Madonna.

Many of the most celebrated painters and sculptors in the history of art have turned their gaze towards the rendering of the Madonna including Leonardo da Vinci, Michelangelo, Raphael, Bellini, Rubens, Dali and Henry Moore. More recently there have been a number of controversial versions of the Virgin Mother. One of the paintings of The Holy Virgin Mother by Chris Ofili, an English Turner Prize-winning artist best known for his paintings incorporating elephant dung, was at issue in a lawsuit between the Mayor of New York City, Rudy Giuliani, and the Brooklyn Museum of Art. The painting was the subject of passionate controversy, a tribute to the continuing stature of the Madonna in our current culture. The artist dared to question the familiar traditional image by introducing sexual imagery into the painting of Mary. Breaking the taboo which focuses on the sexual purity of the virgin mother continues to be a risk that exacts a price, and in the secular, not only the religious world. The attachment to this important image is felt across cultures and throughout history.

Alongside the perfected version of the pure ever virgin Mary, as depicted through Mariology, we see within our culture the development of another mythological Mary; that is the Magdalene. This Mary is given the role of the prostitute in our culture. When we speak of the Madonna and the Whore, a well-known binary way of separating women from each other both intra-psychically as well as interpersonally, it is the ever virgin mother Mary and Mary Magdalene that underpin the binarism. It is helpful to see Estela V. Welldon's (1988) book *Mother, Madonna, Whore* on this subject.

It was several centuries after the writing of the Gospels that Mary Magdalene became conflated with the prostitute who bathed and anointed the feet of Jesus (Luke 7: 36–50). But there is no evidence for the association in the text. What scripture does show is that Mary Magdalene was a close follower of Jesus, who accompanied him on his journeys, learned from him, remained faithful to him even in his darkest hour when his male disciples fell away, was the first to see the Christ after his death and was the person who announced the resurrection. Jesus' inclusion of a woman in such an important role in an era when Jewish teachers almost never had female disciples or taught women is a striking example of the breadth of his embrace. It is fascinating that a woman given such an important role in the life, ministry, death and resurrection of Jesus should be transformed in the way Mary Magdalene was. It is as though someone must pay the balance for the asexual and sinless idealised mother and who better than a sinful prostitute. But constructing such images does not make the images representative of truth or fact.

There exists within the teaching of the Church a strong emphasis on the sexuality of women, notably these two Marys. I want to say a little about the radical prizing of female virginity within the Mariological doctrine. Although women were important within the ministry of Jesus during his life, within a few hundred years their role in the development of the Church was completely eradicated. Misogyny took hold and the most perfect being created by the male theologians of the time was construed as feeling no lust, had no husband, no sex, no children by normal means. It is striking that the vagina is not the only orifice of the woman that must remain closed. She is not to speak except to affirm what the men have said. She is to be shut up in a fundamental sense. The symbolic situation that seeps into the unconscious of all over the centuries is that men make the law in the name of God, the authority and learning belongs to them, the woman is not in an equal relation with them. When she speaks it is to bolster what he has said and she is sexually purified and so represents no threat to his status in the world. Many couples are operating with these ideas informing their behaviour and expectations even today and without their consciously knowing it.

The idealised and denigrated Marys and this relegation of women is not what we find in the orbit of Jesus. In the gospel we see his attitude to a third Mary who barely shows up in religious iconography in contrast to the place given to the Madonna and the Magdalene.

> As Jesus and his disciples were on their way, he came to a village where a woman named Martha opened her home to him. She had a sister called Mary, who sat at the Lord's feet listening to what he said. But Martha was distracted by all the preparations that had to be made. She came to him and asked, 'Lord, don't you care that my sister has left me to do the work by myself? Tell her to help me!' 'Martha, Martha,' the Lord answered: 'You are worried and upset about many things but only one thing is needed. Mary has chosen what is better, and it will not be taken away from her.'
>
> *(Luke NIV, 10: 38–42)*

Women are not defined by Jesus in terms of their adherence to conventional roles as we see in this story. They are as able to listen, think, and learn as men are and are encouraged by Jesus to make this choice of the 'better part' if they want to. Our culture has done a great deal to try to keep women in their place just as the Church did for centuries in the name of God. Sadly, the iconography of Mariology has been an aid to the control of women in many ways. But this cannot be said to comply with original Christian thinking.

I would like to examine the attitude of Jesus towards female sexuality and sin. The following moment is recorded in the Gospel of John (Chapter 8 vv3–11 NIV):

> The teachers of the law and the Pharisees brought in a woman caught in adultery. They made her stand before the group and said to Jesus, 'Teacher, this woman was caught in the act of adultery. In the Law Moses commanded us to stone such women. Now what do you say?' They were using this question as a trap, in order to have a basis for accusing him.
>
> But Jesus bent down and started to write on the ground with his finger. When they kept on questioning him, he straightened up and said to them, 'Let any one of you who is without sin be the first to throw a stone at her.' Again he stooped down and wrote on the ground.
>
> At this, those who heard began to go away one at a time, the older ones first, until only Jesus was left, with the woman standing there. Jesus straightened up and asked her, 'Woman, where are they? Has no one condemned you?'
>
> 'No one, sir.' she said.
>
> 'Then neither do I condemn you,' Jesus declared. 'Go now and leave your life of sin.'

Jesus, unlike the teachers of the law and Pharisees in the account, does not become excited and judgemental about the adulterous woman. He shows that he applies the same moral standard to the male accusers as to the accused woman. He makes them see that they are no less sinful than she is and in no position to take the moral high ground over her. The Church's later attitude in many ways seems more like that of the scribes and Pharisees of this story than it seems like the just attitude of Jesus.

Conclusion

To conclude, I want to cite here one of my favourite moments in the Gospel, which is to be found in Matt 15 22–28 NIV:

> A Canaanite woman from that vicinity came to him, crying out, 'Lord, Son of David, have mercy on me! My daughter is demon-possessed and suffering terribly.'
>
> Jesus did not answer a word. So his disciples came to him and urged him, 'Send her away, for she keeps crying out after us.'
>
> He answered. 'I was sent only to the lost sheep of Israel.'
>
> The woman came and knelt before him. 'Lord, help me!' she said.
>
> He replied, 'It is not right to take the children's bread and toss it to the dogs.'
>
> 'Yes, it is, Lord,' she said. 'Even the dogs eat the crumbs that fall from their master's table.'
>
> Then Jesus said to her, 'Woman, you have great faith! Your request is granted.' And her daughter was healed at that moment.

What is wonderful here is the emphasis on the intercourse between this Canaanite mother and the Jewish Jesus. Symbolically virginity represents impenetrability and a prohibition on penetration. This mother hears that she is being turned away on the basis of being a gentile yet she stays to fight her corner. She is not offended, does not take herself off in a huff to complain about Jesus to other people and leave her daughter in distress. She stands up for herself and her daughter and it is her faith, her hope, her perseverance that penetrates the heart of Jesus. He is moved by love to help her.

Something creative happens between this man and this woman through their engagement with one another and it is Jesus who takes up the place of listener, receiver, learner, one might even say the traditionally feminine position. This is a transformative moment for him. He shifts his position and agrees to heal her daughter. This is a dynamic and poignant interaction. It offers the opportunity for learning in a way that the more static Mariological dogma does not.

I would like to point to a similarly thought-provoking moment in recent history, where another influential Jewish man from within a male-biased society listens to a societally disenfranchised woman, the hysteric. In Freud's volume entitled *Studies in Hysteria*, we find a paper on his work with Frau Emmy von N. in which he is undoubtedly taking the lead as the doctor in his demand that she remember by tomorrow something that she claims not to know. He goes on to describe how:

> She then said in a definitely grumbling tone that I was not to keep on asking her where this and that came from, but to let her tell me what she had to say.

Freud then tells us: 'I fell in with this' (Freud and Breuer 1991: 120).

In both of these situations women who are in positions where their rights are severely curtailed make their voices heard by powerful men in male-biased fora who in each case are transformed by being able to listen to the woman's words and something new occurs for all concerned.

At the time of the Church's teaching that the Sun moved round the Earth, no large telescope had been invented that might bring further learning into view. Once that invention occurred, the Church was not prepared to look through it as Copernicus and Galileo did. It chose to bury its head in the sand and persecute people for centuries rather than face its own ignorance and shift its position.

Today, with the so-called 'Talking cures' which are, it is worth noticing not referred to as the 'Listening cures' which might be perceived as a more female-valuing description (or indeed ' the talking-and-listening cure', which might value both tongue and ear equally), there exists a specific discourse that has its basis in the agreement to listen, to actually listen, to those who wish to speak including those who had previously been relegated and disenfranchised for whatever reason.

The version of the Mother within Mariology with her perfected and inhuman image offers us all, both men and women, a cruel and impossible standard by which to judge ourselves or our mothers as mothers. It asks that she or we subjugate herself or ourselves to the needs of the other no matter how old that other may be. There is the promotion of an infantilising dynamic, where it is the husband or the person in the position of the husband who is treated like the eternal infant around whom the woman is required to fit herself.

It was through clinical work with devoutly Christian men and women that I first began to notice the unhappy tendency towards the abnegation of the self to the needs of the other as though this were a good thing. This will not be a characteristic specific to those of the Christian faith nor will the reasons for it be simple or singular. However, it is my belief that to understand more fully the origins of the most influential mythical mother within our culture and over centuries may help us bring to consciousness dynamics that may be influencing us and our children unhelpfully without us having any idea about them at all.

The Catholic Church has in recent times been plagued by the problem of child sexual abuse. Perpetrators are people whose emotional development is hampered and whose forms of relating are immature. We all participate in the responsibility for the care of our children, and much of the damage over the ages has been effected through the turning of a blind eye to what we as a society know about and cannot bear to face. Perhaps deconstructing the iconography that supports and even encourages infantile dynamics will open up the path to a greater understanding of what maturity might require of the human subject. The evasion of emotional suffering though the idealisation and consequent denigration of the mother and the woman is not helpful to any of us. To be able to make room for the man and the woman, the maternal and the paternal, the sexual and the celibate, saint and sinner, the parent and the child, Jew and Gentile, the powerful and the vulnerable remains an ever-present challenge.

References

Freud. S. and Breuer, J. (reprinted 1991) *Studies on Hysteria*. London, England: Penguin.

Tabor, J. D. (posted 5/31/13, updated 7/31/13) *Mary – Mother of God or Jewish Mother of Seven?* Taborblog. Available at: http://jamestabor.com/2012/05/25/mary-mother-of-god-or-jewish-mother-of-seven/.

The Holy Bible: New International Version. (1984) Grand Rapids, MI: Zondervan.

The Vatican Website. (1992) *Cathecism of the Catholic Church*. Available at: http://www.vatican.va/archive/ENG0015/_INDEX.HTM.

Toibin, C. (2012) *The Testament of Mary*. New York, NY: Scribner's.

Welldon, E.V. (1988) *Mother, Madonna, Whore*. London, England: Karnac.

6
MOTHERS AND SONS

Melike Kayhan

I presented this chapter at the 'Maternal' seminars which took place at the Philadelphia Association in 2011–2013. There has been little contemporary qualitative research informed by psychoanalytic concepts and one of the aims of this chapter is to address that gap. The chapter presents a psychoanalytic exploration of how masculinity is constructed in society, taking as its focus the experiences of a group of Kurdish men who spent their childhoods in Kurdistan (parts of Iraq, Iran, Turkey and Syria), but moved to Britain as adults. As part of my Master's thesis,[1] I set up and conducted in-depth interviews with these men, excerpts from which are reproduced below. Presented here are some of my research findings relevant to my current title: 'Mothers and Sons'.

The project has a personal dimension. I wanted to reflect on my own experience of growing up as a girl in a Kurdish family, in a society in which mothers teach their daughters that women are inferior and men are superior, and that daughters should serve their fathers and brothers. I guess my lifelong protest against my mother's internalisation of her self-hatred is one reason why I was prompted to write this chapter. Most feminist writings focus on women's experience of oppression within the family and other institutions, as opposed to men's. As the youngest of three sisters, and sibling to five older brothers, I wanted to look at my own observations of mother-son relationships.

Before presenting my findings, I would first like to explain the significance of the mother-son relationship from a psychoanalytic perspective. An obvious starting point is Freud's theory on the Oedipus complex, a term he coined. The key concept here is ambivalence: on the one hand, the young boy gradually moves away from the mother to identify with the father, experiencing separation anxiety and loss in the process, while on the other hand, he resents the father for his possession of the mother and the implied threat of castration. A double-edged relationship is thus set in motion. The boy learns masculine behaviours via the paternal bond while unconsciously wishing for a return to the mother. His relationship to the father is ambivalent, oscillating between feelings of resentment and admiration. The pursuit of the masculine and repression of the feminine is culturally sanctioned. For example, the Kleinian concept of projection (Klein 1988) theorises that stereotypical female behaviours, such as emotional openness, are classified as weak and split off from the male self. This 'weakness' is then projected onto women (Gough 2004), a point of view reinforced by society, for example, by its validation of the strong silent type (Holloway 1989).

Structuring the interviews

Clearly, every mother-son relationship will be moulded not just by internal dynamics, but by the culture in which that relationship is fostered. Bearing this in mind, when conducting the interviews, I wanted to establish the particular influences to which Kurdish men were subject, where, when and under what circumstances. All the participants were educated to at least degree level. Among them there were two medical doctors, engineers in various fields and mature research students. The participants were between the ages of 28 and 57; barring three of them, they all lived in London. Although the interviews followed the same general structure, there was a great deal of flexibility in each conversation. The interviewees were asked for a narrative of their childhood experiences. The focus was on how they were brought up, and who was responsible for different aspects of their childhood, whether they had a happy childhood, the aspects they were happiest and least happy about. They were encouraged to tell their life story, or at least highlight significant early experiences. For example, they were invited to recount their earliest/most important memories, or early relationships with parents and significant others.[2]

The use of English was problematic at times since all the participants were Kurdish and English was not their first language. The transcripts were not edited grammatically because it was important to get an accurate transcription of the interviews.

Research findings[3]

The men's earliest memories, and their account of family relationships revealed conventional upbringings. In all cases, the mother was the primary carer and a full-time housewife. In psychoanalytic terms, the conditions for sustained pre-Oedipal identification with the mother were clearly present. As touched upon earlier, there are pressures that arise for boys accompanying the need to separate themselves from this relationship, and these pressures could be traced in the childhood memories of most of the group.

After experiencing an early primal identification with the mother, all the individuals in my sample went through a process of Oedipal masculinisation under the influence of fathers, brothers and patriarchal institutions. In several cases, there followed some distancing from the idea of 'hegemonic masculinity',[4] through later reunion with the mother, or a recognition and admiration of women's strength. But, in general, by late adolescence, consciously or unconsciously, most of these men seemed well on the way to not only accepting, but approving, men's dominant position in the social hierarchy.

As I interviewed my subjects, three distinct themes emerged, namely, the Idealised/Repudiated Mother, Cherished Sons, and Attitudes Towards Women/ Violence Towards Women. My findings in each subject area are examined in detail below.

Idealised/repudiated mother

All the men in my group described their relationship to their mothers as 'close', but identification with a male figure, mostly fathers, stands out. Despite this, five of the eight men remembered encountering admirably strong women in the course of their personal formation. Admiration for the mother and an appreciation of female strength is particularly explicit in my interview with Kawa. He describes his relationship with his mother as:

> Very close. I can say that as far as I am concerned I never saw a relationship between a mother and a son that was as strong. She was my closest friend until she died in 1991. I never loved anyone like I loved my mum. She was kind and intelligent, open minded, modern, more than the most of her generation. Some simple questions, even sexual questions that children had I could still ask my mother. Compared to other mothers she was very different. She would explain things about female and male gender, specific things, and actually I got most of my education from my mother. She would show me the way to find out. She would never dictate to me … Because of our mother we were not allowed to act like boys and dictate to our sisters. At home among the children and relatives, my mother was very strong…

In contrast, his father is very authoritarian, distant and at times violent with his mother and the rest of the family. In Kawa's words:

> He was used to dictate [to] people around him. No one told him don't do that or don't do this. He never listened to my mother. Until the day we were older my mother was suffering a lot because of my father, he always ignored her and she was like a slave with my father…

Kawa describes his mother as a very unhappy woman, who stayed in the marriage only for the sake of her children and to avoid the stigma of being a divorced woman in their community. As a child he carefully noted his father's treatment of his mother, which in some cases was harsh and sadistic (especially when he was drunk). This probably created the same emotions of fear, flight and avoidance in him as he noticed in his mother. Thus, Kawa's helpless mother is likely to stir similar emotions in her son and instinctively shape him in her own image. This creates an emotional gulf between him and his father.

Throughout the interview, Kawa expressed pro-women views and strongly rejected the practices – which he saw as degrading to women – of seclusion, of 'honour killings' and polygyny in Kurdistan. This rejection is very likely to be a result of witnessing his mother and other women being subject to various oppressive practices in the family and community. At times his tone wasn't just disapproving, but full of anger and revulsion.

In her chapter on 'Paradoxes of Masculinity', one of a series of essays in *Dislocating Masculinity,* the academic Deniz Kandiyoti argues that in the Middle East the subjection of women through various oppressive practices distorts the male child's psyche. Kandiyoti says:

> It is only gradually I started noticing that, quite often, male reformers were not speaking from the position of the dominating patriarch, but from the perspective of the young son of the repudiated or repudiable mother, powerless in the face of an aloof, unpredictable and seemingly all-powerful father. Was I hearing the rage of an earlier, subordinated masculinity masquerading as pro-feminism?
>
> *(Kandiyoti 1994: 198)*

Kawa also told me how powerless and oppressed he felt as a child:

> So my childhood had two sides, I was not punished so much, but on the other hand I had a very limited area to live or talk or to be myself. ... Anyway I was nothing. In our culture, in Kurdish culture, I will tell you, children are nothing, absolutely nothing. They have to eat after everyone has eaten ... and watch TV or do the things they like after everyone else...

He then goes on to give various other examples of how he was disciplined and taught how to be and behave as a boy by his father, brother and teachers:

> Children are not allowed to talk at all. They are not allowed to interrupt anyone at all. And it means that they are nothing. But the way my father told me to respect people I knew he didn't have to dictate to me, it was the society that was like that ... For example if we had guests, or even just the family, if it was the cartoon time on TV, I was not allowed to watch the cartoons or lie down if I wanted to, I was not allowed to interrupt anyone even for an

emergency thing. My father said when you sit you need to be very careful. You are not allowed to play, even if you play you have to be very quiet or go to another room. Once I asked one of my teachers a question about women. I really didn't know why but he just started to beat me up and he took me to the room of the head teacher. I asked two questions actually. One of them was why a man and woman can't have children before getting married. And the teacher told this to the head teacher and he told my father so I got punished for asking a simple question.

I asked how old he was at the time:

I was seven or eight years old. And the second question was about what happens to women or what they do that makes them have children after they get married. I didn't mean anything and that question just came to my mind and I asked them…

Although Kawa goes through a process of Oedipal masculinisation under the influence of his father, brother and his teachers, he also ends up distancing himself from his culture's expectations of men, and its treatment of women, as is explicit in the excerpt below:

Another thing that came to my mind: somebody from Europe sent my brother a card and there was a picture of a girl on the card, among the trees, and she had very tight trousers. I saw that her private places were a bit up. I asked my brother – he was the closest to me, how come they don't have men's tool. That became a really big cause of trouble, I was punished for it. My father took me to the side, he thought he was an open-minded man, he told me how to respect myself, how to avoid those things and that I was not allowed to ask any of those things about men and women. He said you don't need to know about any of these things. He said: 'if you talk to your teacher and the teacher says that you are wrong, don't say things like "I didn't mean it that way." Don't explain; just say "I won't do it again"'. That was the advice and I knew it was wrong. I had to tell my father that he was right and I was wrong. If someone was older than you he is right. By the time I was twelve, I knew that my father was wrong and others can make mistakes and I may be right. The child has his own personality and you have to let the child do what he wants.

His closeness to his mother and his sisters allowed him to build alliances with women. He says he came to value 'feminine' traits such as sensitivity, expressiveness and caring for others, and came to reject the 'masculine things' he was taught at school, by his father and brothers. In his late adolescence, having identified men as the main beneficiaries of existing power differences between genders, he then decides to use his privilege for the benefit of women; in this case his sister:

> Because we were close she told me that there was a guy she loved and he loved her. She said that they haven't talked but they have seen each other from far away. She asked me what to do. I said, 'talk to him'. I said I could arrange that. I arranged an appointment for her. I went to talk to him and said come to our house and try to have a word with my sister because that is not going to be sorted from afar. So that appointment was arranged. After a while I said ok guys I will leave and will return in a few hours of time … After a few weeks or so, my father and brothers found out about the incident. The oldest brother and my father were very angry about the whole thing and I was protecting my sister and told them that I was responsible. I remember my father was pointing his gun at me. He asked me if I thought we did not have dignity or if I thought we opened a whorehouse that anyone outside can come in and you leave your sister there…

Kawa is also critical of Kurdish women for having internalised their subordinate position in the community when he says 'my sister was so scared and worried about what the man she liked would think of her and her family, and also frightened of being found out by others.'

As I discovered, Kawa's formative experiences in the family had profound effects on his adult life:

> I believe only in that love between my mother and me. What is love? It means when you love someone that means you love that person in every aspect or every way, you totally accept that person. My mum loved me even if I was lazy or ugly and so on. If I was away or at home or causing trouble [or not] she still loved me … I never felt safe emotionally with my girlfriends as I did with my mother. I don't trust women … and don't believe any woman can love me the way my mother did…

Kawa's romanticised relationship with his mother seems to have given him unrealistic expectations of his partners. With his mother he was unconditionally loved, adored and accepted. Kawa lost his mother in a house fire at thirteen. In all his memories of her, she is 'perfect'. But he also developed an unconscious fear of abandonment and fear of intimacy after the death of his mother. What followed in his adult life was a series of unsuccessful relationships. In the rest of his interview, Kawa gave indications that he was untrusting towards women, and had difficulty committing to relationships. Although he said he desperately wanted to have lasting relationships with his previous girlfriends, Kawa's 'love fantasy' – that is the true love between himself and his mother – seems to have got in the way.

It's hard for Kawa to acknowledge his anger at his mother for abandoning him at thirteen. But in adulthood, it became evident in his relationship with his girlfriends, as he couldn't allow them to get close to him. In his defense, he would say no woman was as good as his mother. From a psychoanalytic perspective, mother idealisation can result in denying or repressing painful feelings, as well as distorting the cherished figure. The perfect mother in this example becomes an absent presence, an imagined but meaningful figure who influences everything her son is and does.

Cherished sons

The other person who was very explicit about his relationship with his mother was Jamal. The most striking feature of Jamal's case is what we might call 'maternal over-involvement'. Being the eldest, he is his mother's favourite. In his words:

> She has always devoted herself to the family, and keeping a very tight niche and control, if you like, on the family members; always having a lot of black and white and very little grey. What is right in her view would only be right and there is nothing to change her mind on that. I think there is an authoritarian attitude to it, but in a motherly way. Very protective as well and at times you could say protective to an extent it can be viewed as control. Controlling in the sense that she would like to decide how our future would be woven, how our future would be shaped.

Jamal continues:

> I think she would use different tactics really. Initially she tries to persuade and also come up with examples – this is how things are done, this is how we do it and then moving on, at times she gets angry trying to force her views. In that way, she would try and impose her views … When I came to England we were separated for a few years. Later on, they also came here and joined me. I remember my father saying 'we didn't want to tell you, but your mother has not been very well for months now, and medicines were no help. She has been crying all the time. You must talk to her, she will listen to you'. So I spent a lot of time with her and within a month she was fine. I guess she was missing me. She cannot bear to separate from me…

Jamal's conflicted relationship with an overbearing mother is in many ways typical of the power relations between mothers and sons in Muslim Kurdish families. Kandiyoti (1994) points out that in societies with structural patterns that tend to weaken the marital bond, where motherhood (especially of male children) is highly valued, while wifehood and daughterhood are debased, an intense maternal involvement with sons may result. Growing up in this culture myself, I saw this clearly enacted in Kurdish society. While a woman who expresses open affection for her husband is frowned upon, her culturally defined role as a mother (of male children) hugely influences her status within the community. I observed that otherwise downtrodden women are empowered through their sons and, through them, able to impose their authority. Furthermore, if the emotional needs of women are not consumed in the marriage union, feelings for the husband are displaced onto the male child, sometimes with the expression of openly erotic feelings. The mother's expectation is that the son will compensate for her disappointment with her husband. The son may then become the target of both maternal seduction and repressed rage, as the mother alternately builds him up as an 'idealised protector' and rejects and ridicules his masculine pretensions. This is assumed to make for a narcissistic and insecure masculinity (Kandiyoti 1994: 202). According to Kandiyoti, this 'golden son' (cherished son) is a reflection of the mother's internalised self-hatred.

The notion of 'cherished sons' is of course not limited to Kurdish society and goes beyond cultural norms in the Middle East. It is interesting to note that Freud was Jewish and also a very cherished first son coming from a Middle Eastern culture. We might detect some sexism in Freud's emphasis on the Oedipus complex, which is a male model of the development of sexuality that largely ignores female sexuality.

Jamal is in his late forties and has only ever had a serious relationship with two women, his ex-wife and his present girlfriend. Chatting about his late adolescence, he is full of regret:

> I used to get phone calls from the girls in the neighbourhood, but I never got to talk to them. My mother would always pick up the phone and tell them off for calling me and threaten them saying 'Aren't you ashamed of yourself calling a boy in his house? I will talk to your parents, if you call again'. All my other male friends used to get calls, but their mother never interfered. This is the kind of family I come from. Later on, my sister joined my mother in answering calls and putting girls off when she was a bit older. I don't know why they have such a hold over me.

Jamal comments on his failed marriage:

> She [my mother] didn't want my ex-wife (now), and she tried her best to dissuade me from marrying her. I think it was the fact that my wife was English; she didn't think that the marriage would ever work. And I think that my father was also of that line of thinking ... I left Iraq when I was twenty-nine for Britain where I met my wife. Looking back, I can see now very clearly that I had to leave Iraq in order to have some breathing space. My mother was very angry with me for leaving her and she was psychologically sick after I left. Even then, I had to wait for my mother to approve my marriage for

six years. Although we lived in different countries for ten years she had a very strong hold over me. Always dictating her authority from afar…

It is interesting to consider how Jamal experienced his maleness as a young boy, given the control exerted by his mother and his sister, and also how his masculinity developed as a result of those experiences. The importance of mothers' authority over young sons has been noted in most discussions of the psychodynamics of masculinity (Kandiyoti 1994: 202–203). John Bowlby's theory of attachment (1988)[5] and Margaret Mahler's individuation-separation theory (1968) are both crucial to understanding the tensions that can arise in mother-son relationships. In particular, Mahler's theory emphasised the need for a child to achieve a healthy separation from its mother in order to thrive. According to Mahler this 'separation' happens in several distinct developmental stages, as the child learns both to distinguish itself from its mother, and, eventually, to discover its own identity. In her view, these phases were essential for the development of autonomy, independence, and identity. The way in which Jamal's mother has contributed to his difficulties with attachment, separation and autonomy are highlighted above. In Jamal's case, his mother's controlling behaviour pushes him away. The son distances himself from the mother and the mother is at a loss to understand how and why this has occurred. Angry and disappointed, she feels rejected for what seems to her no perceivable reason.

As a practising psychotherapist trained in psychoanalysis, I have observed the consequences of such derailed relationships first hand. From a psychoanalytic perspective, the relationship between the adult son and the mother is ideally a process whereby all participants strive to achieve a balance between attachment, separation and autonomy.

Attitudes towards women/violence towards women

There seemed to be a consensus among the men I interviewed when it came to recognising the oppression Kurdish women suffer in the family and in the community. As I mentioned at the start of this chapter, I myself was taught by my mother that women are inferior and that it was my duty to serve my father and brothers. Clearly, the mother herself is culturally biased towards men. As a result, sexual inequality and submissiveness to men prevails in Kurdish and other Middle Eastern cultures (Lindisfarne 1994). Women grow up with inferiority complexes and internalised self-loathing. Kurdish men, conversely, grow up with notions of superiority and privilege. And although many of the men I spoke to were critical of the subordination of women in the Middle East, they also seemed to feel they were in a position of authority, overseeing these 'childlike' women.

When I asked them to comment on the so-called 'honour killing' cases in the Kurdish community, they all agreed these were acts of murder and that there could be no justification for such crimes. However, they also pointed out that the men who committed them faced cultural pressures. Men who demonstrate weakness, by failing to control women's behaviour, lose credibility in the Kurdish community. Thus, a man may be labelled 'dishonourable' or 'soft' and 'weak', when a daughter elopes and the father is forced to arrange a marriage for her against his wishes.

According to Nancy Lindisfarne, the rhetoric of hegemonic masculinity in Middle Eastern cultures depends on stereotypes of women as weak, emotional, both needing support and potentially deceitful. Female virginity and chastity are valued but seen as hazardous. This is how the control of men, as well as women, is justified in such societies. 'Honour' must be protected and shame avoided, at all costs. There were some striking examples of these themes in my interviews. Aram and Rebwar, for example, both complained about the restrictions placed on their freedom when they were adolescents:

> In my country, or the region that I came from, there were a lot of cases sur-rounding abusing boys and I was a pretty nice-looking boy. My family was a bit protective and didn't let me go out. That caused some bad feeling for me; I felt that I was always behind compared to the other boys of my age in the same school. Even at the time of higher education, I felt I was always behind them – socially and confidence-wise.
>
> *(Aram)*

> There were times that I would go out and I would be asked what time I was coming back etc. and my sisters wouldn't be so restricted. The reason given was that there was much more danger facing young boys … Well I had some tough times as a teenager, I was a very nice-looking, even feminine-looking boy in a quite rough masculine type of society and I was always picked on by older men. They were attempting to sexually abuse me or start a relationship with me, so I always grew up with a fear that meant I was always trying to protect myself.
>
> *(Rebwar)*

Accounts of the dangers faced by young boys led these families to be overprotec-tive of their sons. By guarding their young sons from male predators, these families were protecting their honour. It could be argued that the abuse of these 'femi-nised' young boys by predatory males was a projection of maternal-female hatred. As discussed earlier, when sons become the target of both maternal seduction and repressed rage, it is likely to create a very narcissistic and insecure masculinity. As for gay relationships between consenting adults, homosexual men are only stigmatised in Kurdish society if they receive rather than give sex. As Rebwar explains:

> A homosexual act was seen as acting in a feminine way only [when] recei-ving sex – it doesn't go the other way. So for gay men to live in that society you have to go and have sex with male prostitutes. That's how it is viewed. It doesn't go both ways.

When it comes to female sexuality, Firat, who is doing a Ph.D. in Kurdish history at a prestigious British university, has profoundly contradictory views:

> Virginity is important but marriages should be possible even if the woman is not a virgin. Ideally a virgin would be better. With a divorced woman, it's different because you know she is no longer a virgin. If you're talking about my culture in Kurdish setting I would like my partner to be a virgin and I would wait to consummate my marriage.

In Kurdish culture, female virginity is idealised and penetration signifies possession. Firat's views suggest that taking your wife's virginity is an essential part of being male. However, he had to renegotiate his masculine ideals when confronted with the realities of a new cultural setting in Britain. As he puts it:

> Because of my own personal experiences [of] living here and being single until my mid-thirties, well, my views have [now] changed.

Not only Kurdish women must be 'pure' in body, they must also display 'feminine' qualities at all times. Namo, for example, seems unaware of his double standards when he comments on an 'honour killing' case that took place in London.

> It's a shame on our community … I felt ashamed for being Kurdish when I heard about it. For two reasons, firstly that a Kurdish man could do this, secondly that a community should try to hide such a hideous crime. I certainly cannot justify what the mother has done. If she was a real mother, a real human being, she could have prevented that. There were many arguments between Heshu and her father over this issue, and every time her mother calmed her down and stopped her from contacting the police by saying their 'honour' was at risk.

Although he is critical of the husband, his real anger is reserved for the mother. 'If she was a **real mother**', she could not have done this. Again, while he bemoans the subjection of women, he can't help adopting a position of superiority when it comes to judging their actions and in this case, a woman's 'unnatural' behaviour. It is certainly true that the woman/mother in the excerpt above appears to be complicit in her daughter's eventual death. Despite the risks to her daughter, she colludes with her husband in the protection of so-called 'honour'. This betrayal of her own sex again suggests the presence of internalised self-hatred.

When it came to female activism, the men's views were interesting. Although they all expressed sympathy for the plight of Kurdish women, many of them disapproved of those 'feminists' who go too far:

> I don't like the idea of those women who hate men – feminism; because I am against feminism, but I like equality but not division or segregation. We don't have a 'men army' against a 'women army'.
>
> *(Kawa)*

They [the educated Kurdish women from Turkey] tend to be extreme feminists and rebellious. Basically it takes longer for Kurdish women of this background to mature.

(Fikret)

I would like to see a woman [who] has a wide understanding of feminism. Not a narrow view that wouldn't work in Kurdish society, one that allows men to join in as well. Looking at men as the enemy does not work, and that is why I don't have much faith in the woman's movement currently.

(Rebwar)

In general, the men I interviewed said that they would never resort to physical violence in a relationship, and disapproved of those who did. However, three of the interviewees felt that under certain circumstances it may be unavoidable and one said he was not against it.

I am not a person who says you should never hit a woman.

(Fikret)

How I feel about my friend will depend on the circumstances – did he slap her or punch her? Was it once or did he beat her very badly? Did she hit him first? Was it in self-defense for the man?

(Edip)

I've hit a girlfriend although I was provoked myself … I reject this type of behaviour between adults. As a member of the stronger sex we should never hit women.

(Rebwar)

Fikret doesn't seem to think of himself as deviant. By hitting a woman, he is exercising a right. Edip argues that striking a woman is acceptable unless the woman is badly hurt. Although he admits to once hitting a girlfriend when 'provoked', Rebwar is the only one of the three who feels it is wrong. He is more ambiguous on the subject of rape, however:

I would have some sympathy with the girl if she weren't happy with the outcome, but also with the man because of the situation he was put under, or because of the way she was dressed, maybe not knowingly. If they [women] choose to do so they should be aware of the dangers … there may be dangerous, sexually frustrated men, and the women may then send the wrong signals, particularly when it's mixed with a pint or two of alcohol. It's not an easy issue.

(Rebwar)

A man may not be able to control his sexual urges if a woman sends 'misleading' signals, so by displaying her sexuality, a woman is complicit in her own rape. Rebwar is unconsciously rehearsing the age-old prejudice that shifts blame from the rapist to the victim – 'she gets what she deserves' is the underlying message. There is also the implication that women shouldn't be allowed to express or even have desire; desire belongs to the man.

Conclusion

In this chapter, I have used psychoanalytic concepts to explore the relationships between mothers and sons in Muslim Kurdish families, and the effect these relationships have on the development, and construction, of masculinity. As discussed earlier, sons who witness their father's mistreatment of their mothers and the subjection of women (mothers, sisters) to various oppressive practices can end up having a distorted sense of 'maleness'. As my field study with a group of Kurdish men revealed, these distortions can take various forms; Kawa's over-identification with his 'repudiated' mother almost certainly masks a deeper rage ('I was nothing') at the suppression of his masculinity by a tyrannical father, while 'cherished son' Jamal feels his oppressed mother's controlling hold over him wherever he goes. As I spoke to these men, and later, researched this chapter, I became aware of similar dynamics having been at play between my brothers, my mother and my father. It is now clear to me that witnessing my father's treatment of my mother and other women led my brothers to identify with my mother's self-hatred, resulting in an internalised hostility towards myself, my sisters, and women in general.

Writing this chapter gave me the opportunity to reflect not just on my observations of mother-son interactions, but on myself. Unlike my brothers, I grew up with many restrictions on my freedom. I had to fight to get what I wanted. All my five brothers stayed close to the family while I lived abroad for most of my adult life in a culture in which I felt more accepted, regardless of my sex. I have now returned home after living abroad for 21 years, and am still trying to renew links with family members. As the result of my researches, I can now relate much better to men's experiences of growing up in a culture similar to my own, and their sense of what it means to be a 'man' in such a society.

Clearly, research interviews aren't the same as therapeutic sessions. But when the subjects are recounting and remembering very significant personal experiences, and expressing emotion, as was the case in this study, a quasi-therapeutic quality has been attributed to them (Holloway and Jefferson 2000).

What struck me in this particular group of men was that their masculinity was under threat. They had grown up in one culture and been transplanted to another. As emerged in the interviews, the differences between traditional Kurdish society and British mainstream culture are vast. These men have had to renegotiate their male identities, their sense of what it means to be a man, in this very different cultural setting. In some cases their views on certain subjects had changed. Others were still struggling to define themselves, caught between conflicting constructs of masculinity. This was very clear when some of the men recounted being stigmatised or marginalised in British society.

These men interested me for another reason. I felt their childhood experiences had left a clear mark. Growing up in a society with such rigid gender roles leaves very little room for real emotional growth and development – in terms of having a genuine understanding of oneself and a connection to others. Clearly, it is not possible to delve too far into unconscious motives in a field study. But as far as possible, I looked for clues in the men's childhood histories, their accounts of relationship crises, and their hopes and desires for the future. Not only was psychoanalysis essential to understanding mother-son relationships, and the role of gender politics in society, it also proved to be a very useful analytical tool when it came to examining these men's internal conflicts and gaining a deeper understanding of the human psyche.

Notes

1 This chapter is based on my dissertation entitled: A psychoanalytic exploration of construction of masculinity: A field study of exiled Kurdish men in Britain which I submitted as part of my M.Sc. in Gender, Culture and Politics at Birkbeck College, London University, in September 2006.

2 I looked for further evidence of their views on gender roles and the meaning of masculinity by asking questions on various controversial issues such as homosexuality, premarital sexual relationships, 'honour killings', forced marriage, arranged marriage, chastity, child-rearing, the division of labour in a domestic setting, violence towards women, experiences of racism, Kurdish culture versus British/Western culture, feelings about their ethnic identity and so on. Another aim of this study has thus been to engage with different stereotypes of masculinity, by exploring areas where you might expect gender bias or conflicted feelings or where difficult choices which have a bearing on masculinity must be made.

3 This project forms part of a recent dialogue between discourse analysis – the study and analysis of the use of discourse, and the meanings beyond it – and psychoanalysis. Although there are differences between both perspectives, they share some common ground. Both approaches present subjectivity as fragmented and dynamic; both are interested in the construction of self and identity, both present the speaker as active in producing meaning, and both suggest the shaping of selves by the 'other'. I would suggest that both approaches are valid and can be used together to produce a more rounded, psychosocial analysis; this was my aim in this project. I began my investigation by focusing my attention on the construction of masculinity and one of the main institutions responsible for it: the family. I used a psychoanalytic approach when analysing my interview material, with a view to gaining insights into these men's formative experiences, and to hear the 'voice' of the male child, negotiating and constructing his male identity from his childhood experiences. The views expressed in this chapter about masculinity have been informed both by existing research and by my findings in the interviews I conducted with eight Kurdish men who have come to live in Britain under very different circumstances. In my analysis, I drew primarily on psychoanalysis on the basis that it rejects any fixed sexual identity and exposes the

complexities and internal conflicts of each individual. My aim in using psychoanalysis was to reveal the workings of the individual psyche. I wanted to question conventional notions of what it is to be a 'man', using psychoanalysis as a tool. I feel it is important to explain how I designed the project and implemented it; otherwise, there is a danger that my research findings and analysis may sound arbitrary. For my field study, I tried to identify a group of men whose sense of their own masculinity was under pressure. My assumption was that their masculine identities had been shaken through a loss of social authority, either through a loss of profession, a weakening of their ethnic identity, or simply through exposure to a different cultural setting by living in Britain.

4 Connell suggests that some forms of masculinity are elevated in certain times and places, giving rise to a dominant model of masculinity or 'hegemonic' masculinity (2002).

5 Bowlby postulated that children have an evolutionary need to stay close to one figure (usually the mother) during the early part of their lives and that disruptions to this relationship could cause serious psychological damage.

References

Bowlby, J. (1988) *A Secure Base: Clinical Applications of Attachment Theory*. London, England: Routledge.

Brod, H. and Kaufman, M. (eds.). (1994) *Theorizing Masculinities*. London, England: Sage Publications.

Carrigan, T., Connell, R. W., and Lee, J. (2002) Toward a new sociology of masculinity. In Adams, R. and Savran, D. (eds.). *The Masculinity Studies Reader*. Oxford, England: Blackwell Publishers Ltd.

Chodorow, N. J. (1994) *Femininities, Masculinities, Sexualities*. London, England: Free Association Books.

Connell, R. W. (1987) *Gender and Power: Society, The Person and Sexual Politics*. Stanford, CA: Polity Press.

Connell, R. W. (1994) Psychoanalysis on masculinity. In Brod, H. and Kaufman, M. (eds.). *Theorizing Masculinities*. London, England: Sage Publications.

Connell, R. W. (1995) *Masculinities*. Cambridge, England: Polity Press.

Connell, R. W. (2000) *The Men and the Boys*. Cambridge, England: Polity Press.

Connell, R. W. (2002) *Gender*. Cambridge, England: Polity Press.

Fausto-Sterling, A. (2000) *Sexing the Body: Gender Politics and the Construction of Sexuality*. New York, NY: Basic Books.

Frosh, S. (1994) *Sexual Difference*. London, England: Routledge.

Ghoussab, M. and Sinclair-Webb, E. (eds.). (2000) *Imagined Masculinities*. London, England: Saqi Books.

Gough, I. (2004) *Global Social Policy*. London, England: Sage Publications. 4; 289 DOI: 10.1177/1468018104047489. The online version of this article can be found at: http://gsp.sagepub.com/cgi/content/abstract/4/3/289.

Hallway, W. (1989) *Subjectivity and Method in Psychology: Gender, Meaning and Science*. London, England: Sage Publications.

Herek, G. M. (1987) On heterosexual masculinity. In Kimmel, M. S. (ed.). *Changing Men*. London, England: Sage Publications.

Holloway, W. and Jefferson, T. (2000) *Doing Qualitative Research Differently: Free Association, Narrative and the Interview Method*. London, England: Sage Publications.

Kandiyoti, D. (1994) The paradoxes of masculinity. In Cornwall, A. and Lindisfarne, N. (eds.). *Dislocating Masculinity*. London, England: Routledge.

Kandiyoti, D. (1996) *Gendering the Middle East*. London, England: I. B. Tauris.

Kimmel, M. S. (1987) *Changing Men*. London, England: Sage Publications.

Klein, M. (1988) *Envy and Gratitude and Other Works: 1944–63*. London, England: Virago.

Kvale, S. (1996) *Inter-views: An Introduction to Qualitative Research Interviewing*. London, England: Sage Publications.

Lindisfarne, N. (1994) Variant masculinities, variant virginities: Rethinking "honour and shame". In Cornwall, A. and Lindisfarne, N. (eds.). *Dislocating Masculinity*. London, England: Routledge.

Mahler, M. (1968). *On Human Symbiosis and the Vicissitudes of Individuation*. New York, NY: International Universities Press.

Matson, F. W. (1954) The political implications of psychoanalytic theory. In *The Journal of Politics* 16(14): 704–725.

Silverman, D. (2013) *Doing Qualitative Research: A Practical Handbook*. London, England: Sage Publications.

7

REJECTING MOTHERHOOD

Pat Blackett

Introduction

I was asked to contribute to the Maternal Seminars at the Philadelphia Association in the belief that people might be interested in the viewpoint of someone who has chosen not to have children. I have been careful to choose a title and theme that would not offend women who are in a completely different category to myself, those women who do not have children, but want them. I wanted a title that would not only reflect my situation which involves the life decision not to be a mother, but also alludes to having a rejecting mother and, possibly, one which suggests rejecting my own mother.

I was surprised at how many women I talked to thought that I had chosen an interesting theme to write about. I cannot be sure in every case, but it would seem that the people who said this most often were women who are mothers and this is probably because they cannot imagine how it would be possible to live life without children. Obviously, as I have not had children, I cannot know what it feels like, but I think that if you do have them, then life would seem unthinkable and rather empty without them. I feel the same about dogs! Perhaps you just do not miss what you have never had. It is possible that childfree women might be a growing movement. Apparently, projections for Great Britain suggest that as many as 20 per cent of women born in 1975 and later will remain childless (McAllister and Clarke 1998).

GINK: Green Inclinations, No Kids

The reasons why women choose to remain childless are varied, completely personal and uniquely individual. Some want to pursue a career, some do not want to give up important pursuits, perhaps a partner does not want children and some, like me, have just not felt any great desire for them. My aversion is not so great that I would have gone against fate; had I become pregnant at some point along the line, I suspect I would have chosen to have the child. I am fortunate not to have had to make the choice to terminate a pregnancy. I have known some women who have not had that good fortune and the effects are often painful and lifelong. It is difficult to gauge life satisfaction in terms of what might have been, as I have no idea how I would feel if I had taken a different path.

Even if they are vaguely aware that there are people with children who are not at all happy, many people still think that living without children increases the risk of unhappiness. This may be true for some people, but there is no good reason to think that it is true for *all* people, and plenty of reasons against thinking so. I will provide myself as a case in point. For as long as I can remember, I have not had any great desire to get married or have children; it just did not seem something particularly relevant to me. The few times I have stopped to reflect on this, it did strike me as slightly odd considering that I was a woman and was supposed to want these things. This stereotype of a woman only being fulfilled through being a wife and mother is obviously not as strong these days in terms of defining what a woman is, and this may play into the projection that 20 per cent of women who are in their mid-thirties now will choose not to have children.

I consider myself to have been very fortunate to have been born at the time that I was and to have been given this choice. I am one of the first generations of women born in the 1950s who have directly benefited from the women's movement in the 1950s and 1960s and also the invention of the Pill. I have been able to make life choices that would have been much harder if the women's movement had not questioned the roles that society was forcing women into, prior to the second push for women's rights. For a brief period in history in the 1960s and 1970s, and part of the 1980s until AIDS came along, women were able to have full, sexual relationships with men with no strings attached and no real worries because they no longer had to fear the consequence of getting pregnant, or to suffer much social stigma for being promiscuous. It might be worth qualifying this statement, however, given my middle class background, because this freedom was not universal and varied according to social class, religious background and ethnicity. Luckily, I have been able to question my direction in life and to ask, do I really want to get married and have children? As the answer was 'no' for me, childlessness has not impacted on my life in any detrimental way. This has been an incredibly liberating opportunity for my generation and those that have followed. I have the feminist movement to thank for my life choices and I am truly grateful. Generations of women who have come after me perhaps have no idea how much they owe to those earlier struggles and take for granted how they are viewed in society and the choices they are able to make.

The Pill came into use in 1961 and my mother was on it as soon as it became available. Once I started to use it, it felt like a wonder drug. I know so many women who have ambivalent or even hostile feelings towards the Pill, but that was not my experience. I thought of it as a magic pill that enabled me to remain child-free and happy, free of the fear of pregnancy. I actually felt extremely well on it. I stopped taking it after a couple of decades of continuous use on my doctor's advice and it was with regret.

There have always been role models for successful women who have chosen not to have children and I have always been drawn to these figures myself without being that conscious of why. Women who come to mind are Elizabeth I, Jane Austen, Virginia Woolf, Edith Wharton and Simone De Beauvoir. Throughout history there have been ways whereby women could choose not to be a wife and mother, but it would have only been for the few. The main way out would have been to become a nun. This was a route for many independent minded women like Hildergaard of Bingen, although the communal living might have proved difficult for some. I could speculate that perhaps Sister Wendy Beckett, famous nun, art historian and hermit, opted for her caravan because she found the company of nuns all day long rather suffocating and restricting. Had I been forced down the nun route, I imagine I would have ended up as a hermit somewhere. Even being Queen of England did not necessarily mean that you could opt out. Elizabeth I had to be quite a strategist to avoid being forced into marriage and had to use all her cunning in order to remain single. So I suspect my lot in life, depending on what century I was born, would have been to become a nun or hermit, to be viewed with suspicion, possibly as the local witch, or to be pitied by my neighbours as the village spinster.

Nurturing and the lovely mother

Despite my lack of desire for marriage or children, I do consider myself a rather nurturing person, someone who might be described as maternal. So what is a maternal instinct? It does not only relate to bonding or loving your offspring. In my experience, it has a wider definition. I am drawn to look after my plants, animals and the people around me. I have always loved animals and nature. Nothing calms my spirit like being with animals and plants and that has always been the case from as far back as I can remember. A great sadness in my childhood was that pets were not welcome so I used to make homes and attempt to care for ants, beetles, slow worms and lizards, and at every opportunity would offer to walk neighbours' dogs.

Thus, animals bring out my maternal streak. I used to be someone who flinched when someone referred to themselves as Mummy or Daddy in the presence of an animal. However, with my six adopted rescue dogs I have found myself being one of these sentimental people. It just slipped out one day and I realised that perhaps I should not fight it. There is definitely a maternal feeling towards my animals. I want to protect them, to provide them with the best of lives and to fulfil their needs.

Why that should be does not trouble me too much. It is a source of joy and fulfilment and that is all I need to know. Being in the presence of animals feels incredibly nurturing, peaceful and healing. If I am with any of my animals, I immediately start to feel calmer and enriched. I realise this is not everyone's experience but the draw to be around them is strong. The connection is deep and feels natural. There is now research to back this up. Scientists have discovered that dogs and owners get boosts of the hormone oxytocin, a hormone responsible for maternal caring, when they gaze at each other. The same hormone has been shown to increase in mothers' brains when they look into their children's eyes. This therapeutic bond is something that animal lovers have always suspected but now there is scientific evidence about it (Nagasawa et al. 2015: 333–336).

Moreover, the maternal may not only belong to women. During my childhood, I experienced my father as extremely nurturing and in a way motherly. His presence was very enveloping and affectionate but I felt absolutely no sense of nurturing from my mother, apart from the maternal practicalities of her feeding us, bathing us and dressing us. All my early memories are of being with my father, including my earliest memory of lying on his stomach, hearing it gurgle and feeling warm and safe. He is the one who loved nature and plants and showed me how to care for them and respect them.

I remember quite a few years ago, being scolded by an acquaintance who worked in an area that defended human rights. She accused me of preferring animals to people and said it was positively shameful to be worrying about the welfare of animals when people were suffering. I was rather taken aback and had to reflect on whether this was true. I could see her point of view and partly agreed with her. I understand why she was in such a fury with me, but ultimately you cannot force yourself to feel something that is not there. You have to go in the direction that moves you and, as I said to her, it takes all sorts to work towards a better world. I am extremely glad there are people who feel moved to help other human beings and, equally, I am glad that there are people who care about the welfare of animals. I have managed to combine these concerns to some extent by taking one of my rescue dogs, Herbie, into schools to help children gain confidence with reading. He also visits old people in hospital and care homes and is a qualified Pets As Therapy dog – acronym PAT!

Hand in hand with this nurturing side that appears to come from a maternal source within me is the part of me that I suspect has rejected the whole wife and mother route. This is the extremely independent side that values autonomy and the ability to make my own decisions and act on them without having to negotiate and cooperate with someone else. This is key to my happiness and feeling of wellbeing. Also, I enjoy enormously being on my own for quite long periods of time. My idea of bliss is to have a long weekend of four days or more where I know I am not going to have to see or speak to another human being. It does not happen enough for my liking but these are times I really treasure.

People often say to me 'you would have made a lovely mother'. I suspect I would not, if I was anything like my own mother, who, after years of therapy, I realise I probably am.

I remember a few years ago sharing a joke with some of my friends about my choice in handbags, one of the stereotypes about women is that handbags are apparently considered very important to them. I have never seen much point in them and they do seem to be an awful waste of money. I certainly have never been remotely interested in them apart from their capacity as a useful receptacle to carry things around in and have always argued that a carrier bag functions just as well. Similarly, shoes leave me cold. As long as they are comfortable, cheap and do not wear out too quickly they will suffice. I differ greatly from my mother on these two points. Shoes were her passion and she always liked to have a matching handbag or an expensive, quality handbag. If handbags are in some way linked to the feminine, and one would have to see the direct symbolic link to a womb, I can go with this argument. I do tend to see my womb as a bit of an inconvenience which causes monthly obstacles and difficulties and I would, to be honest, rather be without it. I have thought about having a hysterectomy and having it over with, but as it is a major operation with possible side effects, on balance it is probably best to leave things where they are. The choice is individual and any women reading this might like to consider their own attitude to handbags and what that might mean to their relationship with their uterus.

There are political arguments for choosing to remain child-free, which I could adopt, if I wanted to appear noble and self-sacrificing. On the one hand, producing children is bad for the environment, uses up precious resources and is ultimately selfish. On the other hand, we need children to carry on humanity, support an ageing population and to inject energy and drive forward into the future. Mine is a purely personal choice, a luxury of living in the time that we do, in the country that we do. Yet throughout history, all cultures have had to deal with the place of the Mother in society, and so I turn now to an imaginative approach, that of Greek mythology.

Athena and the virgin goddesses

Myths are endlessly fascinating and full of meaning, but why they should be so profoundly meaningful can be obscure. In this sense, myths have been described as 'things that never happened but always are' (Sallustius fourth century AD). From an early age, I was drawn to Greek mythology and alongside this fascination with the gods and goddesses of ancient Greece, I identified with the Greek goddess Athena. I had an affinity with owls and collected images of them as a child with plenty of owl themed ornaments for my shadow box (a wall mounted keepsake frame that was popular in the 1960s). Athena always seemed the most interesting of all the gods and as a child I was pleased to find out that her bird was the owl. I had other things in common with the goddess 'who never was, but is always there', to paraphrase

Sallustius, in that I privileged my father over my mother, just like Athena. She did not even acknowledge her own mother, the ancient goddess of cunning, Metis. I was further delighted to discover that Athena was born in Libya where I was born. That final fact made it clear that she was the one who needed to be honoured!

Years later, I came across a book called *Goddesses in Everywoman: Powerful Archetypes in Women's Lives* (Bolen 2004). In it Bolen, a Jungian psychologist, argues that women have archetypes that they identify with and that the Greek goddesses can be seen as archetypes that describe different types of women. These are images that go back thousands of years, and yet we are still fascinated by their powerful stories because they are like collective dreams. In this book the seven goddesses fall into three groups: The Virgin Goddesses are Artemis, Athena and Hestia; the Vulnerable Goddesses are Hera, Demeter and Persephone, and the Alchemical Goddess is Aphrodite.

When I read about Athena, a Virgin goddess, I recognised a lot of traits that she describes as being of that psychological type. The Virgin goddesses are described as independent and self-sufficient. These goddesses are not susceptible to falling in love. They are not victimized and do not suffer. They represent the need for autonomy and the capacity women have to focus their consciousness on what is personally meaningful. Artemis and Athena focus their attention on external matters whereas Hestia focuses her attention inward to the spiritual centre.

On the other hand, the Vulnerable Goddesses represent the traditional roles of wife, mother and daughter. They are more relationship oriented. Their identity and wellbeing depend on having a significant relationship. They are much more attuned to others, but also, through this, they are vulnerable. All the goddesses are potentially present in women.

The only one who differs is Aphrodite: the goddess of love and beauty. She is beautiful and irresistible. She has many affairs and many offspring. She enters relationships of her own choosing, and is never victimized. She maintains autonomy like a virgin goddess but also has relationships. Bolen calls her the 'alchemical goddess' because of the way she combines vulnerability with independence. It would seem that Aphrodite is the marrying of the two that brings about the most balanced state for a woman.

Bolen also gives a description of what she calls focused and receptive consciousness. She points out that the Greek goddesses lived in a patriarchal society which remains relevant to modern day, and within this context, the virgin goddesses have their own strategies for survival. Artemis lives separately from men. Hestia withdraws into solitude and contemplation. Athena, however, identifies and joins the world of men. A more psychotherapeutically traditional way of describing these three might be to say they all have a 'masculine complex'. The virgin goddesses represent:

> …Every woman who has wanted 'a room of her own', or feels at home in nature, delights in figuring out how something works, or appreciates solitude.
> *(Bolen 2004: 35)*

Fulfilling the maternal and making Mum chuckle

Could there be another explanation for my childless choice, rather than the proposition that I am a woman who honours the spirit of Athena? Perhaps my choice not to have children is linked to the level of vulnerability that motherhood would entail. It is bad enough losing a much loved cat or dog or for something bad to happen to it and the worry and fretting that goes on when they are ill or lost. To have that for your entire life would be unbearable. Friends with children admit that they had not been prepared for the level of vulnerability they felt once they had given birth.

As women, we have uteruses, and so the whole capacity to be a mother is a biological part of us but one can biologically be a mother, and yet it may not touch the deep archetypal level of the mother. If that happens, biologically a woman becomes a mother but, something deep does not click. This may have been the case for my own mother, although I do not have a way of knowing now.

As my mother aged and developed Alzheimer's disease, I could not help but find myself more and more sympathetic to her, attempting to understand her approach to life and the way that she was. We have a lot of characteristics in common but also many differences, not only shoes and handbags. I often feel that I am pursuing a destiny and am part of a mythical narrative, so despite feeling that I have been a free agent and remained child-free through choice, is the truth more likely that I am actually carrying out my own mother's desire not to have children? Perhaps this was my destiny all along?

My conception and birth may have relevance to the path I find myself on. My mother and father were living in Libya when I was born. They already had three children. The eldest, my sister, was eleven, my older brother was nine and another brother was only eighteen months old. The story both my younger brother and I were told from as far back as we can remember was that neither of us was planned or wanted and that Mum only ever really wanted two children. Mum related the story of how it is said that Libya is where the Romans used to send their barren women to get pregnant. It was believed to be a place where fertility increased. So my Mum blamed living in Libya for her fertile state. Apparently, when she arrived pregnant with me at the British Hospital in Tripoli the doctor wearily exclaimed 'Not you again'. There was a boom in pregnant women which seemed to back up the Roman belief in Libya's ability to induce fecundity. However, to counter the wish of my mother that she only have two children, my father apparently was delighted at the prospect of another child and promised to buy her a gold watch if she had a girl as it would mean that the family was complete and balanced with two boys and two girls. She did have a girl and she named me Patricia after a little girl she knew in Tripoli who she thought was very sweet.

My mother was obviously a woman who did not enjoy the experience of mothering young children and I can never recall having felt cherished or enjoyed by her when I was small. I was aware of her ambivalence to my being there, but my recollection is that I would think 'Well I am here now, so get over it', or sentiments to that effect. I was prone to violent tantrums which did not help. Within the family, stories would be told about how difficult I could be. My mother and I seemed to be at war and, even more infuriating to me, she always won because I was a child. She had quite a severe method of dealing with my outbursts which was to fill a sink with water, place me on a chair and dunk my head in the water until I stopped screaming.

As a child, I was attached to all my fluffy, cuddly toys but was left indifferent towards my dolls, which always seemed rather hard and plastic and unrealistic. I could certainly never see the point in the doll 'Tiny Tears'! Disgusting! But my bright turquoise Wonder Woofer dog seemed alive and real and was much loved for years. I have always wanted to have animals and have fulfilled this wish in later life. Although, as I have mentioned earlier, pets were discouraged as children, my mother did finally relent to my persistent nagging when I was about eight years old and let me have a hamster. When it inevitably died after a long life of four years I was inconsolable and grieved so deeply that I was not allowed another pet.

So with regards to children, other than a tinge of regret towards an ex-partner's wonderful and loveable kids, I would say, hand on heart, that I am happy with the way my life has turned out, mainly because I have managed to find the space to allow animals and plants to be a part of my day to day life. I have also been able to nurture and provide space for rich and long-lasting friendships.

I am vaguely aware of the irony that I may in fact be unconsciously carrying my mother's desire forward not to have children. This fear has more than a small element of truth to it, because my brother who was also 'unwanted' does not have children either. I suspect our dual rejection by our mother hit him harder, perhaps because I came along after him or just because as a man, his relationship with Mother was more Oedipal. A further twist was that when we were adults, he was almost certainly her favourite. He is the one who elicited the most delight from her when he rang or visited, and his brief visits were talked over and remembered long afterwards. This is unlike the visits from my older brother and myself, who were there much more often, my older brother in fact being her main carer. On my regular visits to my Mum, she often reminded me that I was unwanted but by that stage, I was able to respond wryly that if she had not had me, we would not now be drinking a nice cup of coffee, chatting about our week and enjoying the sunshine. This would make her chuckle and she agreed that I was probably right. She told me it was much better having grown up children and that she enjoyed us much more now. And so the rich and diverse aspects of the maternal instinct can reveal themselves in many ways depending on the particular traits and foibles of the human being involved. It is not just about the mother and child.

References

Bolen, J.S., (2004) *Goddesses in Everywoman: Powerful Archetypes in Women's Lives.* 1st Quill ed. San Francisco, CA: Harper Collins Design International.

McAllister, F. and Clarke, L. (1998). A study of childlessness in Britain. In *Joseph Rowntree Foundation.* York: Family Policy Studies Centre.

Nagasawa, M. et al. (2015) Oxytocin-gaze positive loop and the coevolution of human-dog bonds. *Science* 348(6232): 333–336.

Sallustius (Fourth century AD) *On the Gods and the Cosmos* (trans. Gilbert Murray).

PART II

On maternal subjectivities

8
MOTHERHOOD AND ART PRACTICE

Expressing maternal experience in visual art

Eti Wade

FIGURE 8.1 *Bathwomb* (2006).

This chapter is a personal account of my experience of motherhood and the ways in which this personal experience has shaped and informed my creative artistic practice. The personal hardship I underwent as a first time mother is then considered through wider critical frameworks, as well as the personal context of reparative second time motherhood. The insights and critical understandings regarding my experience of motherhood, shaped and framed by social conventions and taboos, are the material from which I develop and create works of art. Some of the creative processes also operate as auto-therapy and offer a personal journey of coming to terms with my perceived failings as a new mother, but I maintain that the value of public exhibition of my work acts as a way of articulating forbidden aspects of maternal experience, expanding and diversifying contemporary maternal narratives.

I am (m)other

I am a mother artist. I am an artist making work about motherhood and a mother who is concerned with articulating the maternal experience through the making and showing of works of art, based upon my personal experiences of motherhood. *Mother* comes first because my motherhood is the basis for my art making and the motivation behind it.

As a mother artist, I am unflinchingly committed to not only examining my own experience as a mother, but also to considering that of other mothers, keeping a watchful eye for social conventions and popular clichés that might affect how I experience my children and myself. I am committed to the expression of my personal experience in its entirety, and to the treatment of all aspects as being of equal importance, which are at the core of my creative practice. I am particularly attuned to those aspects of maternal experience that tend to be hidden, repressed or unacknowledged as a result of the way in which society and culture represents motherhood and refracts perfection. In *Representations of Motherhood,* Bassin, Honey and Kaplan state, 'the predominant image of the mother in white Western history is of the ever-bountiful, ever-giving, self-sacrificing mother' (1994). Rozsika Parker, in her discussion of maternal ambivalence, starts by voicing her own uncomfortable prejudice, stating that 'maternal ambivalence is curiously hard to believe in' (1997: 17), possibly because 'concern for the negative impact of clinical maternal depression on the developing child marries up with cultural representations of the unalloyed joy of motherhood', therefore 'it feels almost sacrilegious to suggest that mothers need to be depressed' (Parker 2007: 29). Stemming from my personal experiences, I feel strongly about making problematic and socially obscured aspects of maternal experience visible so that my audience can come to accept motherhood in all its complexity, not just the idealised, self-sacrificial perfection which Bassin et al. refer to. What I mean is that when one becomes a mother for the first time, the transformation in personal circumstances, personal freedom, economic power and independence is especially considerable and often detrimental for a young woman. The mother's new life often comprises little or no free time, coupled with a requirement to put aside all of her own desires in preference for the child's. I do not wish to disregard the pleasure derived from caring for a baby, which is considerable, but to problematise the sacrifice expected. Such a profound change, along with the mismatch between lived experience and idealised maternal perfection 'often produces either intensified efforts to achieve it or a destructive cycle of self- and/or mother-blame' (Pope et al. 1990: 442). This effect is exacerbated by the silence surrounding the realities of maternal experience, as demonstrated by Susan Maushart in her book *The Mask of Motherhood* (1999), contributing further to the isolation felt by new mothers in their struggle to adjust to a new situation, for which they are often unprepared. The formal representation of motherhood hides all of this behind the promise of personal fulfilment and pleasure, articulated mostly through representations of mother and child as sun drenched and easy going. A young mother is represented as happy and fulfilled, beautiful, slim and almost invariably blonde, whom Douglas and Michael describe as a 'chasm between the ridiculous, honey hued ideals of perfect motherhood in the mass media and the realities of mothers' everyday lives' (2005: 2). To elaborate, they state, 'however much you do for and love your kids, it is never enough'. Cultural and social concealment of the negative emotions and difficulties that new mothers face may affect a denial of such emotions, causing them to ignore and suppress their experiences. This is contrary to the beneficial acknowledgement of negative, difficult emotions as Parker affirms, 'if a mother can hold on to the depression, aggression and grief mobilized by ambivalence it can be beneficial in a number of ways' (Parker 2007: 29). To resist this ideology and the mainstream media representations that come to uphold it, I have committed to following this path and persona of Mother Artist.

My maternal journey began on the 12th of May 1993 when I gave birth to my eldest son and became a mother. Having dropped out of my dentistry training at the Hebrew University in Jerusalem less than a year before, with no alternative career direction, I was led to believe that giving birth and becoming a mother at the age of 24 amounted to failure. Please take into account here that like most Israeli youth, I started my higher education at the age of 21 after having served for three years in the army (IDF). Therefore, when I fell pregnant at the age of 23 I had only just begun what I believed to be my real adult life. Similarly to many Western, educated, high achieving women, motherhood was not something I had thought about or wished for in my early twenties. I had been brought up in middle class, affluent Tel-Aviv and had been aiming at embarking upon academic training and a successful career. Becoming a mother so early into my adulthood was not part of the plan. I had also moved to London at the beginning of the pregnancy; thus, when I became a new mum I was away from the close family and friends who would have supported me and alleviated the loneliness new mothers experience acutely in the first year of their child's life.

I should also add here the following complications, which were: my son's genetic blood condition which required frequent hospitalisations, exacerbating the worries and concerns over a young baby's health that new mothers normally experience; an unstable relationship with my son's father; and most probably (since it was never diagnosed) severe postpartum depression (PPD). All of these combined factors contributed to making my first year of motherhood the hardest and most unhappy year of my life. I know I am not alone in experiencing the transition into motherhood as problematic. Andrea Buchanan, in her book, *Mother Shock*, talks about early motherhood as a profound destabilising experience, describing it, as the title of the book clearly states, 'a shock' (Buchanan 2003). I would go further to suggest that the transition into motherhood could, in many cases, constitute a trauma. The subject of early motherhood is often explored in literature, which analyses the mismatch between personal experience and preconceived expectation, which is born out of social and cultural conventions and mainstream representations of early motherhood (Maushart 1999; Cusk 2001; Wolf 2001).

So for me, several aspects combined to produce a profound sense of failure that had probably contributed to my failure to bond with my baby son: the lack of emotional and mental preparedness for motherhood (having had my son at a very early stage in my life); whilst at a crossroads, which meant that I did not have a clear sense of identity and direction such as could be offered by an identified career path; added to which, the worry and feeling of helplessness over my son's health problems. The failure to bond emotionally was also the probable result of my PPD. In my struggle to cope, I did not seek help because I believed that there was something fundamentally wrong with me that could not be fixed and, therefore, to avoid being found out, I pretended that everything was fine.

Having such a poor sense of self as a mother, I certainly did not think I should contemplate having another child, so it wasn't until my son was six years old that I became pregnant with his brother – yes, another unplanned pregnancy! Thinking back, I can detect a certain level of ambivalence regarding my thoughts and feelings about motherhood that allowed me to be careless enough to become pregnant.

Throughout my second pregnancy and up to the birth I had very low expectations of second time motherhood. I prepared myself for the hard work and sleepless nights, and felt better equipped this time to make the necessary sacrifices. I was also generally more aware, in ways that I was not the first time around, that mothering *changes* one. That the baby's complete dependence, which I found so stifling in the first few months of caring for my eldest son, is in fact a temporary stage and does not last. What I did not know was that my first time mothering experience had severely stunted me, emotionally. I believe that this was as a result of PPD, but could also have been due to other factors such as cultural and social isolation, concern and worry that were caused by my firstborn's health, managing his genetic blood condition, along with the treatments that he had to undergo. Therefore, I could not have anticipated the surprise that second time motherhood held in store for me, which started unfolding shortly after giving birth to my second son. I was flung into the intense and wonderful emotional universe that can only be experienced through early motherhood. The amazing gift that being a mother to a child can be, a full gamut of intense emotional and physical pleasures. This pleasure is derived of a fierce protectiveness, a deep and profound love and an intoxicating sense of a uniquely female power, to create a new life and care for it. It is important to remember here that this rich, powerful and pleasurable aspect of motherhood may not be fully experienced by all new mothers because of a range of possible causes, including PPD.

And so, I found out it was not me, that there was nothing specifically wrong with my emotional make-up or personality as I was, after all, capable of loving my child. In hindsight, a part of me still grieves over what my eldest son and I missed out on and can never be recovered. That loss is, to a great extent, the motivation for my creative practice and academic research activity on the subject of motherhood and art. The insights that I have gained through my own experiences of motherhood, as a result of examining the differences between my first time motherhood (with my eldest son) and my second experience of motherhood, not having suffered from PPD and being better prepared and supported, feeds into the work that I make and guides me in my research of the work of other mother artists.

When thinking back to my first year of motherhood in considering how isolated and lonely I felt in my unhappiness and my failure to derive pleasure and fulfilment from motherhood, I wondered about the prevalent representations of motherhood that I was exposed to. In particular, the representations used to advertise baby related products that I encountered in popular media and in images. These images are presented as a hegemonic, idealised representation of a fulfilled and happy mother, more than content with the joys of mothering. Abbey argues that this representation can be thought of as oppressive, as representations of motherhood create an 'unrealistic conceptualisation which women, attempting to replicate and conform to, are left feeling inadequate, guilt-ridden or confused' (2003: 8).

It therefore feels important that a complex maternal experience should be articulated through my work, touching on issues such as maternal ambivalence, maternal omnipotence, rage, sensuality and corporeality, along with various other aspects that are often repressed by society and as a result, can be experienced as deviancy by new mothers. Aspects of maternal experience that do not conform to the narrow patriarchally prescribed ideal are taboo. I hid my hardship because of ignorance, guilt and shame, preventing me from seeking help. Perhaps if motherhood became widely represented in this complex way and accepted as incorporating (sometimes very intense) positive and negative emotions, an experience such as mine would not feel so lonely and painful.

In becoming a mother, the transition from an independent, self sufficient and free person to a woman who is tied down to a child can be quite overwhelming, and for a mother who is struggling, possibly feeling resentful, unhappy and depressed, it can only make it more difficult to deny and repress those feelings.

In my work I also seek also to represent the inarticulable exhilaration, pleasure and delight that being the source of a new life, giving birth to and bringing up a young child, offers. I maintain that mainstream representations of motherhood in imagery, such as can be found in lifestyle and stock photography, advertising campaigns and popular magazines, images often depicting a smiling young mother holding a happy healthy child, trivialise this most profound of life's experiences – one that is uniquely experienced by women. The intimate relationship between a mother and a child is visceral, physical and bodily and it grips, making us forever changed. It offers a most meaningful connection between two human beings, especially in the early years of a child's life – a joint journey of personal change and growth. It is a revered privilege, which we as women enjoy and being uniquely female it is, to an extent, downplayed in mainstream representations. As identified by Abbey (2003: 8), such representations are mainly generated by males and therefore are likely to uphold patriarchal values. I believe it also tends to represent the positive aspects of motherhood as wrapped up in frills and pastel colours and hence trivialised, or in art world terms, sentimental.

Although my work has been, for the most part, created in collaboration with my second son, it functioned to a great degree as a *photo-therapeutic process*; working through feelings and thoughts I had experienced during my first time mothering. In making the work, I engaged with and came to terms with projected aspects of myself as a 'bad' or 'neglectful' mother, aspects that I believed myself to be guilty of in terms of mothering my eldest son, but had not allowed myself to articulate. This does not detract from the potential significance of the work for audiences offering, as it does, an alternative representation of motherhood, incorporating rejection, anger, violence and aggression as well as intense pleasure and joy.

In 2001, when my baby was a year old, I created *Kisses 1* and *Kisses 2* (see Figure 8.2); two images that show my son's torso covered in blood-red lipstick kisses, with the added twist of showing what appears to be drops of blood on the crumpled white sheet next to his body. I was thinking at the time about the activity that we both enormously enjoyed, of me kissing and biting his naked body, a physically intimate, sensual and exciting exchange between a mother and her young child. I was concerned with how this activity could be easily mistaken for abuse and wondered about what would happen if I inflicted a painful bite or an inappropriate caress, and how it might be perceived if I left a bite mark on his body. I pondered the social perceptions of our pleasurable exchange. I knew I could trust myself not to cross the line, but felt that certain ways of representing our activity would easily attract condemnation. Would society trust me if it knew the pleasure we derive from our play? Would it still trust me with my child's care? I imagined the possibility of my kisses and bites drawing blood, leaving bruises, and exposing our daring pleasures to the world. I used lipstick and fake blood to create a series of images, which I simply entitled, *Kisses*.

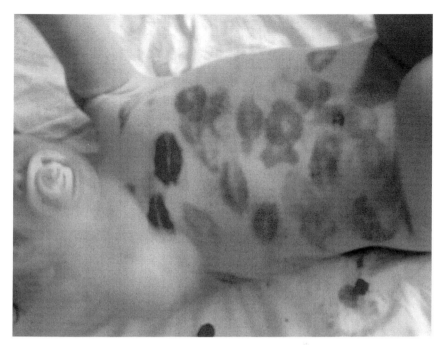

FIGURE 8.2 *Kisses 1* (2001).

Goodnight Boys (Figure 8.3) was created in 2004 whilst on a skiing trip. Every morning the adults happily separated from their children, the children being taken to their own supervised skiing activities, whilst the adults engaged in theirs. We all acted as if there was nothing to worry about, when in fact, injuries happened regularly, with young and old being carried off the mountain on stretchers to the medical centre. Spending the day on the mountain, whilst at the same time worrying for my children's safety made for a surreal holiday experience that related again to my thinking about what is naturalised and repressed in the maternal experience. I felt that this unspoken fear is another social taboo, and is therefore difficult to openly express. The birth of a child introduces into a mother's life the fear of the unspeakable possibility of the child's serious injury or death. The power of this potential, unspeakable loss and the fear of such a tragedy occurring, in the way that it forever shapes the mother's life by introducing constant anxiety into it, was something that I wished to articulate. Using pristine hotel sheeting to create a diptych, I used my children's bodies and covered them whilst curled up in the foetal position. The white shapes also served to echo the pristine, snow-covered peaks on the resort.

As an artist it is important for me to acknowledge and consider what position I am speaking from, since artistic expression is often thought to emerge from the subjective. To claim for myself a position of a mother artist requires me to insist that I am articulating a maternal subjectivity, but the notion of maternal subjectivity is

FIGURE 8.3 *Goodnight Boys* (2004).

in itself questionable. In her book *Feminism, Psychoanalysis and Maternal Subjectivity*, Alison Stone challenges the psychoanalytic assertion that there is no such thing as maternal subjectivity. Stone invokes Irigaray's argument that 'the subject has commonly been viewed as emerging in a break with the maternal body as a female body' (Stone 2012: 5), along with Irigaray's insistence that subjectivity is premised on a masculine model. The Western understanding of a subject as an autonomous agent, the author of his or her experience and meanings, stands in opposition to the nature of maternal experience where a woman becomes subservient to the child(ren) for whom she cares. The psychoanalytic requirement for the child to separate from the mother in order to become a subject further problematises the mismatch between the Western, psychoanalytically derived conceptions of both the subject and the mother.

Stone distinguishes the locus of maternal subjectivity in the conceptualisation of maternal body relations, invoking a more recent philosophical preference for identifying a subject position that is firmly located in the body. She further argues that the mother is a subject, because 'significance, within maternal body relations, emerges from a self organizing and self forming intelligence intrinsic to matter itself which prefigures the more conscious, fully developed forms of human intelligence' (2012: 5). Centrally positioning the body in our understanding of maternal subjectivity links to the current philosophical drive to reject the split Cartesian subject and allows us to address the problematics and inadequacy of language for maternal experience. Communicating maternal experience, through my practice as a visual artist, allows me to communicate within, but also beyond language. I agree most strongly with Luce Irigaray's assertion that language is patriarchal, where she states, 'the sexes are now defined only as they are determined in and through language. Whose laws, it must not be forgotten, have been prescribed by male subjects for centuries' (1985: 87). To that end, creative practice and artistic expression can potentially allow a better representation and communication of maternal experience.

Lisa Baraitser considers another way of accounting for maternal subjectivity, suggesting that we ask, 'What is it like to be alongside a child?' and invoking Sara Ruddick's description of a child as an 'open structure' which suggests the irregular, unpredictable and utter otherness of the child, the proximity of which shapes the experience of maternal subjectivity (Ruddick 1989; Baraitser 2009: 25–26). This proximity can at times be productive of complex emotions, which my work titled *2004–2007* addresses (see Figure 8.4). In this series I made visible the fear of maternal omnipotence, which is linked to maternal aggression and hatred. It is an exploration of the fantasies of maternal aggression, invoked in relation to the complete dependence and vulnerability of the child. The child's body is depicted as small and helpless, unaware of the potentially powerful maternal gaze. This sense of problematic and frightening power was particularly evoked for me at bath time, a fraught, tense and emotionally draining part of the child-caring day when preparing a child for sleep. Often a time of conflict, when 'a mother's love might be overwhelmed by persecutory anxiety, promoting the impulse to attack the persecuting baby' or child (Parker 1997: 27–28).

FIGURE 8.4 *2004–2007* (2005).

Another body of work, which I began making at about the same time, deals with similar issues, but makes extensive use of the mother's body within the work and allows for a clearer statement of maternal subjectivity. In 2004 I began using a scanner to create what would later become the body of work called *Jocasta* (see Figures 8.5–8.7). Created over a period of two years, the scanner, a simple domestic A4 document and photograph scanner attached to my laptop computer, was used to create the raw materials and the scanning activity that mostly took place whilst sitting with my son on the rug in the living room, watching TV. The scanner and laptop were portable enough to be used in working to create images of my son and myself and was a mode that was easily incorporated into our domestic space and everyday activities. The scanner was chosen as a tool that enabled me to overcome a few of the formal and ontological problems I often struggled with while photographing.

The camera is a distancing device, placing the photographer/artist at a distance from the subject, creating an objectifying and controlling gaze, which is often counterproductive to raw expressivity. As a mother artist I often felt the need to record and express mothering in a way that allows everyday emotions to be captured and expressed in the work. Working with intuitive expression was made easy through creating the opportunities to make use of an embodied, expressive mode. Not only through representing my viewpoint (behind the camera), but also through the presentation of myself, in conjunction with my child, as part of my effort to create an alternative representation of motherhood. Both by using the scanner and working with my child to represent my motherhood, by enacting our relationship and my maternal position onto his body, allowed me to be present in the work. It is also interesting to think of the scanner plate as a kind of stage and the duration of the scan as the duration of a (short) performance of maternal subjectivity. In this work the child is used as a form of prop through and onto which I performed aspects of my ambivalent maternal subjectivity.

In the work, I take the role of *Jocasta*, acting out significant subjective maternal positions. I perform my deep passion towards my male child and the joyous immersion in the sensual pleasure of the physicality of his body. I enact my fearful anticipation of the imminent loss of the intimacy and closeness, which occurs as the child grows out of the Oedipal phase. *Jocasta* is a fairly self-evident choice for the name, especially considering that my son was going through his Oedipal phase at the time (ages 4 and 5) and my maternal experience was enhanced by the intense pleasure of being the subject of infantile infatuation, coupled with the bittersweet knowledge of the immanent separation that is, at least according to Freud, inevitable.

The process of creating the raw materials for *Jocasta* (the initial scans) turned out to be so effective as personal auto-therapy, allowing me to work through some of the guilt and shame I felt in regard to my first time mothering, that the work became too personal for me to show or to contemplate showing for a long time. As a result, it was not until 2008 that the materials were fully edited into the final form that *Jocasta* now takes.

FIGURE 8.5 *Jocasta 11* (2008).

FIGURE 8.6 *Jocasta 13* (2008).

FIGURE 8.7 *Jocasta 2: detail* (2008).

In 2009 my third and youngest son was born. Third time motherhood was on the whole a positive and happy experience. The decision to have another child had been carefully considered, but this time conception had not been easy and it took two years to conceive. Since my son's birth I have created several motherhood-related projects, the most prominent ones being *57 Baths* (Figure 8.8) and *The Ikea Lack Coffee Table Family Portrait Series* (Figure 8.9).

57 Baths is a web-based video project, recording the maternal viewpoint of a daily and repetitive chore – the evening bath. The videos were recorded using a micro digital video (DV) camera, which I wore on my forehead. The camera lens was located in the middle of my forehead creating a maternal third eye and giving audiences access to an authentic and unedited maternal viewpoint. The nightly video footage was posted onto YouTube shortly after being created. Being posted so swiftly after being shot, with no editing, gave a performative flavour to the project. Through the recording video camera, a potential global audience observed the private daily routine of our bath time. The videos take a very consistent format with the recording always beginning just before I turn on the taps and ending with my son, in his pyjamas, being put to my breast just before going to sleep.

The 57 videos were created and uploaded over a period of four and a half months, starting in late May 2011 and ending in early October 2011. Many of the videos are repetitive, following a standard routine, but at the same time some unusual events are recorded; such as the short period when I was in a plaster cast having fractured a metatarsal bone and had to move about with the help of crutches, which made giving my son his bath particularly challenging, and several baths where, in trying to get rid of the head lice my baby son had contracted from his older brother, I had to comb his hair with a nit comb, which he found unpleasant.

A few of the recorded bath times are indeed lovely, where my son is in a playful and happy mood, but this is more the exception as in many of the videos he is fractious and tired. My own behaviour also changes. Sometimes I engage with him, playing and talking to him; at other times I am busy, fitting in many other activities, taking advantage of the distraction that the water and bath toys provide in order to catch up with mundane chores, such as folding the laundry or tidying up the bedroom next door. There are also some occasions where I lose my temper, talk in an angry voice and treat him unkindly and efficiently.

The purpose of *57 Baths* was to present an authentic 'raw' maternal experience. Bath time is a particularly difficult part of the child caring day. It is often experienced in isolation, the mother alone with her young child(ren) and because both child(ren) and mother are tired, the child(ren)'s behaviour is often challenging. The repetitive nature of the experience further adds to the potential hardship. As a result, bath time is often the time when maternal ambivalence is most acutely experienced and, as in my previous project *2004–2007*, the fear of potential harm inflicted is enhanced.

Following *57 Baths*, *The Ikea Lack Coffee Table Family Portrait Series* also operates in a performative mode, creating images and posting them online at regular intervals, shortly after being created. For this work I asked my family members to pose with me for an early morning family portrait every day, for a period of three months. With the camera set on a timer, we posed whilst standing precariously on two small, flimsy Ikea (*Lack*) coffee tables, which were moved incrementally every day. Eventually we covered the entire area of the house. The two tables formed a

FIGURE 8.8 *'57 Baths', Monday 4th of July: showing me in the mirror with the camera on my forehead and holding my son upside down on our way to the bath* [Still] (2011).

mini stage, further enhancing the performative aspect of the work. I regard both *57 Baths* and *The Ikea Lack Coffee Table* as performances for two reasons: Firstly, because of the way the audiences were involved, in that they regularly looked forward to receiving the latest instalment of video or still photograph, as in a scheduled performance event. Secondly, presenting the material with minimal editing (or in the case of the video, none at all), or being limited to selecting one of a handful of photographs, as in the case of the photographic project, introduced a live and unprocessed quality to the work.

Working with what I think of as the 'raw' materials of motherhood, recording maternal experience and using it in my creative work in a relatively unprocessed way, is a creative strategy designed to overcome the challenge of fitting in art practice into a full life of maternal and professional work. The selection of works presented and discussed in this chapter is a partial, but representative selection of my 15-year creative practice that draws upon my experience of motherhood. Exploring the work, I think it is easier to see how my practice follows and brings forth aspects of maternal experience that are normally kept private.

As a practicing artist, my aim is to expand the cultural framework regarding maternal experience. I wish to counteract the taboos regarding maternal ambivalence, making space within culture and society for what are very real feelings experienced

FIGURE 8.9 *The Ikea Lack Coffee Table Family Portrait Series* (22nd–23rd April 2012).

by many new mothers. These feelings, which in my personal story felt like deviancy, but which in fact were the result of my personal struggle, can be helped through acknowledgement and recognition as opposed to repression and secrecy.

I make my creative work about motherhood in order to help generate a new cultural space for maternal subjectivity; representing it as a multi-hued, emotional experience, encompassing many shades, and at times presenting it all at once. This requires the development of an aesthetic vocabulary that can bring maternal subjectivity, in all its complexity, into the everyday.

My practice incorporates the raw maternal every day, sometimes in an unedited form as I am keen to avoid the type of kneejerk reactions that cause me to hide away what is not normally shown, but what is at the same time so common and experienced by mothers everywhere. This means including (with no self-censorship) the times when I am not at my best, the times I do or say something that I regret. My claim to represent maternal subjectivity requires me to be highly attentive to the parts of maternal experience that are socially invisible and, as a result, often become repressed and self-censored. Maternal ambivalence is not fun. It is not a choice. To hide maternal ambivalence does not make it go away; it only makes the personal experience more difficult. Representation and public exposure are at the core of generating a change, hence my commitment to working on the slippery borders of social taboos regarding motherhood.

References

Abbey, S. M. (2003) Deconstructing images of mothering in media and film: possibilities and trends. *Future Journal of the Association for Research on Mothering* 5(1): 7–23.

Bassin, D., Honey, M. and Kaplan, M. (eds.). (1994) *Representations of Motherhood.* New York, NY: Yale University Press.

Buchanan, A. J. (2003) *Mother Shock.* New York, NY: Seal Press.

Cusk, R. (2001) *A Life's Work.* London, England: Fourth Estate.

Douglas, S. J. and Michaels, M. W. (2005) *The Mommy Myth: The Idealization of Motherhood and How It Has Undermined All Women.* New York, NY: Free Press.

Irigaray, L. (1985) *The Sex Which Is Not One.* New York, NY: Cornell University Press.

Maushart, S. (1999) *The Mask Of Motherhood.* New York, NY: New Press.

Parker, R. (1997) The production and purposes of maternal ambivalence. In: Holloway, W. and Featherstone, B. (Eds.). *Mothering and Ambivalence.* London, England: Routledge.

Pope, D., Quinn, N., and Wyer, M. (1990) The ideology of mothering: disruption and reproduction of patriarchy. *Signs* 15(3): 441–46.

Ruddick, S. (1989) *Maternal Thinking: Towards a Politics of Peace.* London, England: Women's Press.

Stone, A. (2012) *Feminism, Psychoanalysis, and Maternal Subjectivity.* New York, NY: Routledge.

Winnicott, D. (1950) *The Ordinary Devoted Mother and Her Baby.* London, England: (Pamphlet).

Wolf, N. (2001) *Misconceptions: Truth, Lies And The Unexpected On The Journey to Motherhood.* New York, NY: Anchor Books.

9

THE PARADOX OF THE MATERNAL

Barbara Latham

After an introduction where I point out what I am not attempting to discuss, this chapter is in two distinct parts, in which I consider the maternal only in a very specific sense. Since this series aims to include the personal, I have brought together two strands: my rereading of John Heaton's book *The Talking Cure* (2010) influences the section on therapy, while a project, of sorting decades of notes to and about my long dead mother, is the source for the final part.

Introduction

Most of us have plenty to say about mothers if we have been anywhere near psychoanalysis. The very word 'maternal' brings a shudder to many who feel grateful at having put at arm's length the one who had total power to protect or destroy. Not only were we within her body, but were incapable of looking after ourselves for a prolonged period. We relied on being cared for and could only gradually join in the language in use – language partially shaped to suit whoever was initiating us – language being used by others to decide who we might be or what was good for us.

Others sigh at those endless psychoanalytic papers on mothers and babies, on attachment and dependence, for it is grown adults who come to our consulting rooms, not just big babies reducible back to one original mould – a mould which usually takes little account of social context, siblings, or the subtleties of temperamental differences. In the astonishing range and complexity of what people say of their mothers, or being a mother, one overriding thing is certain – it does not all fit any one pattern and changes over time.

I liked being a girl – rather it never occurred to me to wish it otherwise – but, until nine or ten, it hadn't dawned on me I might also be expected to follow my mother and take up some particular place as a woman. To that I said a firm

'No, thank you!' asserting resolute disinclination to acquire what were considered important feminine skills. When asked, 'So what will you do when you have children?' I answered grandly, I wouldn't have any, but adopt when I was 50. I didn't quite know what I was saying, or why, yet was articulating wanting something other than what seemed to be on offer for girls in small town New Zealand of the 1950s.

The maternal, like the paternal, is deeply implicated in social and economic structures, in the political, and in the way of thinking of any era. We have a continuing fight over responsibility for those in need of care — where the hard work of giving one's flesh, one's time, one's life, to caring for others is not much valued. And then there is the distribution of what are called feminine and masculine characteristics. Here the edge was taken off battle lines for me, by having a father drawn to looking out for others and emotionally more available for intimacy, while my sparky mother liked a big stage to thrive.

But this whole complex area (along with the enormity of being a mother and inevitably hurting one's children or worse, damaging them) which I'm sure will be taken up elsewhere in this series, is *not* what I'm attempting to consider. I put all that aside — since what I want to look at is our mammalian start — a beginning in water and also in inarticulacy. There is a play with sounds early once we move into air, but language is slow learning. Like our mothers' bodies, language is about us and forever remains that which is of us and also beyond our skin. It is outside full mastery in that, however we come to express ourselves, we can never get behind the available language, or get back to before we could use it. It is this paradox, which is also at the heart of the maternal, that is my focus in this chapter.

Becoming a mother was another re-opening to that which is beyond, and not just through the passion of childbirth to which one is subject, for despite the scientism around us and belief that soon all will be explained, mothers do not know how to make their own babies. A new life takes shape within our bodies by simply absorbing what is needed, as the baby then absorbs the culture and language. Also becoming a mother — and thankfully I was not kept to my childhood intentions — made me responsible for someone. Once replugged back into life outside myself, there was no longer the option of ending it all in a fury of retaliation towards my dead mother.

Our culture emphasises the separate, the individual and the rational — as if we are to make everything just our own. We don't keep our eye on where we are rooted in the collective — for example, in the complicated game of money there is little acknowledgement of the fact it can only be played because it *is* the shared game. Each is to grab what money they can, without responsibility, and those living with excess, displaying huge wealth, are admired — a need for luxury fuelling the economy — yet now there is also a move to add on something lost, as it becomes the fashion for the rich and for business to 'give something back'.

The word 'separate' is used with such approval, being an individual is set up as a good, as if it's not a profoundly subtle matter. After all *sep*arate comes from *separate*, which in the thesaurus equates with cleave, break up, come apart, disjoin, disconnect, unattach. Much of what we claim to be expressions of our unique individuality are likely to have been absorbed from the zeitgeist. Then there is the range of phenomena we call intuition and the uncanny, which draw attention to the fact that we cannot be half as separate as we mostly assume.

Nor are we as much creatures of reason as we hope. Anglo-Saxon culture seems particularly drawn to elevate reason, not just as a crucial language to learn, which it is for us, but as if it's the *basis* for all life. It has a long history of taking sons, who might be expected to have power and influence one day, right away from the maternal while still young – as if to wipe out that in which their life is rooted.

Freud, like Jung, became fascinated by the area where reason did not hold sway. They took up an interest in the occult. Freud saw we could not be conscious of all we are immersed in – we are embodied and subject to our bodies' extraordinarily subtle workings, we are in language, and a particular era, we are subject to desire and to a need for sleep where we are not in our conscious mind.

Nevertheless Freud decided to put, as he said, 'a bulwark against the black tide of mud', and redefined all which cannot be brought to consciousness as the UNCON-SCIOUS. Bion argues that the theory of the conscious and unconscious is extremely useful but

> becomes a bit of a pest after a time because it gets in the way of being able to see other things one doesn't know – stands in the way of one's own ignorance, so that there is very little chance of investigating this realm of ideas that have never been conscious and this state of mind that is not available when a person is talking to you with his wits about him in broad daylight, and you are listening to him with all your wits about you.
>
> *(Bion 2005: 21)*

Certainly Freud, growing attached to his own description, proceeded to use his rational theories as if they decoded mystery, so that we are no longer inevitably creatures of the symbolic but, like Oedipus, faced only with a riddle. A riddle, psychoanalysis itself might answer. This confusion continues within psychoanalysis – is the analytic tradition one of getting behind dreams and the defined unconscious to give a decoding from theory? Or is it addressing the original recognition that we are in more than we can grasp, since we can never be sufficiently outside to fully formulate it? Freud acknowledged forces to which we are subject, and then shifted gear so that his metaphors became 'facts'.

If we take a brief look at dreaming, it's obvious we do not stay awake to reason while we also dream. Even if words bubble up, briefly on automatic, as one wakes, which may be the best access one gets, or if we are left with vivid images to play with, the dream has faded. That weave of strangeness, with possibly a haunting presence, has gone – a mode of connectedness has been shed, not brought into the day, even though meditating on it may throw light on matters. To quote Bion:

> I don't think that Freud, in talking about the interpretation of dreams, really considers the fact that the patient who has a dream had an experience in what I would consider a very different state of mind from that in which he is when he is awake. Therefore the story the patient tells you, consciously, is his version of what happened last night, but he doesn't really know. (2005: 21)

What we cannot do is gain dominion over dreaming by cracking any one particular, deciphering code. That we try to do so reveals our mania for explanation. Our relation to the maternal is much the same – we come out of dreaming as even more fundamentally we came out of our inarticulate beginnings. Driven to catch where we have been, we start retrospectively applying constructions. Some might be well imagined. We may look to descriptions of attachment, or read Winnicott and find it makes sense to us, just as any good fiction does. What has a ring of truth is, then, too readily mistaken for explanation. This process of generating 'explanations' is helped by reification. Of course, there is no such thing as 'the maternal'; there is a birth mother and someone who has to care for an infant.

Slippage into explanation and other category confusion is not trivial, nor a cold matter of 'just grammar and logic': once descriptions slip into accounting for our history, we lay claim to conceptualising more than is justified and turn ourselves, our patients, and the maternal into objects of knowledge. Also we generate the unfounded illusion of being able to get hold of ourselves through rational theory, even though we were fully present, alert and responsive to the world around us, our senses in good order, long before reasoning, which is necessarily a late development in language. How far we can sniff one another out, tuning in in a myriad of ways, sensing where we are with one another and getting our bearings, long before we can use reasoning – and, thankfully, these ways continue along with speech an increasing belief in 'rationality'.

Language introduces meaning and makes possible a future and a past tense – a past tense that may go to our head if we superimpose some theoretical picture. This is obvious in Klein's misuse of language to decree what is going on conceptually in the minds of prelinguistic infants, who cannot possibly yet have any concepts. These require language. Klein's theory encloses the baby within particular structures, as if no other life force is of any relevance. It is as though the child forms within a seashell, with Klein knowing exactly the shape of those firm sides shutting in the developing life. In her picture, there is no ocean; yet if sea shells do not open to the flow of water, any life within shrivels and dies. Winnicott, in his struggle with Klein, to be allowed to express what he understood in language other than Kleinian theory, used a different metaphor to argue that she sounded as if she knew how to make daffodils flower and that was not what psychoanalysis could know. All we can see is how we might better nurture the bulb, in the hope that it may flourish.

Since therapy is an attempt at honest speech, the therapists' correct relation to the words they use is fundamental. Slippage into pseudo-explanation and confusion of categories, which imply or establish a spurious knowingness, is either unthinking or unscrupulous. It generates power and fake authority for our practice. This is not to suggest a collapse into 'we can't say anything', nor is it to endorse that 'it's all about feelings and words don't matter' – the struggle to move into a more correct relation with what we can and cannot say of ourselves requires rigorous attention. Just as what it is that we can capture of having been mothered, when much of it took place before language, requires consideration.

Wittgenstein's questioning of language misuse seems particularly relevant here. As I have said, we human mammals, who were once within what remains beyond our group, also find ourselves joining a shared language beyond our confines, and the many ways we get drawn into confusions with language is the essence of therapy. Most of us come to therapy with, at least, some of our 'language-on-holiday' (Heaton 2014), that is, we speak with a degree of disconnection from what we have already lived, or perhaps only half understanding what it is we are trying to say. That is, having become caught up in debased language, with varying degrees of dissociation, rather than being able to speak our distress we come in search of it. Often at the start the words used are bland generalisations … 'there is something wrong with me', or 'I have depression/anxiety/low self-esteem'. Out of such shared phrases as if we are an object with a condition defined by experts, begins a struggle in a search for the meaningful which is particular, for we can only come alive to our own temperament and face our specific lostness. As Ortega y Gasset says:

> The man with the clear head is the man who frees himself from … fantastic 'ideas' and looks life in the face, realises that everything in it is problematic and feels himself lost – he who accepts this already begins to find himself, to be on firm ground. Instinctively, as do the shipwrecked, he will look round for something to which to cling and that tragic, ruthless glance, absolutely sincere, because it is a question of salvation, will cause him to bring order into the chaos of his life. These are the only genuine ideas; the ideas of the shipwrecked. All the rest is rhetoric, posturing, farce. He who does not really feel himself lost is without remission; that is to say, he never finds himself, never comes up against his own reality. (1972: 120)

For many the wish to have difficulties heard might be a beginning to therapy, but soon there is a question of our own unreliability. For example, where we have constructed a coherence from a not fully acknowledged grievance, or from a determination that we 'need' to get hold of a systematic picture if we are to understand, and so keep to a belief about ourselves and others.

There is the task in therapy of listening to oneself as one is being heard, with a slow recognition of words that are empty, or are really a demand, that is, 'parents should have done x', 'life ought to be y'. And attempts to explain ourselves or our past usually cover over what we have been unable to adequately question. This includes much of the language used in and about therapy. It's easy to say 'self' and 'ego', making claims as to what we believe to be good for them, but what are we actually talking about? They aren't objects to be taken out and assessed like an appendix. That in time we learn to say 'I' is part of the process of initiation into using the shared language and cannot be reduced back to a singular possession. Similarly many speak of separation from mothers as if we know what this is and that it's a 'thing to achieve'. Obviously we don't stay in her belly but do we think we must separate from shared genes and language, from her values and all her way of life?

The task of finding a way out of proliferating vain talk towards more honest speech is, crucially, a move towards accepting complexity and is a move towards seeing how much of ourselves can never be caught with words. Perhaps we begin therapy as a search, hopeful of *an* answer, *the* meaning. Expecting to grasp ourselves and others with understanding we pursue this quest until we are forced to recognise the limits of our language.

Many of us also begin expecting to extricate ourselves from strong mothers and take a long time to surrender to the fact that the maternal, like language, is the ground of our being – and we cannot reason our way out of being subject to it. This brings me to the second part of this chapter – to my own notes as I tried to get hold of my mother. I have taken a tiny selection, from masses of scraps of paper, bits of diary, which I eventually gathered together to put in two big folders.[1]

Perhaps, I began writing to her when surprised by the intensity of longing to show her my newborn son, though she had been dead 10 years. I can't really say what I was hoping to clarify – and it changed – but I sought to make more sense of the woman who left life dramatically, just as I assumed myself to be leaving her. Who was she? What did I think of her? And why did I seem unable to refind ease of connection, except in extremis, out at sea. I had gone to look for something of her, nine grim months after her death, in the city she came from and where she'd returned on holiday and been killed in a car crash.

There seemed to be no doubt that she was present in the deep. She had been all around me as I grew into life inside her and I, like many, felt her profoundly about me as I was almost drowning. In between my coming into life and nearly leaving it, what had she been?

These fragments are not in the order in which they were written, over four decades. I have chosen those that seem to connect with the first part of this chapter and restricted myself to an alphabet length of A to Z. My mother is the 'you' in these notes, my father the 'he'.

A. Had you lived, there would have been ways to meet, with everyday frustrations. In the resounding absence, I foraged, perhaps finding only dried bones, but also made my way into much you left unspoken.
B. Decades on, it is still possible to gag on the fact that you are never coming back – and that you, who were all too present to existence, could just leave with no goodbye.

C.   There was nothing to be done to keep you. It was all over and not a single thing could make it different. That was the crushing defeat and how I struggled to forgive it.

D.   When death came for you, I had no importance – yet it remained an outrage you didn't send a message.

E.   For you were at the mercy of forces I no longer believed in – the power of life and death, like fairies, were outgrown. Till you showed me – dying to do it!

F.   The air thickened with misery and confusion. Weighing heavy, it pushed us down through surface crust, over which we'd previously skated.

G.   You whisked away the ground we stood on, proving every lullaby a lie – *you* couldn't keep us safe – you could not save yourself!

H.   Having assumed any difficulty ahead would be standing up to your strength – asserting my own way – I never doubted you'd be there to fall back on. If I was about to move out on a long rope, of course, you'd stay firm behind me.

I.   We lived side by side, no longer close, I'd probably have replied, if asked – you cooked, I ate good food, and failed to notice I might be rooted in you still – not so autonomous after all.

J.   You died and that was fact, if also indigestible. Your mothering proved to be no object to catch – whatever still lived was not for extermination – and continued beyond that barely believable cremation.

K.   With him it was easier – never having been within his flesh, he couldn't swallow me back. And it never occurred to try and seek all strands of fathering – he was there in person – not to be pinned with words.

L.   Death was dressed in euphemisms and you draped in hyperboles. The 'you' I recognised was gone and, after bewilderment, I began to hunt you – to catch those primrose sandals at the beach – the way you flung yourself backwards into water – my pride in your sparkling ball gowns – your relish of oysters and foreign foods. I sought your character, asking embarrassed friends and your reluctant sisters. I got given clichés.

M.   I missed knowing you as adult – so much I want to ask – and all I'd like to tell. But would you have ever listened?

N.   Like most, I hatched to cocoon life, within a family – added in and sharing residence, fears, a bedroom, meal routines and ways of speaking, ways of doing to grow in us as forming bones.

O.   Your structuring days were through my way of being, not detachable as I'd supposed.

P.   My flesh began as part of you, though I considered myself distinct, but your crashing out proved more than could be taken in, through confusions of what must be you and what was me, until I found I could not go where you had gone, except by wilful destruction. And, yet, how soon I went abroad, shoulders pushed up in declaration of managing without you, and went exploring, just as you made plans to do the night before you borrowed a car, not knowing it was faulty.

Q. Though I thought it was you reduced to pieces in a smash, it was our expectations lying in bits. But, cruelly, our bodies looked whole, in an illusion of completeness, while having to bear comprehension of your death only in small fragments.

R. You were the earth for the seed of me, even if that idea displeased. I grew despite you is the claim, yet cells developed through no will of mine. Not that you spoke to me of our beginnings, even though the complications lingered.

S. Shared existence shattered, like some shell, leaving me apparently freed, if with a running yolk. You as the container were fragile too, though I'd certainly failed to notice. Astonishingly his comfort outlives his ordinary death – while your end was too disruptive of who I took my teenage self to be.

T. Alongside our colonial, daily life was always that wide ocean. Even landlocked days kept a watery edge – liquid, from which we emerged, there in perpetual motion – a power beyond the confines of town. Our several rivers led the way in merging again, into vast and salted sea.

U. And when its pulse fades into tales of its existence – having no force except in the pitfalls of memory – we are stranded high and dry in constructions of the mind.

V. Sedate like you I've never been, and move still in tides and with the moon. The flow of water might be hard to collect and yet I have felt gathered, in etching words to you, across what stays filmy between us.

W. Phrases come alive in the writing – that quick move to show the unseen – but what do they net when put on repeat?

X. Who can speak that move out of water into air, before there is any talking? You told me only what you wished, of thunder at my birth. Then left before I could question your version.

Y. While you lived, some of our history never got a word in – which put much else on semi-disconnect between us. In nearly drowning, months after your death, finding you at sea, it seemed an absolute that language for us must begin again, from scratch!

Z. Eventually, therapy gave a gradual re-association with some of what we'd lived. I didn't get hold of you, as probably I'd hoped, but learned to talk with someone else – making space for a way of speaking, inconceivable while beside you.

Note

1 These notes are taken from the author's book, *Dancing after a Dead Mother,* currently under preparation.

References

Bion, W. R. (2005) *The Tavistock Seminars.* London, England: Karnac Books.

Heaton, J. M. (2010, 2013) *The Talking Cure: Wittgenstein on Language as Bewitchment & Clarity.* London, England: Palgrave Macmillan.

Heaton, J. M. (2014) *Wittgenstein and Psychotherapy: From Paradox to Wonder.* London, England: Macmillan.

Ortega y Gasset, J. (1972) *The Revolt of the Masses.* United Kingdom: Unwin Books.

10

NOT-SO-GREAT EXPECTATIONS

Motherhood and the clash of private and public worlds[1]

Melissa Benn

A writer friend was recently asked to give a talk at a prestigious university about the politics of parenthood. She arrived be faced by a room full of clever young women 'who had all their plans ready... they had already figured out how they were going to work for so long – then marry – then take so much time off for the first and subsequent baby ... and so on.' My friend didn't have the heart to tell them that no life can be sketched out on an envelope in quite that fashion, particularly not when children might be involved. Yet we both knew that these undergraduates were expressing, and placing their faith in, a set of spoken and unspoken rules that govern how successful women are supposed to live, love and work in the United Kingdom in the early twenty-first century: a set of rules that, given the way society is organised, are bound to let them down, sooner rather than later.

Today's girls are more highly educated than ever: they outperform boys at almost every point in the education system, right up to postgraduate level. From teachers to features, from Sheryl Sandberg to Michelle Obama, the message is: aim high, change the world, the only thing blocking you is your own lack of confidence, your inner reluctance to 'lean in' towards ever greater achievement. Yet the truth is, very few young women will go on to elite occupations or change the world and few, in reality, are given the tools to do so. When in 2014 the Equality and Human Rights Commission undertook a major survey of female pupils aged 14–18, they found a depressing lack of self-belief among working class girls, most of whom 'still believe they will fail' and whom are encouraged, even by well-meaning teachers, into jobs like hairdressing or the three Cs: catering, childcare or cleaning (Benn 2013: 41).

But whether a woman is highly educated, with great expectations of her future work life, or leaves school with a handful of qualifications, the experience of motherhood will shape, and indeed damage, her working life in ways that the ambition/ achievement narrative simply hasn't prepared her for. It is through having a child that most women come to realise, often over a lifetime, that mothers can rarely play the 'game' of economic and public life as conventionally agreed. Nor do many of them want to. Becoming a parent faces us with the potentially infinite, complex needs and demands of other human beings, and while there is always some ambivalence about responding to these demands, very few mothers question the depth and significance of the ties that bind or the need to cherish rather than deny or offload them. Indeed, for many women, parenthood will be one of the most significant and meaningful experiences of their lives.

For some, the inevitable clash between a rich, demanding private experience and the accepted rules and rhythms of the public, working world sets up a sense of enduring failure and frustration; for others, it leads to a decision to *appear* to play the game, to hide their family or personal life, whatever the cost; for many, it leads to a stoic acceptance of limitation, particularly in terms of intellectual or professional development.

But there is also a growing movement, disparate in origin and aim, to challenge and change the rules of the game itself. In essence this movement asserts that, if we seriously want women to be individually fulfilled and involved, in whatever work or whatever level of the economy or public life that suits their nature and ambitions, we must do no less than change the rules of our 'man-made' system: the way it measures out work and time and success and meaning itself. As Eva Tutchell and John Edmonds argue in their new book *Man-Made: Why There Are So Few Women at the Top*, 'In short we either fix the women or we fix the system' (2015: 199). Put like that, we glimpse the absurdity of carrying on as we are.

Only experience can measure for us the true weight of involved parenthood, and so paint a realistic portrait of what needs to be conserved and what needs to change. Like many educated women of my generation, I had children relatively late in life: my daughters were born when I was 37 and 39. I felt enormously blessed, and still do, by them both: from that simple truth, all else follows. But, judging from much modern writing on motherhood, I was also typical of my generation (and those efficient, hopeful undergraduates) in that I was woefully underprepared for the intensity or demands of the experience. Rebecca Asher writes of her shock at:

> ...The loss of autonomy ... the self-abnegation ... instant and absolute. The independence, affirmation and daily purpose that I'd been used to, gave way to gruelling, unacknowledged servitude. My life became unrecognisable to me. (2012: 3)

For the novelist and memoirist Rachel Cusk it was as:

> ...If I had boarded a train and could see through the window the road on which I had always been, a road with which for a while my train ran parallel before gaining speed and moving steadily away to east or west, to a vista of unfamiliar hills, leaving everything vanished behind it. (2001: 25)

To some extent, life remains forever on this parallel track to what went before. The shock of labour and the visceral intensity of the early months fade, but the ties of relationship only multiply and strengthen through the succeeding years. I was lucky in my vocation. As a writer I could, in theory, control the timing and place of my work: be a hands-on parent, and continue my professional life. Even in the blur of the days and months after birth, there was no question that that was what I wanted, and needed, to do; it just had to be on fresh terms.

I had not realised how difficult I would find it to leave my children when they were young. I remember going to Bristol for the day, to conduct some interviews for a feature in a national newspaper, when my elder daughter was eight months old, and crying in the carriage, unsure whether it was because I missed my baby or feared that she was missing and needing me. Another, even more painful, memory: meeting my younger daughter in the street, when she was in the care of a capable childminder. Straining in her pushchair, arms outstretched, she cried for me to pick her up and go 'Home with you mummy! Home with *you!*' Her anguish pierced my soul. At that moment, my need for even a modicum of freedom felt utterly selfish.

That I felt tired, on and off, for years, is hardly worthy of comment. What interests me now is how I reacted to my own fatigue: refusing its messages, in the name of a more profound form of survival. After my second daughter was born and I was juggling life with a newborn and a wary toddler, I longed more than anything to take six months off and do nothing but enjoy my babies. Yet I did not dare, on any level: financially, professionally or personally. I must have feared I would disappear down a dark hole and never emerge again. The values of a man's world had me in their grip. I had to keep going, I had to keep working, to put myself out there. I had a book contract, a deadline, an advance: these were fixed and precious points in my landscape, proof of hard-earned adult, professional status. Yet the effort exhausted me. When one high-flying mother said of herself that 'I never looked so awful as I did when my children were young', I could heartily concur: at times of extreme work stress, I was drawn and ashen faced.

I always knew that I wanted to be with my children, to spend significant time with them, as much of it aimless as directed, living time not the dreaded 'quality time.' I rebelled against the idea of fitting this relationship into some preset timetable, dictated by deadlines and debts, employers and expectations. But I also longed for, resented and envied the freedom of my pre-baby self, single women and pretty much all men. The wish to pursue a different timetable altogether, dictated by myself only, or the needs of the work was like a never slated thirst. This clash was never fully resolved; one learns only to live with it, even draw on it.

School provided some welcome free time – a defined timetable – while weekends, oddly enough, were the worst, even with a supportive and domestically involved partner. In my pre-baby life, Saturdays and Sundays were periods of recuperation and fun. Now they felt relentless and claustrophobic in a home that teetered perpetually on the edge of grubby chaos. Slowly, I patched together two different kinds of lives – the responding-mother one, and the autonomous work one – largely by stealing from my own time, especially my own rest. (Bad idea; don't try this at home.) Impecunious self-employment was the only way not to feel a slave to everyone's rhythms but my own. It is also why high numbers of mothers choose self-employment: a need for freedom from official surveillance.

Worrying comes with the territory. I am so used to it, now, the endless free floating, mostly manageable, anxiety about my children's health and happiness, friendship and work, personal safety and self-fulfillment. Maybe it's the novelist in me, but as the 'girls' take ever greater control of their own lives, I feel ever more responsible for their fate, only now the worry is of an increasingly abstract, elusive nature. But a sensitive parent surely fears and feels the weight of the past in the unfolding present and not yet realised future: the anxiety that a wrong decision or a failure to act in years past might be the cause of some problem up ahead. I suspect that mothers are more prey to these kinds of ongoing thoughts than fathers. I have long believed that maternal worry, even if it seems pointless or exaggerated to others or even ourselves, is merely a highly emotionally charged way of paying close attention. The worry may be surplus to requirements; the attention is absolutely vital.

I describe these intense, emotional aspects of having a child because it's a way of refusing neater narratives that ultimately serve no one. Certain truths need repeating: motherhood changes everything, sets up new priorities and panics, but doesn't alter, one jot, our need to be creative, effective, a significant part of the world. We have made enormous strides through the generations in terms of reconciling these different sides of a woman; a mother's right to work, to have an outside, other life, is now clearly established. It's just that the price she – we – pay for it is now much more subtle, almost submerged, for a whole host of reasons.

Numerous studies and statistics confirm the freefall in status and income consequent on motherhood. We learn from one newspaper report that for:

> ...Each year ... she is absent ... from the workplace, a mother's future wages will reduce by 5%

and from another that

> A mother's earnings decrease by roughly 13 percent per child.
> *(Gentleman 2009)*

Even for high-earning women the motherhood penalty is striking. According to a submission on the situation of women in the workplace by the Chartered Management Institute in 2012, female executives who follow identical career paths to men earn nearly half a million pounds less (£423,390 to be exact) over their lifetimes than their male peers (Chartered Management Institute 2012: 2). For once the headline 'Motherhood "Devastates" Women's Pay' was no exaggeration (Gentleman 2009).

It is not hard to find accounts of the struggle that many women face in the immediate period when they return to work after having a baby. It is illegal to discriminate against pregnant women or to make a woman redundant while she is on maternity leave, but according to recent research, almost a third of new mothers feel they don't fit in anymore, and significant numbers report increased stress, a lack of support, problems with their partner, and a small minority losing their job altogether (McVeigh 2013).

Experiences such as these arouse little public outrage but are, particularly in these times of ongoing economic crisis, considered just one more minor manifestation of capitalism's multiple malfunctions. Unlike sexual harassment or sexual violence, unacceptable breaches of justice in a public space, work is now considered a semi-private space, almost beyond the reach of politics itself. We have become inured, resigned to numerous instances of more so-called 'ordinary' unfairness. No new mother, probably at one of the most vulnerable points of her life, is going to undertake a campaign in her own defense, and the isolating nature of motherhood itself makes it a time in life when one is least likely to gather with others.

There is possibly a form of covert misogyny and/or fatalism at work here too. A largely, small c, conservative, male dominated world (political, corporate, media) remains at worst uneasy, at best uncertain, about the role and rights of the working mother. Few question the right of mothers to work, but there are mixed feelings at work: beliefs, possibly, that family benefits from a stay-at-home mother or irritation at the deep gravitational pull of the mother towards her child which makes her unavailable to an increasingly frenetic round-the-clock working world. Tired and insecure new mothers, full of the strong but chaotic feelings that I described above, will pick up on this patriarchal bass line and feel genuinely unsure about what is best for their baby, their employer and themselves.

It is not often until much later on that they realise the many forms of low level discrimination, or rank injustice, that they have endured in trying to balance out these different needs. From my own acquaintance, it is not until women get to their late forties and fifties, as if surfacing from a long period underwater, that they realise how much having, and caring, for children has held them back, curtailed their work opportunities and even severely impoverished them. Women in their fifties earn less than women in any other decade of their life: a large majority work part time, and a majority of these earn less than £10,000 a year.

There was a period in the 1970s and early 1980s when the tail end of second wave feminism, a strong trade union movement and a more visible equal opportunities arm within government campaigned for greater 'work life' balance. Important advances were made in both policies and attitudes, including a greater understanding of the need for, and advantages of, flexible working: more parental leave, particularly for fathers, and better funded childcare. But this movement stalled, as progressively more economically liberal, deregulating, governments urged employers to make changes on a voluntary basis, and economic crisis weakened the bargaining power of all employees. Nowadays, discussion, such as it is, has shifted to the more liberating (sic) possibilities of the new technology (text, email, Skype) and novel approaches to the working week from compressed work to annualised hours, the job split to the mini-job (this last promoted, apparently, by a company called Slivers of Time) (TUC Report 2014: 4).

At the same time, there is a new all-pervasive, if largely informal, assumption of men's growing involvement in domestic life and more gender-neutral working patterns. Unlike our fathers' lives, men today, we are told, cook, shop, and take their children to the park. Public figures speak openly about their families, and their pleasure in spending time with them. I have lost count of the number of conversations I have had with successful men in their thirties or forties, often with young children, who tell me, 'it is all different now', how when this next job or busy period is over, they fully intend to play an equal part in their children's upbringing and swap roles with their female partner, and how deprived they feel that they can't be at home more. The recession has made the decision for some: according to the Office of National Statistics, the number of fathers who now stay at home has doubled over the last 20 years – from 111,000 in 1993 to 229,000 in 2014 – and is now at a record high. This change is mirrored by a fall in the number of women who chose to stay at home: a drop of 45,000 from 2013–2014 has taken the overall figure to 2.4 million. It is this sort of shift in the statistics that encourage some popular writers, mainly in the United States, where they love nothing as much as a new storyline, to talk about *The End of Men* and *The Rise of Women* or even *The Richer Sex*.

I remain skeptical. For all the new excitable narratives about top women and domesticated open-hearted men, the figures suggest that it is still women who are forced to choose between a satisfying level of involvement with their children and career satisfaction and conventional success. A report by the Equality and Human Rights Commission found that women 'are significantly more likely to be in part-time employment than men and this pattern has remained relatively unchanged over the past ten years' (2013).[2] They pointed to an interesting paradox: while childcare is no longer *seen* as largely a woman's responsibility, most women continue to *be* the primary carers. Even those who maintain high pressure jobs and earn high incomes will continue to take greater responsibility for the care of their children.

So, for the majority who work part time, there can be decades of a kind of twilight professional life. Many women work enough to 'get by', or to 'keep their hand in', professionally speaking, but they do not significantly progress in either their pay or prospects, thus making it easier for employers to shed them at a later date. Economic crisis has not helped, particularly for those, whom through divorce, separation or death, become, in effect, single parents: simply desperate to hold on to their jobs. This 'neither one thing nor the other' kind of life might be viewed as balanced and satisfactory but for two factors. Firstly, in a society that still judges personal merit on professional status and visibility, those who remain on the 'mommy track' feel themselves to be demeaned and unseen.

Secondly, if in a partnership, the mother who works part-time is probably still taking on the majority of domestic and child related work. That domestic work and childcare is a form of unpaid labour, vital to the economy, was one of the simple but brilliant insights of second wave feminism: an insight that has become, once again, submerged. There is a widespread assumption that looking after a home and children is a form of labour that takes care of itself: that love makes, and marks, it out as something different from work as more widely understood. In one sense, that is true: but its implications for other kinds of employment or personal satisfaction can be catastrophic. All the figures show that once children come along, women, on the whole, take on more of the housework and caring work, while men increase their time in paid work. In one US study, of 30 working-class cohabiting couples, the researchers found that even when the men weren't earning, they didn't see domestic labour as a means of contributing. In fact, they did even less of it, since to contribute more at home would, in some way, challenge their masculinity. Conversely, even when women paid most of the household bills, they were rarely awarded the privileges of male providers, such as retaining control of household finances (Miller and Sassler 2012).

We severely underestimate the compound effect on many women of this common, still highly gendered, deal. I recently came across an anonymous blog by a female scientist, which seemed to sum up what many women feel, not at the outset of parenthood, but a decade or two on: a complex and often toxic mix of resentment and realism, gratitude and self-criticism:

> I have beautiful and smart children, who are unfortunately prone to ear infections and food allergies that make the early years of each of their childhoods very challenging. I love them dearly, but there is a lot of work involved. A lot of worrying, and a large mental load involving scheduling various doctor's appointments, taking time off work for each, making lunches, getting them all ready for school, picking them up from school, making dinner, doing dishes, giving baths… Why doesn't my husband do more? He does things around the house, cleaning and laundry. But I cannot battle over chores anymore. Also, he is happy. He has time to play World of Warcraft to his heart's content, he can sleep in on weekends. Who am I and how important is my career really that I would have the right to ask him to sacrifice much more of his comfort and happiness? For all I know, I could be working even more and I would still not be happy. The difference would be that I would never see my kids or him, and that he would likely be miserable too. Now, at least one of us is happy, that's something I suppose.

It is for all these reasons that we need a new approach to the private/public world, particularly in terms of children. We need to stop pretending both that it is easy to fit authentic human relations into existing economic and political systems, and yet at the same time too difficult to solve the issues at hand. We need to be honest with our daughters about the depth and demands of becoming a mother (back to those undergraduates) but encourage them to fight for their due: to take on the world, not to retreat from it, seeking only individual solutions.

Big changes are needed in both the home and in public life. Yes, there are aspects of having and raising a baby that only a woman can perform: but these, after all, last for only a relatively short period. In contrast, it is time to question, once more, the non-existent biological imperative that says only women can cook, clean, do laundry, shop and clear up. For all the fanfare around the new fatherhood and women's rising economic power, domestic life, as I have already argued, remains largely unchanged. According to special briefing produced by the Institute for Public Policy Research (IPPR 2012) patterns of housework have shifted only slightly over the last half century or more. The analysis found that 8 out of 10 women born in 1958 say they do more laundry and ironing than their partner, while 7 out of 10 women born in 1970 agreed. It is clear, the revolution in gender roles is unfinished.[3] Yet if we do not achieve domestic democracy for future generations, women will continue to be severely and progressively stymied in other areas of their development.

There must be equally substantive changes in the conditions of employment and here senior women may lead the way. US academic and policy advisor, Anne-Marie Slaughter, came to political radicalism through her experience of motherhood:

> I strongly believe that women can 'have it all' (and that men can too). I believe that we can 'have it all at the same time.' But not today, not with the way America's economy and society are currently structured. My experiences over the past three years have forced me to confront a number of uncomfortable facts that need to be widely …acknowledged—and quickly changed.
>
> (Slaughter 2012)

Politics is a disparate business these days: countries can be toppled with the help of Twitter, companies can be shamed out of regressive practices, while governments still hold some sway over the public sphere. We need to gather examples of creative, workable ideas from employers and policy makers and spread the word, support their expansion. Social entrepreneur pioneers like Karen Mattison, who set up Timewise and the Part Time Power List, is working to 'grow the supply' of well-paid flexible or part-time jobs for the thousands of people – men as well as women – who want to develop a life outside work, including spending meaningful time with their children.

There has been much discussion about how effective an employee can be working from home, with some high profile women arguing against it. But other capitalist entrepreneurs have seen the wisdom of allowing highly motivated women and mothers flexibility in terms of when and where they work, especially when their children are young. In the United States, PowerToFly president Katharine Zaleski has created a company based on flexible and remote working. In a recent article for *Forbes* magazine, she spoke about how, by enabling women to work from home, they could be valued for their productivity rather than time spent sitting in an office or at a bar bonding afterwards. Mothers could have a third option that would allow them to either remain in the workforce or be a part of it even from areas with few job options. All the tools exist for remote work – Slack, Jira, Skype, Trello, Google Docs – and remote workers can be more productive.[4] Zaleski's recognition that even those without children want the opportunity to opt out of a relentless 24/7 work culture is crucial here, part of the means by which we can build a bigger coalition to tackle Business as Usual.

What of governments? As Rebecca Asher, a fierce advocate for more Nordic style, parent-friendly employment policies, argues:

> …We have so much good evidence in policy terms about what works. We could cherry pick the best policies around the world. We know that flexible parental leave is really important. We know that paid leave works. And that's so important because it is in those early weeks and months that habits and dynamics get set up, particularly between fathers and children. We know that 'the right to request' (flexible working) isn't enough. In lots of European countries, they have a right to flexible working. We have a wealth of research which shows the benefit to business of working flexibly, in terms of what parents put back into the work force in terms of commitment, productivity and longevity. And childcare, of course.'[5]

In their recent book *Man-Made: Why There Are So Few Women at the Top,* Eva Tutchell and John Edmonds argue for a system of (government funded) regular work breaks of up to three years at a time, available to all employees throughout a working life. Parental leave would become one such 'mini sabbatical' among many, making women or men who take time out to care for their children feel less isolated.

I repeat: politics is a disparate business these days. Changing work practices, says Anne Marie Slaughter, means 'fighting the mundane battles—every day, every year—in individual workplaces, in legislatures, and in the media' (Slaughter 2012). The changes required may appear prosaic, but in our current climate they are nothing short of revolutionary. Slaughter writes:

> My longtime and invaluable assistant, who has a doctorate and juggles many balls as the mother of teenage twins, emailed me while I was working on this article: "You know what would help the vast majority of women with work/family balance? MAKE SCHOOL SCHEDULES MATCH WORK SCHEDULES (Slaughter 2012). The present system, she noted, is based on a society that no longer exists—one in which farming was a major occupation and stay-at-home moms were the norm. Yet the system hasn't changed.
>
> *(Slaughter 2012)*

Slaughter's 'invaluable assistant' is onto something. Once you start to argue for an approach to work that genuinely accommodates human needs and wants (and not just those that relate to children) it takes us into new territory: a territory where we stop trying to find ways of bending our lives around a needs-blind economy, or sketching down a neat life plan, without reference to the contingencies of love and attachment, but one where we can sensibly balance the different sides of ourselves.

This rebalancing will help us to think of equality in wider terms: in particular, to find ways to close the income gap that has widened so alarmingly in recent times. Why not argue for an overall reduction in the working week, balancing out the excessive hours of some, and the perennial and permanent unemployment of others? Writing a few years ago in the Guardian newspaper, Anna Coote of the New Economics Foundation invited us to:

> Imagine a new 'standard' working week of 21 hours. ….more time with the kids, more time to read, ….hang out with friends, make music, fix lunch, walk in the park. While some are overworking, over-earning and over-consuming, others can barely afford life's necessities. (2010)

Wouldn't working less make many people far more efficient as well as happy? Wouldn't they make better decisions, develop new sides of themselves? Wouldn't this allow fathers a far greater role in their children's lives and partners, spouses, extended families and friends a chance to spend meaningful time together, which would be good for everyone, adults and children? Wouldn't this free many women to develop themselves beyond an endless joyless race to keep up with the circular demands of home and understimulating work?

Coote agreed that:

> A much shorter working week would help us all to live more sustainable, satisfying lives by sharing out paid and unpaid time more evenly across the population. Ideas about what is normal can sometimes change quite suddenly … the weight of public opinion can swing from antipathy to routine acceptance. (2010)

New evidence. Changing conditions. A sense of crisis. We could be moving in the right direction. … Certainly, we will never solve the 'problem' of motherhood until we accept that it is not actually mothers that are in difficulty but that it is the man-made world they – we – are trying to fit into that needs reform. As more women are educated to make a significant contribution, demands for a more radical perspective will, I hope, become more insistent. This, in turn, will shift public opinion, promote new forms of practice and alter public policy.

Time to fix the continually underperforming system, and leave the already over-worked women be.

Notes

1 Many thanks to Indra Adnan and Paul Gordon for careful readings and helpful comments on this piece.
2 http://www.equalityhumanrights.com/about-us/devolved-authorities/commission-scotland/legal-work-scotland/articles/women-men-and-part-time-work.
3 http://www.ippr.org/news-and-media/press-releases/eight-out-of-ten-married-women-do-more-housework-than-their-husbands.
4 Katherine Zaleski, March 3, 2015, Female company president: 'I'm sorry to all the mothers I worked with', *Forbes Magazine*.
5 In conversation with the author, early 2015.

References

Asher, R. (2012) *Shattered: Modern Motherhood and the Illusion of Equality.* London, England: Random House Books.

Benn, M. (2013) *What Should We Tell Our Daughters? The Pleasures and Pressures of Growing Up Female.* London, England: Hodder & Stoughton Ltd.

Chartered Management Institute. (December 2012) Submission on 'Women in the Workplace'.

Coote, A. (17 February 2010) 21 hours: A new working week? *The Guardian.*

Cusk, R. (2001) *A Life's Work: On Becoming a Mother.* London, England: Fourth Estate.

Gentleman, A. (10 July. 2009) Motherhood devastates women's pay, research finds. *The Guardian.*

IPPR (Institute for Public Policy Research). (2012) http://www.ippr.org/news-and-media/press-releases/eight-out-of-ten-married-women-do-more-housework-than-their-husbands.

McVeigh, T. (March 9 2013) One in seven women are made redundant after maternity leave. *The Guardian.*

Miller, A. J. and Sassler, S. (2012) The construction of gender among working-class cohabiting couples. *Qualitative Sociology,* 35: 427–46.

Slaughter, A. M. (July-August 2012) Why women still can't have it all. *The Atlantic.*

TUC report. (2014) Age Immaterial, Women Over 50 in the Workplace.

Tutchell, E. and Edmonds, J. (2015) *Man-Made: Why So Few Women Are In Positions Of Power.* England: Gower Publishing Ltd.

11
LEARNING TO BE A MOTHER

Lynda Woodroffe

When it was suggested to me that I think about the maternal from a personal point of view, a thousand thoughts invaded my mind. These thoughts comprised the styles of motherhood of the women I had known, my relatives, my friends, neighbours, women from my everyday life and the stereotypes of mothers in the media. What I focussed on were the personal experiences of my journey into motherhood, whatever form that took, how I learned from these experiences is not only how to be a mother but also how, after 40 years, to feel confident in that role.

While researching academic definitions of motherhood, an article by family therapist, Dr Stephan Poulter, caught my eye. He proposed that there are five types of mother: the perfectionist, the unpredictable, the best friend, the me-first mother and finally the complete mother who encapsulates the best of the other four (Poulter 2010).

This simplistic breakdown of mother-types shows some truth, if a little crassly. Be that as it may, in the full version types 1–4 include the possible detrimental effects on children of each type. We can learn from this. Nevertheless, Poulter suggests that the fifth type is the ideal, exemplifying it as the 'complete' mother and something that encompasses aspects of the other four types.

It is a crass analysis because he omits the likelihood that, in her maternal behaviours, a mother acts unconsciously. Poulter also defines the 'ideal', which as we all know is unachievable, and which, he states, is achieved by only 10% of mothers. How he reached this figure is puzzling. From this article we know nothing about the sample for his research and yet, even without the background information, it can affect us mothers and make us question our own performance as mothers … as if we don't feel guilty enough already.

Many versions of motherhood exist both in reality and fantasy (fairytales) and behind these lie complicated psychological exemplars inherited from mothering, both adequate and inadequate. This chapter is my personal take on motherhood and I hope it explains how I reached a kind of contentment in my own maternal feelings and skills.

Learning from past mothers

My own rich legacy emerged from two mothers who came before me, my mother and grandmother. This story will describe the complex issues that entwined us and how, after rejecting their ways, I came to discover my own route to feeling I was a *good enough* mother. My story cannot be told without describing my strong connections to theirs.

The circumstances of these three generations of mothers reflected the culture and resources of the times, spanning more than a century. My grandmother, a Catholic Italian and the youngest of thirteen children, was born in 1896. She married my grandfather, a red-haired Protestant from Kent (UK) when she was seventeen years old. It is rumoured that the marriage was arranged. She suffered many deaths during her life, including her father, several siblings and three of her own children.

Selflessness and sublimation

My grandmother's maternal drive was an 'unthought known' (Bollas 1987, in Wallin 2007: 115), uncontrollable, unconscious and powerful. She battled through many obstacles to procreate and accepted every child that she bore and gave birth to as a gift. Her role, therefore, was not considered, but taken for granted and she acted accordingly. There was no question of wondering what she herself may need.

She had a small frame and was only 5 ft 1 in. Carrying two sets of twins and five other babies put pressure on her health as well as the foetuses' health and survival rate. Being a Catholic meant not using contraceptives even when they became available. Although she was a wonderful grandmother/mother to me, I often wondered how she coped, how she shared out her love amongst her six surviving children. It seems to me, from the jealousies and resentments that I witnessed in my mother and her siblings, that there just wasn't enough to go round.

My mother was the second child from this brood of children, and the first daughter. She was born in 1922, four years after the end of WWI. In the years between the two world wars, she watched her mother go on to bear and deliver seven other children, three of which died. When, ten years after the birth of my mother, my grandmother became pregnant with twins, she was told she may not survive this last birth. This occurred in 1932. There were other factors. Blood transfusions were not brought into use on a more regular and safe level until the First World War, and all of the children were born in a part of India, now Pakistan, where hygiene was compromised. In 1931, the UK infant mortality rate was 60 in 1,000 live births (ONS 2003) and in 1941 the maternal death rate during birth was much higher than it is today. Antibiotics were not widely used until the 1940s, so, at the time when my grandmother was having her children, the chance of dying from blood loss or infection was quite high.

My mother was aware that her mother could die from carrying these babies and she watched her throughout the pregnancy as she set about making clothes for them. I can only imagine the fear and murderous anger that my mother may have felt for her mother, much like I felt for mine.

The twins were born in January 1932 and, fortunately, my grandmother survived along with her babies. After the birth, her eighth, she was ordered by the doctor not to get pregnant again. A devout Catholic, my grandmother sought the advice of a priest who gave her special permission to seek contraceptive aid and ensure she would remain alive to nurture her children. She was measured for a Dutch cap. She would have been 36 years then, still some years to go before menopause ceased her fertile era.

The depressed mother

My mother grew up jealous, angry and insecure. She was lovely looking, but thought her sister, fair-haired when my mother was dark like me, more beautiful. To compensate my mother used flattery, generosity and flirtatiousness in her social events as an attempt to get the attention she craved. This grandiosity stymied her intellectual and emotional growth. She suffered anxiety and I often heard her wish that she was dead. It is not surprising, therefore, that she married a man whose job it was to kill and to be shot at, a risk-taker. My father survived the war years in Bomber Command (44.4% death rate) only to die in an aircraft accident in 1957, during the Cold War years, a relatively peaceful time. Suffice it to say that there must have been something of a theme in the man she chose and the mother who bore her; both took risks with their lives.

My mother met my father in India before World War Two in 1938. They married three years later and my father refused her any children until after the war when she gave birth to my brother in 1946. She loved children, she said, and animals, and the photographs show this. But this love, after the disruption in her mothering of me, was nothing that I felt. I don't remember her loving gaze, her tender hugs, our bonding and her support. What I do remember are negative memories for most of my childhood and much of my adulthood. As she aged she softened and started to appreciate me, but by that time I had distanced myself and could not trust her. Compliments were received with a cynical disbelief.

Thinking about her now, I realise the fear and anxiety she must have gone through, not just during her childhood, but during the war, when my father left the United Kingdom to bomb German cities, each time wondering if she would ever see him again. Under those circumstances, how could she have kept her mind in control for others in relationship with her? In my mind's eye, I can see her, tense, smoking, keeping emotional control by not speaking. This was the same picture I had of her as I grew up.

My father was a domineering man and a controller. He had strong ideas about how children should be brought up and in particular how boys should learn to become men. This overshadowed my mother's maternal instincts and she failed to assert herself against his powers. This phenomenon is not uncommon and is accurately described by Indra Mohan in Shashi Deshande's book, *A Critical Spectrum*, where she writes about the tensions between the mothers and fathers which have knock-on effects upon the children – one mother is unable to have a relationship with one of her daughters; another child takes advantage and tries to become the centre of the dysfunctioning family. Another feels the parental difficulties are her fault and one of the boys runs away (Mohan 2004).

My father was a patriarch and I have memories of some sunny, playful days on my own with him. But his attitude to my brother was harsh and my mother stifled her maternal instincts to collude with this harshness. I can only rationalise this decision of hers to allow herself this passivity because she was economically as well as emotionally dependent on him. She, and then my brother, submitted to his strictures, but at eight years I learned to fight back. I had had a lot of practice fighting with my bullying brother. At this age, the age when children start to separate, I became bolder, using defiance as my chief weapon. But this boldness was shot down when my father was suddenly killed in an aircraft accident.

This led to a deep and long lasting depression in my mother. She became distant. I didn't know what she was thinking or feeling and I missed her. I was alone with my grief as was my brother who was left at boarding school. Since we took our cues from our mother, we were lost. I remember looking for and at her, seeing her face crumpled with grief, turned away from me, producing almost soundless, stifled whimpers. Judith Nelson refers to this crying style as 'detached inhibited' (2005: 159).

It is thought only humans cry, although there is some evidence that elephants, gorillas and camels also cry from emotion. In children, crying is like a reflex until they are conditioned to hold back. Crying involves all the bodily systems – respiratory, cardiovascular, skeletal, nervous and endocrine. It can be spontaneous as well as controlled. In 'sophisticated' cultures, crying is often frowned upon. This has a detrimental effect on the psyche. Not responding to one's emotional urges can cause a mind-body split. From a psychologist's point of view, it follows that if we are given the facility to cry and express pain it is good for us to use it. Tears from emotion shed stress hormones and toxins, stimulate endorphins and are essential to start the process of grieving (Orloff 2010). Unfortunately though, when I was told the news of my father's death, I, like my mother, cried once, but not again until I was twelve years of age, four years later.

From the day my father died, my grandmother stepped in with her loving hugs and caring looks, but I always looked to my mother. In his description of the mother complex, Jung (1875–1961) stated that maternal love is alive when living closely to a woman (the mother archetype) and that, 'In the absence of the mother, the archetype can be activated by any other female who is consistently *in loco parentis* – an aunt, grandmother, nanny or older sister' (Stevens 1990: 32). This was the role taken by my grandmother.

My mother's emotional absence lasted about 30 years. Bollas (2005) wrote about a client who had suffered traumas as a child and at the end of his analysis he asked himself where the place from which he spoke to his client was. His reply was that he spoke to him 'from a place where maternal love vanished' (107). This was my reality then.

> While despair, sadness or frustration sweeps into the psyche of all mothers. ... troubling them to think themselves through moods, the dead mother refuses her own moods, killing off contact with the processes of inner life. As she dissociates herself from her affects, she stands as a continually stricken witness to the unforeseen misfortunes imposed upon her by lived experience and its after–effects. After-effects are not for her; she is dead to them.
>
> *(Bollas 2005: 100)*

My mother wobbled between schizoid and depressive phases (Klein 1975). Socially she was the soul of the party, generous, attentive and friendly. When she didn't have an audience, her fallacious behaviour vanished. At home with me and my grandmother, she would hide away, closet herself and act angrily, irritated. She told me to be silent when elderly relatives visited us, to be a good girl and not to criticise my grandmother. I was not allowed to offload my own aggression, something which would have enabled some healing in me to take place (Klein 1975).

Friends from school tell me that I was a quiet person, often alone and that, when they visited me at home, they hardly ever saw my mother. They believed she was upstairs in a bedroom on her own. She was very obviously suffering prolonged grief, as were I and my brother. The well-attuned mother would have helped us grieve, would have shared her grief and shown us to manage our difficult feelings. Wallin (2007) states that when affects in a child are deemed manageable and acceptable by the caregiver, a stronger attachment and 'a visceral sense that connection to others can be a source of relief, comfort and pleasure' develops between both (Wallin 2007: 100). Unable to do this, my grandmother was there to help, but she also lacked those skills. Since my mother had not been taught to manage her own feelings and, indeed, had grown up in an age of *the stiff upper lip,* when public displays of grief were thought to be unseemly, how could she possibly help me to manage mine?

To please her very English army officer husband, my grandmother had rejected the sharing of emotions. It is certain that her children also had to learn these cultural traits. I once heard an army officer talk on the radio about soldiers who had experienced therapy. He complained that afterwards they were of no use to him because they had learnt *to feel* and a soldier who could feel could not do his job. Of course this is true. Two world wars, a combined loss of approximately 678,000 mostly young men could not have gone ahead if feelings had come into the equation. The author Pat Barker (1943–) wrote short novels about WWI 'shell-shock', now more commonly known as Post Traumatic Stress Disorder (PTSD), which, for obvious reasons, prevented injured or frightened soldiers from going back to the trenches. Frightened soldiers were considered to be cowards. Cowards cannot fight wars.

Similar to her own mother, my mother married a British services man, one who also thought of tears and grief to be a waste of time. After his death, my mother could not help us. It is difficult to forgive her for that inadequacy. All of this took place in the 1950s at a time before trauma in children had been fully acknowledged and before Alice Miller (1923–2010) wrote extensively about the effects of childhood trauma (Miller 1987). Anthony Stevens wrote (after Bowlby 1951): 'The sad truth is that just as children suffering from Vitamin D deficiency grow up with bowed and distorted limbs, so children deprived of a mother's love are prone to develop rickets of the soul' (Stevens 1990: 80). The impact of this loss was to later affect the health of both my brother and me, thus confirming Stephen's quote.

Resurrecting maternal feelings

Losing my father and missing my mother's attention so young led me to numb myself. I cut off feelings which I, at eight years, could not face, and I lost my 'true' self (Winnicott 1984). I drifted through my adolescence, with few friends, feeling as if I was not part of my own body, until I was 15 years when hormones awoke me to my sexual existence.

Other mother archetypes that played a big part in my life were at school – nuns. They were the cruellest people I had ever come across. Our painful experiences seemed to elicit no sympathy from them. In fact the more we hurt, the less sympathetic they became. The nuns became targets for our secret hatred. The one positive outcome was that our mutual hatred united us.

Cloistered in the convent school, we learned little about the realities of life. Almost as soon as I left school, I became pregnant. When I had my first son, I was in two minds. I felt clever as well as helpless, mesmerised as well as anxious. And along with these came restraints; the hospital, my mother and a young mother's ignorance.

Since he was born prematurely, the hospital staff took control over my baby boy. Since I was no longer in a relationship with the baby's father, my mother felt she should take control at home. And since I had no experience at all of child care, despite witnessing all my aunts nurturing and breastfeeding their babies, I gave in to all mothers who I believed knew better than me.

Learning about being a mother at that age was mostly a practical activity – four-hourly feeding, nappy changing and daily bathing. The emotional side of mothering was not taught or learned nor, for that matter, entirely present. Much of that had been suppressed. But emotionally I was re-integrating; I would suddenly burst into tears for no apparent reason. Holding my sleeping baby each evening and sitting with my angry mother, I felt confused by both my delight and her apparent resentment. She looked sideways at me holding him and told me to put him to bed. She could not share my obvious pleasure and berated my maternal instincts. It was as if she could not bear the attention I was giving him, attention she was not getting. The bonds that we had created seemed to be the bonds that she longed for. Over the next six months, I grew ambivalent to her and had to get away.

Sadly, unresolved grief and PTSD had left me short of empathy for my child. I felt uncertain about my ability to feel maternal. Research shows evidence that maternal instincts do not always emerge at the birth of a child; Fiona Gibson, for example, describes how she waited for the instinct to engulf her... 'But nothing happened' (Gibson 2002). Maternal feelings are thought to arise from a rapport between mother and baby, like a survival tool, with the baby appealing to the mother to take care of him or her (Hamer 2012). Additionally, the empathic mother will feel her nurturing instinct physiologically – she will undergo autonomic responses, an increase in the stress hormone cortisol and a raised heart rate (Stallings et al. 2011). Overall, maternal instincts for *all* women are debatable, and I did not feel confident in mine. My mother exhibited aggression and moods consistent with a depressed person and, as my role model, this had taken its toll on my personal education. She seemed unable to relate to me. Although I didn't feel exactly the same as Gibson, I knew something in me was missing.

When I left home, I did my best to provide a decent environment for me and my child. As my son grew older, my maternal style became unpredictable and inconsistent. It was a difficult period and my son will have experienced not only the discomfort from a poor standard of living, but also, because he lived in my aura, my tensions and anxieties. Much as I loved him, I had needs too which were invariably unmet. Therein lays the point of this tale – that a child who has a mother who suffers unmet needs grows into an adult who also suffers unmet needs. The narcissistic wound untended is, therefore, unintentionally passed on.

My first son went to university when he was 19. I drove him to his next destination wondering what to say, how to say goodbye to him, and, like my mother with me, was unable to cry in front of him. I cried all the way home alone in the car. I dreamt about him. At the same time, my biology was screaming at me; I have to have another child. It felt as if my existence was incomplete without one. My partner gently explained *empty-nest* symptoms. Although what he said made some sense, I was in denial of this and I convinced him that a baby would enhance our lives. My urges were still a long way from rational thought and despite them, I could hardly recognise myself.

I yearned for another baby. I was married and secure in a relationship. A major concern then was my age, I was 41. But the chance to have a child along with the protection from a male partner addressed something that was missing all those years ago. It also meant I could be relieved of the guilt of a past transgression; single mothers in the 1960s, the decade during which I first became a mother, were stigmatised. This time the pregnancy was planned and longed for. Mapping the path of the hormones was a monthly agony. Discussing the possible names even before conception was all part of the fun. Then… what could go wrong? Supposing there were problems? We were both the wrong side of 40. The likelihood of a baby with Down's syndrome was quite high. The decision was made; we would abort.

Then the worst happened. My partner was killed that summer on an Alpine mountain. I was now alone and six weeks pregnant. As he died, he didn't know this fact and I had been robbed of the chance to tell him. He had been robbed of the chance to be a father; my child had been robbed of a father.

Being a single mother again was not part of the grand plan. I'd managed this once already and did not want to go through it alone again. But, like everything, nothing is so clear. I needed to have this baby. My urges told me so. I needed to care for someone, to have someone care for me. I couldn't remember such a strong desire for a child, even when my partner was alive.

Attaching to an ultrasound image

I saw my baby in an ultrasound scan. I immediately attached to him and I fell in love. Falling (in love) is not quite the correct word for that feeling; it felt more like a pulling, at the chest, the stomach, the breasts. Jung described this love as 'not a matter of willpower or social conditioning; a woman does not choose to love her child. It is something that happens to her' (Stevens 1990: 78). For me, this was a new experience.

The death of my husband suddenly, like the sudden death of my father, seemed to resonate with the dormant wound inflicted in 1957. Emotionally I became alive, erupting like a dormant volcano. I felt excruciating pain, fear, anxiety and anger. Through earlier therapy I had understood that unexpressed grief had been strangling me for most of my life. Although the therapy had helped me understand that I was suffering prolonged grief, I was still partially numb. I did not feel safe enough to go deeper into the power of the repressed feelings of the 30 years before. With the loss of my husband, I seemed to be in an emotional loop, repeating a past event. Eventually, after this event and the help and support of more therapy, I was able to recover from my losses and, with that, I could allow my natural instincts to emerge.

Giving birth seemed precarious; the world had taken my father and husband. It was not a safe place. I had read that boy babies are more vulnerable than girls. I felt that hospitals are not ideal places for childbirth; there are many possible sources of infection and dangers. Although I badly needed to meet my child, I feared the danger of childbirth and the possible damage from it to him or me. I feared also the separation from him. While he languished inside me, I felt he was warm and cared for, protected by the waters that surrounded him, fed by our umbilical cord, for as long as I was healthy. With all of these thoughts in my mind, I lay back on the hospital bed as an attempt to slow down the labour, hoping that in lying down gravity would lose its pull. Needless to say, this was not possible and he was born naturally, a little underweight and with a good strong scream.

Recovery

I have been in therapy for many years, mostly with women who were mothers themselves. Two were Kleinian therapists. I have now experienced *the good breast* as well as bad (Klein 1975). I eventually decided that I needed to challenge myself to trusting a male therapist. The one I chose helped me complete the grief cycle and to re-integrate. I no longer feel the need for therapy.

Maternal feelings had returned fully when my second son was born and I was able to judge my own mother as an inadequate mother, someone who had left me helpless not only as a child. I determined not to be like her. I breastfed this new child as and when he demanded it. When she visited me, my mother tutted in disapproval and told me to stop fussing around him, put him down. I retaliated: '*This is my baby and I'll bring him up the way I want to'*. Also, I was not going to be a mother like my grandmother, subservient to all her children's needs to the detriment of her own. Lastly, never was I going to be like the surrogate mothers at school.

There is a song by the Spice Girls, *Mama*, whose lyrics resonate with me particularly when my mother died. It describes the difficult relationship with the mother, the shame, the guilt, and how now they understand her. Over the years, my attitude to her softened and on her deathbed I apologised to her for being a 'bad' daughter, but this was not the true picture of our relationship. Being thrown together after my father's death was suffocating. At the same time, the connections of tension and disagreement bound us. We could not escape each other. It was these that I thought a lot about after she died. Forgiving her inadequacies became part and parcel in forgiving myself for failing to be that perfect daughter. Writing this now I feel sad, remembering it all, but I no longer feel guilty.

Thinking again about the maternal styles of my two mothers, I can now admit it was not all bad. I was fed, clean, clothed and sent to school. My mother taught me how to spell and to use the English language correctly, even if that excluded expressing myself. My grandmother taught me some French and Italian. They both taught me to sew, knit and put on make-up. I eventually acknowledged them as strong women. My grandmother could manage a demanding husband and six children with little help from him or anyone else. She was a widow at 60 years. My mother was a single mother at 35 years. With no men around the war had been instructive for women. Together, they could change fuse wires in the fuse box, wire a plug and produce colourful flowers in the garden at the drop of a trowel. Additionally, they were both excellent cooks and could put on a mean party.

Remembering these talents with the love that I now feel for them helps me to realise that they had done what they thought was right and, under those very difficult circumstances, it was their best. Ironically, it was their shortcomings that taught me how to be a good mother.

In this chapter, I have described how I came to accept myself as a good mother, to understand how, through lack of attunement, my mother taught me about the necessity to attune with my own children. While at first glance I condemned the mother types described by Stephan Poulter as crass, since thinking about my own experience, I can now identify with Poulter's definitions. My mother was over-controlling, anxious, moody, self-absorbed and critical, all characteristics Poulter listed. But she was also a mother of her time, subject to the expectations of women during the years when she was alive. The point is we are all subject to expectations of our time. Being maternal is not always 'natural'. It does not always emerge at childbirth. It can suffer stops and starts. For me, motherhood is a melting, an unfurling, developmental and evolutionary.

References

Barker, P., (1991–95), *The Regeneration Trilogy*. (Regeneration, The Eye in the Door, The Ghost Road). London, England: Penguin.

Bollas, C., (1987) in Wallin, D., (2007), *Attachment in Psychotherapy*. London, England: Guildford.

Bollas, C., (2005), Dead mother, dead child. In *The Dead Mother*, the work of Andre Green. Ed. Gregorio Kohon. London, England: Routledge.

Gibson, F., (2002), Go play in the garden, *The Observer*, 6 October 2002. http://www.theguardian.com/theobserver/2002/oct/06/featuresreview.review1. Accessed on 1 July 2015.

Hamer, C., (2012), NCT Research overview: Parent-child communication is important from birth perspective – NCT's journal on preparing parents for birth and early parenthood. March 2012. https://www.google.co.uk/#q=Hamer%2C+NCT+research. Accessed on 1 July 2015.

Indra Mohan, T.M.J., Ed. (2004), *Shashi Deshpande: A Critical Spectrum*. Atlantic. Dehli, India.

Klein, M., (1975), *Love, Guilt and Reparation and Other Works 1921–1945*. London, England: Hogarth Press and the Institute of Psychoanalysis.

Lyrics of *'Mama'*, by the Spice Girls. http://www.azlyrics.com/lyrics/spicegirls/mama.html. Accessed on 27 May 2015.

Miller, A., (1987), *For Your Own Good: The Roots of Violence in Child-Rearing*. London, England: Virago.

Nelson, J. K., (2005), *Seeing Through Tears: Crying and Attachment*. London, England: Routledge.

Office of National Statistics (ONS), (2003), Twentieth Century Mortality Trends in England and Wales. http://r.search.yahoo.com/_ylt=A0LEV7wAbTxXni8AAxgnnIlQ;_ylu= X3oDMTEycGlzdXNuBGNvbG8DYmYxBHBvcwMyBHZ0aWQDQjIwN- DRfMQRzZWMDc3I-/RV=2/RE=1463606657/RO=10/RU=http%3a%2f%2fweb.

ons.gov.uk%2fons%2frel%2fhsq%2fhealth-statistics-quarterly%2fno--18--summer-2003%2ftwentieth-century-mortality-trends-in-england-and-wales.pdf/RK=0/RS=zdI742kTpfH6CafkDt3dfE95rvo-. Accessed on 21 May 2015.

Orloff, J., (2010), The health benefits of tears. *Psychology Today.* URL: https://www.psychologytoday.com/blog/emotional-freedom/201007/the-health-benefits-tears. Accessed on 21 May 2015.

Poulter, S., (2010), The five mother types. *Psychologies Magazine,* https://psychologies.co.uk/family/the-five-mother-types-2.html. Accessed on 27 May 2015.

RAF Bomber Command. Details from Wikipedia, http://en.wikipedia.org/wiki/RAF_Bomber_Command. Accessed on 21 May 2015.

Stallings, J., Fleming, A. S., Corter, C., Worthman, C., and Steiner, M., (2001), The effects of infant cries and odors on sympathy, cortisol, and autonomic responses in new mothers and nonpostpartum women. *Parenting: Science and Practice* 1(1–2): 71–100.

Stevens, A., (1990), *On Jung.* London, England: Routledge.

Winnicott, D. W., (1984), *Deprivation and Delinquency.* C. Winnicott, R. Shepherd, and M. Davis, (eds.). London, England: Brunner-Routledge.

12
MUSIC AND THE MATERNAL

Alison Davies

There are three aspects that I want to illustrate in this chapter. Firstly, my own experience both as a mother and a daughter; secondly, illustrations and examples from my clinical work as both a music therapist and a psychotherapist; and, thirdly, theoretical thinking and considerations. Much of what I am going to say has been greatly enriched by talking to Rosalind Mayo over the years, as we travelled home from Philadelphia Association meetings on the Cambridge train. I thank Ros for very stimulating discussions, which often seemed to be drawn towards thinking about the maternal.

About myself, my mother and music therapy

Before I trained at the PA as a psychotherapist, I worked as a music therapist mainly in psychiatry. Music as a therapy is practised in an interactive and improvisational way to relate to people who have difficulties in various ways in connecting to others. Music seems to help ameliorate a sense of loneliness and a feeling of disconnection often associated with mental health problems and disabilities. Being met through sound and music can often go a long way towards allowing people to emerge from this isolation. Further into this chapter, I will be more specific about the nature of music therapy practice.

I worked at Fulbourn Hospital in Cambridge in the 1990s. At that time, the arts therapies were flourishing and our department, as well as having four music therapists, also had two art therapists, a drama therapist and a dance movement therapist. Sadly at this present time, few arts therapists are employed in the Mental Health Services, despite the realisation that these therapies are extremely valuable as therapies for people with deeply entrenched communicational and mental health problems. However, after working as a music therapist for some years, I decided to seek an additional training in psychotherapy, my own experience of psychotherapy having been life changing.

On memories of being mothered

Much of my thinking, I see in retrospect, is firmly based on my own experiences as a child. I have been asked and I have also asked myself, why, if music is so central to my life, I chose to train as a psychotherapist, which has spoken language as its currency of relating. When considering this question I go back to a sense I have had for most of my life, and that is to achieve a balance between feeling and thinking. I realise now that I had unconsciously cultivated and prioritised feeling over thinking out of a necessity to address this imbalance that seemed part of my feeling 'out of kilter' with the rest of my family. I came from a family where my mother and later my brother were journalists and whose intimate and bonding connection was through the play of words.

Encouraged by our mother, my brother edited a family newspaper during our school years and, following my mother's footsteps, ended up in Fleet Street as a journalist. My mother, a graduate in classics and for whom words were always exciting and of great importance, offered to give us children half a crown if we could find a word she couldn't spell or did not know the meaning of. None of us three children ever did manage this task and it seemed that without the fairy tale goblin or the magician to come to our aid, we would never find a word to fox her, and we didn't.

An early photo is very telling of me and my older brother Hugh. I am about five months old and my brother is about two. I am lying on a settee propped up by pillows, eyes fixed on Hugh, studying his expression intensely whilst he appears to '*read*' to me from the telephone directory. It seems to me that he was learning that words, even from a telephone directory, were the connecting factor between people. However, what I might have been learning, as a baby of a few months, was the sound of my brother's voice that connected me to him.

Crucial to my own early years and my survival growing up was my capacity to find a place of sanctuary within my family life that wasn't necessarily dependant on verbal communication. I think there was a fear in me that I would get submerged within these family members who, as I felt then and see it now, prioritised words.

Music, for me as a teenager, was my haven. My mother didn't appear or seem to need music around as I did, although she would have denied this vehemently. I can visualise her now playing the piano on occasions in a thumping, rather aggressive way. Her legendary rendering of Edward German's 'Henry the Eighth's Dances' played with gritted teeth was a rather terrifying spectacle. The piano was to be my entry to my world of feeling and I didn't like sharing it with anyone. My father played various instruments badly but could be moved to tears by music. Looking back, my father, a man of few words but ferocious outbreaks of anger, was nearer to my non-verbal states than my mother, although it was my mother with whom I have always had the closest bond.

My mother's two favourite expressions were; '*Let me think about it*' and '*If I were you*'. The first '*let me think about it*' seemed to absolve me from thinking. In other words, I left the thoughts to her and awaited her responses. The second '*if I were you*' meant that she most often did not listen to my experience which I have to say was hard to articulate. She would translate what she thought I wanted into what it meant for her. She would then give her answer to me. I am mindful of the Winnicottian idea here of the mother metabolising the child's experience and fears and handing them back in a digested form. I feel that my mother often handed back her own undigested fears to me rather than a thought through, or eased version of my own. All this led to a confused symbiotic relationship, which I was to spend many years as an adult trying to understand and move away from. I deeply loved my mother, but she did live through me or I, by default, through her, however you like to look at it.

Later, training with the PA taught me about the specificity of the lived experience and suffering of the lives of others. This helped me to understand my mother's position of identification and my own propensity to live vicariously through the desire of the other. I am reminded here of Francois Roustang's chapter entitled 'Towards a Theory of Psychosis' (1982) in *Dire Mastery*. He describes how the psychotic lives on the stage of others, being thought *for* rather than being thought *of*, with a resultant feeling of being appropriated or taken over. Although not psychotic, this was a place I knew well with my mother. I think in some ways my ability to turn to music and also painting, the nonverbal creative arts, to some extent held me a little safer from the worst catastrophes of merging. Her inability to understand these artistic aspects of me finally led, long into adulthood, into a degree of separateness from her that was both a re-emergence for me, but also a loss.

Some of my earliest memories around music are ones of anxiety. I could never listen to music in the presence of my mother without a feeling, coming from her, of a huge uncontrollable emotion welling up in her as she sat beside me. This was 'suffering' for me, as I could never free myself on these occasions from a preoccupation with this potentially explosive event, which might erupt at any moment and was clearly to do with a sort of hysterical identification with me. The emotional impact of this and a sort of fusional state that came with it could never be spoken about. She was enormously sensitive to criticism and this was never alluded to or spoken about. For my part, I felt I was left just to bear the anxiety and tension of it all.

I loved going to concerts and, until a certain age, I had to be accompanied by my mother, my father being frequently absent. I looked forward to these musical events with a certain amount of apprehension. Would her emotions in the form of suppressed hysteria manifest themselves during the music? How would I manage the embarrassment? I certainly wouldn't be able to listen to the music as well as worry about my mother's emotional state. However, over time, I became very skilled at booking tickets for a concert myself. I would say to my mother that all adjacent seats were sold and that we would have to sit rather far from each other. With relief, I could wave to her from the opposite side of the hall and then enjoy the music on my own. Silence also produced the same problem. My mother was a Quaker and accompanying her to Quaker meetings as a young person was tricky. Here again my strategy was to linger in the hallway to delay going in with her and then, pretending not to notice her, finding a seat as far away from her as possible. Music and silence, or the music of silence, were sort of dissociative emotional states for my mother, in the sense of being ungrounded. It wasn't until she was very old and my own middle age, when, after a long period in therapy and finally reaching a degree of emotional separateness where I could begin to think and speak on my own behalf, that this way of being lessened between us. She married for the second time in old age and I lost her to another in a more final way than it had ever been with my father.

However, one particular aspect of my mother is lovingly remembered. In this memory she did get it right. I was a rather depressed and sulky teenager and prone to periods of black times of 'nameless dread' (a term of Bion's that I particularly relate to). At these times, my parents, especially my mother, would try and '*chivvy*' me out of these moods, often getting exasperated with my lack of response.

Snap out of it was my father's phrase and my mother's was, *Just try and act normally!*

Firstly, the ability to '*snap out*' of an emotional experience is so far from the deep introspective place of depression and secondly, in this sunken state, trying is impossible. However it was when, having been left or allowed myself to languish in this place of disconnection for a few days, my mother would come up to my room and very gently, ask me what the matter was. Her voice on this occasion was soft, un-theatrical and slow. It was then that I really felt she was present for me and as a result of this, I finally felt a connection with her. Very often, this would result in a spontaneous lifting of my depressive mood. I did not need to respond to her question, I just needed to hear her voice and to be able to feel, through the music of her words, her sense of concern, real concern (at last!) and I suppose her willingness at that precise moment to try to enter into my experience.

On empathy, attunement and music

Daniel Stern (2010) writes about attunement and vitality affects. He speaks about the language of sound and gesture that the mother and baby share. Firstly, between the mother and baby, there is the awareness of movement, and then a communicative repertoire encompassing vocalisations and facial expressions. This is a playful partnership and socialisation through sound. He speaks about the:

> …Understanding at a deep level that allows each partner, mother and baby to know that the other is fully 'there' for them. These moments could be

described as both partners having an emotional feel for each other. A feel for when and how they get angry or if they are fully attentive or not, or that the gesture is one of love. (2010: 111)

Christopher Bollas (2000) remarks that the vowel sound in 'love' lifts the expression, 'opens the mouth wide and cracks up the face. It is preferable to consonants, which bear the knowledge of reality' (p. 43). It was when I was in those 'dark' places as a teenager that the 'music' of my mother's voice was what I responded to.

Thoughts on nonverbal communication, the mother and 'tuning in'

As well as auditory, there are visual and the tactile gestures available for nonverbal communication. Although the mother most often instinctively knows how to respond, it seems that there is a great responsibility for her to get this right. If the mother gauges it wrongly, is too forceful and not sensitive enough, the baby might appear to engage but in real terms "switches off" or turns away as if to reduce the impact. The stronger the impact the more the infant has to regulate herself by turning away or rejecting the source of stimulus. The overloaded baby could be the 'smothered' baby whose separateness is not acknowledged. The understimulated baby who is not aroused may become the baby who turns away and uses sleep as a protection from too much 'otherness', resulting in emptiness or disconnection. Perhaps these two extremes of 'smother' and 'other' are actually quite close in the sense of missing the mark for the baby.

Recently, playing with the word '*mother*', three positions occurred to me. Firstly, putting an '*s*' in front of the word becomes *smother*, secondly, taking the '*m*' away gives you '*other*'. Thirdly, returning to '*mother*', we have a word beginning with '*m*', a soft consonant sound that babies really enjoy exploring bringing the lips together in a slapping watery sound, a primitive early place of experience

As a psychotherapist and having trained as a music therapist, I am interested in how these shadows or images of early interactions and attunements show themselves in the therapeutic relationship. If affect attunement is the basis of empathy, it follows that this ought to be of interest to the therapist. Empathy, very simply put, is the ability to put oneself in another's shoes, so to speak, and to have a desire to connect with another's emotions or feeling life and respond appropriately. This is an attribute that is closely linked with the maternal and care giving. Simon Baron-Cohen (2003) writes:

Empathising leads you to constantly search people's tone of voice and to scan people's faces, especially their eyes, to pick up how they might be feeling or what they might be thinking. You use the 'language of the eyes' and intonation as windows to their mind! (p. 22)

Vitality affects are connected to attunement. Music therapists refer to vitality affects as part of the experience of aliveness. Vitality affects are present in dynamic forms in all the time-based arts where the vitality expressed by one person resonates with another. Louis Zinkin (1991), who was a Jungian and a Group Analyst, spoke about vitality affects not in terms of readily available groups of emotion such as anger, sadness, joy, fear, or disgust but rather understanding them as more kinetic qualities such as exploding, fading away, accelerating and so on. He wrote in his paper *The Search for Origins*:

> Vitality affects seem to me like the musical signs that are not the notes to be played but indicate how they are to be played. The musician learns the shape of a crescendo, diminuendo, sforzando, calendo, subito piano, accelerando, con fuoco, allegro ma non troppo and even 'con amore'. (52)

Zinkin (1991) writes extensively about a meta communication, irrespective of the content of the manifest message, that forms the primary communication. This secondary or latent message, which may be nonverbal, is one that gives information to the other about the nature of the relationship between the two. It is the *manner* in which one is being told what one is hearing that I think of and tune into as the music of communication. Bringing to mind the idea that 'T'aint what you say but the way you say it'.

Zinkin remarks that it is well known that patients after a long analysis do not remember much about the interpretations they were given, although they may be effective at the time. What is more likely to be remembered, he says, is the quality of the relationship and most probably the manner in which the interpretations were delivered. In my practice, what interests me is attending to the '*music*' of the therapy session: the tone of voice, the melody (closely linked with what infant researchers call '*prosody*'), the timing, the pacing and many other nonverbal messages which are communicated, received and responded to mutually between patient and therapist during the analytic encounter.

Christopher Bollas (2000), in his chapter 'In the Beginning is the Mother' from his book entitled *Hysteria*, touches on the sensual when speaking of the mother/baby attunement. He draws our attention to the seduction of the mutual sounds of infant and mother playing together. He writes:

> It is not only through the breast feed that the mother conveys her eroticism. She bathes the infant in seductive sonic imagery, oooing and aahing, luring the infant's being from autistic enclave into desire for this voice. As the mother words her infant gestures, with the onomatopoetics of ooing and aahing, she extends his or her body through this sonic imagery, which is maternal parole. ... Her speech attaches itself to the moving parts of the baby's body, driven by her affective sense of its requirements. (43)

Bollas (2000) suggests that maternal speech links language to desire long before words in themselves are used by the child to express his or her desire. He puts it beautifully by saying:

> In 'voicing over' the infants body, the mother touches her infant with acoustic fingers, precursive to all conversions of word to body, and likewise accomplishing its reversal, as the body is now put into words. (43)

In speaking about music, in relation to words and thought, Susanne Langer (1941) writes:

> The assignment of meanings (of music) is a shifting kaleidoscopic play, probably below the threshold of consciousness, certainly outside the pale of discursive thinking. The lasting effect is ... to make things conceivable rather than to store up propositions. Not communication but insight is the gift of music; in a very naïve phrase, a knowledge of 'how feelings go'. (243–244)

It is common that people experience with joy a song or a piece of music and have no idea what the words mean. For me, the countess's love song in the second act of The Marriage of Figaro is an example. It doesn't matter what language it is sung in, what the music conveys to me is the most exquisite expression of love, longing and the potential anticipation of loss.

Music and words in clinical practice

I would like to illustrate the therapeutic use of music and words by first looking at how I see these two elements at work in music therapy. The following are examples of recurring dynamics from my music therapy practice that I have experienced in sessions. Music therapy takes many forms; my particular interest has been the interface between music and words. For those unfamiliar with how music therapy works, it is most often practised as an interactive therapy with both the therapist and the patient playing music together. The instruments used are tuned and untuned percussion instruments. The patient does not have to have a practical knowledge of music. The sorts of instruments offered to the patient are accessible to all. The music therapist however has a particular skill on his or her instrument whether it is the piano, violin or singing voice, for example. Their therapeutic and musical skills, as well as accompanying the patient's music, take on many aspects according to clinical need. It may be to support or put into context the patient's music or it may be to challenge or to help extend the repertoire of communication through music. The following are some examples from my work as a music therapist. In the interests of confidentiality, these examples have been disguised whilst keeping the dynamic of the interactions intact.

One patient, suffering from schizophrenia, would not easily engage in a therapeutic relationship but could relate through shared musical improvisation together. He would place himself with his back to me and play the large xylophone whilst I accompanied him on the piano. Rarely could he be drawn into what I would understand as meaningful dialogue in words. His own world was circumscribed and enclosed. Our connection came through the music we played together. Although the music was often chaotic and discontinuous, together, distinct moments of connection were clearly felt by us both. Musically they took the form of shared rhythms, dynamics and timing. I would try to tune in to his freeform playing, sometimes underpinning with a harmonic structure and at other times just freely matching his sounds, expanding them or echoing them. This felt at times close and intimate but at other times distant, as if we couldn't find any mutuality in the music we played together. Over time we developed a musical language that was able both to embrace closeness and to tolerate the discordant. As I saw him around the hospital in a world of his own, my feeling was that the music we played together might have gone a small way in bridging his isolation.

Another patient, who had an extensive command of verbal language and many words to describe her life, historically and factually, clearly had few means to tell others of her feelings or emotions. Music was a release for her. She improvised mainly on the drum whilst I played a variety of tuned percussive instruments. We made a tape of our music together and on one particular occasion, after she had reached a massive ear splitting crescendo on the drum, there was silence followed by a huge sigh and a burst of laughter. This was often referred back to in subsequent sessions. It seemed a clear moment of natural release that we both experienced together. Here, music had resulted in laughter and this had both a sense of connectivity as well as an ordinariness in its release of tension.

One very isolated long stay patient could often be seen drifting around the hospital in his silent world. In a room with two somewhat dilapidated grand pianos (yes, this was the NHS!) he and I would improvise music together. He had some ability in piano playing. However, it was often hard for me to find a place in the harmonies he played or to follow his rhythms. But occasionally we would hit on the same harmonic base, beat or sequence of notes and he would stop and look over towards me. His look, as I remember, was one of amazement. It was a sort of recognition of meeting, or a sense of wonder at a connection. In fact, he often used to refer to Alice in Wonderland. I took this to be a reference to my name. However, these moments were short, intense and easily broken. I felt we had experienced together a certain intimacy that I think this patient really longed for, but also feared at the same time. A sudden switch of mood, resulting in unrelated music and chaotic playing, would follow these moments. The feeling of closeness passed all too quickly. But at these times, I began to understand a little clearer the difficulty that he had in placing himself alongside another person.

Early maternal memories around a feel for music would often seem to be present with people with dementia and, in particular, Alzheimer's disease. Words may appear to have long receded but many of the hospital patients that I worked with could sing songs or hymns from their earliest childhood. One lady in her eighties who had lost her powers for meaningful verbal communication could sing all the verses of the hymn *Abide with Me*. The words may have lost any meaning but what was retained was a response to music. Through music this patient could feel connected to me in a way that she may not have done otherwise.

In my psychotherapy practice, I often attend to a 'musical' sense in the relationship. I listen to the patient who presents in a seamless verbal way with no breaks or pauses, as if to keep a running commentary on every thought that occurred to them. This solipsistic and self-referential way of being distances them from others. There is a fear of letting others into a relationship with them, a fear of what might happen if mutuality developed. I might sense a critical mother here, a need as an adult for protection by trying hard not to let anyone in that might appear to replicate an early maternal experience. I try to notice this musically and attend to my musical countertransference. I am reminded of hypnotic music.

With another patient, the 'music' or feel of the session, so to speak, might be all in the head. The heart might seem occluded with every word 'figured' out and carefully placed. These patients might describe a feeling of emotional disconnection in relationships. They might seem to be working everything out on their own and presenting me with the conclusion. Any sense of exchange between us is hard to get a sense of. I might ask myself where the playfulness and improvisation of emotional exchange is. I could find myself thinking of the emotional outpourings of Mahler or the expansive symphonies of Brahms and this would give me a clue to the direction that might be good to head towards. In this way, I get a sense of what might relieve the tyranny of the headiness that I can see as my patients' dilemma.

Then there is the music of the patient whose voice fades at the end of a sentence as if she does not believe there is a listener, or the patient with the monotonous voice that seems to put me to sleep in order for me not to experience her angry feelings. There are, of course, simple gestures such as opening a door to a patient and registering their mood or noticing the delaying tactics at the end of a session or the timing of abrupt endings. All these things are valuable to notice. From the point of view of a psychotherapist, they are not just peripheral, but often central to understanding the world of the patient and I associate them with musical feelings in their timing and their melody.

For me, employing my musical ear, these patients are expressing a way of being that might possibly be the repeat of a preverbal experience or experience with mother. This may be in terms of perhaps an over-intrusive mother, a need to protect against criticism or being taken over, a maternal absence where vigilant thinking and reasoning now has had to guard against deep emotional emptiness or loss.

On feeling, sensing and imagining

The psychoanalyst, Gilbert Rose, in his book *Between Couch and Piano* (2004), writes that words seem to cluster towards the 'knowing' end of the intellect-feeling spectrum, and music towards the opposite pole, 'feeling'. He states that words and music are both rooted in the body. He quotes Freud *On Aphasia* (1891) saying that

> …Every word has been bathed in sensory sources coming from parental speech and intonation. (1)

For Rose, it is clear then that (backed up and well documented by neuroscience) cognition and feeling are basically inseparable and not only in infancy. However, in the course of development, he argues they become more differentiated from each other. Rose explains how images are important in forming mental representations. Imagery and emotions are associated with the nonverbal system. But as thought depends on mental imagery, which is stored in the nonverbal system, it follows that the nonverbal system is closely implicated in thinking.

These experiences of another person in psychotherapy practice can, as Rose puts it in his chapter entitled "Between Words and Music':

> …Sensitize a therapist to non-verbal cues and thereby do more skilfully what he or she may do intuitively, such as bring out a non-verbalized affect, introduce a new facet of personality or prevent a premature closure. (2004: 7–8)

Rose also says that:

> …Verbal interpretations, useful as they are at times, often leave untouched the emotional material that has not been linked to words. (2004: 6)

He speaks about material from a person's life that comes from a place when words were not available. His examples are, for instance, painful aspects that are delinked to, somatised and associated with a nonverbal system, which has never had the opportunity of being expressed in a verbal manner. In these instances he describes how the emotion linked to this experience can first of all be most easily understood in a nonverbal way. However, he goes on to say that it is important to employ verbal expression in a session in order to

> …Disentangle faulty verbal connections that reflect emotional confusion. (Ibid 2004: 6–7)

At a recent trauma conference reported to me, it was stated (backed up and well documented by research in neuroscience) that traumas that happened to the child under the age of seven were experienced on the right side of the brain, the seat of the emotions and the nonverbal. After about seven years of age, these experiences were placed or located on the left side, which is that of words. It would therefore follow that for understanding early trauma, treatment that is based in the nonverbal might be highly appropriate. This, I think is where the arts therapies have a valuable role to play in helping people with trauma experience. The use of improvised music together in music therapy or the use of images in art therapy, closely associated with free association and dream work in psychotherapy, seem to me to be a highly effective way of working with trauma.

On the nature of music

George Steiner (1997) writes about the nature of music in relation to language. He states:

> Its forms in motion are at once more immediate and freer than those of language … music can house contradictions, reversals of temporality, mutually denying moods and pulses of feeling and all these can coexist within the same overall movement… (1997: 65)

In my practice as a music therapist these above elements, especially within free improvisation, often in contradiction to one another (like aspects of life!), are clearly present. They are also evident in attending to the nonverbal dimensions of a psychotherapy conversation such as tone, rhythm, tempo, volume, gesture, the soothing regularities or jarring irregularities of pitch, the singsong way of speaking and so forth. Paying attention to all these elements, both in their musicality and spoken language, helps me to place myself with the suffering of others. It connects with my own experience and allows me to be, in some way, alongside.

Finally, the words of Khan (1923):

> The word in itself is frequently insufficient to express meaning clearly. The student of language by keen study can discover this. Even modern languages are but a simplification of music. No words in any language can be spoken in one and the same way without the distinction of tone, pitch, rhythm, accent, pause and rest. A language, however simple, cannot exist without music in it; music gives it a concrete expression.

References

Baron-Cohen, S. (2003) *The Essential Difference*. New York, NY: Basic Books.

Bollas, C. (2000) *Hysteria*. London, England: Routledge.

Khan, H. I. (1923) Cited and referenced in: Knoblauch, S. H. (2000) *The Musical Edge of Therapeutic Dialogue*. Burlingame, CA: The Analytic Press, Inc.

Langer, S. (1942) *Philosophy in a New Key*. Cambridge, MA: Harvard University Press.

Rose, G. (2004) *Between Couch and Piano: Psychoanalysis, Music, Art and Neuroscience.* United Kingdom: Brunner-Routledge.

Roustang, F. (1982) *Dire Mastery: Discipleship from Freud to Lacan* (Trans. Ned Lukacher). Baltimore, MD: The John Hopkins University Press.

Steiner, G. (1997) *Errata; An Examined Life.* London, England: Phoenix.

Stern, D. (2010) *Forms of Vitality.* Oxford, England: Oxford University Press.

Zinkin, L. (1991) The Klein connection in the London School: The search for origins. *Journal of Analytical Psychology* 36: 37–61.

13

THE MATERNAL AND THE EROTIC

An exploration of the links between maternal and erotic subjectivity

Christina Moutsou

For my children, Marcus and Violet who teach me how to be a mother every day.

LOSS[1]

A baby with staring eyes in a room full of afternoon sun
Breasts full of milk
Come baby, I am ready for you
Dribbling, dribbling, dribbling with milk
Eat baby eat
Fragile skin against my skin
Gently rocking you in my arms
How I miss your baby smell
Ice cream texture, vanilla and berries
Jaws that open looking for milk
Kleinian nonsense, breast is only good
Listening to your little cries makes me feel alive
My baby talks to me
Nothing in the world compares to this
Oval face attached to my breast
Praying that it will last forever
Questions creep in: How will it end?
Rock a bye baby in the tree top
Strong little legs kicking up the floor
Tired big eyes shutting again
United still, we are drifting apart
Violet shadows all over our face

Weaning you for now, but not for ever
You are asleep snuggled up in sweet powder smells
X factor beauty in your dreamy face
Zzz, sleep baby, sleep.

Introduction

The image of a baby sucking at the breast is the prototype of all relationships
of love.

(Freud 1940a [1938])

I wrote the poem above in the context of a therapeutic writing workshop, which
I attended in the summer of 2011, in an attempt to get to grips with some very
powerful feelings that I was experiencing at the time. We were asked to write a
poem using all letters of the English alphabet in the right sequence and trying
to describe all the senses involved as close as possible. Writing it proved both
therapeutic and poignant, as the title came before I knew what the content of the
poem would be, yet the breastfeeding experience is I would argue, when it works,
one of the closest to the adult feeling of falling in love and both breastfeeding
and falling in love can be connected with loss in the anticipation of the inevitable
ending of such blissful state.

I am using the poem above as a preamble to what I want to say in this
chapter in relation to the maternal, which in many ways is what matters to me
the most. In the first part, I will explore the myth of Athena as a disavowal of
the maternal and its links with my personal history. I will also look at some
of the common stereotypes of the maternal in psychoanalysis and in popular discourse. Such stereotypes had resonance in my own upbringing and the
ways in which I developed a gendered identity. They are also heavily relied on
and used within the psychoanalytic discourse and cultural constructions of the
maternal in Western societies. I will argue that such stereotypes move within
the Madonna-Whore axis, which inhibits women from finding creative ways to
inhabit maternal subjectivity.

In the second part of the chapter, I will explore Winnicott's idea that the baby's
hallucinating of the breast is the base of human creativity. I will slightly twist this
idea by suggesting that the baby's hallucination that he can produce a breast full
of milk as a result of the power of his mind is also the base of erotic connection
with another, to which human creativity has obvious links. Breasts are powerful
in cultural imagination as well as in psychoanalysis, yet their link with the erotic
is often underexplored. I will look at the links between the Kleinian breast and
patriarchy as well as a possible alternative of women reconnecting symbolically
with their breasts and primal creativity through supportive relationships with
other women.

I use the term 'erotic' and 'erotic subjectivity' in his chapter in the way Mann (1997) defines them, as separate and to a large degree autonomous from sexual expression and activity. For although sexuality, as Freud suggested, is the adult expression of the working through of these first infantile longings, 'erotic subjectivity' is a universal human experience which is and can be independent from sexuality, and yet it is often confused with sexual expression, and as a result, it is often feared and censored as potentially destructive.

Psychoanalysis became known in popular discourses for its struggle to tackle issues around the erotic transference. In its early days, Freud almost brought it to a premature end because of his 'discovery' of the erotic transference. Part of my thinking in this chapter is that the so-called erotic transference is not only an occasional complication of psychoanalytic practice, but that the erotic and one's erotic subjectivity are inevitably implicated in some way in any therapeutic relationship that is worth having. I do not mean by that that there should always be an 'erotic transference' in the therapeutic relationship and certainly this is not the case in my clinical experience. What I mean is that questions around longing, vulnerability, one's connection and attunement (or lack of) with an other are all linked with our primal senses and bodily subjectivity and they are all absolutely central in any significant and potentially transformative relationship as well as implicated in our creative engagement with the world.

Stereotypes of the mother

Some thoughts on the myth of Athena

The story of Athena is the story of my coming to the world. Athena was gestated in her father's head, after he swallowed her pregnant mother, Metis, the goddess of the ocean. She was born as a grown woman fully armoured and ready for the battle. Athena was her father's favourite child. She was a cerebral goddess, the goddess of wisdom. Athena had no mother. She did not need one. Amber Jacobs remarks on the myth of Athena:

> [The myth of Athena] I consider to be the prototypical patriarchal myth representing the obliteration and appropriation of the mother's capacities in the service of the masculine project of the colonisation of knowledge and generative power. It can be read as a story of the origins of patriarchy. By introducing the famous myth of Zeus' parturition into the discussion of the Oresteia, I suggest that an examination of the links between the phantasy of male parthenogenesis and the phantasy of oral incorporation bring us closer to a theoretical understanding of the subordination of the mother in Western discourses and the cultural imaginary ... Athena, the literal brainchild of her omnipotent father, Zeus, has a very special relation to matricide. It is her

birthright. That is to say, her unique status as her father's daughter, born from the head of the god of gods, came about through a brutal act of violence against her mother (Metis), whose name neither she, nor Zeus, nor Freud (who was very interested in Athena, as I shall discuss later) will ever mention.

(Jacobs 1997: 62–63)

The message in the story is: who needs a woman in order to bring a child in the world? Also, who needs a mother in order to be a powerful woman? Who needs a mother in order to be loved and favoured? Athena was a one-dimensional woman. She was powerful and influential, but she did not have an erotic side to her personality. She was also never to become a mother herself. Athena was uncomplicated and successful in her life. In that sense, one could get the message that to the degree that a woman can abstain from the maternal, to the degree that a woman can avoid getting entangled in the mother-daughter dyad at either end of the spectrum, she can afford to be a grown woman in her own right, fully armoured and in charge of her life. Athena's mother, Metis who was swallowed up and vanished ruled the realm of water, emotions, vastness, chaos, fluidity. We can exist, the myth tells us, in the world of adulthood, we can even be endorsed, if we are to fully accept patriarchal rationality and reason and suppress the dark side associated with womanhood, the fluid world of emotions.

Jacobs' analysis of the myth points out its significance in establishing patriarchal authority as opposed to more archaic systems celebrating the goddess of fertility, Mother Earth. Jacobs focusses on the story of Metis, Athena's mother, which has become silenced and incorporated in the myth of Athena. Here it is in her words:

> Zeus took as his first wife Metis the Titaness, priestess of all knowledge and wisdom. In Hesiod's words, 'Zeus lusted after Metis who did not reciprocate his feelings. In order to escape his advances, Metis changed into all different forms but was unsuccessful and was subsequently caught by Zeus and got his child'. Before she gave birth to Athena, Zeus, 'with slippery words, coaxed Metis on to a couch and there and then swallowed her whole. In his belly Metis then gave him council, spoke to him from inside of him giving him all her knowledge and wisdom' ... And that is the end of Metis. She is never heard of or referred to again. She will remain in the belly of Zeus, source of his knowledge and wisdom, incorporated and digested into the lining of his stomach. (1997: 63)

Jacobs remarks:

> Zeus achieves his power through rape, incorporation, and appropriation of the woman/mother. He cannibalises Metis in order to rob her of her

knowledge and wisdom, together with her reproductive capacity. From then on, she is silent and invincible, an internal source of power that Zeus will claim as his own. Her existence is obliterated so that not even her daughter will ever know of the maternal body in which she was originally conceived. Zeus, in his violent operation, succeeds in taking total possession of the (m)other, whose power he both envies and desires. His initial lust or desire for Metis quickly turns into aggression that results in rape, followed by incorporation. He moves the womb of Metis into his brain. (63)

Jacobs makes an important distinction between the notions of incorporation and introjection. She remarks that incorporation is a fantasy while introjection[2] is a process:

> Incorporation defends against introjection. In the process of introjection, the loss of the loved object is acknowledged and mourned, allowing for the loss to be converted into words. It is through the process of introjection that loss becomes generative. Incorporation however, is a phantasy that functions to deny that there has been any loss at all ... The name of Metis signifies the eradicated: she is the limit of representation, the negative, the empty foundation of meaning – the point at which knowledge reaches its blindness. (64–65)

In my family, there was no possible imagery of the Mother as a good model for me to grow into, the kind of mother I could grow up to be. This gave me the place of Athena within the family, the blessed one who could escape from the struggle of motherhood, from her own desire to be mothered and her impulse to mother others. Going back to the story of Athena, I would suggest that Athena was constructed as an ideal, an improved model of her father, and consequently of the male imaginary. Like him she was powerful, intelligent and wise. Unlike him, she had not had to struggle with the longing for a mother and its possible consequences of managing one's desires, one's sexuality, one's complicated relationships with intimate others. It was precisely intimacy that Athena lacked, and such lack of intimacy and a need or a desire for it was what made her invincible.

Like most people, I found my way to therapy when my repressed vulnerability caught up with me; when I could no longer pretend that I did not need a mother or that there was a safe distance between me and desires and longings that felt dangerous and threatening to my equilibrium. It was at that moment that the question of the maternal opened up for me. It was not that I then started to desire to become a mother myself (although it took that form as well), but it was that by going to therapy, I placed myself in relation to the maternal and its implications of opening oneself up to deep connection, vulnerability and loss.

The Madonna-whore axis through the lens of a Greek fairy tale from Skyros

A friend of mine who has studied Modern Greek literature brought to my attention the following fairytale from the Greek island of Skyros, as she thought that it relates to my personal history and some of the main arguments in this chapter. Here is an abbreviated version:

> A young girl of seven is very fond of her teacher who wants to marry the girl's father. She persuades the girl that if she were to be her mother, she would treat her much better. The girl says: 'But I already have a mother!' She then persuades the girl to kill her mother by asking her to fetch walnuts from a marble case and letting the heavy lid of the case fall on her mother's head as she is leaning down. The teacher then marries the father, and becomes increasingly mean towards the girl. She forces the girl to marry a snake. The girl visits her mother's grave who gives her council advising her that she will have to suffer for her crime. Her mother tells her how to marry the snake and protect herself from the snake biting her. The snake turns out to be a prince and the girl falls pregnant with him. Her stepmother though badmouths the girl to the prince who asks her to leave. As she wanders pregnant in the wild, she meets a man who is a shadow, lives in the underworld and vanishes during the day. She manages to transform him into a prince; she has her baby and lives happily with him. The snake-prince eventually discovers that he was wrong to ask her to leave and looks for her. When he finds her, the girl is presented with the dilemma of having to choose between the snake prince and the shadow prince. She says that she loves them both and cannot choose and she then drops dead (suicide).
>
> *(Ioannou 1990)*

I am not in a position to know whether a version of the above fairytale can be found in any other European countries, however, although the murder of the daughter, usually by the stepmother, is a common theme in fairytales, matricide is not. For the purpose of this analysis, I would like to pick out some relevant themes. The girl is trapped in having to choose between two mothers that I would say, move in the Madonna-Whore axis. The teacher is ruthless and eager to seduce her father. Her mother is self-effacing and eager to please to the detriment of her comfort. She then finds herself in a similar dilemma in adult life, having to choose between the aggressive husband that she has managed to tame and rescuing the second man from the underworld. The impossibility of choosing between these two could be seen as the impasse young women face when having to place themselves at either end of the Madonna-Whore axis. An impasse that can only lead to self-destruction; so, in this case, matricide clearly leads to suicide or death of self.

In my childhood, as in psychoanalytic literature, there were many constructed images of the Mother. There was the 'the ice maiden mother', distant and remote, a control freak, obsessed with household duties and order. There was the 'whore mother', the mother for whom her sexuality and desires for self-pleasure were more important than her desire for the mothering work. These were the examples of a bad mother in my childhood, the ones that were to be avoided.

There was also 'the power mother', the mother who could sort it all out for you, and have it all under control and take care of you. And the 'doormat mother', the one who would absorb all bad feelings and acts of aggression, who had no identity of her own, she was there to be dumped upon. These last two mother images were more linked with my actual mother who was both a goddess and a dumping hole within the family. These were the images of a good mother. The last two images of a mother are also, I think, very powerful constructions of the 'good enough mother' within psychoanalysis, the mother who absorbs and the mother who takes care and processes.

Through looking at the myth of Medea, Welldon argues that the Whore mother and the Madonna mother are two facets of the same cultural tendency to idealise and denigrate motherhood, which leaves women subject to possible perversion in the form of self-harm or harm of their children.

> Medea ... exemplifies not only the power of motherhood, but also how the 'biological clock' determines a woman's actions. Medea is highly intelligent, in power, loved and in love. When abruptly and unexpectedly dispossessed of all this, she becomes aware of the only power left to her: her children, who become the targets for her revenge against their father, Jason. (1998: 83)

According to Welldon, Medea is not that different from the idealised image of the Madonna mother who can be completely selfless and a buffer for the baby's feelings. She says:

> My argument is that motherhood as a perversion occurs as a breakdown of inner mental structures, whereby the mother feels not only emotionally crippled in dealing with the huge psychological and physical demands from her baby, but also impotent and unable to obtain gratification from other sources. She sees the world around her as nonexistent in any helping, supporting way. It is then that she falls back on inappropriate or perverse behaviour ... Our whole culture supports the idea that mothers have complete dominion over their babies; thus we encourage the very ideas the perverse mother exploits. (83)

All the stereotypes of a mother flying around in my family followed the Madonna or Whore axis that Welldon eloquently describes, stereotypes imposed in the family culture through my father's unresolved issues with his own mother. Therefore, like the girl in the fairytale, I was trapped in the Madonna-Whore axis or I had to be coerced into being my father's exclusive gestational product, like Athena. Thankfully, through the process of therapy, I contemplated for the first time the possibility of becoming a mother and that it would not have to be part of the above destructive and self-destructive axis. Below, I will explore the question of maternal and erotic subjectivity, as an alternative to the stereotype of the mother in the Madonna-Whore axis.

The link of the maternal and the erotic as an alternative to matricide and suicide

Winnicott's idea of illusion and disillusionment and its links with the erotic

Many of the core concepts of classic psychoanalytic theory do not make sense to me when I try to match them up with my own development or my experience of being a mother. This is especially so in relation to Kleinian ideas, which often appear to me as a projection of the mother's depression and struggle onto the baby.

Winnicott's concept of illusion and disillusionment in relation to the breast not only makes sense to me, but it helped me explain and conceptualise my experience of breastfeeding two babies for almost two years each. Winnicott argues that the baby has to start with no concept of the breast as a separate object from her. Unlike Klein's conceptualisation, the breast for Winnicott is not an object that is offered and then withdrawn. The baby, Winnicott says, hallucinates of the breast, i.e., she conceptually creates a warm object full of milk as a response to the feeling of hunger. 'Good enough' mothering in early life is for Winnicott the ability to offer the Breast[3] in a way in which the baby understands that she is able to create/produce the breast as a result of her desire and the power of her mind.

> The mother, at the beginning, by an almost 100 per cent adaptation affords the infant the *illusion* that her breast is part of the infant. It is, as it were, under the baby's magical control ... Omnipotence is nearly a fact of experience. (1971: 11)
>
> ...the breast is created by the infant over and over again out of the infant's capacity to love or (one can say) out of need. A subjective phenomenon develops in the baby which we call the mother's breast. The mother places the actual breast just where the infant is ready to create, and at the right moment. (11)

Disillusionment is for Winnicott a gradual and developmental process, through which the baby realises that the breast is indeed a separate object and that it can be withdrawn temporarily or permanently.

The intermediate area to which I am referring is the area that is allowed to the infant between primary creativity and objective perception based on reality-testing … The transitional phenomena represent the early stages of the use of illusion, without which there is no meaning for the human being in the idea of a relationship with an object that is perceived by others as external to that being. (1971: 12)

Unlike for Klein however, for Winnicott disillusionment can only be a healthy developmental stage to the degree that illusion has become internalised and it has established itself as a potential state of mind throughout development.

The mother's eventual task is gradually to disillusion the infant, but she has no hope of success unless at first she has been able to give sufficient opportunity for illusion. (11)

Winnicott argues that establishing illusion is the source of human creativity. In other words, the belief that one can produce a good object as a result of the power of one's mind allows one to engage creatively in the world. As Adam Phillips remarks:

The infant in Winnicott's account discovers the world by first creating it; he is born an artist and a hedonist.

(Phillips 2007: 101)

The breast and patriarchy

One of the problems with classic psychoanalytic texts, and Winnicott is no exception here, although he shows significant distancing from classic theory in other parts of his writing, is that, in these texts, the Mother, and later on in Klein's theory, the Breast become the backdrop against which the development of an individual unfolds.

To the degree that the Mother in certain psychoanalytic texts is the only vehicle for the facilitating of human development, such representation of the Mother is not one of a real human being with weaknesses and vulnerabilities, with an ailing body and a subjective engagement with the world, but that of an omnipotent and yet, fallible being, who becomes the source of all human ailments.

Equally, in Kleinian theory, the Breast is the backdrop for the infant's frustration and paranoia and eventually for achieving the depressive position (Likierman 2001: 112–118). One could say that there is at least implicit here the acknowledgement that it is the Breast, as linked to women's capacity to produce milk and babies, the Breast as linked to women's primal creativity that is the object of murderous attack and envy on an interpersonal, political and cultural level. The Breast here is opposed to Freud's penis envy and Lacan's phallus, both implying that it is only men's potency that matters. Yet, the Breast is a function that in classic Kleinian theory is often there to reinforce patriarchy, to teach the raging infant its place in the world. The baby's desire for the breast is experienced in Kleinian theory as an attack on the mother, an attempt at introjection:

> Greed is an impetuous and insatiable craving, exceeding what the subject needs and what the object is able and willing to give. At the unconscious level, greed aims primarily at completely sucking out, scooping dry, and devouring the breast: that is to say, its aim is destructive introjection.
>
> *(Klein 1997[1975]: 181)*

Subsequently, the mother's place, right from the beginning of life, is to introduce separateness, to resist the baby's attacks through introjection and envy (1997 [1975]: 176–235). In this account, the baby is there to demand, guided by sadistic impulses right from birth, the interplay of the life and death instincts, and the mother is there to resist the baby's demands in order to survive its attacks. The baby is the Subject and the mother, and by extension the breast, is the Object. In other words, the Kleinian Breast is detached both from maternal subjectivity and from the acknowledgement of the mother's vulnerability that can only come to the fore, in my view, if she is to give in, even if temporarily and partially, to the infant's demands.

I have never become more consciously aware of patriarchy and its demands on women to preserve its values than when breastfeeding my toddler son on demand, during a summer family holiday in Greece, where I have been brought up. Before he reached that stage in his development, the full meaning of 'feeding on demand' had not become apparent to me in what had felt like an intersubjective dance of me offering and him seeking out the breast, often, but not invariably, in a way that felt very similar to Winnicott's description, in that he seemed to expect to find the breast when he wanted it and most of the time, he did. He was lucky to be a first born under relatively comfortable circumstances and so when at the beginning of his life he would often be at the breast for hours throughout the night while I dipped in and out of sleep, it had not felt like an intolerable impingement on me.

During that holiday, he was coming on his own, being a highly active sixteen-month-old, who was both vocal and keen to explore. When in between his explorations, he would run back to me and lifting my top, he would seek my breast, our encounter provoked an array of looks from bystanders, that at times seemed as shocked as if they were witnessing a scene of incest. I was not keen to make a deliberate hippy statement, and the issue had not cropped up before, when I had discreetly breastfed along with friends in London cafés. Yet, the outrage I sensed in the onlookers' faces during that holiday provoked the rebel in me. It felt like the message was clear, breasts were sexual, and as such the private objects of men, not something that women could choose to offer in public to active and mischievous toddlers. My mother-in-law discreetly gave me a lecture, how the boy was active and quite thin and should rely solely on food now, and not on my breast, but I felt the message, even if thinly disguised, was the same, it was ok for women to offer their breast privately as an object of sexual pleasure, or for that matter, as an object for the baby's nourishment, but not as part of an intersubjective dance of desire and attachment between a mother and a son (or daughter).

In her brilliant exposition of the phenomenology of breasts, Iris Marion Young remarks that the sexualisation of female breasts, as an object of desire and possession for men, results in the alienation of women from the multifaceted nature of their sexuality and also, from the links between female sexuality and motherhood. She observes that not wearing a bra is a taboo in Western societies, not because of the possibility of exposing the breast, she says that exposing cleavage or even a large part of the breast is both desirable and sought after in certain contexts, but because of exposing both the fluidity and misshapen nature of the female breast, but also, and primarily the nipple. She says:

> Breasts are a scandal because they shatter the border between motherhood and sexuality. Nipples are taboo because they are quite literally, physically, functionally undecidable in the split between motherhood and sexuality. One of the most subversive things feminism can do is affirm this undecidability of motherhood and sexuality.
>
> *(Young 2005: 88)*

Women and breasts

I would like to make a link here between the state of falling in love and the experience of breastfeeding for women and the intensity of feelings it can evoke. The experience of bliss that breastfeeding can give to women when it goes right as well as the experience of heartache when it goes wrong are surprising in intensity and can be remembered for a lifetime.[4] I have often been part in conversations where wry smiles were exchanged between breastfeeding mothers about the effects of oxytocin, the orgasm hormone, apparently released during breastfeeding. Such good experiences of the breastfeeding process by the mother agree with Lisa Baraitser's description of maternal love as an answer to the question: Why love a child?:

> Here we see that the mother is maintained as an actual other person, a person with sexual phantasies, with thoughts and feelings about her child. She is not just a container, a mirror or breast. Neither is she romanticised as part of a loving dyad or nursing couple. A transmission of something enigmatic and sexual takes place between mother and child prompted by the child's presence. In other words, the child calls something forth in the mother (the sucking experience affects the mother at physiological, psychological and

unconscious phantasy levels) that in its turn is returned to the child in coded form. Both parties are actively involved, although neither 'knows' what is going on. I think this usefully moves us closer to a description of *maternal love* that can include the unexpected, the enigmatic and unknowable, without reducing the mother to an object in the child's world, or romanticising the union between them. (2009: 96)

On the other hand, the experiences of women who found breastfeeding and/or other aspects of the early maternal physical connection to the baby torturous could be seen as a failure of the erotic. A friend of mine still talks with tears in her eyes, more than 10 years after the event, about how she could not produce enough milk for her daughter. Another said to me: 'I would give him my blood, but I could not give him my milk'. Another talked, again with tears in her eyes, about how she abruptly stopped breastfeeding when the baby kept biting her breast. She said that she felt attacked when at her most vulnerable. Bollas in his book *Hysteria* offers us an understanding of hysteria and the hysterical personality based on the failure of the erotic connection between mother and baby. He describes eloquently the many forms such connection takes in normal development:

> The mother's pleasure in breast-feeding joins the infant's pleasure in feeding, registered through the mutuality of gaze that is as star-crossed as any lovers. (1999: 42)
> It is not only through the breast-feed that the mother conveys her erotism. She bathes the infant in seductive sonic imagery, ooing, cooing and aahing, luring the infant's being from autistic enclave into desire for this voice. (1999: 43)

In her recently published in the UK novel, *After Birth*, Elisa Albert offers an alternative and potentially refreshing view:

> The main character, Ari wanders alone in desperation in the streets of NYC, pushing the buggy with her sleeping baby, following his birth by C section, a birth which was a disappointment to the mother. She is in what is described as a 'good enough' relationship with a supportive partner, yet it does not prove to be a remedy for the loneliness and intense depression she experiences as the enormity of the maternal task weighs on her along with being haunted by images of her super critical, now dead mother. The character's transformation comes through meeting another woman in despair following the birth of her own son who is failing to thrive through breastfeeding. Ari offers to breastfeed her friend's shrivelling baby and it is the camaraderie between the two women that lifts her out of her depressive state.
>
> *(Albert 2015a)*

In an article in the Saturday *Guardian Magazine* the day before mothering Sunday, Elisa Albert reveals the truth behind the story in the novel. Her baby son was failing to thrive in the postpartum period during which she felt increasingly neglected and unsupported, yet determined that breastfeeding was the only way. It was a friend's remark in passing that she could breastfeed her baby for her that created an opening through her impasse. Allowing her friend to breastfeed her baby took her by surprise, not only because she managed to acknowledge it as an act of kindness, but also because her trust in her relationship with other women, including her own mother, had been historically low. This, she argues, left her with idealised hopes about what she could get from other women she wanted to be close to, and mistrust in exposing herself when feeling vulnerable for fear of being let down. She says:

> I began to understand women better – that there are those of us who have a nurturing resource in our own mother, and those who do not; those who can talk about inhabiting their bodies, and those who cannot; those who are open about their struggles and ambivalence, and those who feign control; those who are lucky enough to be loved and cared for in vulnerability, and those who are not.
>
> *(Albert 2015b: 29)*

Finally, she concludes the article with an account of the potential of female friendship to harbour vulnerability and through it to create a profound life-changing experience:

> …The more vulnerable I remained, the clearer my vision became, and what I could see, at long last, was a circle of woman comrades, offering me fortitude and nourishment… (29)

In conclusion: maternal and erotic subjectivities

To conclude, I would like to suggest that it is the mother's erotic link with the baby through connecting with the primal creativity in her birthing, mothering, breastfeeding capacity, that is, through wonder and love of her own body in its vulnerability that can provide an alternative to matricide or the Madonna-Whore axis. Whether she finds this through her relationship with a supportive partner or in allowing the possibility of trust to emerge in her relationships with other women or in giving space to her subjective and imperfect engagement with the baby, and usually through a combination of all three differs according to the circumstances of individual women.

Winnicott's weakness as a theoretician, as it has been argued, is the almost complete lack of mention of sexuality as well as the lack of conceptualising the importance of the father in his writing (Phillips 2007: 6–7). As a result, 'the good enough' mother sometimes appears to be not an ordinary woman but a figure of extraordinary perfection. However, another reading of Winnicott is that he was the first to observe the process of maternal subjective engagement with the baby and its links with erotic love (Phillips 2007: xi). This comes across very clearly in his rather humorous list of the reasons for which a mother hates her baby. Here they are:

A. The baby is not her own (mental) conception.

B. The baby is not the one of childhood play, father's child, brother's child, etc.

C. The baby is not magically produced.

D. The baby is a danger to her body in pregnancy and at birth.

E. The baby is an interference to her private life, a challenge to preoccupation.

F. To a greater or lesser extent, a mother feels that her own mother demands a baby, so the baby is produced to placate her mother.

G. The baby hurts her nipples, even by suckling, which is at first, a chewing activity.

H. He is ruthless, treats her as scum, an unpaid servant, a slave.

I. She has to love him, excretions and all, at any rate at the beginning, till he has doubts about himself.

J. He tries to hurt her, periodically bites her, all in love.

K. He shows disillusionment about her.

L. His excited love is cupboard love, so that having got what he wants, he throws her away like orange peel.

M. The baby at first must dominate, he must be protected from coincidences, life must unfold at the baby's rate and all this needs his mother's continuous and detailed study. For instance, she must not be anxious when holding him, etc.

N. At first, he does not know at all what she does or what she sacrifices for him. Especially he cannot allow for her hate.

O. He is suspicious, refuses her good food, and makes her doubt herself, but eats well with his aunt.

P. After an awful morning with him, she goes out and he smiles at a stranger who says: 'Isn't he sweet!'

Q. If she fails him at the start she knows he will pay her out for ever.

R. He excites her but frustrates her. She mustn't eat him or trade in sex with him.

(Winnicott 1949: 355)

It is not a long leap between Winnicott's list of Mother's reasons for hating her baby and the states of mind familiar to most people from love stories, where there is culminating frustration at the torturous experience of being in love with an often unavailable or ungratifying subject. I want to argue here that the most obvious link to Winnicott's concept of the baby hallucinating and magically producing the breast is with erotic subjectivity as often experienced in mental states of 'falling in love'. Classic psychoanalysis is mostly suspicious and critical of falling in love as well as the erotic transference, which starting from Freud and even further accentuated through Klein's work is seen as a defence and a disavowal of the death instinct. Johnson puts the question forward:

> Why does falling in love provoke such intense, negative feelings, such as jealousy and possessiveness, greed, rage, sadism and masochism, rivalry and competition, and extremes of idealisation and denigration?
>
> *(Johnson 2010: 3)*

Much has been said about the hallucinatory nature of erotic feelings. It is not a coincidence that most classic love stories end up in the death of the lovers. One possible interpretation of this is that the lovers are being punished for seeking out bliss, or that loss and death are inevitably entailed in the erotic connection as well as the experience of erotic subjectivity.

This felt evident to me when writing the poem on loss. The end of breastfeeding had sadly become intertwined with other previous significant losses I had experienced in my life, such as the fact that I had never been breastfed myself and the recent death of my father. It felt at the time that the fact I had allowed myself to become vulnerable through bonding with my children and giving myself and body to them would almost inevitably bring about my own death, if not literally, which at times I feared, at least in the sense of suffering an intolerable and unrecoverable loss. Of course, partly the experience of being a mother is about allowing for the connection while submitting to and facilitating a series of losses of one's identity and potential claims over the baby. Yet, the hope is that through allowing for the vulnerability that a close connection with another inevitably entails, women can connect and access their primal creativity as a source of joy and pleasure.

Notes

1 I can strongly relate to Elisa Albert's statement that: '…I seemed to want so much more from women than I ever wanted from men – I wanted the world. So I was often that much more disappointed' (Albert 2015b: 27). Taking this into account, I would like to thank three women who, in different ways, were pivotal in the writing of this chapter. Barbara Latham for being there as my therapist at the time I first became a mother, Ros Mayo for years of intense, heartfelt and at times challenging collaboration and friendship that gave birth to this book and Sofia Makri, for life-enduring friendship and insightful conversation as well as letting me know about the Greek fairytale analysed in this chapter, just at the right moment. I would also like to thank Adam Phillips for providing a stimulating and inspiring environment during the time I wrote the first draft of this chapter.

2 Introjection has been used as a term extensively in Kleinian theory. Here, it is referred to quite literally as a dyadic process that acknowledges the existence of a(n) (M)Other, as opposed to incorporation that aims to eradicate the (M)Other.

3 What is referred to here as 'the Breast' is, I am assuming, the presence of the mother who provides nourishment in a way that is sensitive to and attuned with the baby's needs.

4 There is very convincing and now widely known research that shows that breastfeeding gives the best chance of a good start in life for the baby as well as the best medium for mother-child bonding. However, it is worth remembering that breastfeeding per se, such as many other forms of mothering, are culture, class and historicity specific. In the 1970s when I was born, much fewer middle class women in the Western world would breastfeed their babies. Breastfeeding was portrayed as inferior and primitive as well as restricting of the mother's freedom from a feminist perspective (see Lucy King's chapter in this book). The medicalisation of the mother's body including the birth process and breastfeeding were and still are significant factors in problems with establishing breastfeeding after birth. See Fairbank et al.:

> Much of the widespread early discontinuation of breastfeeding that has occurred over the subsequent decades may be attributable to practices that medicalised breastfeeding, such as separation of mothers and babies, restrictions of 4-hourly feeds, test-weighing, and giving of supplementary bottles of artificial food to breastfeeding babies. (2000: 4)

In contemporary Britain, the table is reversed and increasingly the general consensus between middle class women is that breastfeeding is the only way, but this is much less so among their working class counterparts (Ibid 2000: 3). The danger here is that breastfeeding seen as the only way can become a tyranny, like so many others that young mothers put themselves through rather than a chance for creative engagement between mother and child. Lastly, breastfeeding most often takes place between an infant and its biological mother, yet it is not my intention to assume that any other form of mothering such as adoption or same sex parenting is inferior.

References

Albert, E. (2015a) *After Birth*. London, England: Chatto & Windus.

Albert, E. (2015b) Mother's milk: Why my friend fed my baby, *The Guardian Magazine* 14/3/15, 20–29.

Baraitser, L. (2009) *Maternal Encounters: The Ethics of Interruption*. London, England: Routledge.

Bollas, C. (1999) *Hysteria*. London, England: Routledge.

Fairbank, L., O'Meara S., Renfrew M.J., Woolridge M., Sowden A.J., and Lister-Sharp, D. A. (2000) Systematic review to evaluate the effectiveness of interventions to promote the initiation of breastfeeding. *Health Technol Assess* 4(25).

Ioannou, G. (1990) *Fairy Tales of Our Country*. Athens, Greece: Hermes.

Jacobs, A. (2007) *On Matricide: Myth, Psychoanalysis and the Law of the Mother*. New York, NY: Columbia University Press.

Johnson, D. (2010) *Love: Bondage or Liberation? A Psychological Exploration of the Meaning, Values and Dangers of Falling in Love*. London, England: Karnac.

Klein, M. (1997 [1975]) *Envy and Gratitude and Other Works 1946–1963*. London, England: Vintage.

Likierman, M. (2001) *Melanie Klein: Her Work in Context*. London, England: Continuum.

Mann, D. (1997) *Psychotherapy: An Erotic Relationship*. London, England: Routledge.

Phillips, A. (2007) *Winnicott*. London, England: Penguin Books.

Welldon, E. V. (2004) *Mother, Madonna, Whore: The Idealization and Denigration of Motherhood*. London, England: Karnac.

Winnicott, D. W. (1949) Hate in the countertransference. *International Journal of Psychoanalysis* 30: 69–74.

Winnicott, D. W. (1971) *Playing and Reality*. London, England: Tavistock Publications Ltd.

Young, I. M. (2005) Breasted experience: the look and the feeling. In: *On Female Body Experience: 'Throwing Like a Girl' and Other Essays*. Oxford, England: Oxford University Press.

14

HOW SHALL WE TELL EACH OTHER OF OUR MOTHERS?

Rosalind Mayo

Maternal epistemologies

> When my boat comes in we'll have some of those pink fondant sweets with the hazelnuts on top.[1]

At the kitchen table, stories of the past, the living and the dead, were told and retold. The telling was a remembering, and a reminiscing. Unwelcome beginnings and lost childhoods, the sacrifices, and the getting by the best you can. Stories of worlds that had passed leaving only their memories and their wounds. And sometimes, that awful wishing, that maybe, if things could have been different. And the rest – it was all the bits and pieces that make up all lives. Perhaps it was a way many people went over and collected up those strange fragments that had been, and were their lives, and from the telling made a recognizable story, one they could see themselves in, and live with.

A story my mother told

The woman settled down
And the child,
sensing something of importance to come
grows very still,
and the woman begins her story.
It was the day before Empire Day.[2]
Kathleen O'Shaunessy leant her tired body against the gate, and turned her face
    towards the late afternoon sun.
The thin awkward looking child was in no hurry and approached slowly.

'You've got a visitor Lillia, a man, been there some time.'

A visitor was an unusual event, but the girl's mind was on food, she was often hungry. She did not reply.

'I'll come and see Jimmy Boy later Mrs O'Shaunessy'.

Jimmy had his legs in irons, and did not go to school. Lillia helped him with his reading, and afterwards she was allowed to play their piano.

Kathleen O'Shaunessy was a woman of few words and trusted in the small community.

Like her mother, and grandmother, she was a seamstress, which kept her and her son in the things that were needed, and no more. She had one small secret pleasure, her piano.

At quiet moments when everything else was done, she sat down to play.

It was, for anyone watching her, a visible experience of pleasure which rippled down her dimpled arms, to her pin pricked finger tips, and as her toes touched and tipped over the piano pedals, her face became smooth, as if someone had recently run the flat iron across the deeply etched frown lines of her usual cautious look at the world.

An extraordinary sound filled the small room, like a feeling of something set free, and it ran through the whole of that dark damp building with its long and heavy memories.

The neighbours said nothing. Very few of them had a piano left to play these days, but they too experienced the feeling, like something soaring.

For the child, this would become her secret pleasure too.

Inside the long dimly lit hallway the smell of stewed apples and moth balls hung in the air, she was almost beside him before she realised someone was standing there. She felt the smell of him, the way men smell, though she didn't know many men beside her uncles, and they always smelt of shaving soap and shoe polish. The damp air clung to the coarse wool of his jacket and she caught his slow deep breathing, as though he was sleeping, his arms folded, he leant against the half open parlor door, looking like the men who wait outside the saloon door of The Worlds End, waiting for opening time, or just waiting.

He did not speak to the girl, but glanced at her, sideways; she thought long afterwards, he didn't actually look at her, or see her. Her aunt appeared in the doorway and pointed her towards the kitchen, through the half open parlor door she glimpsed her mother with her head on the table crying. Cold apples were pushed towards her.

'They are left over from the Maud's lunch'.

Aunt was in service with the Maud's she was their head cook.

'Who is the man aunt, why is mum crying?'

Her Aunt's neck was covered in pink blotches, a look the child knew well enough to keep quiet, it usually led to her aunt saying things were all too much for a maiden woman who never asked for any of this.

She ate the apples in silence.

'Your mother will be alright, she's had a shock that's all.'

Sensing it might be alright to say something, the girl asked again, 'Who is the man aunt, what does he want, is that why my mum is crying?'

'He's your father Lillia.'

The child didn't really like stewed apples.

'But my father's dead. We've just got uncles.'

'His name is Walter Trelawney and he is your father, for what it's worth,' she added, almost to herself.

'Does he know who I am, does he want to see me?'

Long after that day, the girl thought that she didn't really know if she did want to see him anyway. The front door slammed.

'No Lillia he doesn't know you, or want to see you'.

The girl remembered crying but didn't know why, and remembered her aunt comforting her. Later, when aunt had gone to the Maud's, she went to see Jimmy Boy. Jimmy's Dad went missing before he was born. After his reading, she played the piano.

She didn't tell Jimmy her father had been to see her.

And this was the way the nine-year-old girl came to remember it.

Years later when she had wanted to ask more about that day, it was too late, and the one person who she had loved more than anyone in the world, her aunt, had died too.

And with her, the story of who she was.

But in the meantime a story had grown up about him, as stories do in families. Walter Trelawney was Irish from County Mayo, a freedom fighter for Ireland's independence, a hero.

The question was Lillia.

Who was she for, why was she here.

Questions that stayed with her throughout her life.

The woman finished

The story ends

And the child

Who is me

Gets up and moves away.

Not knowing what to do with a story about my mother's life.[3]

Each of us is a story largely told by others, and our living is its telling.

We are born into a world of M/others: Into the desires and embrace of others.

We belong to other times, other than the present. The history, stories, dreams and longings, unlived lives, and lost lives of others, are a part of the ground of our being, embodied in our desires and choices and loves, and where we find ourselves unloved, or cannot love. These m/other lives will colour the texture and tenor of our own life, consciously and unconsciously.

Whether we recognize that we owe these m/others something, perhaps a great deal, that is, and will always remain, unknown and unquantifiable, will depend on many things. Recognition of difference, recognition of lives lived at a specific point in time and culture, which will have shaped those lives, as it now shapes our own: recognition of failure and disappointment, recognition of their loss, and ours with them, and mourning. And the recognition that we are already, from the start, given over, beyond ourselves (Butler 2006: 22–23), beyond the I and the other, and the other of the I, implicated in the lives of many others, their helplessness and vulnerabilities, and our own, intratwined.

One of the central focuses of feminists' early consciousness raising groups in the 1970s was the practice of speaking about one's own experience and history as a woman. It struck me as a rather scary practice. Some women were inevitably more outspoken, brave perhaps, and bold, less inhibited, I was not one of those.

Speaking, in a sometimes large group of women, about one's history and personal life and experience, which often focused on relationships and family, could be empowering, the word used in those days. But if you thought speaking to a group of women was going to be easy you could be mistaken. Responses were not always as generous as one might have secretly wished for, but blame was not usually a feature of the groups, and more often support was given, to overcome doubts and fears. On the whole, it was a strangely satisfying moment of hearing oneself speaking about one's life and experience, however self-selected and guarded. It was a revealing act, one in which you stood open before and to others, vulnerable and exposed, and this sense it was a relational act, one which could flounder or flourish.

From it there came a sense of connectedness, and of differences, many differences, and the struggle to find ways to think and speak about these, although these were frequently pushed aside, or talked down, in the eagerness, and fear, to share and feel united. And it did mean that many questions and difficulties, and differences of views and experience, were either denied or silenced, one of these was the feelings of rivalry and envy that from time to time surfaced in the groups. But one of the points of the group, if not the main purpose, was to create a space to speak, to tell one's story. It was a political space, and a social space in which to imagine and discuss other possibilities, to create new vocabularies, to imagine change and create changes, for political action and engagement, other visions and ideas for our lives and society, other images of women's lives and experiences. The narration of one's own story acted at many levels: personal, political, ethical, social, pedagogical, psychological and creative – a co-generative act.

Whilst some women were already mothers, the focus then was the legal rights over one's body: women's sexuality, birth control, abortion; and women's rights for work, equal wages, education, and equality under the law, particularly in marriage and divorce and property law. There were lots of discussions about relationships with mothers, and fathers, and whilst some women pulled no punches, many were uncertain and uncomfortable. It often appeared to be easier to speak about fathers, and to express ambivalent feelings; whereas talk about one's mother seemed to present even then, some unfathomable obstacles that were not easy to think about, let alone articulate and define for most women, especially where it related to sexuality, and having, or wanting, a different life than one's mother.

Feelings of betrayal and anger sat uneasily with the wish for independence, freedom and the wish to be different; mothers it seemed 'held you back', either in reality, or fantasy, or both, passing on her own unconscious compliance, resentment and sexual repression, through expressions of criticism, envy and aggression. Somehow she had to be got free of and left behind. So much we had yet to learn!

At this time most feminists (except in France) were very ambivalent about taking up psychoanalysis. And yet the aims of the feminist project at this time to uncover repressed female histories, myths, stories, images of other women's lives, and to push sexuality to the front of the political agenda, ironically shared some of the intentions and scope of psychoanalysis.

In the United States, Freud was rejected, until a reworking began in the 1980s, whilst many British feminists were influenced by socialism, of one kind or another, drawing on Marx and class history and the formation of female subjectivity. A surge in women's/feminist writing about mothers and daughters began in the late 1970s and early 1980s. Looking back now to this vibrant period, the narratives and discourse on the mother, where not drawing on the psychoanalytic narrative, seemed to fall into two distinct questions: The mother was either someone who had to be got away from, and free of, either because she was too powerful and controlling – the phallic mother. Or because she was too passive, weak, and self-effacing – the abject mother.

Both of which rather eerily pick up the psychoanalytic story of the mother. This particular trajectory on the mother continued in some form for many years despite the much earlier groundbreaking text of Adrienne Rich, *Of Woman Born*, and her powerful insight that what all women really needed and longed for was a mother who could love them unreservedly. The resistance to this powerful message has been persistent through the years that followed, as if none of us dared to admit to this longing and its risks.

But alongside of this was another idea, one with a much longer history, stemming from the philosophy of the enlightenment period that found its way into psychoanalysis: Attaining adult subjectivity and maturity, sometimes referred to as individuation, or autonomy, is premised upon separation from the mother. What this word separation meant and went on to mean within this discourse, whilst very different for men and women, has been the central and driving force of the succeeding years in any discussion of the mother and daughter relationship, and female-maternal subjectivity. No matter how misunderstood the concept, its history, and its interpretation, and tragic its implications.

Despite all the variations on the theme of mothers and daughters it seemed as if all daughters were inevitably condemned to being disappointed, at the least, in their mother. And she, who was she, this woman constantly summoned up as the cause of her daughter's sadness, badness, abandonment, depression, anorexia, hysteria and dysfunction of any kind. No one asked.

Some of the United States black womanist/feminists had a different story. The mother was and could be someone whose life and history should and could be remembered and drawn upon for one's own life, however different. Her history and her stories were meant to inspire, and to enable her daughters to recreate new images for the present and the future. But more than this, they were histories and stories of women/mother lives not to be forgotten and discarded as no longer of any use to the present; here was a redemptive power to memory, for the past and the future.

This same impulse was also being drawn upon by feminists in theology at the time, not as a glorification of the past and its pain, but the recognition that comes from reclaiming the stories of the past, something that Alice Walker and Toni Morrison, among many others, embodied in their work, something that was needed for the present, in order to live. The most significant difference then, about womanist theories of female/maternal subjectivity, was that it did not present the development of adult subjectivity as dependent upon separation from the mother, indeed the very opposite![4]

A story of a mother and a daughter

Landscape for a Good Woman (LFGW) was first published in 1986, against a background of texts on mother-daughter narratives, predominantly from white, middle class contexts, detailing middle class maternal-daughter experience and subjectivity. And this was one of the motivations for Steedman's book. I read the book then, and many times since, because it offered to me as a feminist socialist a narrative not much in evidence then of the complexities of the lives of women and mothers from other cultural backgrounds.[5] I was researching the closing of the coal pits in the East Midlands, North of England and Wales, and the effects of this on the lives of the women.

At the time Steedman's text offered a radical critique of the then acclaimed *Ethics of Care* (Gilligan 1982), a text that was much influenced by the work of Nancy Chodorow (1978) and others. *LFGW* describes a world I was born into: Ration books, listening to the wireless, queuing for food, ice cream as a treat on a Sunday afternoon, few new clothes, and so sewing, darning and repairing, shoes polished and repaired, and small treats, a fresh peach, if I was good girl from the man with no legs.

It was a world still living through the effects of two world wars, particularly the effects on individual lives and memories. I grew up in this world in my early years, safe and loved, in the then genteel backwaters of Cambridge, with a maternal grandmother, and a much loved aunt and uncle. Stories were a part of my life, what I heard from the adults talking at the supper table and together in the evenings.

I grew up convinced that somehow I had been a part of the Second World War, so present were the stories and memories that those kind, quite ordinary people still remembered, and I overheard. Later it was stories from my mother, and later still, a little, from my father.

Historians have focused on the 'heroes and heroines' of those years, and the larger pictures, and rarely taken into account just how much those events shaped and effected the lives of ordinary people who had lived through it, long after it was all over.[6] There was a country to rebuild, and people wanted, understandably, to move on, but memories and their effects stayed. The world of my early childhood is now gone, but it was one that never quite existed in the way it is remembered, making its memory now all the more intense and bittersweet.[7]

Steedman's text is complex, with its interweaving of economics, politics, class, autobiography and memoir, and an analysis of psychoanalytic theory on the mother-daughter relationship, and female desire. Her primary purpose in the book was to detail the specific economic, cultural and social context of her family, and their lives, to its psychological inscription, and their effects.

At the time the book was published almost all the texts available that articulated some form of working class culture and life were authored by men. These authors had usually 'moved on' from their backgrounds to other lives. And their perceptions, whilst not wholly inaccurate, were shaped as much by gender, as by a nostalgia and romanticism of the period and that culture, in particular their experiences and images of maternal subjectivity (Hoggart 1959).

These narratives produced the 'story' of the 'old working class' as decent, clean, respectable and passive. Reference to the sensibilities and feelings that economics and class inscribed was usually absent, with the result that a uniformity and sameness of experience was represented, held together by their material vicissitudes and struggles. This was a simplistic and appealing picture that many black and white films reinforced until the 1960s. It is to some extent anyway an ahistorical picture, and yet one that still has appeal today, for different and quite complex reasons.

This was particularly true when applied to fantasies and ideas of the mother, where the dominant images were passivity, goodness, patience, self-effacing, sacrificial – 'our mam'. From a daughter's experience and interpretation, Steedman tells the story of her mother's life. A mother who desired a better life than her own mother had experienced, a woman who desired the things of the earth, security, a home, nice clothes, all the things she did not possess, and was not expected to want, or expect from her background.

'Never have children dear', she said, 'they ruin your life'.

(Steedman 1986: 17)

It is a story of social status, belonging, identity, and exclusion. And a mother's body as a site of desire and rejection.

> Loving a baby costs very little. But feeding us during our later childhood was a tense struggle between giving and denial. (Ibid 1986: 93)

Steedman makes two central claims:

One that the central narratives that describe maternal subjectivity, and maternal experience, arise from particular socioeconomic and cultural contexts which subtend and perpetuate the main cultural and psychoanalytical theories of female-maternal subjectivity and desire. One of the consequences of this is that all other maternal experience and maternal subjectivity remains marginalized, and is frequently pathologised. Steedman's text is an argument for the recognition of the differences produced by cultural, social and class specificities, and their psychological inscription and internalisation to female-maternal subjectivity, experience, and desire.

Her second claim is that theories of female desire which propose that all women have an inherent desire, or wish, to produce babies require closer examination and theorizing. In particular, the specificity of maternal history across generations, as well as the psychological and economic contexts in which women might refuse reproduction.

This is a part of Steedman's own story, and one that she claims is little understood.

> My refusal of my mother's body was ….a recognition of the problem that my own physical presence represented to her; … At the same time it was a refusal of the inexorable nature of that difficulty, ….., that I would become her, even come to reproduce the circumstances of our straightened unsatisfying life. (1986: 95)

A woman's desire

> I was born in the year of the New Look (coat), and understood, that dresses needing twenty yards for a skirt, were items as expensive as children… (Ibid 1986: 29)

The landscape of the book is South London and 1950s postwar Britain; a country hungry for food, in need of housing, and longing for things to get better. Steedman's mother is a weaver's daughter, from the cotton mills of the North, who escapes to London to improve her chances. She is a woman who knows the value of good clothes, which promise more than keeping you warm against a cold world: the cut and fall of a skirt, a pair of good leather shoes, a good winter coat, a passport and a boundary to another world. It is the beginning of the welfare state, and the NHS, free orange juice and vitamins for babies, Winnicott on the wireless.

> My mother did what the powerless, particularly powerless women, have done before, and do still: she worked on her body, the only bargaining power she ended up with, given the economic times and the culture in which she grew. (Ibid 1986: 141)

As many women before her have done, Steedman's mother makes a bargain with her life; one which she thought would gain her security, and the material possessions she wanted. Carolyn Steedman was the bargain, a baby was to be the way to a better life.

It is an old story.

What follows is the story of Steedman's childhood with a father that was sometimes present, more often absent, and the financial and emotional struggles by her mother to keep things going, and the effects this had on Steedman and her younger sister.

> It matters then, whether one reshapes past time, re-uses the ordinary exigencies and crises of all childhoods whilst looking down from the curtainless windows of a terraced house like my mother did, or sees at that moment the long view stretching away from the big house in some richer and more detailed landscape. (Ibid 1986: 5)

Following the birth of her sister, the district nurse had called to see the new baby. Standing in a bare front bedroom, the district nurse pronounces the room unfit. 'This house isn't fit for a baby'.

> And then she stopped crying, my mother, got by,.....It says, it's like this, it shouldn't be like this; it's unfair; I'll manage. (Ibid 1986: 2)

Many women have stood in that place, with their child watching its mother's exclusion, and its own, and known where they stand in relation to the rest of the world.

> And I? I will do everything, and anything, until the end of my days, to stop anyone ever talking to me like that woman talked to my mother? (Ibid 186: 2)

In Kathleen Woodward's book, *Jipping Street*, Steedman says she read of her own experience of her mother.

> Kathleen Woodward's mother of the 1890's was the one I knew: Mothers were the people who told you how long they were in labour with you and how much it hurt,... ....and who told you to accept the impossible contradiction, of being both desired and being a burden, and not to complain.
>
> *(Steedman 1992: 31)*

Published in 1928, *Jipping Street* is the story of growing up as a daughter, who is working class, and of a mother who is not the sacrificial saintly 'our mam', of traditional working class male narratives; and of her daughter Kathleen Woodward, who is bound to her mother, not by love and gratitude, but by resentment, anger, hatred and debt.

Adrienne Rich has asked what happens to girl children in these circumstances:

> What of a women who has to toil so hard for survival that no maternal energy remains at the end of the day. … The child does not discern the social system or the institution of motherhood, only a harsh voice, a dulled pair of eyes, a mother who does not hold her, does not tell her how wonderful she is.
>
> *(Steedman1986: 95 and Rich 1976: 248–9)*

The ambiguous law of the father

> We need a reading of history that reveals fathers mattering in a different way from the way they matter in the corpus of traditional psychoanalysis, the novels that depict the same familial settings…
>
> *(Steedman 1986: 18)*

After the birth of her sister, Steedman's father takes her to a wood where bluebells grow on a fern-covered slope, he picks bluebells, making a bunch, she cannot remember if he gave them to her. This scene is violently broken up by the arrival of the forest keeper who shouts at her father for picking the flowers, and sends them both away.

The memory of this scene, and of her father's expulsion, and his evident vulnerability and powerlessness in the face of the forest keeper's authority, becomes for Steedman the moment which holds all her disappointment, anger and longing, for a father who did not, would not, or could not, count as father with her mother, and with his children.

But who also did not count as a father in terms of the social and cultural law and practices. Steedman questions the accounts of the father as the paternal 'law', in the family and society, and her father who did not signify in either places and her own ambiguous position. Social class was defined according to the Registrar General's records by a father's occupation, the breadwinner. This was recorded on the birth certificates of children. Steedman's mother had at an earlier stage falsified their birth certificates.[8] In Steedman's family, it is her mother who is the breadwinner and a single woman. Her father only sometimes present, more often absent, lived with his first legal and authorised family, which was discovered much later, although known to her mother.

> The new consumer goods came into the house slowly and we were taught to understand that our material deprivation was due entirely to my father's meanness.
>
> *(Steedman 1986: 36)*

All the attempts by Steedman's mother, including a later seduction which produces a second daughter, fail to gain the legal and paternal authorisation, and the security of the social and economic status, of being his authorized and legitimate children. They found out later, after his death, that he had paid all the bills, and the rent, and seven pounds housekeeping a week, and given them pocket money. They were not as bad off as it seemed.

> I wish I could tell him now, even though he was really a sod, that I am sorry for the years of rejection and dislike…
>
> *(Steedman 1986: 35–36)*

Years later when Steedman is at university, her father meets some of her friends in a pub; they see him as an authentic South London wide boy, old but gritty, with a rich story and jokes to tell of his past life: reality collides with abandonment and loss. And the wish, that the circumstances might have been different. And the memory, that pre-lapsarian moment in the woods, picking the bluebells, before their expulsion by the forest keeper, leaving the picked bluebells strewn on the bank, their milky white transparent roots pulled from the earth.

A daughter and a mother

> Each daughter … must have longed for a mother whose love for her and whose power was so great as to undo rape and bring her back from death. And every mother must have longed for the power of Demeter, the efficacy of her anger, the reconciliation of her lost self.
>
> *(Steedman 1986: 88)*

> The sense of being absent in my mother's presence, was nothing to do with illness, it was what it had always been like…
>
> *(Steedman 1986: 142)*

Central to this text is Steedman's childhood and adolescent experience of her mother, and what she believes to be one of the consequences of this; her choice not to have children, her refusal to reproduce herself, and the circumstances of her own childhood. She asks, what is it that a woman refuses when she says no to having children. For Steedman the answer is her own mother; and her childhood.

> Part of the desire to reproduce oneself as a body, as an entity in the real world, lies in conscious memory of someone approving of that body.
>
> *(Steedman 1986: 95)*

Steedman says she has no conscious recognition or memory of her mother's approval and confirmation of her, as a girl, or of her body. Excluded in this way, she suggests, girls do not develop self-love, and it is this self-love that lies at the heart of the wish for a child.

> To know that, whilst one exists, ... that things might be better if one wasn't there at all, presents all the ingredients of contradiction ... the integration of the self ... that provides the basis of sensuality, dies in the little girl... (Ibid 1986: 96)

The economics of desire and maternity

Steedman makes a plea that accounts of non-mothering, such as her own account, be recognized, and reckoned with, and the implications for the development of self-understanding and self-worth.

> I think that my mother's half conscious motive in producing me was the wish that my father would marry her, though I did not understand the economic terms of my existence that this motive dictated, until long past my childhood.
> *(Steedman 1986: 88)*

LFGW Conclusion

> An absence of discourse, relegates certain lives to unmournability, not a life at all, and its death therefore not quite a death.
> *(Butler 2004: 20)*

Landscape for A Good Woman is almost 30 years old since its publication. A lot more is understood now regarding the differences produced by culture, class and economics, race and gender. Although how much attends to the implications of Steedman's questions and conclusions with regard to maternal subjectivities is still woefully inadequate. Maternal experience from other cultural and economic backgrounds is still frequently pathologised, especially by clinicians.

The psychoanalytic narratives of female-maternal subjectivity still hold immense persuasion and power. It is not my intention in this brief discussion of Steedman's text to argue with her understanding and sense of her own experience and interpretation. Steedman's analysis is complex, and in some places she does tend towards some overdetermined answers; for example, her own refusal to have children. But many of the questions she asks are still with us.

I have one reservation:

Steedman asks her readers to recognize and reckon with, and to begin to theorize, woman-maternal subjectivities within their cultural, social and economic contexts, and the kinds of self-understanding these experiences produce. It will not do, she says, to go on producing the same narratives from the same cultural backgrounds, with little reference to other contexts, and their influence and inscriptions, which produce different experiences of female-maternal subjectivity.

And yet, in a paradoxical circular gesture, Steedman's conclusion to her mother's story and life is to say that it cannot count as history, made as it is, out on the border lands, and a part of all lost childhoods. She refuses to let it be absorbed by the central stories, refuses to celebrate it, and so consigns it to '*the dark*' (Steedman 1986: 144).

Although Steedman does in fact after the book's publication go on writing and speaking about 'the book' – (her mother). She is frequently, she claims, with some exasperation, asked to talk about the book and her experiences. And so there is a revisiting for her of the 'subject', and a returning to the matter/nal, and its continuing mattering, and her own ambivalence and ambiguity.

Whilst today's concerns and questions on the woman-maternal-daughter subjectivity and the symbolic were not explicitly Steedman's narrative and focus, she nonetheless does raise exactly some of these questions, whilst coming from a different period, perspective and purpose. And yet, her opening gesture to move from the narratives of autobiography, memoir, and biography, and the formation of female and maternal subjectivity, into eschatological futures of narratives: epistemologies, ethics, philosophy, and the pedagogy of the maternal, becomes subsumed by the patriarchal logic she sets out to question. A phallic oedipal foreclosure of female-maternal subjectivity and its connections – a matricidal conclusion.

But what of the cost?

My mother: a life to grow old in

She telephoned and left a message on the answering phone. She had spent the morning baking cakes and washing curtains, and she was feeling much better, and on her way to see the doctor so that she could return to work. She hoped I was alright. She would ring later. A warm May afternoon, a cloudless blue sky. A few yards from the doctor's surgery, she collapsed and died.

For a long time afterwards I looked for her. I searched for a face that was like hers. If I saw a woman of a similar shape, the hair, or clothes, the shape of the shoulders, or neck, or overheard a voice – the way my mother looked when she was very tired and carrying shopping home. I would follow the woman through the shop or street, so that I could go on looking at her, for just a little longer. After a time, I would stop and look at the woman-stranger, and face what I already knew, she was not my mother. That moment was unbearable. One day, I don't know when, it stopped. But sometimes, even now, after all of these years – if I see a woman, who for a moment … Time and space lends a kind of distance and acceptance, but they know nothing of longing.

The gift of the fragile moment.

(Cavarero 1997)

She had just turned 62 when she died. I don't think that she had expectations or thoughts that she would live into an old age. She never spoke about it, and anyway there were no models for her of what it was like as a woman to grow old. All the women in her maternal family had died quite young, her own mother at 53. She saw herself as someone who had to work to stay alive, money was the small reward offering some kind of security, and without being able to do that, life was precarious. Love was a very practical thing, especially in those days, utilitarian. She was fed, clothed, kept clean, shoes mended, sent to school, and then out into service at 14, a war changed what came next.

Love is not just these things: A smile, the look of recognition in the eyes of the other, those moments of shared laughter and talk about nothing in particular, just for its own sake and the pleasure it brings: The touch of a hand on the shoulder, for no other reason than *you* are there, and it is good. Small invitations into such finite life.

And when death comes we might still be afraid, but such beginnings of tenderness may be what is remembered in us.

> Maman had an open hospital night dress on and she did not mind that her wrinkled belly criss-crossed with tiny lines and her bald pubis showed. I turned away and gazed fixedly into the garden. The sight of my mother's nakedness had jarred me. No body existed less for me. None existed more.
>
> *(Beauvoir 1964/73)*

These reflections by the 'Mother' of modern feminism, about her dying mother have always puzzled me, even allowing for the fact that this daughter wrote a powerful and moving account of her mother's death. This is the woman who refused to become a mother, and whose connection to her own mother had long been fraught with ambivalence. And yet this is the woman philosopher who claims women's lives in all their messiness and complexity: sexuality, desire, reproduction, abortion, prostitution, menstruation, relationships, work, ageing, and death, as the rightful proper ground for philosophy!

But why does this daughter notice her mother's lack of pubic hair? A sign of ageing, of being old? Or the opening and the threshold, which birthed and other/ed her child? That archaic memory and connection to another world in which this now famous woman, once was held, bathing in its warm life-giving waters, nourished by its body, tuned to the rhythms of its beating heart.

Are the criss-crossed lines the marks of childbirth or stretch marks, or age? Is she embarrassed by her mother's semi-nakedness, and her unawareness of it; evoking the nakedness and helplessness and vulnerability of all our births, and of giving birth, and our death?

A whole world is disclosed in this meeting; A world of meaning, value and significance.

A world unsymbolised! A world that has infused and permeates through endless unfathomable connections to each female – woman's unconscious; the archaic connection to another woman that the daughter also shares. The potentiality for holding and generating an/other/s into life and futures.

Or there is the Oedipal reading; i this dying mother's body the sign to her daughter of a woman's body as no longer erotic, desirable, sexual, and fertile, all of which implies youthful. The conditions that constitute and construct woman as feminine in the patriarchal Oedipal order, and a reminder to the daughter that the same fate awaits her too.

What can we now as women, who also share this same fate in all its vulnerabilities, say to each other of this scene? Is there a story that will help and heal us, to find other ways, to live with other possibilities, to live and flourish creatively with each other?

What becomes of Demeter?

The feminism of the late 1960s and 1970s was concerned with questions that were relevant to the social and political context of those years, and the age group of the majority of women who participated reflected this. Although not all of the women were young, meaning of reproductive age. I can remember seeing 'older' women and wondering what they were doing there! And I suspect thinking that I would not become like them, who seemed wrinkled and old and very far from me! In fact, I went on to find some of the warmest and most empowering relationships from some of those so-called older women. Now missed very much.

By the 1990s, it looked as if going *In Search of our Mother's Gardens*, and *Thinking Back through Our Mother*, as Alice Walker and Virginia Woolf had called for, had seen its day. And it became apparent by the 1990s that generational warfare between feminists of the 1960/1970s and the next generation was rife.

There had always been fierce differences of definitions: sexuality, women's bodies, the relationship to men, political and economic identifications, but this was a generational conflict, it was about age, and ageing, evoking anxiety, fear, repression, anger and denial.

The journalist Susan Faludi wrote:

> A generational breakdown underlies so many of the pathologies that have long disturbed American feminism alongside the battle of the sexes rages the battle of the ages. ...
>
> *(Segal 2013: 71)*

She also reported that the newer feminist activism and scholarship not only spurned the work of older feminists, but that surveys carried out in 2008 reported that young women overall neither wanted, nor trusted older woman bosses, whilst many younger women opposed Hilary Clinton on the grounds that she reminded them of their mother!

At a feminist 'mother-daughter' dinner party, which degenerated into bitter hostilities, Faludi observed, many of the younger women announced they were sick to death of hearing about the glory days, whilst the older women declared they were sick to death of being chucked into the dustbin of history! It seemed that the mother had returned with a vengeance, and it seemed intractable, an ancient archaic battle once again being played out between the generations – mother and daughter, and the fears of the engulfing mother. We had come full circle.

Part of this problem was that the mother referred to in many, if not all, of the earlier feminist texts was often without context. *LFGW* was a success in illustrating this absence – or matricide. Many of these faceless texts and theories on the maternal and maternal subjectivity, both psychoanalytic and feminist, focused on the pre-Oedipal maternal experience, and even when narratives appeared documenting the 'empty nest', and menopause, with questions on female-maternal subjectivity and identities, it seemed as if the questions and connections still lay waiting to be recognised and asked. And when later still feminists of the 1960s and 1970s began writing on postmenopause, ageing and death, sexuality and desire, ill health, loneliness and depression, and creativity, still the connections across time and generations to the maternal lay waiting.

Demeter

> Let's face it.
> We're undone by each other.
> And if we're not, we're missing something

(Butler 2004: 23)

In all its different versions, the central core of the myth of Demeter and Persephone remains the same. Demeter and Persephone are mother and daughter. Persephone is abducted to the underworld by Hades. Demeter the mother goddess and deity of fertility – linked to the earth and its fecundity and creativity – is distraught, she searches for her lost daughter, going out of her mind she wreaks havoc and destruction on the land causing famine, the people go hungry. Eventually Hades intervenes, and Persephone is restored to her mother, after a bargain is struck that she spend six months of the year in the underworld and six months with her mother.[9]

Can we make anything life giving and creative from this most famous and popular patriarchal myth? In all the other variants on the myth, with their various interpretations, there is still the question of Demeter. And this is usually the point where some therapists, and others, respond with depressed, powerless, vengeful, narcissistically wounded, hysteric or psychotic mother.

In her very poignant poem *Demeter,* Carol Ann Duffy (1999: 76) describes Demeter's loss of Persephone as her heart had turned cold, turned to stone – and is broken, which even her tough hard words will not melt. But then, she sees her at last, her daughter Persephone, coming from a long, long way off, walking across the fields, and with her footsteps, bringing all the spring flowers (life and love) to her mother's broken heart.[10]

I think this picks up another lost story, or one never told, of the love between mothers and daughters. In the New Testament story of the prodigal son (KJV Luke 15), the father sees in the distance his long-lost son returning home, and he runs out to meet him, and calls all of his household to welcome his son and to share his happiness that his son is restored to him and all can be well. It is beautiful story, of the love between father and son, and I think it is also intended to convey that in the absence of this son, the father has been sad and lost too.[11]

But my question is about Demeter, the mother, what is her 'identity' now? What does she do in the intervening six months of Persephone's absence? Who is she now without her daughter? Does she desire anything else for herself, or indeed desire anyone else? Does she have her own questions about her life? I imagine her asking herself, 'Did I see my life now like this, what do I want now?'[12]

I think it is worth recalling Freud in this context on his future mother-in-law. He begins by speaking of his affection for her and praising her 'high' accomplishments.

> Because her charm and vitality have lasted so long, she still demands in return her full share of life – not the share of old age – and expects to be the centre, the ruler, an end in herself.
>
> Every man who has grown old honourably wants the same, only in a woman one is not used to it. (!)
>
> As a mother she ought to be content to know that her three children are fairly happy, and she ought to sacrifice her wishes to their needs. This she doesn't do…
>
> *(Woodward 1991: 27)*

Freud was 27 years old; the mother he describes was 53. Re-inscribing the Oedipal complex, he sees the strength of a man of the same age as good, but in a woman of the same age, it is unnatural. She does not know her place, power belongs to the man, as a mother who has had a full life, she is, it would appear hanging on to it, instead of sacrificing herself!

Demeter's role and function was to survive the loss of her daughter; survive without hatred or destruction and be prepared to be left behind, no retaliation is permitted, she is required to remain silent; she is no longer needed to mirror anyone, the magic mirror can be broken. But Demeter's response was anger, revenge, grief and mourning. Here is a real living mother, with feelings, responding to the abduction of her daughter. Here she is a subject, not an *object,* and that is part of the problem.

In psychoanalytic theory the mother is an object, an object to be left behind. Persephone no longer needs her mother and all of those unfathomable archaic connections, we are told, can now be severed. Circumcision of the daughter!

Foreclosure of the maternal connections and appropriation of the female-maternal body/life. Persephone's longing and loss of her mother is denied.

And Demeter?

Why are we all so convinced that separation from the mother will not cost the daughter dearly, that matricide is not also a death to the daughter! Bracha Ettinger (2006) points to the possible irreparable pain and harm done to daughters (and sons) when therapists speak of the toxic mother, or abject mother, or destructive mother, or phallic mother. The implication is that the therapist, male or female, or therapy, can and will in some way 'compensate' or 'make up' for the *lack, or not enoughness,* of the real mother.

Whilst there may indeed have been 'difficulties', perhaps very serious ones, this is not about denying these, but describing the mother in this language can only leave the daughter (son) with the lasting sense that her mother was not good enough, and damaged her.[13]

Conclusion

In *The Coming of Age*, Beauvoir writes:

> As men see it, a woman's purpose in life is to be an erotic object, when she grows old and ugly she loses the place allotted to her in society: She becomes a monstrum that excites revulsion and even dread.
>
> *(Beauvoir 1978: 184)*

The male and female fear of woman as the all-engulfing mother is exacerbated when women grow old, she becomes subject to a double marginality – a double bind: Desire for the mother is taboo in psychoanalysis and culturally, and so the older woman necessarily occupies the position of the mother or grandmother.

Virginia Woolf looked around her and asked, where are all the mothers, in history, in literature, in poetry, in politics, in writing, in life? 'Why,' she asks, 'isn't there a tradition of the mothers'? It is a complex question with no easy answers.

The fact is we cannot even begin to build a maternal genealogy without the recognition of the intimate connections between age-identity-sexuality-desire – and the (place) intentional parenthesis – of the postmenopausal woman-mother, and the recognition of our internalised hatred against ageing women. And the recognition of the fear of the mother, her power, but especially her vulnerability.

We need to recognise the latent aversion to *the mother*, within psychoanalytic theory and clinical practice, but also feminist theory and practice. Without this, psychoanalytic theory and practice and feminism collude with the patriarchal consumer led obsession and focus on 'youth', and the power/gender dynamics implicit to it; and its collusion with the wider social, economic and political dominating narratives, which in the end damages us all as men and women.

Notes

1 Fondant sweets: This was something my mother used to say to me when I was a child. It meant that when she could afford it, we would have some of these sweets, which were her favourite. We did not have them very often. It was meant to comfort, and I think to give hope.

 The metaphor is taken from the boats coming in many years before, she might have remembered those times when ships brought in their goods, particularly food, and families waited on them, and maybe for the men to arrive home as well. Nowadays it is likely to mean the lottery, if it is used at all.

2 Empire Day was May 24th. It was a national holiday and celebrated, a bit like a Coronation. It stopped after the end of WWII.

3 According to Alasdair MacIntyre, I can only answer the question, 'What am I to do?' if I can answer the prior question, 'Of what stories or story do I find myself a part?' (1984: 216).

 Taking stock of stories is the activity through which we 'make sense' of the world and render it intelligible. For MacIntyre, a meaningful life is one that is embodied in our 'quest' for, as well as ordering of, the numerous narratives (stories) that compose the self throughout our lives. These stories or narratives are embedded and embodied in communities and families, traditions and practices – and for others writing with the same concerns, rooted in the natural world (environment) and work, that is connected intimately with the land, and natural world. (See Wendell Berry, Bill McKibben, Oliver O'Donovan, and Norman Maclean.)

 MacIntyre insists that narratives and stories are so essential (integral) to how humans come to know and recognize their place in the world, that quite literally, 'we flourish or fail to flourish, live or die' as our stories live or die (1990: 201).

 And the fact that we exist among a multiplicity of traditions, practices and beliefs does not afford us a multiplicity of perspectives among which we can choose and move, or intelligibility gives way to incoherence.

 'To be unable to render oneself intelligible is to risk being taken to be mad – is, if carried far enough, to be mad. And madness or death may always be the outcomes which prevent the resolution of an epistemological crisis' (MacIntyre 1977: 140).

 Writing at the end of the twentieth century, MacIntyre said we are now living in an epistemological crisis, a time of incoherence where most people can make no sense of the world in which they live, as lives and stories, communities and practices become ever more fragmented, incoherent, unintelligible and unrooted.

4 I am unable to draw out the many examples of how and where African American Womanist literature, poetry and art have and still do, differ from what is still produced in Western Europe on maternal female subjectivities. Toni Morrison, in particular, but also Alice Walker have documented over the years the ideas of what constitutes human subjectivity in the West is a discourse that is identical to a white, capitalist, ownership, power-status-sexuality and gender – and more recently includes youth – as a denial of death and the earth, which is seen as exploitable. In her novels, Morrison constructs a female subjectivity which is maternal based – through families – and their histories and traditions, across generations and through stories and memory. Echoing the earlier words of Elizabeth Barret Browning and Virginia Woolf, Morrison recounts a conversation with a young black girl, 'They have grown up these days as if they had never had grandmothers, or if they had then they never paid any attention to them and their stories'. Morrison claims that the white culture of the United States and Europe is a life denying culture which maims us all, men and women, disconnecting us from each other, and the earth. See Reilly (2004).

5 For an excellent and still relevant analysis of the psychological inscription to subjectivity and class see Sennet and Cobb (1977) and Rubin (1976).

6 The advent of the People's History is something Steedman refers to in *LFGW*. My reading of her on this is that she does not see it as 'real' history. See also Steedman in *Past Tenses* (1992).

7 The last 10 years or so have seen a renewal and revival of interest and remembrance in the First and Second World Wars and their historical and social contexts, witnessed in the many new books, films, poetry and drama. Whilst this has in part been about the recognition that a section of the population who took part in these events is also coming to the end of their lives, and the wish to recall and remember – as well as being the occasions for state/ national purposes – it is also mixed with a nostalgia, and the recognition of worlds now gone, leaving only a backward glance and longing for what is lost, and unrepresentable, except through such iconic images that those events have given us, and the longing for what seemed to be a 'simpler life'– a world far removed from the one we now live in.

8 Birth certificates: This was not an unusual occurrence, particularly when a child was illegitimate. In poorer families, there was often a delay in registering a child's birth, and the date the child was registered was often put down as the child's birthdate.

9 I am aware that there are a number of different variations and interpretations of this myth, and I do not have the space to go into them here, but I believe that the basic core of the myth is as I have given here. Though the interpretations do vary considerably they all recount Demeter as the mother who must be parted from as integral to the myth's function and meaning.

10 Demeter shows she is *at a loss*, over the loss of her daughter, who is *lost*, and she, Demeter, *is also lost*. I am not suggesting anything like some kind of symbiotic relationship, even supposing this were possible. I believe this theory-concept also demonstrates our fears of the/our Mothers. For me, this demonstrates at a profound level what it means to understand that we are as human beings in our subjectivity constituted by Other/s, by our connections to Others, as Judith Butler says, and so, exposed and vulnerable to Others through our attachments. Our real suffering is that we are unable to admit to these as fundamental to our nature, and the dominant narratives and neoliberalist world we live in requires that we all emphatically deny any such vulnerability, with the result that it is both projected onto the elderly, dying or sick, or to children, and women, as a sign of weakness. There is no way around this, and the loss of someone we love and care for shows us this at a profound level. See Butler (2006). This questions the whole concept of what the word separation means when applied and interpreted the way it usually is in relation (sic) to the mother and daughter. It is word that is used more often in the context of mother and daughter, and less with the son, and I think it signals very loudly our fears of merger and engulfment, and also our longing!

See also Adriana Cavarero (2000) (*Relating Narratives*) who writes that it is not because we are reasoning beings that we are connected to one another, but rather because we are *exposed* to one another.

11 I am not able to enter into the other theological meanings attributed to this Christian parable here. There are numerous other stories that also pick up these themes in the NT and OT almost all referring to the relationship between father and son (to symbolize the relationship between God and his son/humans). The only comparable story that comes to mind of mother and daughter is of course Ruth and Naomi (The Book of Ruth verse 16 KJV).

I am not saying this was Duffy's intention, only that her poem would seem to attune with the sentiment and tenderness expressed in the book of Ruth.

12 Judith Butler's account is I believe much more faithful to most people's experience of loss, death and mourning. And see Kathleen Woodward, *Ageing and its Discontents* (1991) which also picks up these themes in a nuanced analysis. Lynne Segal's *Out of Time* (2013) is also excellent on loss, mourning and learning to live again through loss, particularly in relation to Demeter/mothers – 'older' women.

13 Selected references: Balint (1952), Bollas (1987), Winnicott (1947).

References

Balint, M. (1952) *Love for the Mother and Mother Love – In Primary Love and Psycho-Analytic Technique*. London, England: Hogarth Press.

Berry, W. (1990) *What Are People For?* San Francisco, CA: North Point Press.

Bollas, C. (1987) *The Shadow of the Object*. London, England: Free Association.

De Beauvoir, S. (1972) *The Second Sex* (trans. Parshley, H.M.). Harmondsworth, England: Penguin Books.

De Beauvoir, S. (1964/73 reprint) *A Very Easy Death* (trans. O'Brian, P.). New York, NY: Pantheon Books.

De Beauvoir, S. (1986–1996) *The Coming of Age* (trans. O'Brian, P.). New York, NY: Norton.

Butler, J. (2006) *Precarious Life: The Powers of Mourning and Violence*. London, England: Verso.

Cavarero, A. (1997 Italian, 2000 English) *Relating Narratives: Story Telling and Selfhood*. London, England: Routledge.

Chodorow, N. (1978) *The Reproduction of Mothering: Psychoanalysis and the Sociology of Gender*. San Francisco, CA: University of California Press.

Duffy, C. A. (1999) *The World's Wife*. Oxford, England: Picador.

Ettinger, B. L. (2006a) *The Matrixial Border Space: Theory Out of Bound*. Minneapolis, MN: University of Minnesota Press.

Ettinger, B.L. (2006b) From proto-ethical compassion to responsibility: besideness and the three primal mother–phantasies of not enoughness, devouring and abandonment. *Athena Philosophical Studies* 2:100–135.

Fiorenza, E. S., (1983) *In Memory Of Her: A Feminist Theological Reconstruction of Christian Origins*. London, England: SCM Press.

Gilligan, C. (1982) *Ethics of Care: Psychological Theory and Women's Development*. Cambridge, MA: Harvard University Press.

Grosholz, E. R. (ed.). (2004) *The Legacy of Simone de Beauvoir*. Oxford, England: Clarendon Press.

Hoggart, R. (1959) *The Uses of Literacy*. London, England: Penguin.

Irigaray. L. (1993) *Sexes and Genealogies*. (trans. Gill, G.) New York, NY: Columbia University Press.

MacIntyre. A. (1977) Epistemological crisis, dramatic narrative and philosophy of science. *The Monist* 60(4): 453–472.

MacIntyre, A. (1984) *After Virtue*. 2nd ed. Notre Dame, IN: University of Notre Dame.

MacIntyre, A. (1990) *Three Rival Versions of Moral Inquiry*. Notre Dame: IN. University of Notre Dame.

Maclean, N. (1976) *A River Runs Through It*. Chicago, IL: University of Chicago.

McKibben, B. (1989) *The End of Nature*. New York, NY: Random House.

O'Donovan, O. (1989) The loss of a sense of place. *Irish Theological Quarterly* 55: 39–58.

Olsen, T. (1980) *Silences*. London, England: Virago.

O'Reilly, A. (2004) *Toni Morrison and Motherhood: A Politics of the Heart*. New York, NY: State University.

Phillips, A. (2002) Coming to grief. In *Promises, Promises: Essays in Literature and Psychoanalysis*. London, England: Faber and Faber.

Rich, A. (1976) *Of Woman Born: Motherhood as Experience and Institution*. New York, NY: Norton.

Rubin, L. B. (1976) *Worlds of Pain: Life in the Working Class Family*. New York, NY: Basic Books.

Segal, L. (2013) *Out of Time: The Pleasures and Perils of Ageing*. London, England: Verso.

Sennet, R. and Cobb, J. (1977) *The Hidden Injuries of Class*. Cambridge, England: Cambridge University Press.

Steedman, C. (1986) *Landscape for A Good Woman*. London, England: Virago Press.

Steedman C. (1992) *Past Tenses: Essays on Writing Autobiography and History*. London, England: Rivers Oram Press.

Walker, A. (1983) *In Search of Our Mothers' Gardens*. San Diego, CA: Harcourt, Brace, Jovanovich.

Williams, R. (1984) *Keywords: A Vocabulary of Culture and Society*. London, England: Fontana.

Winnicott, D.W. (1947) Hate in the counter-transference. In *Through Paediatrics to Psycho-Analysis*. London, England: Hogarth Press.

Woodward, K. (1928) *Jipping Street*. London, England: Virago.

Woodward, K. (1991) *Ageing and Its Discontents: Freud and Other Fictions*. Bloomington, IN: Indiana University Press.

INDEX

Taylor & Francis eBooks

Helping you to choose the right eBooks for your Library

Add Routledge titles to your library's digital collection today. Taylor and Francis ebooks contains over 50,000 titles in the Humanities, Social Sciences, Behavioural Sciences, Built Environment and Law.

Choose from a range of subject packages or create your own!

Benefits for you

» Free MARC records
» COUNTER-compliant usage statistics
» Flexible purchase and pricing options
» All titles DRM-free.

Benefits for your user

» Off-site, anytime access via Athens or referring URL
» Print or copy pages or chapters
» Full content search
» Bookmark, highlight and annotate text
» Access to thousands of pages of quality research at the click of a button.

REQUEST YOUR FREE INSTITUTIONAL TRIAL TODAY

Free Trials Available
We offer free trials to qualifying academic, corporate and government customers.

---

eCollections – Choose from over 30 subject eCollections, including:

Archaeology	Language Learning
Architecture	Law
Asian Studies	Literature
Business & Management	Media & Communication
Classical Studies	Middle East Studies
Construction	Music
Creative & Media Arts	Philosophy
Criminology & Criminal Justice	Planning
Economics	Politics
Education	Psychology & Mental Health
Energy	Religion
Engineering	Security
English Language & Linguistics	Social Work
Environment & Sustainability	Sociology
Geography	Sport
Health Studies	Theatre & Performance
History	Tourism, Hospitality & Events

For more information, pricing enquiries or to order a free trial, please contact your local sales team: www.tandfebooks.com/page/sales

 Routledge
Taylor & Francis Group

The home of
Routledge books

www.tandfebooks.com

THE TOFF AND THE CURATE

John Creasey

CHIVERS
THORNDIKE

This Large Print book is published by BBC Audiobooks Ltd, Bath, England and by Thorndike Press®, Waterville, Maine, USA.

Published in 2005 in the U.K. by arrangement with Tethered Camel Publishing.

Published in 2005 in the U.S. by arrangement with The Tethered Camel Ltd.

U.K. Hardcover   ISBN 1–4056–3293–3 (Chivers Large Print)
U.K. Softcover   ISBN 1–4056–3294–1 (Camden Large Print)
U.S. Softcover   ISBN 0–7862–7630–4 (British Favorites)

The text of this Large Print edition is unabridged.
Other aspects of the book may vary from the original edition.

Set in 16 pt. New Times Roman.

Printed in Great Britain on acid-free paper.

British Library Cataloguing in Publication Data available

Library of Congress Cataloging-in-Publication Data

Creasey, John.
    The Toff and the curate / by John Creasey.
       p.   cm.
    "Thorndike Press large print British favorites."—T.p. verso.
    ISBN 0–7862–7630–4 (lg. print : sc : alk. paper)
    1. Toff (Fictitious character)—Fiction. 2. Private investigators—
England—Fiction. 3. London—(England)—Fiction. 4. Clergy—
Fiction. 5. Large type books. I. Title. II. Series.
PR6005.R517T616 2005
823'.912—dc22   2005004879

Foreword

RICHARD CREASEY

The Toff—or the Honourable Richard
Rollison—was 'born' in the twopenny weekly
Thriller in 1933 but it was not until 1938 that
my father, John Creasey, first published books
about him. At once the Toff took on
characteristics all his own and became a kind
of '*Saint* with his feet on the ground.' My
father consciously used the Toff to show how
well the Mayfair man-about-town could get on
with the rough diamonds of the East End.

What gives the Toff his ever-fresh, ever-
appealing quality is that he likes people and
continues to live a life of glamour and
romance while constantly showing (by
implication alone) that all men are brothers
under the skin.

I am delighted that the Toff is available
again to enchant a whole new audience. And
proud that my parents named me Richard
after such an amazing role-model.

Richard Creasey is Chairman of The Television
Trust for the Environment *and, for the last 20
years, has been an executive producer for both
BBC and ITV.*

It was John Creasey who introduced him to the

world of travel and adventure. Richard and his brother were driven round the world for 465 days in the back of their parents' car when they were five and six years old. In 1992 Richard led 'The Overland Challenge' driving from London to New York via the Bering Strait.

CHAPTER ONE

THE CURATE MAKES A CALL

Jolly brought the caller's card into the bathroom where Rollison was brushing his teeth. Nothing in Jolly's expression gave a clue to his thoughts, although he would have been justified in thinking that 11.15pm was an unreasonable time for a stranger to pay an unexpected visit, even on a summer night.

Rollison glanced down and read:

The Rev Ronald Kemp
Curate
St Guy's Church, Whitechapel

then looked up into Jolly's eyes.

'Why?' he asked.

'Mr Kemp would not explain the reason for his call, sir,' said Jolly. 'He insisted that he is prepared to wait all night to see you, if needs be.'

The manservant looked as if he were fighting a losing battle with dyspepsia. His appearance often gave rise to the baseless accusation that the Toff—by which soubriquet the Hon Richard Rollison was widely known—had dubbed his man Jolly, inspired by some whimsical fancy to give him a cheerful name to

1

offset his gloomy expression.

'Is that all?' asked Rollison.

'If you are asking me to give you my impressions of Mr Kemp,' said Jolly, cautiously, 'I would say that he is in a state of great agitation. He is a large young man, sir.'

'We don't know him, do we?' asked Rollison.

'I haven't met him before,' said Jolly, 'but when I was in the district a few weeks ago, I understood that a new curate had arrived at St Guy's. You may recall that the vicar, the Reverend Cartwright, is seriously ill and that the curacy has been vacant for some time.'

'Yes,' said Rollison. 'Kemp has certainly taken on a handful.'

'He looks as though he is beginning to realise it,' said Jolly.

Rollison smiled drily but he was interested and sent Jolly to tell the Rev Kemp that he would see him soon.

He wore a silk dressing-gown of duck-egg blue and maroon-coloured pyjamas and slippers; gifts from aunts. The sash about his waist emphasised his tall leanness and the pale blue threw his dark hair and tanned face into relief. He started brushing his teeth again, needing a few minutes to refresh his memory about the parish of St Guy. It was not a parish in which the Church was likely to thrive, although there were several mission houses and the Salvation Army Hostel had a large, if changing, list of clients. It was poor, even in

2

these days when the workers were receiving more money than they had for a long time past, and 'dock-worker' was no longer synonymous with occasional work and long periods of enforced idleness. Its inhabitants, hardy, hard-swearing Cockneys with a sprinkling of Indians, Pakistanis, Chinamen, Jamaicans, Irish and various others, had taken the air-raid blows sturdily and aroused the admiration of the rest of the country.

The Vicar of St Guy's was more than an estimable man; he was godly. His physical courage and endurance had been an inspiration to his neighbours, who could by no stretch of the imagination be called his flock. Yet St Guy's, being one of the few churches remaining in the district, had a fair membership. Until Cartwright had worked himself to exhaustion, it had been a considerable power for good.

Rollison, being so fond of the East End and its people, greatly regretted Cartwright's illness. Now, it seemed, a youthful cleric had descended upon the parish and was in trouble; few people came to the Toff unless they wanted help.

He went into the small drawing-room of the Gresham Terrace flat.

The Rev Ronald Kemp jumped to his feet and Rollison saw that Jolly had not exaggerated when he had called him massive. Kemp towered above the Toff, who was over

3

six feet. He was a fair-haired, rugged-looking man, clad in a well-cut suit of pin-striped flannel and wearing a limp-looking clerical collar. Rollison judged him to be no more than twenty-three or four.

'Thanks for seeing me,' said Kemp in a powerful voice. 'You're my last hope, Mr Rollison. *Will* you help me?'

'I might,' said Rollison, cautiously.

'For the love of Mike, don't put me off with pretty phrases,' boomed the curate. 'If you're not prepared to help, say so.'

His fine, grey eyes were stormy. He seemed to be fighting to keep a firm hold on himself and his large hands were clenched. He looked at the Toff as if he were sure that his appeal would be turned down.

'It would be a help if I knew what you want me to do,' Rollison said mildly. 'I can't commit myself in advance.'

'I didn't think it would be any use,' said Kemp, bitterly. 'I never did believe in your reputation.'

'Don't talk like an ass!' said Rollison, sharply enough to startle Kemp into silence. He offered him a cigarette and Kemp took one without shifting his gaze. They lit up and Rollison turned to a corner cupboard.

'Will you have a drink?'

'No, thanks,' said Kemp, and boomed out again: 'It's really serious, Rollison.' Angrily he watched the Toff pouring out whisky and

4

adding soda water.

'Sure you won't have one?' he asked.

'Well—yes, I will,' said Kemp. He stood with ill-concealed impatience while Rollison rang for Jolly and asked for ice. Rollison sipped the drink appreciatively, while Kemp swallowed half of his in a gulp, then spoke in a more composed voice.

'I'm sorry I let forth like that but I'm worried stiff and I was told you were the only man likely to help me.'

'Exactly what is the trouble?' asked the Toff.

'One of my church members has been charged with murder,' said Kemp, abruptly. 'He was arrested a couple of hours ago. I couldn't make any impression on the police, they practically told me to mind my own business.'

'Either you met a poor policeman,' said Rollison, with a twinkle in his eye, 'or else one who didn't like being told what a fool he was!'

Kemp coloured. 'Perhaps I was a bit hot-headed.'

'Who is the accused?' asked Rollison, tactfully.

'A man named Craik,' answered Kemp. 'He's a damned good fellow and I don't mind admitting that without him I would have been absolutely lost.' He smoothed down his short hair and went on abruptly: 'Craik was mixed up in a fight early this evening. One of the men was killed. He'd been stabbed. The police say

5

that the knife was Craik's.'

'Was it?' inquired Rollison.

'I don't know but if it was, it was stolen.'

'It might have been,' conceded Rollison. 'Do you know what the fight was about?'

'As far as I can gather, there was a lot of foul talk going on, and some of the fellows baited Craik—apparently they didn't approve of me. I know he shouldn't have taken it so badly but—well, I don't believe that he used a knife.'

'So Craik started the fighting,' remarked Rollison.

'I don't know about that. He answered them pretty stoutly, as far as I can gather, and before anyone knew where he was, the scuffle started. There are dozens of such brawls every night and no one would have thought much about it but for the—er—accident.'

Rollison regarded the young parson thoughtfully.

'I'll do what I can,' he said, cautiously, 'but I must warn you, it's no use calling murder an accident and no use whitewashing a man because you happen to like him. I don't say you're wrong but you've got a tough crowd in your parish and you'll find a streak of violence in unexpected people. Don't get this thing out of perspective. The English law has a curious habit of doing the right thing in the long run, too.'

Kemp spoke reluctantly.

'I suppose you're right but—well, what with

one thing and another, I feel pretty sore.'
Rollison allowed that understatement to pass
without comment. 'You're serious?' added the
curate, more eagerly. 'You will try to help?'

'Yes,' promised Rollison.

'Good man! I—' Kemp looked embarrassed.
'I'm afraid I was extremely rude just now.'

'Don't worry about that,' said Rollison. 'Just
what do you mean by "what with one thing and
another"?'

Kemp shrugged his big shoulders.

'Don't get the idea that I'm complaining,' he
said, 'I knew that I was going into a pretty hot
district. A friend in my previous church
suggested it and it rather attracted me. My
father is an old friend of Mr Cartwright, too.
Since he's been ill, things have rather run to
seed. I've been trying to get them going again,
but—' he drew a deep breath. '*Can* you see the
sense in it?' he demanded helplessly.

'In what precisely?' asked Rollison, patiently.

'Breaking up meetings, pilfering from our
reserve of old clothes—it seems as if there's
someone in the district who wants to wreck
everything we try to do.'

'I see,' said Rollison, and added
unexpectedly: 'The Devil works hard, doesn't
he?'

Kemp looked startled. 'I didn't expect—' he
broke off. When he coloured his fair skin was
suffused and he looked like a boy.

'You didn't expect that kind of talk from me,'

7

Rollison completed for him. 'I don't see why not. Crime is evil, evil springs from somewhere, why not add the 'D'? Where are you living?'

'I've converted a room at one of the mission halls,' answered Kemp. 'Housing's still a problem near the docks and I thought I'd be wise to try to manage on my own. Will you come with me?' he added, eagerly. 'There are one or two people who saw the fight and you might learn something from them.'

'I won't come with you,' said Rollison, 'but I'll join you in about an hour's time. Which hall is it?'

'In Jupe Street. Oughtn't you to have a guide?'

Rollison chuckled. 'I can find my way about! You get back, Kemp, and stop thinking that Craik is half-way to the gallows!'

He ushered the young parson out and, when the door closed, turned to see Jolly approaching from his bedroom where, doubtless, he had been listening.

'I've laid out your clothes, sir,' said Jolly. 'A flannel suit will be all right, won't it?'

'Yes, thanks. What do you make of him?'

'I think he is in a somewhat chastened mood now, sir, and it should be beneficial,' said Jolly. 'It is rather an intriguing story, isn't it?'

'Yes. Do you know Craik?'

'I seem to have heard the name,' said Jolly. 'I think he owns a small general store near St

Guy's.'

'We'll know soon,' said Rollison. 'Try to get Grice on the 'phone, will you? If he's not at the Yard, try his home. Oh—find out first who arrested Craik.'

'Very good, sir,' said Jolly.

Superintendent Grice of Scotland Yard was neither at the Yard nor at his home—he was away for a few days, on a well-earned holiday. Det Sergeant Bray of the Yard had detained Craik and Inspector Chumley—an easy-going, genial individual from the AZ Division—had charged him.

'A curious mixture,' Rollison reflected, 'Bray from the Yard doing work in the Division and handing it over to Chumley. Chumley's usually all right, although he's a bit of a smiler. I'll look in and see him after I've been to Jupe Street.'

'Will you want me, sir?' inquired Jolly.

'Come, if you feel like it,' said Rollison, 'but I don't expect much tonight'

They set out together and were lucky in finding a taxi in Piccadilly with a driver who put himself at their disposal for the night.

'I 'ope that's long enough, sir,' he said out of the darkness. 'If it isn't, I'll pay you overtime,' promised Rollison and was rewarded by gusty laughter and the comforting knowledge that he had put the man in a good humour.

Jolly opened the windows to admit a cool, welcome breeze. 'I wonder how the bellicose

9

curate is getting on?' said Rollison, *sotto voce.* 'Did you or did you not take to him, Jolly?'

'I did rather, sir, yes.'

'If you hadn't, you wouldn't have admitted him,' said Rollison. 'But I doubt whether you could have kept him out. That young man is militant-minded and he seems to be getting a raw deal.'

'I expect he has invited it,' murmured Jolly, primly. 'I can't imagine the people near the docks taking kindly to being driven by a parson.'

'No. And he would try to drive,' mused Rollison. The journey took a little more than half an hour. On the last lap, Jolly had to direct the driver to Jupe Street, a narrow thoroughfare leading off Whitechapel Road. The Mission Hall was at the far end. They passed row upon row of mean houses and some bare patches and did not see any light until the taxi stopped. Then a streak of light from an open door shone right across an alleyway.

'Tell 'em to put that light aht,' growled the driver. Rollison and Jolly hurried down the alley to the door and, as they drew nearer, they caught sight of Kemp standing just inside the room.

Jolly stood outside the door as Rollison went in.

Kemp must have heard him but did not turn round.

10

He was standing quite still, his chin thrust forward and his face set. He was looking at the wreckage of chairs and forms and benches, curtains and pictures. The hall was not a large one and at the far end was a stage with doors on either side; they were open and inside both rooms Rollison saw further upheaval. Whoever had been here had worked with frenzied malice. Most of the chairs were broken, the side walls had been daubed with white and brown paint and, on the wall behind the stage, written in badly-formed letters in red paint, were the words:

Clear out, Kemp. We don't
want yore kind ere.

CHAPTER TWO

EVIDENCE OF MALICE

'Who is that?' asked Kemp, without looking round.

'Rollison,' said Rollison.

'Oh.' The younger man turned slowly and looked into the Toff's face. His own held a curiously drawn expression—as if the past hour had put years on to his life. 'Someone doesn't like me,' he said, harshly.

'That can cut both ways,' said Rollison,

lightly.

He wanted to see how the other would react and watched him carefully. After a long pause, during which his face was quite blank except for the glitter in his eyes, Kemp's lips began to curve.

'You're a good cure for depression,' he said, in a lighter voice. I was to have met two parishioners here. Instead, the door was open and, when I switched on the light, this is what I found. They've made a thorough job, haven't they?'

'Not bad,' admitted Rollison, 'but there isn't much that can't be repaired, as far as I can see, so perhaps they want to keep you busy. Who were the two people whom you expected to be waiting for you?'

'A Mr and Mrs Whiting,' Kemp said, absently. 'Probably they got scared and I can't blame them. I shouldn't imagine I'm going to have many friends in the near future!' The edge was back in his voice as he proffered cigarettes. Rollison took one.

'You don't know your people yet,' he said. 'Those who were lukewarm towards you before will now rally round and people who've never set foot in the church will probably come in on your side. You've a chance in a thousand, *if* you'll take it.'

Kemp looked at him incredulously.

'Are you serious?'

'Yes,' said Rollison, 'I've been acquainted

12

with these people for years and I don't think you need worry about lacking friends—you can count on it that those who aren't for you now are against you, which will be a help.' He stepped to the door and called Jolly, who entered without a change of expression; he bowed to Kemp. 'Move around a bit, Jolly,' said Rollison, 'and try to find out something about this. Freddie Day might have heard a whisper, or else—'

'I think I know whom to approach, sir,' said Jolly, faintly reproachful.

Rollison grinned. 'So you should! If I'm not here when you've finished, I'll leave a message.'

'Very good, sir.' Jolly went out and Kemp's gaze followed him, as if he were too good to be true.

'Who is Eddie Day?' he asked.

'Freddie,' corrected Rollison. 'He's the manager of the pub on the corner of Jupe Street.'

Kemp frowned. 'I don't know the licensed victuallers.'

Rollison stared. 'The—' he chuckled and went on jocularly: 'If you call pub-keepers licensed victuallers, you'll make your people think they've got to learn a new language—it would be easier for you to learn theirs!' When Kemp looked slightly shocked, he went on in a sharper voice: 'The pubs are part of your parish, aren't they?'

13

'Yes,' admitted Kemp, uncomfortably, 'but I—er—I—I always thought—'

'That they were dens of vice and iniquity in the East End,' said Rollison. 'Yes, I suppose you would but the quicker you get the idea out of your head, the better. You'll find the good as well as the bad go regularly for their pint and if you try to make 'em give it up, you'll come a cropper. None of which is my business, strictly speaking,' he added, more lightly. 'This job is. Have you got anything in mind?'

'I suppose I'd better tell the police,' said Kemp, slowly.

'Why such reluctance?'

'I didn't get on with them very well before,' said Kemp. 'I mean, about Craik.'

'If that were the only reason, I'd say go to see them,' said Rollison. 'But it might be a good idea not to tell them yet. They'll hear about it but unless you approach them officially, they'll do nothing. If you ask them to investigate, they'll probably start a round-up and they might pick up half a dozen of the people concerned but your stock would go down with a bump.'

'I wish I could understand you,' said Kemp, after a short pause.

'Taken by and large,' said Rollison, 'East Enders don't like the police. Oh, they rub shoulders and get along all right but it's an uneasy peace. A man who runs to the police if he's been beaten up or had his pocket picked

14

doesn't win much favour but if he finds out who does it and repays him in kind, that's a different story.'

'Confound it, *I* can't go round wrecking people's homes!'

'Need you take me so literally?' asked Rollison. 'Ever done any boxing, Kemp?'

'A bit, at Oxford,' Kemp answered.

'I thought you looked as if you could pack a punch.'

'I suppose you do realise that I'm—'

'A parson, yes. Is that any reason why you shouldn't behave like a human being?' asked Rollison. 'You want to get on top of this trouble and you want the people friendly, don't you?'

Kemp said: 'Yes.' He spoke with restraint, as if he had difficulty in preventing himself from saying just how badly he wanted both those things.

'Then give my way a trial,' advised Rollison. 'You'll soon find out if it flops.' He stepped forward towards the stage and looked at the writing thoughtfully, murmuring: 'A nice taste in capitals. Now, let's get busy,' he said more briskly. 'It's personal but it isn't aimed at you because you're Ronald Kemp, recently from Oxford and trying to muscle in on a new district. It's because of something you've done or you want to do, which is upsetting someone's applecart. Have you any ideas about it?'

15

'Not the faintest!'

'Try to think some up,' urged Rollison. 'Go over everything that's happened since you arrived and find out whose corns you've trodden on. What kind of reforms have you tried to start?' he added drily. 'You haven't seriously had a shot at turning the pagans teetotal, have you?'

'Great Scott, no! I don't know that I've done anything that could offend anyone,' Kemp went on worriedly. 'I've started one or two of the mission halls going again, there hadn't been any meetings or social evenings for some time. And I've tried to step up the collection of old clothes for some of the poorer people. Do you think they resent that kind of charity?'

'They'd be queer fish if they liked it,' Rollison said. 'But they don't resent it, especially if they're clothes for the women and children. Kemp, get one thing firmly fixed in your head. Most of your parishioners have exactly the same ideas of right and wrong as you have, although they differ in degree. They like a fighter, even if they don't like what he fights for. If a man doesn't drink or smoke, that's his affair, but if he tries to convert others to his way of thinking, it's a different matter. That goes for any kind of habit, vice or crime—the one way you might get some of them to look at it differently is by example— only by example. Do you see what I'm driving at?'

16

'Yes,' said Kemp, slowly. 'As a matter of fact, Mr Cartwright said something on the same lines but I haven't been able to see him for several weeks.' He looked rueful. 'I didn't pay much attention at the time.'

'Try to, now,' urged Rollison. 'What was I saying? Oh—item one: you've upset someone badly and you're the only one who can find out how. It may be simply a matter of having trodden on someone's corns but it doesn't look like that to me,' he admitted, thoughtfully.

'What does it look like?' asked Kemp.

'A much bigger motive,' said Rollison. 'But that's guesswork and won't help us. This Mr and Mrs Whiting—where do they live?'

'In Little Lane—it's off Jupe Street.'

'I know it,' said Rollison. 'Let's go and see them.'

Kemp obviously did not see much point in them both going but he raised no serious objection and, after closing the door, the lock of which had been broken by the wreckers, they walked through the blackout towards Little Lane.

They had not gone fifty yards before Rollison knew that they were being followed.

He said nothing to Kemp until they reached the corner and then spoke in a whisper.

'Walk straight on and make as much noise as you can. Don't argue!'

He heard Kemp's intake of breath as the man was about to speak but obediently the

17

curate crossed the end of the lane and stamped towards Whitechapel Road. Rollison slipped back into the lane and, after a few seconds, two men passed; they made little sound and the soft padding of their footsteps told him that they were wearing rubber-soled shoes.

He wished that he was, too.

He moved after them, drawing closer. It was too dark for him to see Kemp but he could just make out the figures of the others. Both were short men who moved easily and silently.

Kemp's footsteps rang out clearly and the two short men quickened their pace.

Rollison followed suit, caring less now about being heard, but the others appeared too intent on their task to keep on the alert for anyone else.

Rollison suddenly shone his torch full on the two men who were within a few feet of Kemp. One of them had an arm upraised, and was holding a cosh.

'Look out, Kemp!' cried Rollison.

He broke into a run as Kemp swung round; the cosh appeared to strike him on the shoulder but with nothing like the power with which he struck at his assailant. The man toppled over before his companion swung round to get away—only to run straight into Rollison.

He tried to dodge aside; Rollison put out a leg and tripped him up.

18

'Are you all right?' he called to Kemp.

After a pause, Kemp called back in a strained voice.

'Rollison, I think I've hurt him.'

'Even if you've broken his neck, it wouldn't rate as manslaughter! Is he unconscious?'

The man he had tripped up was foxing as he lay motionless on the floor and he kept the beam of light on him.

'Yes,' called Kemp.

'Make sure, then pick him up and take him back to the hall,' said Rollison. 'I—ah!'

His own victim sprang to his feet like a spring-heeled-Jack and made to dart down the street but Rollison shot out a hand and caught his coat, yanking him back. He fended off an attempt to kick him in the stomach, got a grip on the man's arm and held it behind his back in a hammer-lock. The man began to squeal.

'The more you wriggle, the more it will hurt,' Rollison said quietly.

No one appeared to have heard the scuffle and the only sounds were their voices and Kemp's footsteps. Kemp came up, carrying a man in his arms and Rollison spoke mildly.

'I don't like ribbing you all the time, old chap, but if he comes round he could get his hands on your throat, or gouge your eyes out or knee you in the stomach. Put him over your shoulder in a fireman's hold and keep a grip on one of his wrists. That's better!' Although he could not see clearly in the light of the

19

torch, he approved the speed with which Kemp took his advice. Together, they went to the hall. The squealing of the Toff's captive grew louder. Still no one appeared to hear them and they entered the hall without having encountered a soul.

Kemp lowered his victim to a broken bench.

'Surely *some*one heard us?' he said.

Rollison chuckled.

'Half Jupe Street heard us but it wasn't their business. We haven't done so badly, have we?'

'Did you expect this?'

'I wasn't altogether surprised,' admitted Rollison, 'but I didn't hope for a brace of them. Nasty-looking brutes, aren't they? Have you ever seen either of them before?'

'No,' said Kemp.

Looped round the right wrist of his victim, who was still unconscious but not badly hurt, was a cosh—a weapon not unlike a rubber truncheon but smooth and round at one end and narrow near the wrist. He pulled it off; it was flexible and he swished it through the air, letting it go perilously close to the man who was cowering back against the wall. The weapon missed his head by inches.

'No!' he gasped. 'No!'

'Sorry,' said Rollison, perfunctorily. 'Do you know this weapon, Kemp?'

'No,' said Kemp again.

'It's a common or garden cosh,' Rollison told him, 'and it's as popular here as the knuckle-

20 √

duster, razor and flick-knife but less dangerous. Feel it.' Kemp fingered the thicker end. 'It's filled with lead shot,' went on Rollison, 'and is made like that so that it will knock a man out but leave no permanent injury, probably not even a bruise. So they didn't intend to kill which should console you.' He smiled crookedly at Kemp but, before the curate could reply, he swung round on the conscious man and spoke in a rough voice. 'Now! It's time you talked. Who sent you after Mr Kemp?'

CHAPTER THREE

TALK OF HARRY KELLER

The man's mouth dropped open and he tried to back further against the wall but only succeeded in knocking the back of his head against it. The Toff moved the cosh again, not violently, but close to his frightened eyes. The man was undersized, round-faced with a broken nose and an ugly scar over his right eye. From his cauliflower ears the Toff classed him as an ex-prize fighter. He was a man of perhaps forty and, in spite of his fear, there was a cunning glint in his eyes.

He drew in a hiss of breath.

'I—I just 'appened to be—'

21

'You just happened to meet a friend and you were walking along with him when all of a sudden he jumped out at someone in front of him,' said Rollison, sarcastically. 'I know all about that one, I've heard it before. I'd followed you far enough to know that you were both involved, so don't lie. Who told you to . . .'

'I dunno!' squealed the man.

'You dunno, don't you,' said Rollison. 'Kemp, I'm going to give you a lesson in how to make a stubborn man talk. You might find it useful but don't say who taught you!' He raised the cosh as if he meant business and Kemp actually put out a hand to restrain him.

'I'll tell you!' gasped the little man, rearing up against the wall, ' 'Arry Keller gimme a quid to come along wiv Spike!'

Rollison glanced at the man on the floor.

'And is he Spike?'

'Spike Adams, that's his name, mister.'

'And what's your name?' demanded Rollison.

'I—I don't 'ave to tell yer *my* name, do I?' asked the little man, in a wheedling tone, 'I've told yer the names of the others. Gimme a break. I never did nothing, I only drifted along with Spike, that's all.'

'When you've given me your name and waited for half an hour, you can go,' said Rollison.

'You *mean* that?' The man's little eyes lit up.

'Yes,' said Rollison—and released a flood of

talk.

'My name's 'Arris, mister, Tom 'Arris. I live dahn in River Row, everyone knows Tom 'Arris—me name's an 'ouseold word. Never beaten, I wasn't. Had two hundred and two fights an' never beaten, that's me. I'm dahn on me luck, mister,' went on Harris in maudlin tones. 'I wouldn't have done such a thing as I done tonight if I 'adn't been. A quid means a lot to me an' I never knew what Spike was going to do. That's Gawd's truth.'

'I don't think!' said Rollison. 'Go and sit on the stage and don't move until I tell you to.'

'Me wife'll be expecting me,' declared Harris, pleadingly, 'I promised I wouldn't be no later than one o'clock. You wouldn't let a woman be left alone at night these days, would you?'

'Some women, gladly,' said Rollison. 'Get on the stage.'

Harris shrugged his shoulders and slouched off.

'Keep an eye on him,' Rollison said, *sotto voce*, 'he might start throwing the chairs about.'

He spoke loudly enough for the man on the floor to hear, if he were conscious, and stepped towards the other wall. The man bounded to his feet and darted for the door. Rollison picked up a chair and threw it so that the man went sprawling.

'Now, Spike,' said Rollison, chidingly. 'Foxing won't help you. He strolled over to the

23

man, who made no further attempt to get up, and smiled at him. 'So Harry Keller sent you, did he?'

Adams glared up.

'So you're not a talker, like Harris?' said Rollison, 'I suppose I couldn't expect to find two on the same night.' He glanced at Kemp who was trying to watch him and keep an eye on Harris at the same time. 'I don't think we need worry about this customer, do you? The police will look after him, he'll probably get twelve months for using the cosh.'

Adams broke across the words.

'If you run me in, I'll see you get beaten up. Got me?'

'It's like that, is it?' asked Rollison, thrusting a hand into his pocket and swinging the cosh with the other. 'I don't think you've recognised me, Spike.'

'I don't give a damn who you are!'

'You should, you know,' said Rollison. 'For now I come to think of it, I've seen and heard a lot about you. Try using your memory.' When Adams kept silent, he went on in an amiable tone: 'Come! You should be able to do better than this!'

A remarkable change came over Spike Adams's face. One moment he was glaring defiance; the next he was staring incredulously and defiance seemed to ooze away from him. His body relaxed and his lips began to move but he only managed to stutter. Rollison stood

24

smiling down at him. Kemp gave up all pretence of watching the man on the stage.

'Gawd!' exclaimed Spike, at last, 'you're the Toff!'

'That's right, Spike.'

'*You—you* ain't in this affair.'

'Didn't Harry Keller tell you I was,' asked Rollison. 'He should be fair, shouldn't he?' His voice changed. 'Let's have it: what do you know?'

Spike began to talk freely.

'I dunno much, mister, that's a fact. Keller gimme the orders, said I was to beat the parson up. That's all. He never said I might run inter the Toff. Listen, mister, you wouldn't run me in, would you? I 'ad to do it, if I hadn't, Keller would've put some of the boys on me.'

'Which boys?' asked Rollison.

'He's got a dozen in his mob!'

'Harry Keller and his dozen, is it?' mused Rollison. 'Where can I find Keller?'

'I—I dunno,' said Spike and his voice became a squeak. 'I don't, I tell yer—that's Gawd's truth. He's not one who stays in the same place for long. Last I heard, he was at The Docker but he ain't there now. I seed 'im in the street ternight, that's when he gimme the job.'

Rollison weighed the cosh in his hand and deliberated. Harris was staring fixedly from the stage; the name 'Toff' had affected him as much as it had Spike Adams. Only the heavy

25

breathing of the prisoners broke the silence.

Kemp looked from one to the other, incredulous.

'All right,' Rollison said at last, 'I'll take your word this time but if you've lied to me, I'll fix you. Don't forget it. The police will be glad of a chance to put both of you inside,' he went on, turning to include Harris in his homily. 'If Keller wants you to do any more of his dirty work, send word to me.'

'Okay, mister!' Spike gasped.

He scrambled to his feet and Harris jumped down from the stage and joined him. Rollison nodded towards the door and the men nearly fell over each other in their eagerness to get away. Harris closed the door carefully behind them.

Kemp drew a deep breath.

'Great Scott, Rollison! I've never seen anything like it!'

Rollison smiled. 'I hope you often will. They know we could land them in jail for a year and added to it they have a curious idea that I'm unbeatable and infallible.'

'But that man's face when he recognised you!'

Rollison laughed.

'Once upon a time someone started a legend about me and I've kept up the illusion ever since,' he said, lightly. 'We're making progress. We want to interview Mr Harry Keller as soon as we can. A curious business,' he added. 'I think Adams told the truth when he said he doesn't know where Keller lives and that he's not one of the mob. So Keller wanted to make quite sure that if things went wrong, no one could say much about what he's up to.'

'Can you see any sense in it?' demanded Kemp.

'There is sense but no reason for it,' said Rollison. 'Who first suggested that I might help?'

'The Whitings,' said Kemp.

'We really ought to go to see them,' said Rollison, glancing at his watch. 'It's half-past one, but—'

'We can't knock them up at this time of night!'

'That won't worry them,' said Rollison, confidently.

'Look here!' said Kemp, 'never mind the Whitings—why did you let those men go?'

'Is that still worrying you?' asked Rollison. 'They'll run straight to Keller and tell him about me,' said Rollison. 'It's one thing to persecute a newcomer to the district—and there's a peculiar idea that curates can't hit back but Spike knows better now!—and another thing to operate against me. I know the East End and I've a lot of friends here. It will be interesting to see what happens when Keller gets to know I'm involved.'

'I give up!' exclaimed Kemp.

'Not you, you've only just started! Let's see

27

the Whitings.' Kemp protested half-heartedly but Rollison was firm. This time, no one followed them from the hall. The stars were still out and a breeze from the river made it cooler. Rollison walked leisurely and Kemp towered beside him, occasionally starting to speak but always thinking better of it. They were halfway down Little Lane, shining their torches on the numbers of the houses, when Kemp said abruptly:

'I say, what about your man?'

'He'll be all right.'

'But you were going to leave a message for him!'

'He won't be finished for another hour or more,' said Rollison. 'If he should get back and find us gone, he'll telephone my flat. Don't worry about Jolly. What was the Whitings' number?'

'Forty-nine,' Kemp told him.

'Forty-three-five-seven-nine,' said Rollison. 'Here we are.'

The house was one of a long, narrow terrace which, in daylight, looked dreary and dilapidated. There were no pavements in Little Lane and the road was cobbled. An odour of decay and stale cooking hung about the lane but there was no chink of light from any window, no sign of anyone awake.

Rollison knocked sharply on the door.

'I hope they don't think it's an awful nerve,' said Kemp.

'I hope you think Craik's worth the trouble,' said Rollison, tartly.

'Oh—sorry!' Kemp made no further comment and Rollison knocked again but there was no answer.

'Do they live here on their own?' asked Rollison.

'There's an old lady—Mrs Whiting's mother—and three children,' said Kemp.

'No boarders?'

'I've never heard of any.'

Rollison knocked again. The sound echoed along the street and faded into a brooding silence but brought no response. Rollison rattled the letter box, bent down and peered inside. A faint glow of light showed at the far end of the passage.

'That's peculiar,' he said. 'Stay here, Kemp—don't go away and don't let anyone distract your attention.'

'Where—' began Kemp but he spoke to the darkness, for Rollison had disappeared, soundlessly.

Rollison hurried to the end of the lane then along Jupe Street to a narrow alley. There were tiny gardens here, back and front, for Jupe Street had been built when some measure of enlightenment had permeated Victorian minds and even East Enders had been allowed room in which to breathe.

There was no gateway to the alley.

Rollison counted the wooden gates as he

29

passed, shining his torch until he reached Number 49. He put it out and opened a gate noisily. He left it open and walked with heavy tread for a few yards then switched off his torch and went on again stealthily, counting the houses by their roofs outlined against the starlit sky. He stopped at Number 47.

He thought he heard voices.

The back gate was open and he heard a man stirring—as if he were waiting inside the tiny yard and getting impatient. Soon a door opened and a sliver of light showed. It disappeared as the door closed.

'Okay?' a man asked, softly.

'I've scared the lights out of them,' said another, in a cultured voice which carried a hint of laughter. 'They won't go to church in a hurry!'

Rollison stood in the doorway as the men approached, holding his torch in front of him. As they drew within a yard or two of him, walking side by side, he switched on the torch and the dazzling light brought them abruptly to a standstill.

'And which of you is Mr Keller?' inquired Rollison, politely.

CHAPTER FOUR

THE MEN WHO UTTERED MENACES

'Don't make the mistake of moving,' continued Rollison without a pause, 'because I've brought a gun with me. Which of you is Keller?' he repeated.

Neither of them moved. Probably they realised that if they doubled back into the house they would do little good; more likely, they were afraid that he really had a gun. The light of his torch showed their hands as well as their faces.

The taller of the two was well-dressed and good-looking with short, dark hair and a heavy moustache. He was hatless and wore an open-necked shirt. Obviously he was the man with the cultured voice. The other, shorter and thick-set, had a pugnacious but not an evil face—he was very different from the ex-prize-fighter and Spike Adams. His large eyes stood the light better than his companion and he was the first to speak.

'Who the hell are you?' His voice was rough but not Cockney.

'A friend of Kemp,' answered Rollison.

'If you know what's good for you, you'll tell Kemp to clear out,' growled the thick-set man. 'He's not wanted here.'

'So I gathered when Spike Adams tried to beat him up,' said Rollison. 'The Rev Kemp is tougher than you realise.'

'I've warned him,' the man growled.

'Are you Keller?'

'Never mind who I am!'

'I don't think we understand each other,' said Rollison, mildly. 'I'm helping Kemp who is here to stay. Anyone who tries to get rid of him will run into much more trouble than he expects.'

'Anyone who helps Kemp will be lucky if he doesn't get his neck broken,' said the thick-set man.

Then, with one accord, they jumped at him.

Rollison was prepared for the rush. He switched off his torch, stepped to one side and shot out his foot. The simple method worked. The thick-set man fell heavily and the other tripped over him, gasping. Rollison drew away, not certain that the worst was over. The night's silence was broken by the sound of footsteps approaching from both directions.

He slipped into the yard of the house next door and stood by the gate. The men on the ground picked themselves up, muttering, as a newcomer drew up.

'You okay?' he asked, hoarsely.

'Yes,' grunted the thick-set man. 'If I come across that man again, I'll break his neck!' He uttered a stream of expletives as he dusted himself down while Rollison backed further into the yard and other men arrived.

None of the newcomers saw him. He kept close to the wall, trying to estimate the chances of climbing into the next yard if they should start to search for him. In the darkness, climbing would not be easy but there were at least three newcomers and odds of five to one were too heavy.

He crept further away, although he could hear their heavy breathing. There was a furtive air about them all and they spoke in whispers.

'Who was he?' asked the man with the cultured voice.

'Some fool who fancies himself,' muttered the other. 'I didn't think Kemp would ask any of his posh friends to come and help him. We'll have to put a stop to that.'

'I never see no one,' one of the newcomers said.

'I think I seed him go Jupe Street way,' volunteered another.

'He's scared stiff,' said the man with the gruff voice. 'Let's get away.'

'Oughtn't we to look for him?' asked the man with the cultured voice.

'On a night like this? Have some sense!'

They moved off, two of the newcomers going ahead of the couple whom Rollison had met and the third following. Rollison waited until their footsteps had faded then pushed a hand through his hair, looking very thoughtful as he walked to the back door of the Whitings' house and tapped.

After a long pause, the door opened. A faint glow of light shone from another room. A thin man was outlined against it, but Rollison could not see his face.

'W-what do you want?' His voice was unsteady.

'If you're Mr Whiting, I want to see you,' said Rollison. He pushed his way past and closed the door. He heard the hissing and popping of a lighted gas-jet and widened the doorway from which the light came. It shone on a weedy-looking young man with thin hair, pale features, a harassed expression.

'Who-who is it, Erny?' asked a woman from another room, in a quavering voice. 'Are—are they back again?'

'I don't know,' muttered Erny Whiting. 'I— No! They're not!' His voice rose and his troubled expression cleared. 'Why, it's the—'

'Hush!' urged Rollison.

Whiting stood and gazed at him in silence while a little anxious-and-tired looking woman came from the other room. She stopped abruptly when she saw Rollison, a gleam of recognition in her eyes.

'The others might be listening outside,' said Rollison, 'I'll make sure. You let Mr Kemp in—he's at the front.'

Mrs Whiting turned to obey after only a moment's hesitation. Rollison went into the yard again but found no one. He returned to

34

the house and was ushered into the tiny parlour. Kemp was inside, stooping slightly because the ceiling was so low. In an armchair in one corner sat a very old woman, her hair drawn tightly back from her forehead. Her face was so thin that her skin was a mass of lines and wrinkles. She looked at Rollison with bright, beady eyes—both suspicious and wary.

'Who is he?' she squeaked.

'It—it's Mr Rollison,' said Whiting, nervously. 'I—I somehow didn't think you would come, Mr Rollison.'

'We can go on from there,' smiled Rollison, leaning against a piano which took up most of one wall. 'Why didn't you open the front door as soon as we knocked?'

Whiting licked his lips.

'They—the men told me not to.'

'Do you know who they were?'

'No, I've never seen them before,' answered Whiting. 'They came about ten minutes before you—came the back way.' He licked his lips again. 'They said we wasn't to help Mr Kemp or go to the church—if we did, they said, they'd—' he stopped, tongue-tied.

Rollison's eyes held a steely glint.

'The men who uttered menaces!' he murmured. 'Whom did they threaten? Your children?'

'Yes!' Whiting gasped.

'We had to promise we wouldn't help Mr Kemp!' Mrs Whiting cried, 'we don't want

35

anything to happen to our children, Mr Rollison!'

'Of course you don't and nothing will,' Rollison assured her. 'Why do they want to keep you away from church, Whiting? Do you know?'

'They—they only just told us that,' said Whiting, 'but I think I know why. I was—I was with Joe Craik,' he added with a nervous rush. 'We was walking down to the hall together and two men bumped into us. They went off and Joe said they'd picked 'is pocket but the only thing missing was his knife, he said, and he might have left that at his shop.'

'Go on,' murmured Rollison.

'Well, we hadn't got much further on when three more were waiting for us, near the hall,' Whiting said, sending a troubled glance at the old woman in the corner, who clearly disapproved of his frankness. 'They started leading off about Mr Kemp. It wasn't fair, the things they said—it just wasn't fair. I didn't want any trouble but Joe answered back and before we knew where we were, they was on us. We *had* to hit back,' Whiting added, defensively. 'The police come and one of them was on the pavement—I thought he'd knocked hisself out. Instead—'

'He warned you, didn't he?' squeaked the old woman in the corner. 'He told you wot would 'appen if you squealed!'

'Be quiet, Ma,' pleaded Whiting.

36

Rollison was on the point of leaving when a taxi drew up outside and Jolly arrived.

He had little information. No word of the trouble at the hall had yet reached Freddie Day or others whom Jolly had seen but the hostility towards Kemp was already well known. Not until they were in the taxi, the driver of which was still in a good humour, did Jolly confide that the majority were taking a neutral attitude. Kemp had not yet made a very good impression among his parishioners.

'He will,' said Rollison, confidently.

He told Jolly what had happened before they reached the flat. Rollison paid the driver off, adding a pound to the fare and walked upstairs with the man's gusty thanks ringing in his ears.

Jolly had gone ahead.

Afterwards, Rollison knew that he should have been prepared for some such development, although he had not thought of the possibility of a visit to the flat so early. As it was, he stepped inside the little hall and saw Jolly standing motionless with his back towards him, just inside the drawing-room.

'What—' he began.

'That's enough from you, Rollison,' said a voice from behind him.

Rollison forced himself not to turn too hastily but his heart began to thump. The voice was that of the thick-set man whom he had seen at the back of Whiting's house. He caught a glimpse of the owner of the educated voice, standing in front of Jolly. He got the impression that Jolly was being held up at the point of a gun, as he turned to look into the curiously docile looking brown eyes of the man with the growling voice.

CHAPTER FIVE

'I'M KELLER.'

Once he had recovered from the surprise, Rollison smiled into the man's face.

'Harry Keller, I presume,' he said.

'I'm Keller, yes,' answered the thick-set man. 'When are you going to stop nosing into other people's business?'

'It's a congenital failing, I'm afraid,' said Rollison, sadly, 'I can't help myself.'

'You'll help yourself this time,' said Keller.

His assurance in itself was puzzling. If the visitors had planned an attack it would probably have been made when Rollison had walked unsuspectingly into the hall. It appeared more likely that Keller had come to reason with him and that was puzzling.

'What makes you think so?' he inquired politely.

'We don't want that big parson around and we don't intend to let him stay, Toff or no Toff. Nothing you can do will make any

42

difference but if you don't lay off, you will get hurt.'

'Oh, dear,' said Rollison, blankly.

'I mean *hurt*,' repeated Keller, harshly. 'It won't help you to run to the dicks. They can't get at me and I'm too powerful for you on your own. It's time you stayed where you belong.'

'Where do you think that is?' asked Rollison.

'In the West End with all your fancy tarts and your wealthy friends,' said Keller. 'This isn't a game for you, Rollison. You might get your hands dirty.' Rollison watched his mobile features, seeing the way his lips curled and his eyebrows rose. Keller was an impressive personality, it would be folly to underestimate him. 'You stay in Mayfair, Rollison, and if you must stick your nose into things that don't concern you, there's plenty of cleaning up to be done in your own back yard. But you wouldn't try that, would you? You might find your precious friends are mixed up in it.'

'In what?' asked Rollison, obtusely.

'You know what,' rasped Keller. 'I'm telling you to stick around your own back yard and not meddle in mine.'

'A whole world, all of your own?' asked Rollison.

'If you won't take a warning, don't blame me for anything that happens. I don't want to interfere with you. You let me alone, I'll let you alone.'

'Now who could say fairer than that?' asked

43

Rollison, lightly. 'What would you say if a policeman were to walk into the flat this minute?' He studied the man curiously and thought he had him guessing. 'I don't suggest that it's likely but I have all sorts of queer friends. I'd say to him: "Bill"—or Percy or whatever his name happened to be—"this is Harry Keller. He employed Spike Adams and Tom Harris to beat up the Rev Ronald Kemp. He employed others to wreck a mission hall and do some hundreds of pounds worth of damage. He stole the knife belonging to a man named Craik and killed a third party with the said Craik's knife."'

The atmosphere had grown noticeably more tense while a movement from the drawing-room made him glance at the man with the cultured voice who was pushing past Jolly. He held a gun.

But no one spoke.

'Shall I go on?' Rollison asked. '"Having committed murder," I would add, "Keller worried because a man named Whiting knew about the stolen knife, so he visited Whiting and uttered threats and menaced the lives of Whiting's children. After that, he heard from Spike Adams or Tom Harris that I was a friend of Kemp, so he came here, burglariously entered my flat, threatened my valet with a gun and uttered more menaces." Then,' continued Rollison, smiling faintly, 'I would ask him how many years in gaol you'd be likely

44

to get.'

Keller spoke in a thin voice. 'You don't know what you've done, Rollison.'

'Oh, but I do,' said Rollison. 'I've frightened you and your friend. Queer thing, fear. I've made a study of it.'

'Once and for all, Rollison, I'm telling you to stick to your own back yard!'

'But Whitechapel *is* mine,' protested the Toff. 'I was a frequenter of Jupe Street before you knew the difference between Whitechapel and Bethnal Green. What time did Grice say he'd be here, Jolly?'

Jolly answered with hardly a pause, as if he had been expecting the question and Keller stiffened.

'At four o'clock, sir. I think he's a little late.'

'Grice is on holiday!' Keller growled.

'He was—but he would make any sacrifice in a good cause,' said Rollison, as if gratified. 'When I asked him to come back, he promised to start right away. Of course he'll be alone, so you might prefer to stay. One Superintendent of Scotland Yard won't make much difference to you. Besides, you are above the police.'

'I know what I'm about,' rasped Keller.

'That's splendid,' declared Rollison.

'If you don't—'

'Oh, go away!' snapped Rollison, losing patience. 'You and your empty threats—what do you expect to gain? You've already lined up half of Whitechapel behind Kemp. Before

45

tonight they hadn't much time for him, now they're on his side. Go away and assimilate a little common sense!' He sounded almost pettish as he turned away, passing Jolly and the second man and, pushing the latter roughly to one side, he strode into the drawing-room and picked up the telephone.

The success of the trick he had planned depended upon Jolly—who dodged back into the drawing-room and slammed the door. Rollison dropped the telephone and jumped to the door, putting his full weight against it as Jolly turned the key. Three heavy thuds shook it; then the men outside ceased trying to break it down.

Rollison and Jolly stood either side of the door so that, if Keller or his man fired into it, they would be out of harm's way.

Rollison spoke in a loud voice.

'Nicely done, Jolly!'

'Thank you, sir,' said Jolly, soberly.

'I hope Grice doesn't run into them,' Rollison went on, sounding anxious. 'He's an impetuous beggar and might start a riot. I'd better ring for someone else from the Yard,' he added. He walked heavily round the room then lifted the telephone and banged the receiver up and down several times.

The hall door slammed.

Rollison grinned. 'That might be a pretty trick to make us show ourselves again, we'll stay where we are . . . Hallo, is that Scotland

46

Yard? . . . Rollison speaking, give me Inspector Mason, please.' After a pause, he went on: 'Yes, Sergeant Hamilton will do . . . hallo, Hamilton? Send a couple of your liveliest men round to the flat, will you? I'm locked in my own drawing-room with two homicidal maniacs in the hall, threatening to . . . yes, of course I'm serious!'

The startled sergeant promised that he would send men immediately and Rollison replaced the receiver.

The flat was on the first floor and it would be possible to climb out of the window and surprise Keller from the rear. But he had no weapon and had a healthy respect for the other's gun. Even if he only tried to follow them, it was so dark that they would probably shake him off. It would be best to stay where he was, confident that the flat would be clear of the intruders by the time the police arrived.

He and Jolly conversed in whispers but that soon palled. They heard nothing for five minutes, then a car drew up outside and heavy footsteps came thumping on the stairs. Not until the police were outside the flat did Rollison unlock the drawing-room door and let them in.

Sergeant Hamilton, tall, fair and brisk, hoped Rollison had not been pulling his leg.

'I have not!' Rollison assured him, fervently, 'I expected the men to try to break the door down but they heard me telephoning you and

47

decided not to wait.'

'Who were they?' demanded Hamilton.

'I haven't the faintest idea,' said Rollison.

Afterwards, when the police had gone and as dawn was breaking, he told Jolly that he did not propose to mention Keller's name to the police until he knew more about the man. For one thing, Keller's certainty that he was in no danger from the police was a remarkable thing. For another, he wanted to feel the pulse of the East End before he stirred up police action. He had been perfectly serious when he had told Kemp that it would be better to fight on his own for the time being—the masses of the district would rally round him when it was seen that he was trying to fight single-handed—or even with help from the Toff.

At a quarter-past five, Rollison went to bed.

At a quarter-to eight, Jolly called him for Rollison, an acting Colonel, was due at his office in Whitehall by nine thirty. He had the week before him, for it was only Tuesday, and there was little chance of getting leave; the only way of doing that, he complained to Jolly, was to go sick.

'Won't you await events before taking that step?' asked Jolly.

'You mean won't I give you a free hand?' said Rollison, smiling unamusedly. 'I suppose I'll have to. See Kemp and the Whitings and keep me in touch with what happens. I'll lunch at the club, so ring me there.'

48

'Very good, sir,' said Jolly.

And the Toff, sadly, set out for Whitehall.

Twice, in the course of the morning, a colleague said with some exasperation that he was not giving his mind to the subject under discussion and twice he apologised and tried to pull himself together. In truth, he was apprehensive lest the Whitings had been made to suffer for their boldness. The one reassuring factor was that Bill Ebbutt had sounded as if he knew what kind of proposition he was up against with Keller and would take elaborate precautions. It was absurd that Keller should be able to inspire such apprehension and equally absurd that he should be so self-assured.

'But he isn't!' exclaimed Rollison, aloud.

'Now look here, Rolly,' said plump, bespectacled Colonel Bimbleton, 'you know perfectly well that he was.'

'Eh?' asked Rollison.

'Oh, you're impossible!' declared Bimbleton, then peered at him with sudden interest. 'I say, Rolly, is something up?'

'Up *is* the word,' said Rollison. 'I'm sorry, Bimble, but I can't concentrate on this report. Would you care to have a shot at it yourself?'

Bimbleton regarded him curiously.

'Well, I don't mind trying,' he conceded, 'provided you'll look through it afterwards and make sure I haven't pulled a boner.'

Rollison promised this and Bimbleton went

off to wrestle with a report on pilfering from army stores depots, a task which Whitehall, in all its wisdom, had ordained to be eminently suitable for a man known to associate with the police.

Jolly did not telephone the office or the club.

After lunch, Rollison hurried back to the office but his clerk, a plump ATS sergeant, had no message for him.

In his cogitations, Rollison had got no further than that Keller *was* afraid of the police taking action against him but had reason to think that a lot of prodding would be needed to make them. Keller had been at great pains to try to make sure that Whiting said nothing about the episode of the stolen knife, although there was nothing original in his methods. There were occasional outbursts of intimidation in the East End and, sometimes, a terror-wave which rarely lasted long once it was discovered by the authorities but which might have gained a powerful hold before the police learned of it. Many a man had been frightened into refusing to give evidence, even to committing perjury, by threats such as Keller had made to Whiting.

Two inescapable facts troubled Rollison most.

One was that a man whose name he did not yet know had been murdered and—judging from the evidence so far available—one Joe Craik had been framed for the murder. The second was that Keller had a very powerful reason for wanting to drum the curate out of the St Guy's district.

He dictated letters and signed them, made a brief report on a matter he had been handling by himself, went over Bimbleton's prosy report with its author and made a few comments and left for Gresham Terrace.

Jolly was not at the flat.

Rollison began to feel worried about his man; even if there was nothing to report, Jolly should have telephoned by now. When at last the telephone rang he hurried to it, hoping to hear Jolly's voice. Instead, he heard Kemp's— and Kemp sounded excited.

CHAPTER SIX

MORE NEWS FROM KEMP

'Great Scott, Rollison, I've been trying to get you all the afternoon!' exclaimed Kemp. 'Where the dickens have you been?'

'I should have given you my office number,' said Rollison. 'You'd better take a note of it.'

'Never mind that! Can you come here at once?'

'What's the trouble?'

'I've had a visit from a most astonishing fellow,' said Kemp, amazement making his voice shrill. 'I don't know his name but you should have heard the way he talked! He told me that if you didn't stop interfering, he would mighty soon make you!'

'Did he have brown eyes and a gruff voice?'

'Yes, he did. How did you know?'

'He calls himself Keller,' said Rollison. 'Don't worry about his threats—did he do anything?'

He heard Kemp's sharp intake of breath.

'He didn't actually do anything,' said the curate. 'But—he made the most astonishing offer. He offered to replace all the damaged goods at the hall and give five hundred pounds to St Guy's Relief Fund, if—' Kemp grew almost incoherent.

'If you resigned?' asked Rollison.

'Yes!'

'What did you tell him?'

'I told him,' said Kemp, in a deep voice, '*exactly* where to get off!'

'That's the spirit!' acclaimed Rollison, feeling considerably relieved, 'I was afraid you might have fallen for it.'

'I might have done yesterday,' said Kemp, 'but not now—I've heard a lot about you today. Last night, I only had your name and the little I'd heard about you from the Whitings but today—'

'Spare my blushes,' said Rollison. 'How did you part with our brown-eyed briber?'

'Well, as a matter of fact,' said Kemp, less

52

boisterously, 'I felt a bit uneasy. He's a funny customer, isn't he? He went out breathing threats and said he would give me forty-eight hours to change my mind. He also said *you* would have forty-eight but I'm not particularly worried about *you*.'

'So he's given a time limit, has he?' asked Rollison. 'Don't let yourself be caught napping any time during the next forty-eight hours. Did he have anything else to say?'

'No.'

'Have you thought of anything that might be the cause of the trouble?'

'I've racked my brains but I can't think of anything,' declared Kemp. 'In fact, I don't think there can be—'

'Of course there is,' interrupted Rollison. 'How are the Whitings?'

'They're all right. Those friends of yours have been to and from school with two of the youngsters. It was really funny this afternoon, one of the children is only eighteen months old and Mrs Whiting and the grandmother pushed him out to the shops with two hefties walking behind them. It caused quite a sensation.'

'Good!' said Rollison. 'Publicity is always useful.'

He omitted to say that Kemp's spirits seemed to be much brighter and asked:

'Have you seen my man?'

'That glum looking fellow, what's his name?'

'Jolly.'

53

'What?' asked Kemp, incredulously, and then added hastily: 'No, I haven't seen him. Should he have come here?'

'No, it's all right,' said Rollison.

He rang down, after promising to see Kemp later. He was worried but smiled from time to time when he thought of Keller's offer. After setting his rough-necks on Kemp, attempted bribery was a climb-down—but it told him how seriously Keller intended to get rid of the curate.

Ten minutes later, the telephone rang again. This time, Rollison heard his man's prim voice.

'Good evening, sir.'

'Well, well!' said Rollison and added sarcastically: 'It's nice of you to ring me.'

'I'm sorry that I had no opportunity of telephoning earlier,' said Jolly, stolidly, 'but my inquiries took me out of London and I had to choose between continuing with them and advising you that I could not do so. I came to the conclusion—'

'Yes, you were right,' said Rollison, hastily. 'Where are you now?'

'In Loughton, sir, near Epping Forest. I—' there was a short pause before Jolly went on in a sharper voice: 'I am quite all right but I must go now. I will telephone again at the earliest opportunity. Goodbye, sir!'

Rollison heard the receiver bang down.

He sat contemplating the telephone for some

time. It was rare that Jolly allowed himself to be hurried and he had taken his time at the beginning of the conversation. Only one likely explanation presented itself—that Jolly was keeping watch on someone who had reappeared sooner than he had expected. Reassured, Rollison did not waste time in more than passing speculation on what had taken Jolly to Loughton.

He looked through the evening papers for an account of the murder of the previous night. It was tucked away on an inside page and contained the statement that the murdered man's name was O'Hara. Joseph Craik, of 1a, Jupe Street, had been charged with the murder and been remanded for eight days. Det Sergeant Bray, of Scotland Yard, had made the arrest. Inspector Chumley, of the AZ Division, was not so much as mentioned.

'I suppose I shall have to find out what they're doing sooner or later,' Rollison mused.

Yet the more he pondered, the more determined he became to let the police make the first move. Craik would come to no harm while under remand—he might even be safer in Brixton than in his shop. Had Superintendent Grice been at the Yard, Rollison would have taken a different course; he could talk to Grice off the record and be sure that confidences would be respected, provided the law was not too openly flouted.

A ring at the front door interrupted him.

He opened it, warily, to see a vision in a flowered frock and a wide-brimmed hat with a radiant smile and a beauty spoiled only by a nose which some called *retroussé*. There were few callers he would have welcomed at that juncture, unless they were concerned in the affair of the harassed curate, but he felt a genuine pleasure at the sight of Isobel Crayne.

'Rolly!' she cried.

'Hal-*lo*!' He took her hand and kissed her on the cheek which she presented laughingly. Then he held her at arm's length and eyed her with his head on one side and a gay smile in his eyes.

'Yes,' he said at last 'An improvement, even in you! Isobel, it's good to see you!'

'What an ass you are!' said Isobel, allowing herself to be drawn through the hall into the drawing-room. She took off her hat and dropped it into an easy chair, looking at him all the time. 'How are *you*, Rolly?'

'I *was* jaded,' declared Rollison. 'In fact I was wondering how I could cheer myself up and lo! I open the door and a vision enters.'

'Jaded?' asked Isobel, quickly. 'Why?'

'Oh, the weather—' began Rollison.

'The weather never worried you yet and I don't believe it ever will,' said Isobel. 'And I don't believe you are ever at a loose end.'

'And I thought you'd come to ask me to take you out to dinner!'

'Well, I haven't, I'm on duty tonight,' said

56

Isobel, 'I haven't had an evening free for weeks.'

'Don't rub it in,' said Rollison. 'I can't dance attendance on you like your young men and—'

'Rolly,' said Isobel, still smiling but with a more serious note in her voice, 'I'm afraid you'll want to show me the door when I tell you why I've come but—well, I felt that I had to. It's rather a queer business. Are you very busy?'

'That depends,' said Rollison, 'if I can help you in any way I gladly will. I—confound you!' he broke off, laughing at her, 'I wondered why you spoke up when I said I was jaded, you thought it meant that I'd jump at any excitements you might be able to offer. Isobel, you're too cunning for beauty!'

'*Are* you busy?' persisted Isobel.

'It still depends on what you want,' said Rollison.

He poured her out a long drink; the weather was still hot, although cooler than the previous day, and there was a breeze fresh enough to stir the curtains at the windows. A clear blue sky was visible above the house-tops and just within sight a barrage balloon floated with lazy majesty, as if disdainful of all that went on below.

To some people, Isobel Crayne appeared disdainful, too, for she had a careless manner, at times one almost of condescension; but the Toff knew her for a warm-hearted young woman who did much good privately. She was working for one of the voluntary organisations and had been doing so since the beginning of the war. Not only did it take up most of her time but it also cost her a great deal of money.

Abruptly, she said:

'I've been working in your favourite hunting ground for some time, Rolly.'

'East of Aldgate Pump?'

'Yes. We've a depot down there.'

'Much good work by the Red Cross?'

Isobel looked at him in astonishment.

'What a hopeless memory you've got! I've told you a dozen times that I do *not* work for the Red Cross. I'm WVS and we're running canteens for dock-workers. I can't imagine how you built up such a reputation as a detective, if you forget so easily.'

'I forget what it isn't necessary to remember,' said Rollison, justifying himself urbanely. 'Whether you work for the Red Cross, Aid to China, Aid to Russia, Book Salvage, National Savings, Bone Recovery, ARP or any one of a dozen other equally worthy causes doesn't matter; that you do the work matters a great deal.'

'I am not impressed,' said Isobel. 'In any case, ARP is now Civil Defence! Are you trying to side-track me?'

'Certainly not. I'm waiting patiently for you to get to the point.'

Isobel made a face at him.

58

'I don't suppose it's anything that would interest you,' she went on, 'but if you can possibly look into it, I would be glad. Honestly, I think it's a deserving case. Don't look like that!' she exclaimed, as Rollison's expression grew long-suffering. 'It's not a girl who's taken the wrong turning or a father of twelve who's been picking pockets. It's about—'

Rollison's expression altered so much that Isobel broke off and stared at him, and then went on:

'A young curate, who—'

'Well, well!' exclaimed Rollison, 'so Ronald Kemp has a way with him!'

'You *know* about it?' asked Isobel, incredulously.

'I've heard about it,' said Rollison. 'And you can set your mind at rest. If the great Richard R can turn the scales, the scales are in the process of being turned. How did Kemp win you to his side?'

'He doesn't even know my name,' Isobel told him. 'I heard him preach in Mayfair some time ago and he came to the depot the other day, to see if we had a few odds and ends that he needed for a rummage sale. Have you met him?'

'Yes.'

'No one should have allowed him to go down there,' declared Isobel. 'He's hopelessly out of place. I felt sorry for him the moment I saw him and in the last day or two I've heard rumours that he's being persecuted. But you probably know all about that?'

'A lot about it,' said Rollison.

'Then I needn't worry any more.'

'I call that praise indeed,' smiled Rollison. 'I say, my sweet,' he went on anxiously, 'you haven't been campaigning on Kemp's behalf, have you? I know that crusading heart of yours might have tempted you.'

'I've learned not to interfere with anything that happens, unless it's right under my nose,' said Isobel. 'The East Enders take me on sufferance as it is but if I started to throw my weight about, they'd boycott me. I just felt terribly sorry for Kemp.'

'Don't waste your sympathy,' advised Rollison. 'He is either just the man for the district and is getting the corners smoothed off, or else he's a misfit and he'll find that out soon enough.'

'I suppose you're right,' said Isobel, looking at him curiously. 'You're much deeper than I realise, sometimes.'

'Thanks,' said Rollison, wryly. 'Now—I hate throwing advice about but don't line yourself up with Kemp just yet on any account. I don't mean that you mustn't be sympathetic if he should come and pour out his troubles, which isn't likely, but don't let yourself be persuaded to take an active interest in the affairs of the parish.'

Isobel's eyes were calm.

'So it's dangerous?' she observed.

'It might be.'

'Look after him,' pleaded Isobel. 'He's only a child.'

When she left, Rollison watched her tall graceful figure as she walked towards Piccadilly. She was about Kemp's age and her: 'He's only a child,' echoed ironically in his ears.

He left the flat ten minutes later.

One pressing need was to see Bill Ebbutt, to find out what Bill knew of Keller and why he had been so silent on the telephone. It was a little after half-past six and he hoped to finish with Bill and spend half an hour with Kemp before getting back for a late dinner and, he hoped, Jolly's report.

He went by tube, got out at Whitechapel Station and walked along Whitechapel Road. Bill's pub, the Blue Dog, was on a corner. Behind it was a large, corrugated iron shed which served as the gymnasium. The pub was closed but the gymnasium doors were open. Rollison bunched his fists, thinking that it would do him good to spend half an hour sparring with one of the younger men, or else on the medicine ball, but he quickly cast all thought of such frivolities out of his mind.

Near the door, he was aware of loud noises.

His smile broadened; it sounded as if half a dozen of Bill's 'lads' were having a set-to at one and the same time, probably a free-for-all show which Bill had introduced at the urgent request of youths who were looking forward to joining the Commandos and wanted to be able to teach the Army its job.

As he reached the door, a man somersaulted backwards into the street and not of his own accord. He fell heavily but picked himself up and scuttled away, towards the docks. He was thoroughly frightened—a little, wizened man who did not look like one of Bill's faithfuls.

Rollison pushed aside a tarpaulin which was used for blackout and stepped inside. A man fell against him but recovered quickly and his fist cracked into the face of a grizzled veteran of the ring whose head went back but whose right arm shot out to land a punch which rattled his opponent's teeth. Everywhere, there was the wildest of free-for-alls. A dozen individual bouts were in progress, the battering of fists on faces and bodies and the harsh breathing of the fighters filled the big room; but no one was wearing gloves and at least two men were using knuckle-dusters.

In the centre of the room, on the floor with two men kneeling on him and battering his face and head, was Bill Ebbutt.

CHAPTER SEVEN

A ROUND TO CLUB MEMBERS

Rollison moved forward but had to side-step two couples engaged in furious battle and, as he passed a man whose right fist wore the ugly, spiked knuckle-duster characteristic of the East End mobsman, he clouted him on the side of the head. The fellow's opponent, a much older man whose right cheek was opened and bleeding, did not appear to see Rollison but went in furiously with both fists.

Rollison tried to reach Bill who was fighting back fiercely. They were using coshes on him but he was avoiding many of the blows.

A little, thin-faced fellow stood up from a man who was gasping on the ground, saw Rollison and jumped at him. Rollison shot out his foot and sent the man reeling backwards. His victim banged into one of Bill's men who tore into him. Next moment, Rollison was hauling one assailant off Bill, using his elbow against a bony chin. The other man was smashing at Bill's head and Rollison gripped him about the waist and hauled him into the air. He put his knee into the small of his back and shot him forward; he hit the ground and lay still.

Bruised but not bloody, Bill blinked up.

'Gaw blimey O'Reilly!' he gasped. 'Ta—Mr Ar! Look aht!'

Rollison turned to see a man coming towards him brandishing a knife. He used his foot again and toppled the man over. The fighting was savage and desperate with the members of the club heavily outnumbered. Since none of them had weapons—except two who were swinging Indian clubs—the odds were against them. Rollison rushed across to the wall, picked up two more Indian clubs and began to swing them. The odds were still heavy but suddenly there was a clatter of footsteps outside and half a dozen men burst in, three of them in khaki. They were reinforcements for the 'club' and they weighed in with a violence which altered the whole course of the struggle.

Realising that their chance had gone, the assailants escaped as and when they could, running the gauntlet towards the door. A massive veteran stood by it and clouted each man as he dodged out.

Rollison put down his clubs, smoothed his hair and went over to Bill Ebbutt who was now standing in the middle of the room and directing operations like a guerrilla leader. He said nothing until only three of the attacking party remained, all unconscious.

'I could do with a pint, I could,' Ebbutt declared, looking at Rollison with one eye closed up and already swelling to huge proportions. 'You come just at the right time,

64

Mr Ar. You know 'ow to work it, doncha.'

'Just luck,' said Rollison. 'I'd no idea what was happening.'

'I noo it was bound to come,' said Ebbutt, philosophically. He was a large man, running to fat but still very powerful. His features were rugged and battered, for he had spent thirty years in the ring, but his ears were curiously small and well-shaped; it was his dictum that a boxer who allowed himself to get cauliflower ears should take up stone-breaking. 'Ho, yes, I noo,' he went on, trying to grin although his mouth was nearly as swollen as his eyes and he uttered the words with great difficulty. 'Charlie!'

'Callin' me?' demanded a little man with enormously wide shoulders.

'Who'd yer think I'm callin'?' growled Ebbutt. 'Fetch some beer and glasses, mate, an' be quick about it. An' fetch me a coupla pound o' beefsteak!' he added. 'Strewth, Mr Ar, wartime's a bad time to get a black eye, ain't it? I don't know wot my missus will say when she sees me.' He made a brave attempt to wink. 'I'd better tell 'er it was your fault, that'll keep 'er quiet!'

He roared again. The beer arrived and the club members, now twenty strong and increasing every minute for an SOS had been sent out when the *melée* had started, began to drink eagerly. Of the three men who had been knocked out, two had recovered and been literally kicked out of the room; the other was still on the floor, conscious but detained for interrogation. He looked terrified and proved to be genuinely dumb.

The fight had started about a quarter of an hour before Rollison had arrived when only half a dozen 'club' members had been present. The purpose, Ebbutt declared with assurance, had been to beat him up; he didn't think Rollison would need telling why.

'No,' agreed Rollison. 'Keller wants to prise you off the Whitings.'

It had been a likely enough move, although he had not expected one to materialise so quickly. The place had been admirably chosen. A beating-up in the street, by daylight, was a risky business for it might bring the police while after dark Ebbutt always had plenty of men with him. Also, Ebbutt told Rollison, as soon as he had known what the job was, he had locked his door and made sure no one could get in at his window. Because:

'I know somefink about Keller,' he remarked, darkly.

'I hadn't heard of him until a day or two ago,' said Rollison.

'No more you didn't want to,' declared Ebbutt. ' 'E's a swine, Mr Ar, I don't mind sayin' so—he's a proper swine.'

'How long has he been about?' asked Rollison.

'Three or four munce,' said Ebbutt. 'No,

more'n that. Six munce.'

'What's he up to?'

'No use arstin' me,' said Ebbutt 'I minds me own business, you know that. 'E's a proper swine, Keller is. It's my business all right now,' he went on and made a comical effort to lick his lips. 'I don't half sting,' he added, and managed to get beer past his lips. ' 'Ave another, Mr Ar?'

'Not yet, thanks,' said Rollison. 'Don't you know anything about Keller's game?'

'I only knows that he's got a mob and is runnin' a racket,' declared Bill, 'I dunno what the racket is. Tell yer somefing, Mr Ar.'

Rollison waited.

'Tell yer somefing wot will surprise yer,' declared Ebbutt. ' 'E's 'ad a go at arf a dozen *other* swine. Blokes I wouldn't-a' minded bashin' meself. Mr Ar, that's a fact. No business o' mine, then, seein' as he was goin' fer swine. But some of the things 'e did to them—it would make yer scalp crawl, Mr Ar, it would reely. There was one fella—Tiny Blow, you know Tiny Blow? 'E was inside fer lootin',' Rollison nodded. 'Well, Tiny come out about four munce ago,' went on Ebbutt. ' 'E started throwin' 'is weight about. Keller hadn't started, it was the first time I 'eard of 'im. I did hear that Tiny started a fight in The Docker and waited fer Lucy—been at The Docker ten yers, Lucy has.' Ebbutt sniffed. 'Don't know that I think much of her but Tiny didn't ough to 'ave waited for 'er. Bad thing for 'im he did, because four of Keller's mob was waiting for him. He's still in the 'orspital. If it 'ad been anyone else but Tiny, I woulda' bin sorry for 'im.'

'And the other cases have been as bad?'

'More-less,' assented Ebbutt. 'Except that I thought he was goin' too far when he started on this parson bloke, Kemp.' Ebbutt sniffed again. 'I got nothin' *against* Kemp but he oughta know that he didn't oughta come down to a place like this. He's a *torf*. Don't take me wrong, Mr Ar!' exclaimed Ebbutt, hurriedly. 'I never meant nothin' personal!'

'No offence taken, Bill!'

'Then that's all right,' went on Ebbutt but elaborated the point. 'I wouldn't like yer ter think I was bein' personal, there are *torfs* an' *torfs*.' On the first utterance, he managed to give the word an astonishingly contemptuous ring, on the second one of unveiled admiration. 'Well, there you are! When you ask me to lend a 'and, I was only too 'appy, Mr Ar. Funny thing,' he added, reflectively, 'I wouldn't 'ave expected Kemp to come to you, 'e looks the kind to run to the dicks.'

'What do you know about Joe Craik?' asked Rollison.

Ebbutt finished his beer, summoned Charlie and demanded a refill, wiped his lips gingerly and then turned his one open eye on Rollison.

'Don't get me wrong, Mr Ar. There's persons

an' persons. Goin' to church never did no one any 'arm wot I can see, except it made hypocrites aht've some o' them. But I've 'ad some good boys, *very* good boys, from the church clubs, scouts an' boys' brigades an' things. I don't hold wiv goin' to church meself, though I don't mind a good Army meeting sometimes, they've got a bit of go, the Army. If it wasn't for them always 'alley uya-ing an' arskin' you to confess yer sins up in front've everyone, I wouldn't mind the Army. My own missus wears the uniform,' he added, somewhat shamefacedly.

'She's got to keep you in line somehow,' said Rollison, lightly.

Ebbutt grinned, then winced.

'Doan 'arf sting,' he complained, absently. 'Yes, I agree, Mr Ar. She has somefink ter put up wiv' but wot I was saying is, I'm not perjudiced against churches an' things. Some persons is sincere, some isn't, and I 'aven't got no time for them that isn't. But I never bin able to make up me mind about Craik.'

Sooner or later, Bill always got to the point.

' 'E's gotta good business,' he declared, 'and he gives his customers fair doos. Ain't never 'eard that he's in the market, 'e don't seem ter touch under-cover stuff. But between you an' me, Mr Ar, I don't like his face!'

Rollison grinned.

'It ain't because it's ugly,' Bill assured him, solemnly, ' 'E's got a face as good as the next

69

man but I just never took to it. Thassall I got against Craik. My missus thinks he's okay.'

'I haven't seen him yet,' said Rollison. 'I'll tell you what I think about his face when I've had a look at it! You know nothing else?'

'Ain't that enough, Mr Ar?'

'No. I want to find out what Keller is up to.'

Ebbutt deliberated and then opined that, just as Keller's mob had beaten up 'swine,' there was evidence that Keller was putting into effect a widespread but often undeclared antagonism to Ronald Kemp. It was a case of oil and water, Ebbutt declared.

'Does Billy the Bull still come in here?' Rollison asked.

'Every night, faithful. 'E'll be 'ere soon. On the docks, 'e is. Maybe 'e *is* past 'is prime,' continued the ex-fighter, a little regretfully, 'but there still ain't a dozen men in England could stand five rounds against Billy the Bull. Why'd you want to know?'

Rollison lowered his voice. At intervals during the next five minutes, Ebbutt emitted squeaks of delight and finally managed to part his lips in a smile which showed his discoloured teeth.

Soon afterwards, Rollison left the gymnasium.

He walked to the mission hall, going out of his way to pass 49, Little Lane—named after a benefactor, not because it was any different from a thousand other long, drab, featureless streets in the East End. Front doors were open, women and old men were talking, children were playing on the cobbles and dirt abounded; but some of the tiny windows looked spotlessly clean and some of the women were as well-dressed as they knew how to be. In spite of every disadvantage, there was an air of prosperity about Little Lane. It revealed itself in new boots on many of the children, in the fact that most of the people were smoking, in the gay splashes of lipstick and rouge on faces which had not known them for years.

A dozen friendly people called out to Rollison, others smiled and nodded and as he went out of earshot there was much earnest chattering. Outside Number 49 were two of Bill's stalwarts. He was glad to see them on duty.

Kemp was in the mission hall with three other men and a woman.

The place was fairly ship-shape again. Only a dozen chairs out of two hundred were undamaged but the men were hammering and knocking them into shape. The walls had been cleaned but they still bore traces of the paint. The warning remained at the back of the stage—a good touch, thought Rollison. He asked Kemp why he hadn't removed or covered it.

The curate, dressed in old flannels and an open-necked shirt, which made him look more boyish than ever, grinned widely.

'I'll take it down when it's no longer true.'

'Happy thought,' said Rollison. 'How are things?'

'There's nothing fresh to report,' said Kemp. 'I told you all about Keller's offer. I'm a bit worried about that,' he added, frowning. 'We could use £500—I mean, the Relief Fund could. I have wondered whether I ought to resign and let—'

'Don't be an ass,' said Rollison. 'You can raise the money if you put your mind to it.'

'I suppose I can,' said Kemp, rather lugubriously. 'Anyhow, I wouldn't leave just now for a fortune. I'm beginning to enjoy myself.'

'Yer don't know what injoyment means,' said a man from the door in a loud voice.

All six people turned abruptly, to see a giant standing in the doorway, almost filling it. His shoulders were enormous and his chest deep and powerful and he held his knuckly hands in front of him. He was remarkably ugly and the most astonishing thing about him was the likeness of his face to a cow's. His forehead, although broad, receded. He seemed to have no chin and his lips were very full and wide.

'I don't think you were invited,' said Kemp, after a pregnant pause.

'You don't, doncher? "*Hi* don't think you was hinvited!"' mimicked Billy the Bull, with a vast grin—and a shrill burst of laughter came from

72

behind him, the first indication that he was not alone. 'Why'nt yer go 'ome, Kemp?'

After a moment's hesitation, Kemp advanced towards the man. Rollison and the others watched—Rollison was inwardly smiling and the three men and the woman obviously anxious.

'I don't know who you are,' Kemp said, clearly, 'but it wouldn't surprise me if you know who wrecked the hall. Do you?'

'Supposin' I do?' growled Billy the Bull.

'If I thought you did it,' said Kemp, softly, 'I'd smash your silly face in!'

Stupefaction reigned among the church-workers and astonishment showed on Billy the Bull's bovine countenance.

The silence was broken by a piping voice from behind Billy. A man who did not come up to his shoulder and was thin, bald-headed and dressed in a dirty sweater with a polo collar in spite of the heat, pushed his way in to stand by Billy.

'I wouldn't let him git away wiv' *that*, Billy. I wouldn't let no one say he'd bash *my* face in!'

Billy the Bull licked his lips.

'Take that back!' There was menace in his manner.

'If you haven't the guts to admit that you helped to smash this place up, you're not worth wasting time on,' said Kemp. 'If you did, I'll—'

' 'It him, Billy!' urged the little man,

73

indignantly.

'I don't fight *h*infants,' declared Billy, scowling. 'But I wouldn't mind knocking the grin orf yer face, parson. Talk, that's all you're good for. Standin' up in the poolpit an' shouting yer marf orf—that's all yer can do. "Please Gawd, make me an' all me flock good lickle boys an' gels",' continued Billy, in a fair imitation of the worst type of clerical drawl. ' "Please Gawd—" '

Kemp said quietly:

'Don't say that again.'

Billy broke off, looking at the curate in surprise. Kemp had gone pale and his fists were clenched.

It was the little man who broke the silence again, piping:

'Strewth! Have yer gorn sorft, Billy? *'It* 'im.'

'I don't like knockin' *h*infants about,' repeated Billy. Something in Kemp's expression had stopped him and he was obviously on edge. It was Rollison's cue and he moved forward.

'You do a bit of boxing, Billy, don't you?'

'A bit!' squeaked the little man. 'Why there ain't a man in London can stand a round against 'im!'

'I can use me mitts,' declared Billy the Bull, on safer ground. 'But this apology fer a parson only shoots 'is mouth orf, that's all. Cissy-boy!' he added. 'You ought to be back 'ome wiv' yer muvver!'

'I'll fight you anywhere you like, under the Queensberry Rules,' Kemp said, tense-voiced.

'Coo, 'ear that?' squeaked the little man, dancing up and down. ' 'E's 'eard o' Lord Queensb'ry. Coo! Ain't 'e a proper little man! Why yer don't know wot fightin' is!'

'Don't be rash,' Rollison advised Kemp, looking now as if he wished he had not mentioned boxing. 'Billy's an old campaigner.'

'I'll fight him anywhere he likes,' Kemp said again.

'You mean that?' demanded the little man, coming forward and peering up into Kemp's face. 'You mean that—no, o' corse yer don't! There's a ring not a hundred miles from 'ere, I'll fix yer up a match 'ere an' now, for tonight. Pound aside, one quid per man but you don't mean it.'

'I'm not a—' began Kemp.

'The stakes to go to charity,' Rollison put in hastily.

'Suits me,' said the little man, loftily. 'I managed Billy the Bull all his life, *I* ain't above doin' a bit for charity.'

'*Does* he mean it?' demanded Billy the Bull, incredulously.

'Try to make them understand that I'm not afraid of his size, will you?' Kemp asked Rollison, earnestly.

Rollison nodded and fixed the details quickly.

Billy the Bull and his companion stalked off,

the sound of the little man's squeaky voice drifting back into the hall. The woman helper looked troubled but the three men eyed Kemp with a new respect. Kemp himself seemed unperturbed. One by one, the others left the hall.

'Do you think . . .' Kemp began, when they had gone and talked almost without stopping for twenty minutes.

Meanwhile, the grapevine of the East End, that remarkable information system rivalling the drums of Africa, began to work at high pressure. It played one refrain only. *'Kemp's fighting Billy the Bull at Bill Ebbutt's—nine o'clock. Kemp's fighting Billy the Bull at Bill Ebbutt's—nine o'clock.'*

News reached many unexpected places. It amazed most who heard it, it alarmed the Whitings, it brought church members post-haste to try to dissuade Kemp from going on with it—all to no purpose—it brought protests from the more influential church members; and it put Kemp's stock up to undreamed-of heights, although he did not realise it.

It reached Keller.

It also reached the dockside canteen where Isobel Crayne was working.

CHAPTER EIGHT

THE PARSON WITH A PUNCH

By a quarter-past eight, there was room for neither man nor boy in Bill's gymnasium. By half-past, there was a great exodus for Bill had made hurried arrangements with the management of a nearby indoor stadium for the fight to be staged there. When Rollison heard about that he telephoned Bill who hardly finished speaking before he was roaring to his men:

'Mr Ar says a bob a time. Charge 'em a bob-a-time-money fer charity. See to it, a bob a time.'

The entrance fee made no difference to the crowd. The stadium could hold four thousand and was packed when Rollison and Kemp arrived. Kemp showed no sign of nerves but was anxious to slip in unobserved. Rollison promised that he would try to arrange it but, by a deliberate mistake, took the curate through the crowded hall. There were roars of interest, not so much of applause as of excited comment.

A sprinkling of women were present and in one corner, near the ring, were the Whitings and a body of people at whom Kemp stared in astonishment.

'Do you see that crowd near the Whitings, Rolly?'

'What about them?' asked Rollison.

'They're from the church,' Kemp said, dazedly. 'They—Great Scott, what's brought *them* here?'

'You want some fans, don't you?' asked Rollison.

Kemp shot him a sideways glance then forced his way through the narrow gangway towards the dressing-rooms. Bill Ebbutt was in his element, his right eye so swollen that it almost doubled the size of his face and his mouth was puffed out but grinning. 'You oughta see the gate!' he chortled. 'You oughta see it!'

'Are they charging?' asked Kemp, surprised.

'The money is for charity,' Rollison said, and added: 'To be chosen by the winner—shall we make that a condition?'

'Can you lay down any laws?'

'I can try,' said Rollison.

The master of ceremonies, a tall, portly man who had hastily donned his tail-suit, entered the ring at ten minutes to nine and announced through the microphone that there was to be a ten-round contest between heavyweights, Billy the Bull and the Parson with a Punch. That new nickname brought down the house. All the profits from the engagement were to go to any charity named by the winner, continued the MC. There was another roar of approval.

The MC concluded after lauding Billy the Bull and doing his best for the unknown contender.

At five to nine, one of Bill's men sought out Rollison who was in Kemp's dressing-room. 'There's a lady arstin' for you, Mr Ar. She can't git in, the stadium's overcrowded already. If we ain't careful the cops will be arstin' what about it.'

'Did she give her name?' asked Rollison.

'Yus. Miss Crine.'

'Isobel!' exclaimed Rollison. He glanced at Kemp who was having his hands bandaged. The curate looked in fine condition,although he was puny compared with Billy the Bull. The other Bill had appointed seconds who were fussing round the curate as if he had been in their charge for years. Whiting had come to join them and his thin cheeks were flushed with excitement.

'All right, I'll come,' said Rollison.

Isobel was standing at the head of a crowd at least two hundred strong, who were shouting to be admitted. Three policemen were on duty by the door, refusing to admit another spectator. On the fringes of the crowd a red-faced man smiled as he saw Rollison.

'Rolly, you can't let this go on!' exclaimed Isobel.

'Oh, my dear,' said Rollison, smiling. 'It's Kemp's biggest chance. He'll never get another like it.'

'*You've* arranged it, haven't you?'

79

'I did set the wheels in motion,' admitted Rollison.

She eyed him without smiling.

'It isn't fair,' she said at last. 'He can't win!'

'Don't take anything for granted,' advised Rollison. 'But come in and see it yourself. You've seen a fight before.'

'Do you really think he stands a chance?'

'I don't think it will be slaughter,' said Rollison. 'Will you come?'

'Yes.' Isobel remained unsmiling although there was a brighter look in her eyes.

As Rollison was about to force his way past the turnstile, the man with the red face touched his arm. He looked round to see Inspector Chumley of the AZ Division, Metropolitan Police. Chumley was still smiling; he looked a genial man.

'One of your little games, Mr Rollison?'

'If you care to think so,' said Rollison.

'I want a word with you about O'Hara's murder.'

'Come and see the fight,' said Rollison, 'and talk to me about O'Hara afterwards.'

'All right,' said Chumley. 'Be glad to.'

He followed as Rollison led Isobel into the stadium.

The crowd was on its feet, roaring as Billy the Bull stepped through the ropes. He was a colossal, impressive figure and, when stripped, he looked even more massive than he did when clothed. The bald-headed little man was

80

hopping about at his side, squeaking advice.

Another roar, friendly if not enthusiastic, greeted the arrival of Kemp who looked a stripling beside the professional. The only time he showed any expression was when he caught sight of Rollison, Chumley and Isobel sitting on camp stools at the ringside. His gaze was rivetted on Isobel, who smiled then looked away.

' 'E ain't gotta chance,' someone said, nearby.

'Won't last a round,' said another.

' 'E don't strip bad,' conceded a third, grudgingly.

'Has he done any boxing to speak of?' Chumley asked, leaning across Isobel.

'He says he's done a bit at Oxford,' answered Rollison. 'I'm told he was in the finals three years running but he struck good years.'

'He can't compete with Billy,' Chumley said. 'The man's made of rock.'

Isobel looked at him sharply and then turned reproachfully to the Toff.

The fight started ten minutes late, to roars which echoed up and down the street and were taken up by the hundreds who could not gain admission. As they touched hands in the centre of the ring and Billy danced back, agile for a heavyweight and always surprising his opponents by his footwork, there was a tense, almost a stunned silence.

Kemp went in with a straight left which

shook Billy and jabbed a right above the heart, stopping a rush. Kemp danced back and Billy seemed to stand still.

Rollison thought, it's a pity that Kemp's started off so well. Until then, Billy the Bull had been inclined to take the bout lightly but, although his smile remained, there was a wary expression in his eyes; the blows had made him realise that he must not be careless. Kemp knew the ring and did not take chances. He kept out of the way of those long arms, only taking two punches of any weight and riding them well. He got in a couple to the ribs, which stung but did no damage, and his footwork was good. He managed to keep the fight away from him without making it a dancing match, sparring rather than fighting but in no way pretentious.

When the gong went, the erstwhile silent crowd let forth; there was a new note in their voices. They knew that they were going to see a real fight, not to gloat over a massacre—for the majority had come to see the complete eclipse of the parson who thought he could punch. The most noticeable change was in the corner where Kemp's friends were sitting. They were eager and almost elated; the whole party seemed to have been relieved of a great burden.

Rollison glanced at Isobel.

'Enjoying it?' he asked.

'You beast!' she said, half-laughing. 'I half

believe you were right!'

The little man in Billy's corner was shrill and vociferous. Kemp's seconds, including Whiting, behaved as if they could not believe what they had seen and they settled down to see their man through. Kemp glanced once towards Rollison's corner and his gaze lingered on Isobel. Then the gong went and he began to fight well, still keeping out of range of Billy's murderous left swing which was the punch which had scored most of his knock-outs. Kemp used his feet as if he were remembering the text book all the time. The round was even.

The change in the temper of the crowd was even more noticeable. Chumley shot a shrewd glance at Rollison and Isobel sat back as if enjoying herself.

Three rounds of hard fighting followed with Billy doing most of the attacking but gaining no noticeable advantage and certainly not gaining ascendancy. Watching closely, Rollison thought that Kemp was beginning to tire; there were red blotches on his fair skin. Billy the Bull showed only one or two, although Kemp had drawn blood first by a slight cut on Billy's lips. At the start of the sixth round, Billy went in as if he meant to finish it off once and for all. In the first minute, it looked as though he would succeed. He brought out a pace which surprised Kemp who backed swiftly but could not ride the punches. One of those famous lefts took him on the side of the jaw and staggered him. The crowd jumped to its feet. How Kemp fended off the follow-up, Rollison did not know. He felt as excited as the others.

Kemp kept the knock-out away but towards the end of the round he was groggy. He staggered into his corner as the gong went.

'That's about it,' said Chumley. 'But he's put up a damned good show, Rollison.'

'He can't lose now!' exclaimed Isobel.

Rollison smiled. 'He's not quite finished,' he said. 'If Billy can keep that up next round, though—' he shrugged and broke off.

Money was already changing hands for dozens had wagered that the curate would not last halfway through the bout. The odds, although more even, were still on Billy who remained smiling in his corner but was breathing with greater deliberation. For the first time, Rollison thought that Kemp might possibly pull it off.

The gong went.

The crowd gasped for Kemp moved from his corner with unexpected speed and landed two powerful punches on Billy's jaw. Before the man could hit back he danced away, came in again and jabbed the professional with three straight lefts, each of which pushed Billy's head back. The crowd was on its feet again, Chumley had forgotten himself and was exclaiming:

'You've got him! You've got him!'

Isobel stared, her eyes glistening and her hands clenched.

Kemp jabbed again and the Bull concentrated on keeping away from that waspish left but left himself open for a right swing; Kemp had not used one before; now, he flashed it round and landed with a crack! which sounded clearly through the hall. Billy staggered, lost his footing and went down. Kemp backed away and stood with his hands down, unsmiling but with an expression of contentment which showed his satisfaction.

'... six—seven,' intoned the referee.

On 'eight', Billy rose cautiously to his feet.

Had Kemp gone straight in, he might have finished him off but Kemp waited just too long. What chance he had was lost in Billy's determined covering-up and Chumley shot a meaning glance at Rollison as the round ended.

Isobel said nothing.

'Give you six-ter-four on the parson,' muttered a little fellow behind them, one who had been shortening the odds for a long time. 'Six-to-four on the parson!'

He hedged when he was taken up by a dozen eager backers of Billy the Bull and was in the midst of a heated altercation when the gong rang. He sat down and snapped:

'Watch the fight, can't yer?'

Rollison smiled but felt a tenseness which surprised him. If Kemp could repeat his

85

performance of the last round, he would yet beat the professional but in a few seconds Rollison saw that Kemp had spent himself on his great effort. If Billy had been less wary, he might have made an end to it that round but he waited until the ninth. A spark of energy came back to Kemp but, as he swung a right which connected too near the end of the swing, he left himself wide open. Billy sent in three killer-punches—right-left-right! Kemp's mouth sagged, he staggered and bent at the knees.

'Get 'im, Billy!

'You got 'im, Billy!'

'Don't wait, you fool!'

Billy the Bull, still smiling, stood back from the curate who tried to pull himself together. He managed to raise his hands but then crumpled up. There was a tense moment of silence, followed by an uproar which drowned the referee's voice but Rollison knew it was all over.

The referee turned to Billy the Bull to acclaim him the winner but Billy stepped past him and went down on one knee beside the curate.

The crowd loved it.

Rollison looked at Isobel and saw a film of tears over her eyes. She fought against them and was smiling when Kemp, sitting up in his corner with Billy standing over him and towels flapping, sent another glance towards her.

Rollison put a hand on Isobel's.

'It's all right,' he said, 'Kemp's paid his entrance fee. Will you come to the dressing-room with me?'

'No,' she said, hastily, 'I must get back, I shouldn't have stayed so long.'

'I'll find you an escort,' Rollison said. Watching her go, he smiled thoughtfully. Then a man bumped against him and he looked round—to see Keller.

'You damned fool!' Keller growled. 'I warned you.'

'What's that?' snapped Chumley.

As if he realised that he had made a mistake, Keller turned and was lost in the crowd. Chumley was about to follow him, but drew back.

'What did he say, Rollison? Did he threaten you?'

'It sounded like it,' said Rollison, perfunctorily.

'Who was it?'

Rollison hesitated.

'I know you like to go your own way but there are times when you can't,' Chumley said. 'If you know that man and he's connected with Kemp's trouble, you must tell me his name.'

'Perhaps you're right,' said Rollison. 'But not here— I'll come to the station in about an hour's time.'

'All right,' said Chumley.

Rollison went through the thinning crowd to

the dressing-rooms. Kemp was on a table, being pummelled enthusiastically by his seconds with Whiting standing by and smiling widely. Ebbutt had successfully overcome the handicap of his swollen lips and was smiling as if the world had fallen into his lap, the bald-headed man who had been with Billy the Bull was here, there and everywhere.

Kemp looked at Rollison.

'You'll do,' he said drily.

'*We'll* do!' said Rollison.

'What abaht the gite?' demanded the bald-headed man, shrilly. 'What abaht it, Billy-boy; Two hundred and forty-nine pounds eight an' thruppence, I dunno 'ow the thruppence come in, must'a been a miscount. That's less tax. Wot about it, Billyboy? Goes to charity, don't it? Charity begins at home, don't it?' He grinned, expectantly.

Billy the Bull came in with his gay dressing-gown tight about him.

'Shut your silly marf, Tike,' Billy said, stepping to Kemp's side. 'I decided what to do with the gite. That's if Mr Kemp won't mind assepting it.'

Kemp eyed him in surprise.

'It must go to charity,' he said. 'That was a condition, wasn't it?'

'S'right,' said Billy. 'You've got a relief fund down at St Guys, ain't-cher? And you've 'ad a lot o' espense lately'—Billy the Bull grew tongue-tied and the others fell silent. 'Just seed the management, I 'ave,' he went on at last. 'They've agreed that they doan want no espenses fer ter-night, so it's all going to charity. Will yer assept it for the church, Mr Kemp?'

Kemp slid from the table and held out his hand.

'I will, Billy. It isn't easy to say thanks.' His one open eye was smiling and he seemed to have become much more mature in the past few hours. 'I'm afraid I owe you an apology. I once thought you knew something about the damage to the hall. I'm sorry.'

'Don't menchon it,' said Billy, bluffly. 'Only my little joke, I—' he caught Rollison's eye and went on hastily: 'I just fought I'd pull your leg, that was all. Never guessed you packed a punch like that. All okey-doke, then?'

'All okey-doke,' affirmed Kemp.

'Gawd save the King!' gasped the bald-headed man. 'Who'd 'a believed it?'

*　　*　　*

Rollison left the big hall just after eleven o'clock. It was not quite dark. Two of Ebbutt's men were standing outside, taking no chances. Kemp had been put to bed with a cold compress over a swollen eye. He had said nothing about Rollison's part in fixing the contest but obviously he knew.

Rollison smiled, as he remembered the

curate's last words. 'I suppose you *are* going to do something about Joe Craik, Rolly—or is this reputation of yours just wool over the eyes?'

'I'll try to see him tonight,' Rollison had promised.

He was not followed from the hall but was wary as he walked to the main road and then to the headquarters of AZ Division. He had telephoned the flat but Jolly had not returned and his curiosity about his man's activities was at fever heat. He showed no sign of that when, at half-past eleven, he was ushered in to Chumley's office. The Inspector looked relieved to see him.

'I was afraid you were going to play one of your tricks, Rollison. Sit down—and have a cigarette? If you'd like a drink—'

'No thanks,' said Rollison. 'Tricks?' He looked aggrieved. 'Now would I ever try to put anything across a policeman?'

Chumley chuckled.

'As a matter of fact, I think you would! What *do* you know about O'Hara's murder?'

'I thought you were sure it was Craik,' said Rollison.

'We *thought* we had him, all right,' said Chumley, looking owlish, 'but I'm afraid we made a mistake, Rollison. He's been released.'

CHAPTER NINE

THE RELEASE OF JOE CRAIK

'Why did you let him go?' asked Rollison.

'Lack of evidence,' said Chumley.

'I thought his knife was used.'

'It was—but it had been stolen. We caught the man who stole it,' Chumley added. 'We heard a whisper and went to see him. He denied it but broke down under questioning. He told us that you had been talking to him—in fact, even allowing for exaggeration, what he said you said is enough to make us reprimand you!'

Rollison sat on the corner of the inspector's desk and lit a cigarette.

'Spike Adams or Harris?' he asked.

'Harris.'

'And he admits having picked Craik's pocket?'

'Yes.'

'Well, well! He wasn't at the scene of the murder, was he?'

'No,' said Chumley, regretfully. 'We can't get him for that. He tells a fantastic story of being told that someone else owned the knife, which Craik had stolen—I don't believe a word of it but I've got to believe the confession and, without evidence that Craik used the knife,

I've got nothing on which to hold him.'

Rollison smiled drily.

'*Now* what's amusing you?' asked Chumley.

'A nice piece of fandoogling,' said Rollison. 'I wondered why you were so careful to let Bray of the Yard detain him and only finish off yourself. You didn't want to come a cropper, did you? The Yard did the dirty work, you handed Craik over to them.'

Chumley grinned, smugly.

'You weren't satisfied that it was Craik even then?' asked Rollison.

'I was not.' Chumley was surprisingly emphatic. 'I think I know this Division. I've been here for fifteen years and Joe Craik is one of the reliables. He might have punched O'Hara's head but he wouldn't use a knife. Young Bray was cocky, so I let him have his head. I thought it might give me a chance to do some quick uncovering but I've drawn a blank.'

'Except that you've been tipped off about the knife,' said Rollison. 'Who told you?'

'A man who gave his name as Keller,' said Chumley and sat back, as if prepared to gloat over his sensation.

Rollison could not wholly hide his surprise.

'So you think Keller's behind it, do you,' said Chumley.

Rollison said nothing.

'Don't be afraid to speak up,' urged Chumley. 'Rollison, I've not been asleep for the last six months. I've never talked to Keller, in fact I've only once set eyes on him, but I've had reports about him. There are times when we have to turn a blind eye down here. Keller's associates have the reputation of having committed several ugly crimes but we've never been able to prove they were Keller's men or that Keller knew anything about the crimes. It's a remarkable fact that in every case the victims have been—'

'Bad men,' said Rollison, unexpectedly. 'Swine.'

'What's that?'

'I'm just quoting,' said Rollison, crossing to an easy chair. He sat on the arm. 'There's no evidence against Keller, and the crimes which rumour accredit to him have been—' he shrugged his shoulders, '—justifiable. Is that your opinion?'

'No, of course not! But they have been a kind of rough justice. *You* know something about that kind of thing, don't you?'

'It has been said,' murmured Rollison. 'You seem to be happy about it all, so why ask me to come here?'

'Why are you interested in the murder of O'Hara?' asked Chumley.

'I'm not,' answered Rollison. 'I'm interested in the affairs of the new Curate at St Guy's.'

Chumley rubbed his fleshy chin.

'You're not seriously asking me to believe that?'

93

'It's the truth,' Rollison assured him. 'It might lead to other things, of course. For instance, why was Craik's knife stolen? Was it to cast suspicion on Craik and even provide evidence against him? If so, why?'

'I can't see any other explanation,' admitted Chumley, worriedly, 'although why anyone should want Craik framed for a murder beats me. Rollison, you've been very active in the past twenty-four hours—surely you know something?'

'I'm a victim of mis-statements,' Rollison declared. 'Or if you prefer it, I've been selected as a gullible stooge to help someone create the wrong impression. Did Harris tell you who paid him to take Craik's knife?'

'He *said* it was Keller,' said Chumley, 'and then he described Keller as a stocky man with big brown eyes. Possibly someone has been passing himself off as Keller who, I'm told, is a little man, and—great Scott!' exclaimed Chumley. 'A stocky man with brown eyes! That fellow who spoke to you at the stadium answers the description—did *you* think he was Keller?'

'He told me he was,' said Rollison.

Chumley stared; and then he began to smile.

'And you believed him—I don't think. *That* isn't Keller! He might be the man who has been arranging these attacks, including the wrecking of the mission hall, but he certainly isn't Keller! I wonder why he wants to make

94

out that he is?'

'To establish Keller as a crook, perhaps,' said Rollison. 'In exactly the same way as he tried to frame Craik. Is that what you think?'

'It seems likely,' conceded Chumley. 'Why didn't you tell me about the mission hall trouble?'

'Not your battle, yet,' said Rollison. 'It's Kemp's. But it will probably become yours. Now—to save you from asking why I arranged for Ebbutt to protect the Whiting family—I thought it would help you out as you're short-staffed! The man who called himself Keller uttered violent threats against the Whitings, to stop Whiting from talking about the stolen knife. As the real Keller appears to have blown the gaff I doubt if the Whitings are in any danger, so that had better remain one of the things at which you wink a practised eye. Have you anyone in mind for the O'Hara murder?'

'Not yet,' said Chumley.

'Do you know why he was killed?'

'Not yet.'

'Do you know anything about him?'

'Not much,' said Chumley. 'He was an Irishman from Eire, one of the many dock-workers who came over from there. There's a sizeable colony of them in Whitechapel. O'Hara was not a leading spirit, in fact rather more timid than most. He'd been in this country about six months. Nothing was known against him and there's nothing at his lodgings to suggest a motive. If I didn't know the cause of the quarrel, I'd say he'd been killed in a drunken brawl.'

'Now you know he was killed so that Craik could be framed,' said Rollison, crisply. 'Or don't you look on it that way?'

'I am inclined to,' said Chumley. 'Is that your considered opinion?'

'It's a considered possibility,' said Rollison. 'I wouldn't put it any higher. You'll follow up the two lines, I suppose—why frame Craik or, if that were incidental, why kill O'Hara?'

'Naturally,' said Chumley. 'This brown-eyed man—do you know anything against him?'

'Nothing very much,' said Rollison. 'Uttering threats might do as a charge but—you don't like making arrests when the accused has to be released for lack of evidence, do you?'

Chumley chuckled. 'You won't forget that for a long time!'

'I shall mark it up against you,' declared Rollison. 'You're slyer than I knew. If you should happen to find out the real name of the brown-eyed gentleman, and cared to tell me, I'd be grateful.'

'I will, provided you undertake to advise me if he does anything which is indictable.'

'I always report indictable offences,' said Rollison, reprovingly. 'The days when I carried out trial and sentence myself are gone—and they existed mostly in your imagination!'

He stood up and Chumley did not press him

96

to stay. Rollison was smiling broadly as he reached the street. Three quarters of an hour later, he let himself into his flat and the first thing he saw was a light under the kitchen door. He opened it and made Jolly start.

Jolly wore a white apron over his best clothes and was operating with a yellow powder which Rollison suspected had something to do with eggs. He also had a frying pan on the electric stove, from which came a smell of sizzling fat.

'What it is to have an instinct!' approved Rollison. 'I only had a bun and a piece of cheese for dinner. Good evening, Jolly. Aren't you tired after your day's journeying?'

'Not exceptionally so, sir, and as you have not had dinner, I will reconstitute a little more egg and make two omelettes. Good evening, sir.'

'While reconstituting, you might also reconstruct,' said Rollison. 'Let's have the diary of a day in the life of one, Jolly.'

'I am afraid I have had a disappointing time, sir,' said Jolly, mixing powder and water industriously. 'At one time I hoped that I would have information of first importance but I was disappointed. You will remember that when I telephoned you, I left somewhat hurriedly?'

'Yes,' said Rollison.

'I saw a man whom I had been following all day,' said Jolly. 'He had gone into an inn and I thought he would stay there for a while but he

97

came out and hurried to a bus and I thought it better to continue to follow him.'

'Who was he?' asked Rollison.

'Not Keller but his companion, sir.'

Thoughtfully, Rollison lit a cigarette. 'Keller isn't Keller, according to my latest information. You mean you followed the owner of the cultured voice?'

'Yes. Are you *sure* the other man is not Keller?' Jolly looked puzzled.

'I'm keeping an open mind,' admitted Rollison, 'but the police are confident and Chumley isn't easy to fool.'

While Jolly made the omelettes, Rollison told him of the events of the evening. Jolly only occasionally looked up from the frying pan. He had laid a small table in the kitchen for his own supper and Rollison brought in a chair from the dining-room and they ate together. Since Jolly's day had been disappointing, Rollison was anxious to get his own story into the right perspective and he knew of no better way than discussing it with Jolly.

'And what is your view of Chumley's opinions?' asked the valet, as Rollison finished. 'Are they genuine or are they intended to mislead you?'

'The main problem, yes,' said Rollison. 'You're good, Jolly, sometimes you're very good. Chumley is showing unsuspected cunning, although he doesn't like being called sly. There always seemed to be something fishy about the detention and arrest and he was making sure that he didn't take what raps were coming. I don't know Sergeant Bray,' added Rollison. 'It might do him good to be on the carpet but it wasn't a friendly thing for Chumley to do.'

'On the surface, no, sir,' said Jolly, getting up and taking the coffee percolator from the stove.

'But Chumley doesn't stop there,' went on Rollison. 'He knows that he is in deep waters. Very ingenuously, he wanted my opinion, hoping that I would either prove or disprove his own arguments. I couldn't do either but he doesn't know that. The curious feature is the identity of Keller.'

'Identity but also character, sir.'

'Enlarge on that,' invited Rollison.

'As I see it, sir,' said Jolly, stirring his coffee, 'Keller has built for himself a reputation of being something of a Robin Hood—an avenger, one might say, almost on the lines of your own activities some years ago! He has selected victims who would get no sympathy from the people or the police.'

'Good point,' admitted Rollison. 'Chumley went as far as to say that only rumour links the crimes with Keller. With the arrival of the pseudo-Keller, an explanation dawns. The beatings-up have been done not by the real Keller but by the impersonator.'

'Undoubtedly the situation is very complicated,' murmured Jolly.

'Foggy, yes,' said Rollison. 'But intriguing. Going further and guessing wildly, we might say that (a) the reputation for Keller was deliberately built up by his *vis-à-vis*, that (b) the assaults on the 'swine' were initiated so that when a victim was ready for attack, the police would be reluctant to assume that it was one of the same series and (c) that it has all been built up with great and admirable cunning, in order to confuse the police, confuse the people, and—'

'Rid the district of Mr Kemp,' Jolly completed.

Rollison did not smile.

'Do you think that's possible?'

'I do, sir. As I listened to you, I came to the conclusion that it is the most likely explanation. I hold no brief for Mr Kemp but it is a fact that he has been in the district for six months, that the Keller-crimes, as we may perhaps dub them, have also been in operation for six months. That is right, sir?'

Rollison began to smile.

'I'm glad we think alike. You see where this takes us?'

'If my memory serves me, Mr Cartwright has been ill for nine or ten months and he had been without a curate for some months before that,' Jolly said. 'It is just possible that—'

'Stealing thunder,' said Rollison, 'but go on.'

'Thank you, sir. I was about to say,' Jolly went on with gentle reproof, 'that as I understand your surmise, between the time that Mr Cartwright fell ill and the time that Mr Kemp arrived, some crime, or series of crimes, was planned and put into effect. I do not think that they are necessarily the individual acts of violence. They are more likely to prove something of much greater importance or, perhaps I should say, much greater profit. The arrival of Mr Kemp made it possible that the crimes would be discovered and perhaps prevented, so it was decided to get rid of him. Is that your opinion, sir?'

'You know very well it is.'

'I certainly share it,' said Jolly, warmly. 'I must say that I think it a great pity, Mr Kemp—'

'You needn't worry about Kemp,' said Rollison, with satisfaction.

'I don't understand you, sir.'

'Tonight, he lasted nine rounds against Billy the Bull and four thousand people saw him. Forty thousand know about it by now. If you're thinking of going to St Guy's on Sunday, you'd better reserve a pew!'

'Mr *Kemp*—and Billy the Bull?' gasped Jolly.

'So you can be surprised,' said Rollison, cheerfully.

'But I can't believe it, sir! How could such a contest be arranged? How on earth did Mr Kemp realise the possibilities of such a—

oh, I *see*, sir! You had a hand in it!'

He broke off and they began to laugh. When they sobered up Jolly told his story.

He had made some fruitless inquiries during the morning and had then gone to the dockside pub, The Docker, understanding that one of the men whom Rollison had caught the previous night had said that Keller had once lived there. Jolly had seen the man with the cultured voice coming out and had decided to follow him.

The unknown had gone first to Barking, where he had had lunch in a small coffee-shop, and then made his way by bus to Loughton, where he had paid a visit to an inn, then gone from Loughton to Epping which was not far away. There he had had a drink at another pub and visited two more before he had returned, on the last bus, to London. There the black-out had swallowed him up, near Piccadilly.

'A protracted pub-crawl,' said Rollison. 'But you've made a note of the names of the pubs and other places he called at, I hope?'

'I noted each one down, sir.'

'Good!' said Rollison, briefly. 'Now to bed, Jolly.'

'I hope we are not disturbed, sir,' said Jolly. 'But for that coffee, I would have had great difficulty in keeping awake.' He stifled a yawn, apologised, and asked Rollison what he intended to do next day.

'In the evening, I hope to see Joe Craik,' said

Rollison. 'Two things to ponder, Jolly. The warning to Kemp was misspelt, a 'here' without its aspirate and other glaring errors but 'clear' spelt correctly and not with the double-ee which might have been expected. Would a man who knew where to put commas fail to know where to put an 'h'?'

'It isn't likely, sir. It was a further attempt to confuse, perhaps?'

'As with Joe Craik's knife,' said Rollison.

He was soon asleep in bed and was woken up by Jolly at a quarter-to eight.

After a long day at the office, without being interrupted by the more pressing affair, he learned from Jolly that no one had telephoned the flat. He went to the East End.

Kemp was in high spirits when he arrived and appeared to regard him as a worker of miracles.

'Because Craik's been released?' asked Rollison. 'Don't thank me, thank the police. What kind of a day have you had?'

Kemp, his one open eye bright, drew in his breath.

'The whole atmosphere has changed. I haven't seen so many smiles or been asked how I am so often in all my life! Now that *is* a miracle, Rolly, and you can't deny that you're responsible for it! I know you fixed the fight with Billy the Bull; I wish I could say thanks.'

Rollison eyed him reflectively.

'Odd fellow,' he announced, after a pause. '*I*

don't work miracles. Nor do you. But they happen. Curious, isn't it? Now I'm going to see Joe Craik!'

He left Kemp staring with a startled expression and walked along towards Craik's shop. On the way, a large number of people hailed him.

Outside Craik's shop, a little woman was tapping at the door. Looking round at Rollison, she said:

'S'funny thing, 'e *said* 'e'd be open until seven o'clock. It's funny. Joe don't orfen let yer down.'

She tapped again but got no response. Rollison's smile faded and he stood back, the better to survey the shop and to see the closed first-floor windows above the weather-beaten facia board across which was written '*Joe Craik, Groceries, Provisions*'. The shop windows were freshly dressed with tins of goods on points, all carefully docketted, and it was impossible to see inside the shop.

'I don't know that I like this,' said Rollison. 'Does he live on his own?'

'Yerse.'

'What about his wife?'

' 'E'd be a long way from 'ere if 'e lived wiv 'er,' declared the woman with a wide grin. 'She's bin dead these ten years, mister! 'Ere! Wotcher doing?'

He could smell gas coming from above his head; it was too strong for him to be mistaken.

Rollison hunched a shoulder and thrust it against the glass panel of the shop door which was pasted over with advertising bills. After three attempts, the glass broke. Rollison ignored the curious glances of passers-by who promptly became spectators as he removed a large piece of glass and put his hand inside and opened the door.

As he stepped inside, a uniformed constable came up.

CHAPTER TEN

JOE CRAIK IN PERSON

No one was in the shop.

There was a smell of bacon and fat, although everything looked scrupulously clean, and the floor was covered with sawdust. Goods were piled high on the shelves, neatly ticketed. Rollison glanced round and then looked behind the counters.

The constable came in.

'What—' he began, and then recognised Rollison. 'I say, sir!' he exclaimed.

Rollison smiled at him fleetingly.

'I'm looking for Craik,' he said, opening a door which led to an over-furnished, drably decorated parlour. This was empty, too. He went through into the kitchen but no one was there.

The stairs led from a tiny passage between the shop and the parlour. Rollison mounted the stairs quickly but hesitated when he reached the landing. There were three doors, all closed.

From one there came the strong smell of gas.

Rollison looked into the empty rooms before finding that the third door was locked. It was a thin, freshly-painted one with a brass handle. Rollison put his shoulder against it and heaved; it was easy to break open. As he staggered forward, the smell of gas was very strong.

'You all right up there, sir?' called the constable.

'Yes!' gasped Rollison, stifling a cough. He hurried across the room, holding his breath, and caught a glimpse of the man on the bed; frightened eyes stared at him. He flung up the one, large window and drew in a deep breath of fresh air.

A crowd had gathered outside and some were standing on the opposite side of the road, gazing at the place.

He turned round; the man on the bed held a length of rubber tubing in his hand and from it there came the faint hiss of escaping gas. Rollison saw that the other end of the tube was connected with the gas bracket. He reached up and turned it off. The little, frightened eyes watched every movement; Joe Craik reminded him of nothing more than a scared rabbit.

Rollison reached his side, making him cringe back, and lifted him from the bed, saying in a low voice:

'Keep quiet, if you want to stop a scandal.'

Craik muttered something that was inaudible.

Rollison kicked a chair into position and sat the man on it in front of the window—he could not be seen from outside.

'Stay there,' exhorted Rollison.

He went into the other bedroom and opened the windows, then went downstairs. The policeman had his hands full for two urchins were standing and grinning at him, one of them holding a tin of beans in grubby hands. Three people had entered the shop in addition to the woman and dozens of curious faces peered through the doorway.

'Put it down and be off with you!' the policeman said to the child. 'Is it all right upstairs, sir?'

The boy dropped the tin close enough to the constable's foot to make him step back then turned and ran with his companion. At the door, one of them put his tongue out and the other drew his hand from beneath his jersey and exhibited a second tin before tearing off. There was a roar of laughter from the crowd.

'Well, then, *I'll* 'elp meself!' declared the woman.

'No, you don't,' said the policeman.

'My ole man—' she began.

'Yes, it's all right,' said Rollison interrupting, 'Craik had a heart spasm but he's got some tablets and he's all right now. It's just as well we came.' He stressed the 'we'.

'Oh, that's good.' The constable began to deal with the crowd, helped by two colleagues who soon arrived.

There was no smell of gas in the shop but Rollison could detect it at the foot of the stairs. He went into the stuffy parlour and opened the window and the door. In the shop again he saw Kemp, still in an open-necked shirt and flannels and with his left eye less swollen.

'Is it all right for me to come in?'

'Oh, yes,' said Rollison and Kemp joined him. 'Don't talk.' He said nothing more until they were halfway up the stairs. Then he looked round at Kemp with a wry smile. 'Craik tried to gas himself but I think I've satisfied the police that it was a heart attack. Can you smell gas?'

'Now you come to mention it, yes.' Kemp looked hard at Rollison but said nothing until they reached the bedroom.

Craik was looking over his shoulder and, when he saw Kemp, he tried to get up.

'Don't get up, Joe,' said Kemp. 'And don't worry—Mr Rollison has told everyone you had a heart attack.'

He closed the door.

108

Rollison disconnected the rubber tubing and coiled it round his fingers. The room was spotlessly clean but the wainscotting had been broken in several places and one stretch had recently been replaced by newer, lighter-brown wood. He looked at it thoughtfully, hearing Joe Craik's voice as if from a long way off. The man talked in a monotonous, frightened undertone as Kemp pulled up another chair and sat beside him.

'I couldn't bear it, Mr Kemp. The disgrace, the horrible disgrace!' He shuddered. 'I've never been so much as inside a police-station before and to be charged with—with *murder*.'

'But you were released,' Kemp said.

'You—you don't know the people around here, sir. They'll say I did it. I daren't show my face in church again—oh, why didn't he let me do away with myself?'

He turned and looked at Rollison.

'Why didn't you? What did you want to interfere for?' He tried to get to his feet. His eyes were filled with tears and his face was twisted like a baby's, his lips were quivering. 'A man's got a right to do what he likes with his own life!'

Kemp said: 'You'll feel better soon, Joe. I'll go and make you a cup of tea.'

'I—I won't never be able to lift me head again,' moaned Craik. 'I'd be better out of the way.'

'Do you want everyone to think you killed

109

O'Hara?' demanded Rollison, as Kemp stood up.

'It wouldn't make no difference to me, if I was dead!'

Rollison glanced at Kemp who nodded and went downstairs. Craik continued to stare into Rollison's eyes, his own still watering and his body a-tremble. Rollison turned to the wall, went down on one knee and was touching the wainscotting when Craik gasped:

'What do you think you're doing?'

Rollison pulled at the new piece of wainscotting; it came away easily. He groped inside the hole which lay revealed and touched smooth and cold. He drew out two bottles and stood up, holding one in each hand.

Craik rose unsteadily to his feet.

'Don't—don't tell the curate, Mr Rollison!' His voice seemed strangled. 'Don't tell 'im!' His voice grew almost hysterical but could not be heard outside the room. 'I—I never used to touch it, only since my wife died—I been so lonely. You don't know what it is to be lonely, I don't drink much, only a little drop now and again.'

'I won't tell Kemp,' said Rollison, quietly. 'What is it?' The bottles were clean and had no labels.

'Whisky,' said Craik. 'You—you promise you won't?'

'Yes,' said Rollison but made a mental reservation. 'You're all kinds of a damned fool,

110

Craik. Not a soul would have believed you were innocent.' When Craik said nothing, Rollison went on sharply: 'Why did you try to gas yourself?'

'I—I was so ashamed,' muttered Craik. 'Me, a respectable man, a member o' the church—you don't know the disgrace, Mr Rollison. As soon as I come back, everyone started saying I was a sly one, why, two men come in and congratulated me on getting away with it!'

'Did you kill O'Hara?' asked Rollison, abruptly.

The man's eyes widened in horror.

'Me!' He gasped. 'No, no, Mr Rollison, I never killed him, I never killed a man in my life! He was a dirty tyke in some ways, always goin' on at me, but I—'

'So you knew him,' murmured Rollison.

Apparently the shop was empty and the crowd had been moved on for there were only the sounds of chinking crockery downstairs. In the bedroom, the silence lengthened and Craik had gone very still.

At last, he said:

'I bought the whisky from him, Mr Rollison. That's why he always had a rub at me. I didn't know from one day to another when he was going to give me away, it was something awful. But—I never killed him! I didn't even know I was going to see him that night!'

'Do the police know about your dealings with him?' asked Rollison.

Craik's expression was answer enough.

'All right, I won't tell them,' Rollison said but again he made a mental reservation he would not tell them unless it became important evidence. He listened but Kemp did not appear to be coming up. He unscrewed the cap of one bottle and smelt it. His face wrinkled.

'Great Scott! It's poison!'

'It—it isn't so good as it was,' muttered Craik. 'But whisky's hard to get, Mr Rollison. Don't—don't let the curate know, please!'

Kemp's footsteps sounded on the stairs.

Rollison replaced the bottles and the stretch of wainscotting and was standing up, empty-handed, when Kemp arrived with a tea-tray. He had brought three cups.

The tea seemed to revive Craik. He remained maudlin and apologetic and very humble. He said that he realised now that the suicide attempt had been wrong but he hadn't thought he could stand the disgrace. Kemp jollied him, handling the situation, as he knew it, admirably. Half an hour later, Craik seemed a new man and Kemp rose to go.

'You'll be all right, now, Joe, and I've a meeting at seven-thirty. Don't come out tonight. But don't talk a lot of nonsense about not coming to church!' He rested a hand on the man's shoulder. 'Are you coming, Rolly?'

'I'll stay for half an hour,' said Rollison.

When Kemp had gone, Craik looked at him steadily.

112

Bill Ebbutt had disliked the little man's face and that was understandable. Craik had a hang-dog look, as if he were ashamed of himself. It was meekness but not true humility. He would be anathema to a bluff, confident character like Ebbutt. Now, however, he took on a strange, unexpected dignity.

'I appreciate your help very much, Mr Rollison. I won't forget it, either.'

Rollison smiled.

'That's all right, Joe! It's none of my business but, if you must drink in secret, don't drink poison like that.' He took out the bottles again and tucked them into his pockets where they bulged noticeably. 'If you must have a drink, I'll send you a bottle of the real stuff.'

'Please don't,' said Craik, quickly. 'This has been a lesson to me, I must try to—'

'If you try to reform yourself in five minutes, you'll slip back further than you were before,' said Rollison. 'How long have you been buying this stuff from O'Hara?'

'About four months, I suppose,' said Craik.

'Who did you get it from before that?'

'Another Kelly,' said Craik. 'I mean, another Irishman!'

'Do you know where they got it?'

'No, I—I didn't ask questions,' said Craik and went on in a thin voice: 'I knew I was doing wrong but I couldn't get it no other way. I used to buy it in the West End but when it got short I couldn't.'

'It's your problem,' Rollison said. 'I'm not your judge. Do you know anyone else who buys it?'

'No,' said Craik, emphatically. 'No one knows about it.'

'Then why should they learn?' asked Rollison.

He smiled and left the room.

Someone was putting a piece of board up at the broken window. It was the policeman who appeared to inquire about Craik's condition and said that two or three things had been stolen when a dozen people had burst into the shop.

'I think it was them kids,' the policeman said. 'They take some handling!'

'If they all get handled your way, they'll be all right,' said Rollison. 'I shouldn't worry Craik just now. He'll be better tomorrow.'

'What about the door?' asked the policeman.

'We'll lock it and go out the back way,' said Rollison. 'The back door's got a self-locking Yale.'

When he parted company with the policeman he walked towards the Whitechapel Road, no longer smiling. The bottles were uncomfortable against his sides and once or twice he fingered them.

He did not think he had much further to look for the motive behind the murder; and he came to the conclusion that Jolly had not wasted the previous day. He was very anxious

114

to talk to Jolly.

CHAPTER ELEVEN

'VERY POOR STUFF,' SAYS JOLLY

Jolly sipped at a glass of Joe Craik's whisky gingerly, ran it about his mouth and swallowed. Despite his caution, he choked. When he had recovered, he looked at Rollison with watery eyes.

'Very harsh liquor indeed, sir.'

'So I think,' said Rollison. 'Craik bought it from O'Hara and, before O'Hara, from another Irishman from the colony at the docks. Bootleg liquor, Jolly!'

'You seem almost elated, sir.' Jolly was mildly disapproving. 'I am,' said Rollison. 'We've won half the battle and your journey yesterday was a stroke of genius!'

Jolly looked puzzled.

'Can't you see why?' asked Rollison.

'I'm afraid I can't, sir.'

'You've been drinking too much fire-water! You followed the pseudo-Keller's cultured companion about yesterday, didn't you? And as far as you know, he didn't realise that he was being followed.'

'I should be very reluctant to think that he had observed me,' said Jolly, with dignity.

'I don't think he did, otherwise he wouldn't have gone round booking orders,' said Rollison.

'Booking *orders* for what?' echoed Jolly. 'I must be very obtuse, or—oh, I see, sir!' His eyes grew brighter and took on an eager look. 'Would you care to elaborate the point, sir?'

Rollison chuckled.

'Making sure you don't steal my thunder this time? Yes, I'll elaborate. The man with the cultured voice went to the various pubs and booked orders for the hooch. His voice would go a long way and he would be a plausible salesman. He made nine calls altogether and if he sold a couple of dozen bottles each time, he didn't do so badly. That would explain why he made it a pub-crawl under difficulties. We should have suspected something like it last night.'

'We were both very tired,' murmured Jolly.

'Yes. Well, where do we go from here?' When Jolly did not answer, Rollison went on in a thoughtful voice: 'We are justified in making some guesses. Kemp told me he is re-opening some of the mission halls which have been closed up for some time. After all, the mob would have to keep the stuff somewhere, wouldn't it?'

'Naturally, sir.'

'Why not in or beneath one of the mission halls which haven't been used for some time. A search is indicated! I wish I could get a few days off.'

'Perhaps it is time for you to fall sick, sir,' murmured Jolly. 'We'll see. Meanwhile, I don't think we should move too fast. You've got one of the men who matters, the salesman of the outfit. You'd better pick up his trail again—you didn't find out his name, did you?'

'No, sir,' said Jolly, apologetically.

'You might find out from Bill Ebbutt,' said Rollison. 'You told me that your man finished his rounds in the West End, although he started from the East End. There would be a useful market for fire-water in the mushroom clubs, even more so than in suburban pubs.'

'A much readier one, sir, yes.'

'Find him and keep after him but be careful,' urged Rollison. 'If they realise we're after them in earnest, they might get really nasty. If they murdered O'Hara, who obviously talked too freely for their safety, they'll do anything.'

'Do you think that's why he was murdered?'

'Probably. He couldn't resist baiting Craik which was foolish. Craik made out that he started the fight because he was anxious to defend the fair name of Ronald Kemp but actually he was keyed up to a pitch of desperation because he was afraid that O'Hara would taunt him and let Whiting know what was behind it. It looks as if we're getting along very nicely! Bill Ebbutt was right in his estimate of Joe Craik.'

'And that was, sir?'

117

'Bill doesn't like hypocrites,' said Rollison.

'Craik certainly doesn't impress as a very sincere individual,' murmured Jolly. 'Perhaps you have already seen the other possibility, sir?'

'What possibility?'

Jolly looked diffident and coughed slightly before saying:

'I have not had the advantage of seeing Craik in person but he did discover that this whisky was available, didn't he? He usually bought his supplies in the West End but switched to the East End. The question I ask myself is, how did he know about it? A chance meeting with O'Hara, or any one of the salesmen, would hardly have brought to light the fact that they were selling illicit liquor. Craik's reputation being what it was, he was not a likely informer. Don't you agree, sir?' added Jolly, anxiously; for the Toff was looking at him fixedly.

'I do indeed,' murmured Rollison. 'I'd missed that one. Craik might know where the stuff is being stored. He might even be conniving at it.'

'It occurred to me as being *just* possible, sir,' said Jolly, modestly.

'It strikes me as being probable,' declared Rollison. 'Nice fellow, Joe Craik—if we're right.' He glanced at his watch. 'It's getting on for nine. I'll go over and find these halls and any other places which belong to the church and might be used for warehousing. You can

118

try to find out the name of our cultured gentleman. Oh—and see that Craik gets a bottle of real Scotch.'

'Very good, sir.'

'There's one other thing,' went on Rollison, rubbing his cheek thoughtfully. 'The order of the day is—be careful.'

'I will, sir.'

'When you look blank like that, you're usually wondering what I'm talking about,' said Rollison. 'I'm not drivelling. Care is essential. Even if we're right, we haven't yet discovered where the stuff comes from. The Irish angle might be a blind—these gentry are specialists in diversions, aren't they? But Jolly, if we're right—how big *is* it?'

After a pause, Jolly said warmly:

'I didn't see as far as you, sir. We might close up the traffic in Whitechapel, or even further around, but still leave a very wide field for its disposal.'

'Yes,' said Rollison, 'and we might as well make a clean sweep of it.' He lit a cigarette. 'As it might be a big-money game, take even fewer chances than you would have done five minutes ago.'

'Is there any particular thing you want me to find out about my quarry?'

'Name, address—oh, yes,' said Rollison, 'and what connections he has in the West End. Big money isn't often found in the East End.'

He paused and Jolly waited, hopefully.

119

'There have been whisky rackets before, haven't there?' murmured Rollison. 'Two or three of them—dummy companies selling good stuff at high prices. Could we be on the fringe of something similar but with hooch as its stock-in-trade?'

'It is at least a possibility, sir,' said Jolly. 'I have just remembered something which the man who called himself Keller said when he called last night.'

'What particular thing?' asked Rollison.

'He recommended you to play around in your own back yard and made it clear that he meant the West End.'

Rollison began to smile.

'Jolly, we'll have to go into formal partnership! I missed that.'

'I am quite satisfied with the present arrangement, sir, thank you,' said Jolly, primly. 'I cannot see that it is of any great importance, although it might—'

'Oh, come!' exclaimed Rollison. 'It might be the most important thing yet.'

'I don't quite see—' began Jolly.

'But you must see,' declared Rollison, 'Keller—we'll call him Keller—was anxious that we shouldn't spend too much time on his beat. He doesn't know just what we have discovered. He might even have been referring, obliquely, to the hooch. He might have been saying, in effect: "Why spoil our little market when there's a big one on your

120

own doorstep?" Remember,' added Rollison, 'there is the real Keller, of the established reputation. Two factions, as we know. What a triumph for our Keller if he succeeded in making us concentrate on the other man.'

'Very subtle indeed, sir,' said Jolly. 'I really don't know how you do it! What time do you expect to be back?'

'I hope, by midnight,' said Rollison.

He let Jolly go ahead, reassuring himself that neither he nor his man was being followed. He came to the conclusion that "Keller" had been sincere when he had offered a forty-eight hours armistice and he went by tube to Whitechapel. When he reached the Jupe Street hall, he found it closed. He went to St Guy's, which was half a mile away, but found it empty as well—it was used as a school during the day. He was about to go back to Jupe Street when a side door of the church opened and Craik appeared.

'Why, hallo, sir!' he said, with enforced joviality. 'I didn't expect to see you again this evening!'

'One never knows one's luck, does one?' said the Toff, ironically. 'Have you seen Mr Kemp?'

'He was here a short while ago but went out. I understand that you might find him near East Wharf. We have a small hut near there, sir.'

Did the man look furtive? Rollison asked

himself and decided that Craik's rabbity eyes held no particular expression unless it were of guilt. His drooping lips were set in a smile.

'I'll look there,' promised Rollison and went off.

Craik stood watching him until he was out of sight and thus increased Rollison's sense of misgiving. He reached East Wharf which was large and bustled with activity. A ship was being unloaded and sweating dockers were at the cranes and the pulleys, at hand-barrows and on electric trucks. The roar of engines and the loud voices of the men echoed across the water.

Rollison stood watching for a few minutes.

Many of the voices were clearly Irish; the rich brogue would have fascinated him in any case and just now was exceptionally interesting. He watched some wooden packing cases being swung ashore with two men beneath to steady and direct them to a great pile. Most of the men were stripped to the waist, or wore only singlets and trousers, and many were barefooted. One little party was singing a folk-song and the harmony was curiously affecting.

'Could there be a crate or two of hooch there, I wonder?' mused Rollison, as he turned away.

He did not know where to find the St Guy's hut—he expected that it was one which had been erected to serve the dockers, perhaps as a canteen or a clothes depot, and was now out of use because the WVS had taken over that work. Looking about him at the sweating, singing men, he reflected that Isobel Crayne would have been horrified, only a few years before, at the very thought of spending much of her time amid such people and surroundings.

Then he saw the mobile canteen and smiled when he saw Kemp standing outside it— talking with Isobel.

'He's no slouch,' murmured Rollison and sauntered towards them. Isobel saw him first.

'Hallo, Rolly! We were just talking about you!'

'There is a law of slander,' said Rollison. 'And I'm jealous of my reputation.'

'We weren't doing it any harm,' said Kemp.

'If you were, I would close up your other eye,' said Rollison. 'Shocking, these fighting parsons, aren't they?' he asked Isobel. 'You never know whether you're going to get a homily or a punch on the nose. Don't let him take you away, he'll talk for hours.'

Kemp grinned.

'This is Miss Crayne's half-hour off!'

'Have you discovered that already?' murmured Rollison. 'You're going to quicken the pace in these parts. When is the half-hour up? Because I have much to discuss with you and—'

'*Hoy, there!*'

A stentorian voice broke across his words and made all of them look up sharply. A dozen men bellowed in warning. All were staring towards the trio while a great bale of wooden cases, enclosed in a rope-net, came swinging towards them as if out of control.

CHAPTER TWELVE

THE APOLOGETIC CRANE DRIVER

Rollison swept his right arm round, knocking Isobel into Kemp who lost his balance and fell heavily with Isobel on top of him. Rollison went flat on his stomach. He saw the load sweeping nearer and dropping fast. He drew in his breath and kept still.

The bale crashed.

He felt something strike the back of his leg and heard the crates breaking open; but little debris flew about, for the net kept all but the smaller pieces in. The crash had made the cement ground quiver, made blast enough to take Rollison's breath away but he straightened up, wincing when he moved his right leg. He saw Isobel beginning to get up, bewilderedly; her dark hair had fallen over her eyes. Kemp had one arm about her and, although he was still on his back, he was looking about.

Rollison twisted round so that he could see his leg. The trouser-leg was torn slightly and there was a small streak of blood but he did not think it was serious; a piece of broken wood lay near him.

He stood up and helped Isobel as a dozen men hurried towards them.

Not far away, a man with a pronounced Irish brogue said loudly:

'Always aslape, I've never known a country where the people slape so much!' He spoke insultingly to a big sweaty docker who glowered at him.

'Keep your trap shut, Kelly.'

Out of the corner of his eye, Rollison saw the Irishman stop suddenly then swing round and aim a blow at the docker's head. On the instant, men began to fight. Two were bowled over by the big Irishman who was landing right and left, others joined him and stood together, breathing defiance.

A little, dark-haired man, better dressed than most of the others and who had been approaching Rollison, roared:

'Stop that fighting!'

No one took the slightest notice.

'Strike me, I'll see the lot of you in jail if—' roared the little man and plunged into the middle of the fray. He did not use his fists but pushed and shoved and shouted and out of the melée there came some sort of order. Before long, the combatants had separated and were standing away from each other. The Irish were grinning widely and there seemed to be no malice in the others.

The little dark-haired man gave orders and some of the dockers, from both sections, went towards an empty lorry and began to load it with wooden crates. Only a few of the men had restarted work, however, but Rollison paid little attention to that. He answered questions reassuringly for no great harm had been done. He smiled at the dark-haired man and at the English and the Irish working together in what now appeared to be perfect harmony.

A disruptive note was introduced by the lorry driver.

'Now then, don't knock me lorry apart, Irish!'

'That's enough, Straker!' snapped the dark-haired man.

'Me name's Smith,' said the lorry driver, truculently.

Rollison would have paid little attention to the exchange but for his interest in the dark-haired man who had shown himself so capable of handling an ugly situation.

'Your name doesn't matter a stripe to me,' he growled. 'You work for Straker. Don't start more trouble on this wharf. If you do, I'll report you right away.'

'All right, all right,' growled the driver. 'Can't yer take a joke?' He lit a cigarette and went slouching off to the front of his lorry.

Two scared-looking women in the green dress of WVS workers came from the mobile canteen.

'Are you really all right?' Rollison asked Isobel.

'I'm scared, that's all.'

'Accidents will happen,' said Rollison, 'we were in luck's way.'

No one had been seriously hurt, although the fence of a wooden hut, standing near, was down. A few pieces of machinery were strewn about the wharf, small parts from the packing-cases; Rollison was almost disappointed because there were no broken whisky bottles. He waited until Kemp was dusting himself down and a plump little woman came out with two cups of tea, before turning to the dark-haired man.

'Are you in charge?' he asked.

'Yes. I'm the foreman.' The man was abrupt.

'I'd like a word with that crane-driver.'

'So would I!' said the foreman, darkly. 'Are you sure that cut doesn't need attention, Mr Rollison?'

'I'll see to it later.' Rollison passed no comment on the fact that he had been recognised but went with the foreman towards the crane. It was drooping towards the ground, as if something had broken, and a man was climbing from its smelly interior. Small and pale-faced, he reminded Rollison of Craik but was young enough to be Craik's son.

'What the hell are you doing? I thought you were a crane-driver, not a—' he went on with unprintables, a flow which showed a nice discrimination and made the driver's lips quiver. Several other men gathered round. In different circumstances, Rollison would have been sorry for the little man.

At last, the foreman stopped.

'I–I–I'm sorry, sir,' gasped the driver, in a small voice. 'I misjudged the distance and tried to swing it back. Then my hand slipped.'

'Slipped? Mine'll slip where you don't want it, you bloody lunatic!' roared the foreman. 'I'm always telling you to keep your eyes on your job and to stop going to sleep. This'll be your last ride in a crane,' he added. 'I'll see you off this wharf if I have to drive the thing myself!'

'I–I'm sorry,' muttered the crane-driver. He looked at Rollison. 'You–you wasn't—no one was hurt, was they?'

'You nearly broke this gentleman's leg,' rasped the foreman, 'and for all you cared, you might have knocked their brains out.'

The apologetic crane-driver could not keep still, evaded the foreman's eyes as well as Rollison's. Once or twice, he put an unsteady hand to his lips and his eyes were suspiciously bright.

'Knock off now and go to my office!' snapped the foreman. As the man turned to go and a path was made for him through the crowd, the foreman looked up like a bantam cock and roared: 'What in hades do you loafing varmints think you're doing? Do we want that ship unloaded or don't we? Double time—why, before I pay you double time for behaving like a crowd of village idiots, I'll burn my shirt!'

The curious threat was effective for the men turned away and work started again. A small party had already taken the broken goods from the net and the foreman himself went to the crane and manoeuvred skilfully until it was in its proper position and the empty net was over the hold of the ship. Rollison watched him with close interest. The smelly, oily fumes were nauseating and the number of buttons and levers were confusing but the foreman had a sure touch.

He finished and jumped down.

'Take it over, Smith,' he said to an oldish man standing by. 'It's time they left this job to men.'

'How old is the driver?' Rollison asked.

'About twenty,' said the foreman. 'Only he isn't a driver any more.'

'What's his name?' asked Rollison.

'Cobbett.'

'And there's nothing mechanically wrong with the crane?'

'No. The fool overshot the mark and pressed the wrong button, lowering it instead of taking it back—my stripes, Mr Rollison, I had the wind up! I thought you were all done for!'

'No great harm done, except to the goods,' said Rollison. 'Are they all the same?'

'No, it's a mixed cargo,' said the foreman. 'I wouldn't care if it had been a bale of feather pillows, he shouldn't have lost his head.'

'Do you know him well?'

'Not so well as I know some of them,' said the foreman, and looked squarely into Rollison's face. 'What are you getting at, Mr Rollison?'

'If you've worked here for long, you've probably heard that the new curate isn't popular,' said Rollison.

The foreman grinned.

'Didn't you see that fight last night. But of course you did, I saw you at the ring-side—my stripes, what a fight and what a fighter! Pity he took the cloth, he might have been a British hope!'

'You haven't quite followed me—by the way, I didn't get your name?'

'Owen. Jake Owen,' said the foreman. 'Where haven't I followed you?'

'Kemp still isn't popular in certain quarters,' said Rollison. 'I think there have been attacks on his life.'

Owen's lips tightened, and for some seconds he just stared. Then:

'You mean Cobbett did it on *pur*pose?'

'I mean, he might have done.'

'*I'll* soon find out,' growled Owen and turned

130

on his heel, his face livid. Rollison stopped him.

'It's better not to voice suspicions at this stage, we might be wrong,' he said quietly. 'Even if we're right, I don't think we should say so yet. We've plenty of reasons for making inquiries about Cobbett without saying why. I'm taking you on trust,' he added with an apologetic smile.

'If you say I'm to keep my mouth shut, I'll keep it shut,' growled Owen. 'I don't want any filthy murderers working on my shift.'

'Good! Can you stand Cobbett off for a day or two?'

'That'll only give him a rest, the lazy young—'

'He might go places,' murmured Rollison, 'and I'd rather like to find out where.'

Owen was very quick in the uptake.

'I get you! You like to do things your own way, don't you?'

'The right way when I see it,' said Rollison. 'Thanks.' He obtained Cobbett's address before he left Owen who went to the little office to interview the crane-driver. Rollison returned to the WVS canteen. Kemp was standing by it, Isobel was serving tea and sandwiches to men who were having a break. The sun was getting lower and the first shadows of evening were over the docks, bathing the distant side of the river in a mellow, softening light which took away the ugliness of brick buildings and cranes and

131

barges and even hid the skeleton shapes of two warehouses which had been destroyed by fire during heavy raids.

Kemp was looking sombre.

'What can I do with her?' he demanded as Rollison drew up. 'She won't give it up for tonight and go home.'

Rollison smiled. 'Nor would you, in the circumstances.'

'It must have given her a whale of a shock.'

'It did me but I'm not going home,' said Rollison. 'I've a story that will interest you,' he added. 'Isobel won't mind if you come with me—will you?'

Isobel reassured him and seemed eager to demonstrate that she could still serve two cups of tea to another woman's one. Rollison refused a cup and left with Kemp. Rollison glanced round, after going a few yards, and saw Isobel staring after them, a cup of tea in her hand.

Rollison smothered a grin.

At the Jupe Street hall he gave Kemp an outline of his suspicions but he did not mention Craik's part in helping him to form them, nor did he go into details. He finished:

'If I'm right, then the stuff is being stored somewhere near.'

'Do you think one of the church halls is being used?' said Kemp, slowly.

'It wouldn't surprise me.

'We've three that haven't been used for some

time. Do you want to search them?'

'Not yet,' decided Rollison. 'I think it had better wait—I'll have someone keep an eye on them, though. You don't let them out, do you?'

'No. They're only wooden huts. Mr Cartwright believed in getting out among the people, he thought it easier than trying to persuade them to walk as far as St Guy's.'

'There isn't much wrong with Cartwright's reasoning,' said Rollison.

'It would just about finish him if he learned about this,' said Kemp, grimly.

Rollison looked his amazement.

'Finish Cartwright? Not on your life! He'd want to get out of bed and be after them with an axe!'

Kemp looked startled.

'Perhaps you're right. I—' he stopped abruptly with his mouth parted and his puffy eye opened. Rollison watched him, not surprised at the sudden change and knowing that sooner or later one possibility would occur to Kemp.

'Look here!' exclaimed the curate, 'was that accident with the crane *really* an accident? Or—'

'Or, I think,' answered Rollison. 'They know that they haven't a chance of driving you out and they're getting desperate. Accidents will happen,' he repeated, ironically. 'They won't want to work up police interest by straightforward murder. The police didn't go so wild over the murder of O'Hara as they would over the Rev Ronald Kemp. Watch your step—literally.'

Kemp began to rub his hands together slowly and his good eye began to glisten.

Rollison made a note of the sites of the halls and then went round to Bill's gymnasium, which he found packed, and where he was greeted with great affability. Soon after he arrived, six men departed with instructions to watch the three halls in couples, from a safe distance, and to report any visits by night or day. Then Rollison mentioned, casually, that he had been served with some pretty potent whisky earlier in the evening.

'There's some raw stuff about,' declared Bill Ebbutt. 'You should 'ave stayed thirsty until you arrived 'ere, Mr Ar—I don't sell poison.' He grinned as well as he could. His face was a mass of bruises, black and blue and purple, and he was obviously in great discomfort. 'How's the Rev?'

'A black eye apart, he's all right'

'Bless 'is heart! Will you 'ave a drink?' asked Ebbutt

'No, thanks, that one was enough for tonight!' Rollison shuddered, realistically. 'Is much hooch sold?'

'There's been one or two fellers in pitchin' the tale—you know 'ow it goes. They've got 'old of a few dozen bottles orf someone who's gone bankrupt—but if you bought the stuff, you'd soon go broke all right! The samples is all right, sunnines, sunnines they gives you a spot've the real poison.'

'Can you remember any of the salesmen?'

Bill Ebbutt began to toy with his fleshy jowl. In a very sober voice, he answered:

'Maybe I could. Are you on to sunnink?'

'I might be but I don't want your boys to know about it.'

'S'very thoughtful of yer,' said Ebbutt. 'Very thoughtful indeed. Bootleg liquor, is it? It could be big.' He closed his eyes in an effort to recall who had tried to sell him the stuff and finally opened them and said hurriedly:

'One was a little Irish feller, a proper Kelly. I dunno his name. The other was one o' these eddicated types, all smiles. I soon sent 'im off wiv' a flea in 'is ear. Tell yer what, Mr Ar—if anyone else comes peddling it, I'll buy a dozen an' see what I can find out.'

'Good idea, Bill!' said Rollison. 'This educated fellow—what was he like?'

'Tall–as–you–are–dark–suit–good–looker–clean-shaved–round–erbaht–thirty–five. That do yer, Mr Ar?'

'Wonderful!' said Rollison. 'You've described the man I have in mind. Have you seen him about lately?'

'Nope.'

'Will you find out if he's been to any of the other pubs?'

'Yep. If they've bought the stuff, they won't

talk—if they 'aven't, they'll tell me.'

The description of "Keller"'s' educated companion clinched one thing; the gang was peddling illicit whisky. From the taste of Craik's sample, Rollison thought it was probably made from illicit stills. There was a great deal of similar stuff on sale, especially at the flashier clubs, and members of the armed services bought more of it than anyone else.

'I think it's time I saw the Yard,' Rollison decided, standing on a corner and watching the trams pass by, noisy yet ghostly with their faint lights. There were very few cars or other vehicles, except an occasional bus. He strolled towards Whitechapel Station and, as he neared it, a taxi began to move from the curb.

Rollison hailed it, quickly. The driver pulled up.

'Where to?' he demanded. 'I'm on me way to me garage, can't go far.'

'Scotland Yard,' ordered Rollison.

The pavement was filled with people walking slowly to and fro and some of the shadows seemed to be sinister. He did not think he had been followed but, if he had, then "Keller" would soon know where he was going.

The interior of the cab was very dark and the driver started off too soon.

'Be careful!' exclaimed Rollison—and then stopped short for a hand gripped his wrist and another closed over his mouth and he was dragged into the cab as the door banged. The

136

cab moved off at a rattling pace and Rollison, almost suffocated by the pressure on his mouth, could hardly move.

'Going to Scotland Yard, *are* you,' said the man with the cultured voice.

CHAPTER THIRTEEN

UNEXPECTED JOURNEY

'Keep still!' the man said and struck Rollison across the face. He had released his grip and Rollison was trying to get himself more comfortable. The scratch on his leg troubled him and he was half-kneeling, half-lying, across the legs of the two occupants of the taxi. He could just see their faces, pale in the darkness.

Soon, he managed to ease his leg and stopped moving.

'That's better,' the man said. 'You've made a mistake this time, Rollison. You aren't going to Scotland Yard.'

'Be careful, Gregson!' said the other who was the self-styled Keller. 'He might try to jump out.'

'He won't take the risk,' said Gregson, confidently. 'Sit on one of the tip-up seats, Rollison. Don't forget that we mean business. If you should meet with a nasty accident—well, you wouldn't know much about it.'

Groping in the darkness, Rollison pulled a seat down and sat on it. He had not recovered enough to strike out at the others; he doubted whether he would be wise to. Their confidence now was as great as it had been at the flat with better reason.

Gregson said:

'I've got a shot of morphia here, Rollison; if you get funny you'll have it and you won't wake up again. This is your last chance, if you behave yourself.'

Rollison forced himself to reply:

'Accommodating of you. You're well-equipped, aren't you? Am I going to hear more about my own back-yard?'

'That's enough of that!' snapped "Keller."

He was keeping in the background, the role of spokesman had been switched; Rollison wondered who was really the leader.

He should have been prepared for such an attack. Had the taxi been waiting, he would have wondered whether it had been there fortuitously but, as it had been moving away after dropping a fare, he had not thought twice about it. The incident had been very well-planned.

The only consolation lay in the fact that they still seemed disposed to reason.

The taxi was driving through the back streets of the East End. It had turned round outside the station and was heading further east; he thought they were near the docks. He saw an occasional passer-by from the glow of a cigarette in the darkness. His breathing was easier and he was beginning to feel more capable of tackling the situation.

'You aren't feeling so clever, are you?' sneered Gregson. 'You think you're a lot smarter than you are, Rollison. If there was anything in your reputation, you wouldn't have fallen for this trick.'

Rollison said heartily: 'I couldn't agree more!'

The man exclaimed 'What?' and fell silent. The taxi was going over a cobbled surface which was a further proof that they were in the dockside area.

'You'd better agree with me again,' Gregson said. 'You've gone far enough. Who told you about the whisky?'

'Whisky?' ejaculated Rollison.

'Come on, you know all about that,' said Gregson.

'Don't you know about it?'

'Gregson, he—' began "Keller."

'I didn't know it was a whisky racket,' declared Rollison and then went on in a wondering voice: 'I thought it was something big!' He gave a hollow laugh and wondered if he were overdoing it. There was a startled silence, followed by an oath from Keller.

'Then what the hell *are* you after?'

'I'm simply helping Kemp,' said Rollison,

truthfully.

'You're helping that—' Keller broke off, with an exasperated note in his voice. 'He's been fooling us,' he growled. 'We needn't have worried about him.'

'Who's worried?' asked Gregson but he sounded uneasy. 'All right, so you didn't know. We hijacked a few bottles of booze,' he went on, too quickly. 'We thought you knew about it.'

Rollison said ruefully: 'I could do with a small crate myself.'

The taxi came to a standstill as he spoke.

Any hopes of breaking away were dashed at once for the door was opened by a man outside. As he climbed out, Rollison's wrist was gripped and he saw other shadowy figures crowding round. The man already holding him took a grip on the back of his neck and pushed him forward. He stumbled over a doorstep and along an unlighted passage: there was a faint glow of light at the far end.

'Stop, cully,' ordered his captor.

He stopped. The front door closed and a light was switched on. Three men were in the passage, besides "Keller" and Gregson. They were characteristic East Enders of the tougher breed.

The passage had green distempered walls, the floor was of unstained boards and it looked like part of a warehouse. Soon Rollison was in an office which might have been that of any business firm; his eye was caught by a fine Mirzapore carpet with a round hole in the middle with its edges bound.

Gregson pushed past him and sat at a roll-top desk. Keller also sat down and one of the men stood by the door; the others went out. Gregson, his handsome face clear-cut beneath the light from an unshaded lamp, stared at him, tight-lipped. "Keller's" brown eyes were narrowed and he seemed much more on edge than the other.

'Well, Rollison?' Gregson spoke at last. 'Are you going to be sensible about this?'

'That depends what you call sensible,' said Rollison.

'It's none of your business. Kemp's all right now, we couldn't run him out of the district if we tried, so we won't waste our time trying.' Apparently he took it for granted that Rollison had assumed the crane incident to be an accident. 'You've done what you started out to do and we're doing no one any harm. If you'll undertake to go back to your flat and forget about us, we'll let you go. And we'll give you a dozen *Black and White* into the bargain!'

As he finished Gregson smiled, invitingly.

'Well, it's an attractive proposition,' admitted Rollison. 'But you aren't fools, are you?'

'You'll find out,' growled "Keller."

'Be quiet,' ordered Gregson. 'No, we're not fools, Rollison.'

'So I imagined. What's to prevent me from

141

giving you a promise and then breaking it?'

'I told you—' "Keller" began.

'Oh, be quiet!' repeated Gregson harshly. 'We know you might do that, Rollison but, if you do—well, you know what happened to O'Hara.'

'Yes. Intimidating,' murmured Rollison. 'The thing is, I'm not convinced that you're resigned to Kemp staying on. I mean, what happened to O'Hara could easily happen to him.'

'Now look here,' said Gregson, still reasoningly, 'if we were to kill Kemp, or even you, the police wouldn't rest until they'd turned Whitechapel upside down. We don't want them to do that. This is the reasonable way. You're a man of the world. It doesn't matter to you if a few cases of whisky get stolen and sold at a good profit. That's what we're doing—but it's a dangerous game these days. We'd be charged with black-marketing and we might get seven years. That's enough to make us careful—and to shut the mouth of talkers like O'Hara.'

'So O'Hara talked too much,' said Rollison.

'He couldn't keep his mouth shut when he'd had a couple,' said Gregson. 'It was a coincidence that Craik was there when he was killed.'

'And an accident that Craik's knife was used?'

'It didn't matter who's knife, so long as it didn't belong to the man who actually used it,' said Gregson. 'O'Hara was nothing to you, Rollison. He was an Irishman who's only been here six months and he's a loss to no one. He wasn't even married! Listen to me. We've heard a lot about you. Perhaps you're good and you've just been unlucky this time. It doesn't matter either way. *You* aren't a fool, either. This job isn't one you need worry about, so forget all about it and go home and enjoy yourself with free *Black and White.*'

'Genuine stuff?' inquired Rollison.

He wanted Gregson to continue to reason with him for it gave him more time to size up the situation. There was a snag, they surely wouldn't let him go.

What *would* they do?

'Of *course* it's genuine,' said Gregson. 'I wouldn't cheat—'

Heavy footsteps in the passage outside cut across his words. Rollison thought he heard a shout. "Keller" glanced towards the door as it burst open and a man rushed in.

'Get away!' he gasped and paused for breath. 'The cops are outside!'

"Keller" swung round towards Rollison and pulled a gun from his pocket.

143

CHAPTER FOURTEEN

THE INTEREST OF THE POLICE

Rollison, expecting to be shot, dropped to the floor, keeping his eyes on "Keller." There was no time even to grab at one of the ledgers on the desk to use as a missile. It seemed like his last moment.

Then Gregson struck "Keller's" arm aside.

Gregson said nothing but simply grabbed "Keller's" arm and hustled him forward. The man by the door and the messenger were already in the passage.

Gregson slammed the door and turned the key on the outside.

Rollison picked himself up slowly, choked by relief. Gradually, he became aware of the footsteps. As soon as one lot faded, another drew nearer: the police were already in the building. He looked about the office and opened one of the ledgers. There were entries for various items of groceries, all neatly written up in a youthful hand. He resisted the temptation to look through the other papers on the desk, not wanting to be caught red-handed. He heard someone banging on a door not far away.

'I wonder how—' he began, then snapped his fingers. 'Jolly, of course! He traced Gregson!'

He pulled the ledger towards him. The firm's name was Mellish and Crow Limited and certainly their business appeared to be genuine. He had a feeling that he had heard of them before but could not keep his mind on the book, just glanced through it, thinking:

'If Gregson hadn't stopped him, Keller would have shot me. So I owe Gregson my life. Sensible thing to do—with a corpse on the premises he would have been for the high jump. But he was very quick—and Keller didn't think. Strange metamorphosis, Keller seemed to be the big shot yesterday.'

He stopped, as an entry in the ledger caught his eye.

'*Straker* . . . £107.11.6d.'

Rollison remembered that was the name of the haulage firm which worked for East Wharf.

The police were making a long and careful job of the building. He wondered if they had found some of the men and whether a fight was in progress.

At last they arrived—and Jolly was with Chumley. Jolly's eyes brightened at the sight of the Toff. He stepped forward swiftly.

'Are you hurt, sir?'

'Only a scratch and it wasn't done here,' Rollison said.

'I'm very glad, sir.' Jolly glanced at Chumley whose red face was set, showing nothing of the affability which was his favourite pose. Jolly

145

went on carefully: 'I knew you were being brought here, sir, and in the circumstances I thought it best to send for assistance.'

'In spite of arousing the interest of the police,' smiled Rollison. 'You couldn't have been more right.'

'I'm glad you realise that, Rollison,' Chumley said sarcastically. 'Now perhaps you will stop lying to us. You've lied far too much.'

'Not really,' protested Rollison. 'Afraid of guessing too much and misinforming you, knowing your dislike of doing the wrong thing! However, it's a clear-cut issue for the police now. Two men tricked me into a taxi and threatened to kill me unless I withdrew from the district and went back home. They also said that they were indignant that I should try to interfere in a little matter of stolen whisky and its redistribution.'

'Whisky?' echoed Chumley. His interest, already keen, grew sharper.

'Yes. They tried to bribe me with a case of *Black and White*,' went on Rollison.

'Have you searched this place?' demanded Chumley.

'No. I haven't been here for more than five minutes on my own.'

'You can do plenty in five minutes,' declared Chumley, darkly. 'Sure you haven't touched anything?'

'Frisk me,' invited Rollison, throwing out his arms in an exaggerated gesture. 'I won't make

146

any complaint about illegal searching. Even if I'd had the time to touch anything,' he added, still standing with his arms stretched out, 'I wouldn't have had the inclination.'

'Why not?' demanded Chumley.

'I can't imagine that they would have brought me to a place which, if afterwards located, might yield up its deadly secrets,' Rollison said lightly. 'It wouldn't surprise me to find that the premises belong to some estimable firm, the management of which will be horrified to discover what's going on at night'

'We'll find out,' said Chumley and ordered his men to begin searching.

Jolly found a first aid box in a cloak-room and dabbed iodine freely on Rollison's scratch, fixing lint and adhesive plaster over it and rebuking him for not having attended to it before.

Chumley pressed questions and he told the simple truth, giving the names by which he knew the two men and omitting only that he had known before of the whisky motive. Had Chumley been his usual genial self, Rollison would have been tempted to be more frank. As it was, the policeman became more terse and nearly abusive.

Rollison, smoking and sitting on an upright chair, stared at him coldly.

'I'm beginning to understand why Kemp got such a low opinion of the police,' he said.

Chumley bit his lips and turned away.

Inside an hour, a representative of the management arrived. He was an old, grey-haired, mild-mannered man, at first indignant at the police invasion, then apologetic and obviously puzzled. Thus he laid himself open to some of Chumley's 'pressure.' Rollison stood by and did nothing and Chumley began to raise his voice.

The grey-haired man stood it for some minutes, seeming to grow flustered but, when Chumley called him a liar, he spoke with unexpected sharpness.

'Are you a police officer, sir, or merely an ill-mannered ruffian?'

Rollison caught Jolly's eye. Chumley calmed down but asked more questions. Nothing the man said and nothing that was discovered suggested that the warehouse was being used as a storage place for whisky and the indications were that it had been used, as Rollison had suggested, as a meeting place. The night-watchman stoutly maintained that he knew nothing about it but he cracked unexpectedly. 'They' had made him do it, he declared; 'they' had threatened him with violence unless he let them in. 'They' had been using the office from time to time over a period of six months. He did not know why and he did not know their names but he knew that a number of people called there to see them.

It was three in the morning before Chumley

conceded that there was no need to stay longer.

Walking up the stairs to the flat, Rollison limped noticeably and, when they were inside, Jolly said:

'I think you'd better spend a day in your room tomorrow, sir. Your leg might get much worse.'

'Day in bed be—' began Rollison, then saw Jolly's expression and grinned. 'A day not in the office! Yes, that's more like it! Are you forgetting that I'm a Whitehall Warrior deeply involved in the conduct of the war?'

'I would rate this affair somewhat higher than investigating the pilfering of Army depots,' murmured Jolly.

'Well, well!' exclaimed Rollison. 'How did you manage to find that out? You'd located Gregson, I suppose, and managed to keep behind the taxi?'

'I was nearby, sir, and I heard someone mention the warehouse address, so I telephoned Chumley immediately and hurried there myself. I thought it unwise to try to prevent you from entering the taxi. Had I done so we might not have learned so much.'

'No,' admitted Rollison. 'This is certainly your day. By George, I'm tired!' He stubbed out a cigarette. 'It's a pity but I must go to the office in the morning. There's a Conference of Great Men.'

'At what time, sir?' asked Jolly.

'Eleven o'clock,' said Rollison.

It was ten o'clock next morning when Jolly called him. Rollison looked at his watch, stared at Jolly and was told mildly:

'I think you have good time for the Conference, sir.'

Although his leg was stiff, he felt rested and much more able to cope with the pretentious big brass who were to sit with him round a horseshoe-shaped table and discuss the matter of pilfering from Army depots. Although the pilfering reached alarming proportions and needed close investigation, Rollison disagreed with the attempt to solve it under central direction. As soon as the problem was solved in one place, it broke out in another. He did not agree that it was organised but that, being so spasmodic, it was purely local. Since his particular task was less concerned with stopping the trouble than with arriving at the totals of material and value lost, his heart was not in it and he made frequent attempts to get transferred to another Department; he had almost given up the hope of getting back to active service.

The Conference lingered on until late afternoon. By then, correspondence had accumulated and it was nearly half-past six before Rollison saw his ATS clerk seal the last letter.

'Is there anything else, sir?' she asked.

'Yes,' said Rollison. 'Do you ever go to West End nightclubs?'

'Why, yes—occasionally, sir!'

'What's the whisky like?'

'You shouldn't touch it,' she said, confidentially. 'It's enough to put you out on your feet!'

'How do they sell it?' asked Rollison. 'I mean, could you go and buy me a bottle—tonight, say?'

'I suppose I *could*,' she said, looking at him suspiciously, for he spoke as if obtaining a bottle of whisky would be a great adventure. And then a false light dawned upon her. 'If you really *want* some whisky, sir, a friend of mine is in the trade and I could get you some.'

'That's sweet of you,' said Rollison, smiling. 'But I haven't gone mad. I want a bottle of the stuff I would buy at a nightclub but I don't want to buy it myself.'

Then the true light dawned and she hugged herself as she went off, having sworn that she would not confide in a soul.

Rollison telephoned Jolly, to learn that he had not been able to find Gregson again but that the police were having one of their periodic comb-outs of the East End, that many people were already in hiding and the Fighting Parson was no longer the ruling topic.

'That's better,' said Rollison. 'He doesn't want the limelight. I'll go to see Cobbett the crane-driver, I think.'

151

'Very good, sir,' said Jolly.

Rollison had purposely kept from the crane-driver and not asked anyone else to watch him, believing it would be better if Cobbett lived in a fool's paradise for a few hours. The time had come for the direct approach. But he was not able to go immediately for, as he left Whitehall, a stolid detective-sergeant in plainclothes approached and asked politely if he would mind stepping along to Scotland Yard.

About the time that Rollison was walking towards Scotland Yard with the amiable sergeant, Joe Craik was putting up the black-out shutters at his shop. After every one, he stopped and rubbed his hands, sniffed and smiled his quivering, rabbit smile. He was not furtive, yet gave the impression that he was afraid that people were pointing him out and talking about him.

When he had nearly finished, a youthful figure appeared in front of the shop. Craik turned and looked into the narrowed eyes of Cobbett the crane-driver.

'Now, what do *you* want?' demanded Craik, sharply.

Cobbett sniffed. Two or three people including a monstrously fat woman were walking by the shop and heard the opening remarks. The woman stayed within earshot.

'Have you heard about the accident?' demanded Cobbett.

'Yes, you fool! You might have—'

'Doan rub it in,' pleaded Cobbett and if he were acting he was doing so very well. 'Wot ought I to do, Mr Craik? I never meant it.'

Craik rubbed his hands and then said:

'Well, my boy, if you're really sorry, then I won't make it any the worse for you. *I* know what you can do—go along to Mr Kemp, the curate, and tell him how sorry you are.'

'Do you think—' Cobbett began.

'*He* won't refuse to forgive you, my boy,' said Craik. 'You run along.'

Cobbett still looked miserable but nodded and obeyed.

The fat woman wearing a coloured shawl and a tattered skirt, the hem of which dragged along the pavement, had heard every word. She moved on with a great effort when Craik finished his task, sniffing and saying in an audible voice:

'If I'd have moved off soon's the boy 'ad stopped, he would'a said I was listening to 'im, that 'e would!'

Her fleshy face was set in lines of disgust.

She waddled as far as Little Lane, turned into it and eventually reached Number 49. Outside, two of Bill Ebbutt's men called out good-humouredly:

'What's the latest, Ma?'

She tossed her head at them and was admitted to the Whitings' home by one of the children who called her Mrs Parsons. Then, she regaled the old woman at the house with everything she had heard.

Mrs Parsons was, beyond all doubt, the district's most notorious gossip. Some said there was no malice in her and that she could no more keep information to herself than a colander could hold water. The fact that she talked, and that no confidence was safe with her, was extremely well known—as was the fact that she had one particular crony, Mrs Whiting's mother.

She was not a stranger to Rollison, of whom she always spoke in hushed tones as 'The Torf' and before whom she always curtseyed, but he had not been to see her often recently for he had come to the conclusion that she developed trivial incidents so colourfully and plausibly that they became entirely different from the original.

Soon, she was on her way again and immediately afterwards Mrs Whiting's mother came hurrying out. So two tongues started wagging. Before long, the whole district knew that Cobbett was going to see the curate and wondered why. The story of the accident was already well-known and one of the characteristics of the East End was that when anything happened to the Toff, it had no chance of being passed over; it became an item of general interest.

Rollison, unaware of the significance in the talk, walked along with the sergeant towards

Scotland Yard.

CHAPTER FIFTEEN

THE RETURN OF THE HOLIDAY-MAKER

Rollison was not greatly perturbed as he walked into the familiar hall of Scotland Yard, although a telephoned request would have been more normal. The fact that a sergeant had been waiting outside one entrance of the building suggested that the others had been watched, and that the Yard had been determined to see him quickly.

On the way, he had talked about the weather.

At the Yard, he asked who wanted to see him.

'Superintendent Grice, sir,' said the sergeant.

Rollison was pleasantly surprised for not only did he know Grice well but he was sure that Grice would be helpful whenever he could be. So he entered the spacious office with a smile, as Grice rose from his chair. The Superintendent was a tall, spare man whose complexion was normally very like a woman's and whose skin was stretched tight across his face, particularly at his nose, thus emphasising its high bridge. Grice's complexion and his large brown eyes—not unlike "Keller's"—were his most noticeable features but Rollison was amazed when he saw him.

'Well, well!' he exclaimed. 'The holiday-maker returned—slightly sunburned!'

Grice, his face bright red with sunburn, managed a painful grin.

'Don't rub it in,' he said. 'It's as stiff as blazes.'

'The policeman who never grew up!' Rollison sat down and stretched out his long legs. 'What's brought you back early?'

'You,' said Grice.

'Not I—distrustful policemen elsewhere, I'm afraid.'

'Judging from a 'phone call I've had from Chumley, he's more than distrustful—he's highly suspicious! You needn't tell me that he should know better. You should have treated Chumley more leniently, Rolly.'

'He is rather fond of throwing his weight about and—'

'You could have satisfied him without getting his back up,' remonstrated Grice.

'I rather wanted his back up,' murmured Rollison.

'I expected as much,' commented Grice. 'Well, where will you start?'

'*I* don't start,' said Rollison, 'I was badgered into coming here by a police sergeant whose expression proved that he knew he was doing the wrong thing. Whose idea was that?'

156

'Mine. One of Chumley's men was here and I made him see I really meant business.'

'Good!' said Rollison. 'What business? Whisky?'

'Now you're getting interesting,' said Grice. 'What do you know about the whisky-running?'

'Very little,' answered Rollison, cautiously. 'I didn't believe Gregson when he told me that he was stealing a few cases and passing them on at a profit. I think it goes deeper. Does it?'

'Now you're asking,' Grice said.

Rollison took out his cigarette-case and lit a cigarette—Grice rarely smoked—and carefully replaced the case. After that, he contemplated Grice in silence for some minutes before saying, quietly:

'You and I needn't beat about the bush, need we?'

'What really took you to Whitechapel in the first place?' asked Grice.

'Kemp! Just Kemp! Nothing but Kemp! He was getting a raw deal and he's still in danger, perhaps deadlier than before. So I'm still interested.' Rollison spoke quietly but emphatically. 'I think he's stumbled across a whisky-racket but I know nothing beyond that and I'm not going to theorise for Chumley, you, or the AC himself. The truth is,' went on Rollison, warming up, 'that as soon as the word 'whisky' was mentioned Chumley pricked up his ears and, before I could turn round,

157

you'd cut short your holiday. Presumably, you were working on it before, decided you could take a holiday but came haring back as soon as you knew that trouble had broken out about it.'

Grice's manner relaxed.

'You're pretty well on the mark, Rolly. But the thing I find it hard to believe and which Chumley refuses to accept is that you went down to Whitechapel on Kemp's behalf alone. Was it partly because you'd been working on the case elsewhere and found a lead.'

'It was not. Where do you imagine I would have started?'

'I wouldn't try to guess,' said Grice.

'This last day or two I've guessed that there is a lot of hooch being distributed throughout the West End,' said Rollison. 'Is there?'

Grice leaned forward and spoke with unexpected warmth.

'There is, and it's not ordinary hooch. Much of it is poison. We've had complaints from our own service authorities, from the Americans and from several of the Allied Governments—officers and men in London on leave have drunk the stuff and made themselves ill. There have been two fatalities due to acute alcoholic poisoning. The deaths were directly attributable to the whisky. Do you mean to tell me that you didn't know?'

'Of course. I wouldn't have been working overtime if I had. Do you mind if I use your telephone?' Grice looked puzzled but shook his head and Rollison put a call through to his office. In a few seconds, a weary Bimbleton answered him.

'Bimble, old chap,' said Rollison, 'have you heard about complaints in high places of some of our chaps suffering severely from drinking bad whisky in the West End?'

'Yeh,' said Bimbleton and then articulated more clearly:

'Why, yes, Rollison. I'm sorry. I was just eating a sandwich.'

'Who is handling it?' asked Rollison. 'The drink, not the sandwich.'

'Cracknell,' Bimbleton said.

'Is he on duty, do you know?'

'No, he's left I think—no, wait a minute! I saw him coming in half an hour ago.'

'Put me through to him, will you?' asked Rollison and sat back, beaming at Grice, who looked a little less mystified. Soon, a crisp voice sounded in Rollison's ear and Rollison introduced himself with some circumspection.

'Yes, Rollison,' said Cracknell, who carried much weight at Whitehall. '. . . What's that? . . . Yes, it is quite true . . . Are you sure?'

'I'm quite sure, sir,' Rollison assured him. 'I think, with a little luck, we could see the end of it inside a week. The difficulty is that I'm so tied to the office.'

'This isn't some pet scheme of your own for which you want leave, is it?' demanded

Cracknell, suspiciously.

'I'm in the office of Superintendent Grice, of Scotland Yard,' Rollison told him. 'He asked me to see him about this very business.'

'I'll do what I can to arrange for you to be assigned to it,' Cracknell promised.

'Thanks very much,' said the Toff, warmly. 'I take it that it is regarded seriously?'

'*Extremely* so,' said Cracknell but there was an echo of laughter in his voice. 'Why do you ask?'

'If it's a matter of urgency, I shouldn't waste any time,' said Rollison.

'You can consider yourself assigned to it,' said Cracknell and rang off; the last Rollison heard from him was the beginning of an explosive laugh.

As Rollison replaced the receiver, Grice said: 'One day, you'll wheedle yourself into active service again, I can see it coming. Then what will we poor flatfoots do at Scotland Yard?'

'Wheedle me back!' replied Rollison. 'Grice, you couldn't have done me a better service and Jolly will probably send you a congratulatory telegram! I am now working on this job in an official capacity and, while I am fully prepared to co-operate with the police, I must reserve the right to act as I think best in the interests of men and women of the services who, in their all-too-brief spells of leave, are being raddled with a fire-water sold under the name of whisky, and—'

160

'That's enough!' cried Grice. 'Well, exactly how much do you know?'

Rollison passed on the whole story. Grice made notes on a pad and, when Rollison had finished, they eyed each other thoughtfully. It was Grice who broke the silence.

'Do you think it would be wrong to try to force the case in Whitechapel just yet?'

'Yes. Don't you?'

'Probably,' admitted Grice, 'although it can't be left too long. We'll have to get Gregson and the man who calls himself "Keller" as soon as we can. Chumley has descriptions of them and is already hard at work.'

'I doubt whether he'll get them,' said Rollison. 'My worry is—where is it distributed from in the West End? Have you found any store-places at all?'

'One or two small ones,' said Grice. 'It doesn't appear to be delivered in large quantities, only a few dozen at a time. We've found seven or eight retail suppliers. All of them swear that they buy it legally and believe that it is ordinary stuff—the story is so circumstantial in every case that it seems as if the organisers use a formula.'

'They're not associated clubs, are they?'

'No, they're all quite independent.'

'Then if they use a formula, it's one which they're told to use by the suppliers,' said Rollison. 'What's the story? The bottles of bad stuff were found among deliveries from the reputable companies.'

'Yes?'

'And the reputable companies know nothing about it, of course,' went on Rollison. 'How long has it been worrying you?'

'For the better part of six months.'

'It all seems to have started about six months ago,' admitted Rollison, looking very thoughtful. 'You remember that I told you that Irish dock-workers were concerned?'

'Yes. I'll look into that angle.'

'Not a bad idea,' said Rollison. 'Well, we're making progress of a kind. The main trouble is that I've started working from the wrong angle. They may distribute it in small quantities but there appears to be a lot of it about. Given much thought to distribution?'

'Yes,' said Grice.

He did not enlarge and so gave Rollison the impression that he was holding something back. Rollison did not attempt to force any information but went on thoughtfully:

'East Wharf might possibly be the distributing point as there's a lot of quite legitimate stuff brought in—does any of it come from Eire, do you know?'

'Some, yes,' said Grice cautiously. 'But most Irish goods come in at the West coast ports. Some shipments come direct to London but if you're thinking that the stuff is Irish whisky, you're—'

Rollison laughed.

'Don't insult the Irish distillers. But where are there as many illicit stills as in Ireland? If a manager or foreman of a wharf co-operated, it might be brought off the ships.'

'There's no evidence that it is and I think it's made in England,' Grice said.

'You're probably right,' admitted Rollison. 'However, supposing it is brought in at East Wharf, what happens to it then? It could be loaded straight on to the lorries and—'

He paused.

'Now what's in your mind?' demanded Grice.

'I was picturing a charming little scene at the wharf,' said Rollison. 'A big Irishman ribbed an English docker who promptly called him a neutral and started a free fight. All without malice as far as I could see. But as soon as it had stopped—the foreman handled it well— the combatants were put on to loading the same lorry. They must have been in a big hurry to get the lorry loaded and off.'

'Why?' asked Grice.

'You know, you're not really as dull as this! The obvious reason would be to get whatever they were loading *en route* before the police arrived. Police would be bound to arrive on the scene as soon as word of the accident reached them, wouldn't they?'

'Do you think East Wharf should be raided?'

'Certainly not just now!' exclaimed Rollison. 'If there's anything in the idea, the stuff has been sent away and we'd only put them on their guard. You might care to find out if that was an Irish ship, though, and keep some eyes open when the next one comes in from Eire. A suggestion only!' he added, mildly.

'I know all about your suggestions,' said Grice. 'It's a good one, anyhow.'

'Thanks. Do you know your Sergeant Bray very well?'

'Fairly well,' said Grice, cautiously.

'Is he as hot-headed as he seems? I gathered that he made the arrest a little precipitately.'

'He was right to act as he did and also right to take Craik to Divisional headquarters. Bray's a good chap. He might have made a mistake but, if you're asking me whether I propose to reprimand him for this, I'm not.'

'I should hope not!' exclaimed Rollison. 'Er—Chumley was spry, too, wasn't he?'

'Chumley *is* spry,' said Grice, quietly.

Rollison raised an eyebrow.

'Like that, is it? I was mistaken, I always thought he was one of the better men in the division but he's showing unsuspected qualities of slyness, too. I suppose he wants to keep the glory in the Division?'

Grice made no comment.

'It's a thousand pities that you can't be frank, by reason of the rules and regulations,' Rollison remarked.

Grice smiled and said gently:

'There are no rules and regulations binding you!'

164

'True,' admitted Rollison. 'But then, I'm nearly always frank with you! It's certainly a pity that we can't make a completely fresh start in this business. Seeing that I am in on the ground floor, why not let me have my head without base suspicions of personal motives and dark whisperings about being unorthodox?'

'In other words, will the police authorise you to continue to work your own way!'

'Wrong,' murmured Rollison. 'Will the police authorise the Military Authorities?'

Grice was still smiling, in spite of his sunburn and his reticence, when Rollison left his office.

Rollison felt very much more cheerful as he hurried to Gresham Terrace and regaled Jolly with the news.

'And what will you do now, sir?' asked Jolly, obviously pleased.

'I'll see Cobbett,' said Rollison. 'You'd better have a look round the clubs in the Mayfair area. Don't be too obvious but try to find out whether Gregson has been an intermediary or our man with the big brown eyes. Failing either, try to find out who has been peddling it in this part of the world.'

'Very good, sir,' said Jolly, who was used to attempting the impossible but never complained for Rollison never asked him to attempt what he would not try himself.

Still in a good humour, Rollison left the flat before his man, remembering that he had not yet had dinner. He had missed it two nights running and decided that he could safely afford an hour at his club. He managed to get a single table and thus avoided conversation. Soon after nine o'clock, he was on his way to the home of Cobbett the crane-driver. There, he was told by a sharp-voiced, middle-aged woman—his mother—that Cobbett had not been in all day and she had no idea where he might be found if not at The Docker. When Rollison tried to get more particulars about her son she closed up completely. Did that mean she knew that Cobbett would be in trouble if she talked?

He went to The Docker but Cobbett was not there.

With veiled insolence, the barman told him that Cobbett had not been in all day and the blousy barmaid, who had once inspired Keller's mob to attack a man who had waited for her after opening hours, did not even spare Rollison a glance. None of the customers appeared to recognise him.

On the other side of the road, when he left, were three familiar-looking men and, further along, another three. They were plainclothes policemen, trying to look the part of dock-labourers. That was a mistake. Thoughtfully, he strolled towards Jupe Street and was near it when a police car turned the corner. In it, he saw Chumley.

'So The Docker is going to be raided,' mused

Rollison, and was smiling when he reached the hall.

Kemp was reading in his little room. He put his book down and jumped up.

'Billy the Bull's been asking for you, Rolly.'

'When?' asked Rollison.

'He's sent that bald-headed second round several times since five o'clock,' said Kemp. 'I wouldn't be surprised if—'

Before he could finish the door opened and Billy the Bull's second danced in, squeaked complainingly that he could not waste all day and demanded that Rollison should go with him. He talked shrilly and at length but, by winks, nods and asides, gave the impression that he was aware that he was taking part in a conspiracy of great importance. Rollison humoured him and not until they were out of Kemp's hearing did the little man say:

'Billy said I wasn't to tell anyone *where* we was goin', Mr Ar, 'sept you.'

'Where are we going?' asked Rollison, patiently.

'St Guy's hall, near East Wharf,' answered the bald-headed man. 'Billy and me have bin watchin' it, like you said. Took over at three o'clock, we did. A coupla ruffians—' he brought the word out contemptuously '—tried to start a fight. A fight, wiv Billy!'

'They couldn't have known Billy,' said Rollison, quickening his pace. The little man danced by his side and soon they were within

167

sight of the wharf. There was no sign of activity for the ship had been cleared of its cargo. The WVS canteen was not there and the wooden hall, with its flimsy wire fence wrecked by the previous night's incident, looked small and lonely against the high walls of warehouses some distance behind it.

Billy the Bull was pacing up and down.

'I'm glad you've come, Mr Ar,' he said, worriedly, 'I dunno that I like it. Bill Ebbutt tole me that I wasn't ter come too close an' wasn't ter look inside but if you arst me, it's time someone did.'

'Why?' asked Rollison, hurrying towards the hall.

'Two fellers tried to start a fight,' said Billy, 'but I wouldn't 'ave nothing to do wiv' them, Mr Ar.' He was very serious. 'Soon's I looked rahnd, there was another couple on the other side've the 'all but I never seed them go in. Do yer fink we've found sunnink?'

'It wouldn't surprise me,' said Rollison.

It took him five minutes to pick the lock of the hall, under the admiring gaze of Billy and his companion. He pushed open the door and stepped cautiously inside but there was no need for caution. The only occupant was Cobbett. He had been strangled and his crumpled body lay in the middle of the floor.

168

CHAPTER SIXTEEN

THE ENDEAVOURS OF CHUMLEY

Fresh from what had proved a fruitless raid on The Docker, where all the liquor had been legally obtained and where the occupants had openly derided the police, Chumley went to the scene of Cobbett's murder. He was not in a good mood and was still sore with the Toff. He asked questions, browbeat Billy the Bull, seemed to regret that there was evidence that Rollison had not been there alone and said that he proposed to pull the hall down, if necessary, to find what was hidden there.

'Nothing's hidden here,' said Rollison. 'If there were, they wouldn't have murdered Cobbett on the premises.'

'Even *you* might be wrong,' said Chumley, sarcastically.

But there was nothing hidden in the hall nor beneath it; there was nothing to indicate that it had been used as a storage place for whisky or other contraband. The back door had not been forced; Cobbett's murderers had used a key. There were no fingerprints, nothing that might serve as a clue and Billy the Bull could give no reliable description of the men he had seen.

Chumley will try the other places now, thought Rollison, and one was bound to yield results. He stayed close to Chumley all the evening as they went from hall to hall. Kemp joined them, giving permission for the search freely. No one had the chance to tell Rollison of Craik's advice to Cobbett.

Nor did Kemp talk of his visitor.

There was nothing at the first hall.

By the time they reached the second Craik, Whiting and several other members of St Guy's had arrived with a crowd of sightseers, some of whom jeered and some looked pale and worried. The comb-out of the East End was proceeding fast; suspects were being detained and questioned.

Rollison was prepared to find the store of whisky at the hall and was wondering what his best course would be afterwards but *nothing was found.*

Kemp was relieved. Chumley was obviously disappointed. Craik was smiling, his lips quivering like a rabbit's; that might also have been with relief.

Chumley turned away from a sergeant and said audibly:

'Someone's tipped them off, that's what's happened.'

He looked meaningly towards Rollison who ignored him and walked off with Kemp. As they neared Jupe Street, Kemp asked:

'Do you think they were warned, Rollison?'

'Possibly,' conceded Rollison, 'but if there were stores of the whisky in any of the halls earlier today, or even yesterday, I don't think they could have been moved without a trace. There's something I've missed,' he went on. 'It's something fairly obvious and it concerns you. Be more careful than ever.'

'I suppose you couldn't be wrong in thinking—'

'Cobbett was killed because he might have talked too freely—he was badly scared last night,' said Rollison. 'O'Hara was killed for the same reason. You might be next on the list.'

'But what could *I* talk about?'

'Presumably nothing, yet. It's something you might come across,' said Rollison. He arranged for Grice to send two Scotland Yard men to watch Kemp as unobtrusively as possible then returned to Gresham Terrace where Jolly found him, an hour later, in a mood not far removed from dejection. As the valet entered, Rollison looked up.

'Any luck?' he demanded.

'Not yet, sir,' began Jolly, 'I

'I've been making you waste your time and I've wasted my own,' Rollison said and he went into some detail. 'I thought I had one thing sewn up and when the bag was opened there wasn't even a rabbit inside. We're being played for suckers, Jolly!'

'I can't believe that, sir.'

'I can and do,' said Rollison. 'I've reached the point where I think Kemp might be being persecuted simply to distract attention from

171

the real purpose. Note how carefully everything has been covered up. Keller—and a shadowy individual who might be Keller. Gregson taking orders one night, giving them the next. The Docker deliberately thrust into our faces—and nothing gained from the pub.'

'As you expected,' murmured Jolly.

'Yes but I did expect something from the halls.'

Jolly said, quietly: 'O'Hara and Cobbett *were* murdered, sir. I hardly think anyone would go to the lengths of murder in order to throw out a smokescreen, if I may use the allegory. Both of those men could have betrayed the leaders. That *is* certain.'

'Ye-es. Find their murderers, find the—Jolly!'

'Yes, sir?'

'Did I make a mistake in confiding in that foreman, Owen? Who else knew that I suspected Cobbett?'

Jolly eyed him steadily, seemed about to speak and then changed his mind and suggested that he should make some coffee.

'You stay where you are,' said Rollison. 'What were you going to say?'

'I don't really think—' began Jolly.

'Out with it,' insisted Rollison. 'I don't want concern for my feelings. If I've missed an obvious possibility, tell me. I'm beginning to think I have.'

'I don't think so, sir,' said Jolly, looking

troubled. 'In fact, I feel hardly justified in mentioning what sprang to my mind but, since you insist, I will tell you. You might have been wrong in confiding in Owen but he was not the only man whom you told of your suspicions of Cobbett.'

'Now, come! Chumley may be feeling sour and might have tumbled to it, but—'

'I'm not thinking of the police, sir,' said Jolly, still ill-at-ease, 'and I'm not thinking seriously of Mr Kemp but you *did* let him know that you considered last night's accident might have been an attempt to murder him, didn't you? And, if the mission halls were being used but were emptied in a hurry, it means that there was a leakage of information.'

'Oh, no,' said Rollison, blankly. 'Our fighting parson? Now, be serious, Jolly!'

He neither expected nor hoped to silence his man; in fact his words constituted a challenge and probably nothing else would have encouraged Jolly to explain his reasoning. Nettled, Jolly said:

'The truth is, sir, that we are in danger of surrendering to sentiment which prevents us from considering Mr Kemp as a suspect. After all, the trouble started six months ago—'

Rollison whistled. 'By George!'

'That was when Mr Kemp first took up his position at St Guy's,' continued Jolly, firmly. 'Moreover, although any one of a number of people might have given warning that you

173

thought the halls might be used to store the whisky, only Mr Kemp and Owen could have known that you proposed to visit Cobbett. And there is no reason at all for imagining that Owen knew anything about your suspicions of the halls.'

'The only man who always rings the bell is Kemp,' said Rollison, impressed in spite of himself.

'It *is* a fact, sir,' said Jolly, reluctantly. 'I don't know that I would have thought of it myself, except for a rather strange discovery I made this evening. I visited several of the less respectable night-clubs and at one of them an attendant was extremely impertinent—'

He paused but Rollison kept silent.

'He went so far as to say, sir,' said Jolly, feelingly, 'that I looked a sanctimonious hypocrite. Those were his actual words. He added that he did not want any more visitors who wore their collars the wrong way round during the day. In the end he apologised and told me that some seven or eight months ago a youthful clergyman was a frequent visitor. I described Mr Kemp.'

Jolly stopped.

'And the description fitted?' asked Rollison.

'I'm afraid it did, sir,' said Jolly. 'Naturally it set up a train of thought, so I made other inquiries. I learned that Mr Kemp held a curacy at one of the Mayfair churches, before he went to St Guy's.' When Rollison still did

174

not speak, he went on almost appealingly: 'I did say that our sentiments had blinded us to the possibility, didn't I, sir? In spite of what I learned, I was—I *am!*—reluctant to think that the circumstances are anything more than coincidental. Aren't you, sir?'

Rollison did not answer.

CHAPTER SEVENTEEN

HELP FROM A LADY

After some minutes of silence Jolly, looking deeply concerned, as if moved by the expression on Rollison's face, moved restlessly and asked:

'Are you feeling all right, sir?'

Rollison bestirred himself, lit a cigarette and said:

'Yes. Make that coffee, will you?'

He sat back in an easy chair, smoking, his eyes narrowed towards the ceiling. He did not stir until Jolly came in, placed the tray on a small table and turned to go.

'Bring a cup for yourself,' said Rollison.

'Thank you, sir.' Jolly returned with cup and saucer and Rollison watched while he poured out. On such occasions, it was not Jolly's habit to sit on the edge of the chair—if Rollison suggested a drink together then Jolly rightly assumed that he did not want to stand on ceremony. When Jolly was sitting back and stirring his coffee, Rollison appeared to relax.

'You're quite right,' he said, with a faint smile. 'Kemp is the obvious suspect Number One—a shattering realisation. I should have remembered that Isobel Crayne told me that she had heard him preach in Mayfair. But unless I am badly mistaken, he is developing a fondness for Miss Crayne. Both of them stood in the way of the crane-load last night and both appeared to be in equal danger. On the other hand, if he were expecting it he would have known which way to jump. A quick eye and a quick hand—he could have dodged to one side with her at the last moment and thus lent the utmost credence to the apparent fact that he was nearly a victim. I would probably have been killed and saved a lot of trouble. Even if I escaped, I would be disinclined to suspect Kemp whatever the indications. The accident might even have been planned without any thought that I might be present, solely to make the police and me look anywhere but at Kemp.'

'It is so, sir,' said Jolly. 'But—'

'If that's the truth, he had me on a piece of string,' Rollison interrupted. 'He waited until the last moment to give me a chance of pushing them aside. An unsung hero! The truth is, he appeared to have no more warning than I. I don't remember vividly but he gave

176

me the impression of being petrified as he saw the thing coming towards him. Good acting, perhaps.'

'We mustn't take it for granted that he is involved,' began Jolly, only to be interrupted again.

'We aren't taking anything for granted.' Rollison drank half of his coffee and put the cup down. 'I'm worried, Jolly—apart from the shattering possibility that Kemp's involved and the consequent possibility that I have been completely taken in, it's a very ugly situation.'

'In what way, sir?'

'If you've discovered that Kemp was once a frequenter of night clubs, don't you think the police know all about it? They must have. And they've been very clever,' he added ruefully, 'Grice was even more crafty than Chumley.' When Jolly looked mystified, Rollison went on: 'Chumley has persistently refused to admit that I was interested primarily in Kemp. Grice emphasised the point but both of them have lured me into being more than ordinarily emphatic—"Kemp," said I, "only Kemp! Nothing but Kemp!" If Grice thinks as you do and remembers hearing that from me, isn't he going to assume that I really started from Kemp in the West End and am trying to pull the wool over his eyes?'

'I suppose he is,' admitted Jolly, reluctantly.

'Of course he is! So, if Kemp knows nothing of it he's being shot at from both sides—by

177

Gregson-Keller as well as by the police. Of the two, the police are more dangerous because Kemp would have the devil of a job to live down even a temporary detention. Remember how one affected Craik! Whereas, if Kemp does know—' he broke off, standing up abruptly. 'I can't believe that he does!'

'I can hardly bring myself to believe it,' murmured Jolly. 'But the evidence—'

'Yes, I know. And how clever it would be!' Rollison went to the telephone and dialled a number. 'Hallo,' he said at last, 'is Miss Isobel Crayne in, please? . . . Yes, I'll hold on.' In a few moments, however, he was disappointed for Isobel was spending the night with friends in Caterham. After some trouble he got the number of the friends but, when he put a call through, he was told that there must be some mistake, Isobel had not been there.

'Curious,' commented Rollison, thoughtfully.

'What did you propose to do, sir?' asked Jolly.

'Get help from Miss Crayne,' said Rollison, cryptically.

'Do you propose to do anything about the man Owen?' Jolly appeared disinterested in Isobel's non-appearance at Caterham.

'I think we'll murmur a word into the ears of the police about Owen,' Rollison said. 'There's no reason why we should not be co-operative.'

Grice was not at the Yard but an alert sergeant took his message and promised to see that Owen's record was investigated. Satisfied and apparently in a better humour, Rollison went to bed.

He woke just after seven and was in his bath before Jolly made tea. At nine o'clock he telephoned Isobel again, to be told that she was not expected home until eleven o'clock. At nine fifteen, as he was about to leave the flat, Grice telephoned and wanted to know more about Owen.

'I can't tell you any more,' said Rollison, 'except that I told him I thought Cobbett might have been paid to make that mistake with the crane. Since Cobbett was murdered, Owen becomes an obvious suspect. The moment I realised that, I telephoned you.'

'The very first moment?' asked Grice, sceptically.

'Yes,' said Rollison, 'I'm getting trustful, aren't I? Have you learned anything during the night?'

'No, there've been no developments here,' said Grice.

Rollison rang off and went out. He called on an old friend, the vicar of a Mayfair church, and asked him what he knew of Ronald Kemp. He did not expect to see a frown cross the parson's good-natured face.

'What has he been doing?' asked the parson.

'Trying to put the East End to rights in a hurry,' said Rollison. 'Did you hear about his fight?'

179

'What fight?' The vicar was amused when Rollison told him but quickly frowned again. 'It isn't out of character with Kemp, Rolly, and yet—well, I hesitate to talk too freely. I suppose I can speak in complete confidence?'

'Yes,' said Rollison and added deliberately: 'Either Kemp is in serious trouble or else he's a very dangerous young man.'

'I'll tell you what I know,' the Vicar promised.

Kemp had been the curate at a neighbouring church. He was a promising preacher and, to all appearances, sincere in all he said. Then rumours spread, saying that he was a frequenter of nightclubs and that he did not behave as might have been expected of him. He was warned. He gave no explanation but continued his night-club visits and was eventually taken to task by his Bishop, a scholarly man who might well have little patience with the follies of youth.

'A pedant?' asked Rollison.

'And a theologian,' said the Vicar. 'But I think I am justified in saying that he's out of touch with the modern trend of Christianity. Perhaps another man would have had a greater influence on Kemp. In fact the discussion became heated and Kemp resigned his curacy immediately.'

'Offering no explanation?' asked Rollison.

'Not to my knowledge,' said the Vicar. 'But there is a man who might be able to give you

180

more information. I'm really telling you what he has told me.'

Rollison left, very thoughtful indeed, to visit a Mr Arthur Straker, a wealthy member of Kemp's Mayfair church. The name seemed familiar but Rollison did not place it at once.

The man was an urbane, pleasant individual who received Rollison at breakfast in a luxury flat near Hyde Park. Rollison accepted a cup of coffee and explained why he had called. Straker looked intrigued.

'Is that young rebel making trouble again?'

'Rebel?' echoed Rollison.

'There's no other word for Kemp! Had he found his right medium first, instead of coming to a wealthy parish, he might not have been one—perhaps one should have called him a misfit. It was obvious to me from the start that he would have little patience with orthodoxy. He is not yet old enough to realise that riches and sincerity can go together. Shall I say that he takes many of the passages in the scriptures too literally. "It is easier for a camel to go through the eye of a needle—"' he paused.

'Yes, I've heard the quotation,' said Rollison, drily.

'Kemp read this as meaning that it was impossible for a rich man to behave as a Christian!' went on Straker. 'He's told me so to my face!' He chuckled. 'I liked the young scamp, especially for that. Instead of resigning immediately, as I advised him to do, he

181

decided to crusade amongst the vice dens of Mayfair!'

'Oh,' said Rollison, heavily.

'In fact, he got himself into disrepute by visiting unsavoury places and mixing with some of the more hectic young people,' said Straker. 'I don't know that he did himself any harm. Unfortunately, I think he was reproached rather too abruptly about it and refused to try to explain his point of view to the vicar. His point of view was simply that only by knowing what was happening could a bad thing be fought. I'm afraid he left the parish in a very tense atmosphere and took up the curacy of St Guy's on the rebound. He went from one extreme to the other, genuinely sincere in wanting to find out how the rest of the world lived. I hope he hasn't got into serious trouble?'

'He's giving plenty of people plenty of headaches,' said Rollison, and rose to go. 'Do you think there is any likelihood of your being deceived about his good intentions?'

'D'you mean, was he really sowing wild oats and using high-sounding motives to explain himself?' Straker asked.

'Yes.'

'It shouldn't be ruled out as a possibility,' admitted Straker, 'but had that been the case, he would have defended himself more—gone to a great deal of trouble to explain himself because his conscience would have been uneasy. As it was he felt quite clear in his conscience. Since others preferred to impute the worst of motives, he allowed them to imagine what they liked. I like to think that he was more frank with me than anyone else,' added Straker. 'I often wondered if I could have been more tactful in my handling of him but I was convinced almost from the start that he was a misfit here. He has a better chance of finding his level and crusading where he is now.'

Rollison put his head on one side.

'Do you really think so?'

Straker chuckled, urbanely.

They parted on good terms and Rollison went to Mount Street where Isobel Crayne lived. She had not yet returned but he waited for less than ten minutes when she came in tempestuously, flinging her hat down as she entered the hall, calling 'good morning' to the maid who opened the door and then stopping, astonished, at the sight of Rollison in the drawing-room.

'Why, Rolly—what a surprise!'

'You're very gay for so early in the morning,' Rollison said. 'Have you been places?'

'I've had a busman's holiday!'

'I knew you hadn't been to Caterham,' said Rollison.

Her smile disappeared and she looked at him in sudden alarm.

'You haven't told—'

'I haven't told a soul,' said Rollison. The door of the drawing-room was closed and she was looking at him with an intensity which made him begin to worry. But he went on lightly: 'I got the Caterham 'phone number from your mother but was told that you hadn't been to Caterham. It was not curiosity,' he added, quickly, 'I wanted to talk to you—in fact, I want your help.'

'About what?'

'Ronald Kemp.'

'Then you don't know—' she began and broke off.

Rollison watched her frown as she looked out of the window, obviously collecting her thoughts. The sun was striking through the glass and caught one side of her dark hair, filling it with lights. But for her snub nose she would have been really beautiful; and there was the freshness of youth about her which gave her so much vitality.

'You're uncanny, sometimes,' she said abruptly. 'I suppose I'd better tell you. I went to St Guy's last evening. It was my night off and Ronald had asked me to spend an evening with him. Rolly, don't get ideas! I wasn't sure what time I would get home, so I arranged to stay at a hostel in Mile End Road. We just talked. There's something—magnificent!— about him, isn't there?'

'I once thought so,' agreed Rollison.

'Once?' Her forehead wrinkled and she

looked as if she could easily take offence. 'I don't like the way you said that.'

'I'm not going to make myself popular, I can see,' said Rollison, 'Isobel, when you first came to see me about Kemp, did you know him at all?'

She stared at him in astonishment.

'Of course not! Rolly, what are you getting at?'

'I knew this was going to be delicate,' said Rollison. 'But I can't believe you would try to put anything across me.'

Isobel said quietly:

'I don't know what curious idea you have in your head, Richard, but I don't like the insinuation. I don't know why you should worry about it but the truth is that I had heard Ronald Kemp preach in Mayfair once or twice. Later, I heard a rumour that he had left the district in a huff and I had no idea where he was going. I certainly wouldn't have come to you had I not thought that you might be able to help him. I had never met him personally.'

Rollison's eyes twinkled.

' "Richard" being reproving! Isobel, dear, Ronald Kemp is in a bad spot. The police will probably suspect him of knowing more about the goings-on than he professes.'

'Do you mean *you* suspect him?' Isobel demanded.

'All I know is that there's some circumstantial evidence against him,' Rollison assured her. 'I want to try to make sure of his real motives before going any further. That's where I want your help.'

'I'll have nothing to do with any trickery where he is concerned!' Isobel declared, hotly.

'Not trickery,' protested Rollison. 'A necessary stage in seeing that he doesn't get clobbered for something he didn't do.' He took her hand, 'I've grown fond of Ronald Kemp and really want to help.'

'What do you want me to do?' Isobel asked, reluctantly.

'When will you be seeing him again?'

'This evening.'

'Tell him that at ten o'clock, in my flat, there is to be a meeting which will solve the whole mystery,' said Rollison. 'But don't let him know a minute before nine fifteen.'

'I don't think I like it,' said Isobel. 'I think you ought to tell me more about what you're planning.'

He told her just what he planned, what Kemp's West End reputation had been and just why he wanted to make sure that there was no justification for the *canard*. Isobel heard him out without an interruption and surprised him by speaking with a wealth of contempt.

'You must be *mad*, even to think of such a thing!'

'All I want is evidence that I am mad,' said Rollison, mildly.

'And you think Ronald might come to your flat when he knows that everything is being settled tonight?'

'I think it will help to find the truth about him,' said Rollison. 'You'll amplify that story, of course—say I'm interviewing a man, *one* man, who is going to name the chief rogue.'

'It sounds beastly,' said Isobel.

'Be your age!' exclaimed Rollison. 'If Ronald's mixed up in this affair, it's necessary to find out for the sake of a lot of people—especially that of Isobel Crayne! If he isn't, then it doesn't matter a tinker's curse.'

'I suppose you're right,' Isobel said, reluctantly.

'You'll do it? Good girl!'

'I mustn't tell him before a quarter-past nine you say.'

'No—nor much later.'

'All right,' she said.

She did not say that she might not see Kemp and Rollison assumed that they had a date. If Kemp were innocent, they would make a good couple.

As soon as he reached the flat Rollison telephoned the office, to find that a message had already been received from Cracknell confirming his appointment to the official inquiry into the whisky racket.

'And what have you in mind for me, today?' asked Jolly.

'The same again,' said Rollison. 'Try to trace

the source of supply in the West End.'

'And you will operate in the neighbourhood of St Guy's, sir?'

'Can you think of a better hole?' asked Rollison.

He was at Bill Ebbutt's gymnasium just after half-past twelve but nothing of interest had come in. Ebbutt's men were keeping a watch on the Whitings. Next he saw Kemp in one of the church halls, putting it straight after the police search. He saw the Yard men whom he had asked Grice to send to follow Kemp; so that was all right. He went on to Craik's shop, which was crowded with customers, then visited East Wharf where work was going on apace, unloading another cargo.

Owen came across to him.

'Do you know anything, Mr Rollison?'

'No more than you,' said Rollison.

'I wish I could help,' said Owen. 'What's it about? I *might* be able to strike something if I knew more about it.'

'I don't see what you can do,' Rollison said, 'except tell me what happens to the goods you take off the ships?'

'Most of it's taken to the factories waiting for it,' Owen told him. 'Some of it goes into warehouses. Why, Mr Rollison?'

'How are the contents checked? I mean, are the cases opened here or are they sent off without being opened.'

'Oh, they're all marked,' said Owen. 'I—my

188

stripes! You don't think there's any *smuggling* going on?'

'Could there be?'

'If anything got past me, I'd tear my shirt!' declared Owen. 'I don't think it's likely. The Port Authority police haven't warned me, anyhow.'

'Will you keep a careful look-out?' asked Rollison.

Owen assured him he would, giving the impression that he was genuinely anxious to help.

Rollison was deliberating on his next move when a fair-haired youngster, bare-footed and dressed in a grubby singlet and patched flannel shorts, came racing towards him. The cobbles did not appear to hurt his feet.

'Mr Ar, Mr Ar!' he called and came to a standstill in front of the Toff. 'Mr Ar, Bill ses will you 'phone yon man? He ses you'd know who I mean.'

'I do, thanks,' said Rollison, gave him sixpence and went to a telephone kiosk and called Jolly.

'I'm very glad you've come through so quickly, sir. I have discovered Gregson's West End address.'

'That's good work,' said Rollison. 'Where is it?'

'The Daisy Club, in Pond Street,' answered Jolly. 'I saw him going in and a little questioning of a cleaner elicited the fact that the man whom we know as Keller is also a frequenter of the club. Another thing, sir—a bottle of the—er—firewater was delivered by special messenger this morning.'

'A bottle?' asked Rollison. 'Who on earth—' and then he chuckled. 'Oh, yes, I asked one of the girls at the office to buy me a bottle. Any note to say which club it came from?'

'There is a sealed note accompanying it,' said Jolly.

'Open it, will you?' said Rollison.

After a pause, Jolly spoke again.

'It is signed: "Mabel Bundy, Sergeant," sir, and'—there was the slightest unsteadiness in Jolly's voice—'it says that the bottle was bought at the Daisy Club, as requested.'

'Have you tried it?' asked Rollison.

'I did venture to taste it, sir. I think it is exactly the same brand as that which you brought from Craik's shop.'

'So all things point to the Daisy Club,' said Rollison, with satisfaction. 'Telephone my office, thank Sergeant Bundy for me, then come along to the Daisy Club.'

'Very good, sir,' said Jolly.

Rollison walked to Whitechapel Tube Station.

There was a faint doubt in his mind for, just as everything had once pointed to The Docker and the church halls, it seemed that they were now pointing to the Daisy Club. But this time there seemed to have been no effort on

190

anyone's part to make him pay attention to the place. The purchase of a bottle of the whisky from the club by Sergeant Mabel Bundy was quite unconnected with Jolly's discovery and appeared to have been a lucky stroke.

Pond Street was a dingy thoroughfare off Shaftesbury Avenue. '*The Daisy Club, Secretary F. Legge*', was written on a varnished board nailed to the porch at the foot of a flight of narrow stairs which were fitted with hair-carpet. Jolly was at the far end of the street and Rollison walked to meet him.

It was then that he received the biggest shock he had yet had in *l'affaire* Kemp.

In the doorway of a shop, out of sight until he passed it, two plainclothes men were standing. There was nothing unusual in seeing Yard men in Pond Street but these were the two men whom, not long before, he had seen outside Kemp's hall.

'What is it, sir?' asked Jolly, as he drew up.

'Kemp's shadows. They might have been given a new assignment,' said Rollison, 'but I doubt it.'

They walked past the two Yard men towards the Club, Rollison on edge in case Kemp was upstairs.

CHAPTER EIGHTEEN

THE CURATE AT THE DAISY CLUB

No one was on the first floor landing.

Rollison reached it just ahead of Jolly. He looked at three doors facing him and another flight of stairs. He listened at each of the doors but heard nothing. Jolly, who had gone ahead, stood at the top of the next flight, beckoning. As Rollison reached him, he heard voices.

One was quite unmistakable.

'You know very well I don't!' growled Ronald Kemp.

He was speaking in one of two rooms leading from the landing. The words *'Daisy Club'* were written on the door and there was no other notice. The closed door looked flimsy. Rollison stepped closer, standing on one side with Jolly on the other.

The voice of Gregson came next and Rollison caught Jolly's eye. He hated the implications in Kemp's visit but forced himself to listen.

'Please yourself,' said Gregson. 'You may—'

Footsteps sounded from downstairs. Rollison heard them and turned abruptly—and, on the lower landing, he saw the peeling face of Superintendent Grice. He was taken so much by surprise that he missed Gregson's next words but the shrill ringing of a telephone bell cut them short.

Grice reached the landing.

Gregson said something in a harsh voice; then there was silence in the room.

'Hallo, Rolly!' said Grice with remarkable heartiness, 'I wondered if you'd be here!' He stepped forward and rapped on the door. There was no response—just utter silence.

'You shouldn't have done that,' Rollison whispered. 'They've been warned.'

The door opened abruptly and Gregson stood on the threshold. Behind him was Kemp; "Keller," by the window was a third man who held an automatic pistol. "Keller's" right hand was in his pocket.

'I shouldn't use those guns,' said Grice, mildly.

Gregson swung round on Kemp, his face livid. The curate was staring, as if taken completely unawares.

'You double-crossing swine, you've brought the police. Why, I'd like to cut your throat!'

'That's enough,' said Grice.

Then Keller put a bullet between them and, as they backed away involuntarily, he and Gregson rushed out of the room. Rollison put out his foot. Gregson jumped over it, flinging out his hand and catching Rollison on the side of the head. That alone would not have been enough to put Rollison out but the door opposite opened and two other men appeared, both of them carrying coshes. Almost before he knew what was happening Rollison was in the middle of a furious fight, most of the time keeping off savage blows. He thought Kemp was in the thick of it, too. Grice was stretched out on the floor and Gregson and "Keller" had escaped.

Then the fighting stopped.

Jolly had one of the men gripped powerfully and unable to move and, inside the room, Kemp had knocked the other gunman out. Kemp was looking down at his victim and Rollison straightened up and smoothed down his coat.

'What the devil *is* going on?' demanded Kemp.

'Don't you know?' demanded Rollison gruffly.

'I don't! I—'

Grice, whom Rollison turned to help to his feet, interrupted him. It was not often that Grice looked angry but he did now and his voice held a harsh note.

'I think you know quite enough, Mr Kemp. What are you doing here?'

'I had a telephone call—' began Kemp.

'I see,' sneered Grice. 'You had a telephone call asking you to come to the Daisy Club this morning. You'd no idea what you were wanted for—you are just the innocent victim of a hoax?'

Kemp's face drained of its colour.

194

'That is what happened,' he said, coldly.

'I shall take a lot of convincing.'

'If you prefer not to believe me, that is your affair,' said Kemp, turning to Rollison. 'Do you know this man?'

'He's Superintendent Grice of New Scotland Yard,' Rollison said drily.

'I see that the manners of the police are alike from headquarters downwards,' said Kemp, bitingly.

Grice ignored the rudeness.

'I have a number of questions to ask you, Mr Kemp, and will be glad if you will come with me. I am not at this juncture making any charge against you but you should be warned that anything you say may be used in evidence.'

Kemp stared at him, coldly, then swung round on Rollison.

'Are you going to *let* him do this?'

'I'm afraid I can't stop him. But you needn't go, you know, although if you refuse, he may prefer a charge.'

From amazement, Kemp's expression became one of anger. He looked as if he could hardly keep his fists to himself.

'So you brought the police here. I have no objection to coming with you, Superintendent.' His look suggested that he would have liked to add that he would gladly go anywhere out of sight of Rollison who did not speak again. Grice, slightly mollified, led Kemp out of the room. Several Scotland Yard men arrived and began to search the premises.

Rollison was aware of Jolly's inquiring gaze.

'Quite a morning, isn't it, Jolly? The best laid schemes and all the rest of it. No meeting this evening, no catch, no trap. A curious business from the beginning. It's time we started work!'

One of the plainclothes men looked at him curiously.

'On what, sir?' asked Jolly.

'Disabusing the fixed police mind,' said Rollison. 'Oh, a splendid case has been built up against Kemp and it will take some breaking. Our job is to break it.' He led the way to the deserted street. A car was disappearing round the corner and against the back window he saw the silhouette of Kemp's head. He walked in the car's wake, with Jolly, until they reached Mount Street.

'Are you going to see Miss Crayne?' asked Jolly.

'As a bearer of bad tidings, yes. But also of hope. Come with me, it will save me telling the same story twice.'

Isobel received them in her father's study which she used as an office for voluntary work. She was dressed in the familiar WVS green uniform. There was restraint in her smile as she greeted Rollison and nodded to Jolly.

'Is there trouble?' she demanded before Rollison could speak.

'The police have forestalled us,' said

Rollison. 'Your young man is in a really nasty spot.'

'Did you—'

'I hadn't a thing to do with it,' said Rollison hardily. 'Kemp was at a particularly hot night-club—I should say, at its office. He was overheard talking with men who used violence on the police. There couldn't be much stronger evidence that he was associating with thieves.'

Isobel sat down, slowly.

'There *must* be an explanation,' she said, in a composed voice.

'Kemp was heard talking to them in a familiar manner and, when the police arrived, he was accused by one of them of a double-cross,' said Rollison. 'Believe me, the evidence is there. Only the stubborn pride of your young man prevented him from making convincing denials. Pride is his chief shortcoming.'

'Will you *please* say what you mean?'

'Yes indeed,' Rollison promised. 'I mean that this morning I didn't feel too sure of Ronald but now I'm convinced that he is being very cleverly framed. I think he told the truth when he said that he had been called to the club by telephone and it was done so that the police should find him there. The other men who matter escaped and seemed confident that the police won't find them. They allowed themselves to be seen going in by Jolly, presumably to get me there too. They have realised that the police suspect Kemp and are doing their best to make sure it goes further. We've a big job on our hands and there isn't much time to lose.'

'You're not just saying this to comfort me, I hope,' said Isobel, quietly.

'Now why should I try anything so foolish with a big, fine lass like you! No, this last attempt is so glaringly obvious. Kemp is being framed and it's up to us to prove it. Do you know the foreman at East Wharf?'

'Owen, you mean? Yes.'

'Do you like him?'

'He's quite an inoffensive little man, I would say.'

Rollison grimaced. 'He wouldn't like to hear you say so, he fancies himself as a he-man, a slave-driver, a—but that doesn't matter! Instead of telling Kemp about the meeting in my flat, tell Owen. He's on the overtime shift tonight but you'll have to make the opportunity yourself. Can you do it?'

'I'll manage it somehow!'

'That's the girl!' exclaimed Rollison. 'Don't let him guess that you've been prompted, drop it into ordinary conversation but try to make sure that only Owen can hear you. As for time—well, make your own. Whatever time you talk to him, tell him the meeting is due three-quarters of an hour afterwards.'

'Why?' asked Isobel.

'Because he might try to break up the party,'

198

said Rollison. 'If he does, he'll have to work quickly. In short, if he's really involved and alarmed, he'll send some of his boy-friends and there'll be quite a shiny.'

'Will *you* be all right?'

'I shall be wonderful!' Rollison assured her. 'Don't worry about me! Think of Billy the Bull.'

'Oh!' exclaimed Isobel and began to smile.

'That's the spirit!' said Rollison. 'Let's go, Jolly!'

They left Isobel still smiling. On the way to Gresham Terrace, Jolly asked whether Rollison really meant what he had said. Rollison left him in no doubt. He believed Gregson and "Keller" had seized on his interest in Kemp to fasten guilt on to the curate whose resentment was likely to create a wrong impression with the police.

'And you're throwing a party tonight,' Rollison went on. 'Billy the Bull and three or four of the heftier members of Bill's club—feed them well, don't spare the points! If Owen's our man, be ready for him.'

'Won't you be there, sir?'

'I don't know,' said Rollison, 'we haven't been able to plan far ahead in this show yet. I'll make the arrangements with Bill Ebbutt and the guests will start arriving at any time after seven o'clock.'

'I will entertain them as well as I can,' Jolly assured him. 'If you are right, sir, they are being very clever—almost too clever.'

'That's it, precisely,' said Rollison. 'Too clever by half. I don't believe in such open-handed presents to the police and when Grice is more himself I think he'll begin to have doubts, although he'll have to go on with the investigation into Kemp. On the whole, it shouldn't do Kemp any harm.'

'Provided he gets a clean bill, sir,' said Jolly.

'Yes,' said Rollison, unsmilingly. 'Yes, provided we can clear him. You know one thing.'

'What particular thing have you in mind, sir?'

'From the beginning, they wanted to get rid of Kemp. I'm assuming that he is a victim and not a conspirator! They tried to drum him out, by ostracising him. That failed. They tried to kill him by accident. That failed—and they realised that if he were murdered, it would mean a tremendous fuss. Then I gave them the idea of making Kemp the scapegoat and they didn't lose much time. They have always a scapegoat, from the shadowy Keller who might or might not exist. There's always a dummy, be it a person or a place. *Very* clever, Jolly!'

'Yes, sir. Do you think the whisky is brought in at East Wharf and distributed from there?'

'It could be.'

'I think you told me you had asked the Superintendent to give special attention to the Irish dock-workers, sir—were you serious about that?'

'Partly,' said Rollison. 'But only because O'Hara and the 'other Irishman' whom Craik mentioned, set me thinking along those lines.'

'If Craik has been a party, even to warehousing the whisky,' said Jolly, 'he might be able to give you information.'

'Yes, probably. But the odds are that none of the halls was used to store the stuff. When that theory was exploded much of the case against Craik being hand-in-glove with them was blown sky-high.'

'I suppose so, sir,' said Jolly, reluctantly.

'In other words, your advice is still watch Craik,' said Rollison. 'Yes. We mustn't forget that he tried to kill himself. You're right, Jolly, he wants watching. Lots of people want watching very closely. And we want to start thinking. If the whisky is unloaded at the wharf, it's probably taken away immediately. Therefore, lorry drivers would be involved. Who does the cartage work for the wharf?'

'A firm named Straker Brothers,' said Jolly. 'I have seen the name on a number of lorries there.'

Rollison paused.

'*Straker* Brothers? Jolly, I haven't been very good—not very good at all,' he repeated, softly. 'I think perhaps we're getting places! *Straker* Brothers,' he repeated. 'Jolly, I saw a Mr Arthur Straker this morning and he gave Kemp a very good reputation. Curious fact. Mr Straker lives in South Audley Street. Find out whether he is connected with Straker Brothers, will you? Find out, also, if the same firm do much work for any of the big distilleries. Don't try the police but otherwise move mountains to find out. *Straker* Brothers,' he repeated and went to the telephone.

After he had dialled a Mayfair number, a courteous voice announced that it was the residence of the Rev Martin Anstruther. Anstruther, who had been the vicar of Kemp's first church, spoke to him immediately afterwards and, in a quiet, cultured voice, said that he would gladly see Mr Rollison.

After arranging to go at once, Rollison went to his bedroom and for the first time in this affair put a loaded automatic in his pocket.

Twenty minutes later, at nearly one o'clock, the gentle-voiced Mr Anstruther received Rollison in a spacious room, the walls of which were lined with books and a glance at these showed him that they ranged from theology to philosophy, including works in ancient Greek and Latin. The room was warm, the carpet soft underfoot and the furniture heavy but in keeping with the study of a scholar. That the Rev Martin Anstruther was a scholar was apparent at the first sight of his high forehead and the gentle expression on his lined face. He was an academician, who doubtless had to force himself to take part in the bustle which a church in Mayfair meant for him. There could have been no greater contrast between this man and Kemp.

'How can I help you, Mr Rollison?' he inquired.

'I'm trying to help a friend of mine,' said Rollison. 'He once worked with you, sir—a Mr Ronald Kemp.'

'Oh, indeed. And how is he?' There was no animosity in the old, quiet voice.

'Very fit, very energetic—and in trouble,' answered Rollison.

'I am afraid that young man will always be in trouble until he learns discretion,' said Anstruther, with a charming smile. 'I am afraid that he was rather too boisterous for the curacy here, although I liked him very well. He was surprisingly well-read and *very* sincere. I thought his unconventional methods were unsuited to this part of London and yet—I sympathised with him. Had he stayed with me, I think he would have done a great deal of good—'

'Why did he go?' asked Rollison.

'There were several reasons,' said Anstruther. 'The main one was that in his earnest endeavours to root out vice, he laid himself open to grave suspicion of being addicted to it.' The old cleric smiled again. 'I am afraid that in the world of today, appearances count for too much. Many of my parishioners disliked being guided in their devotions by a man who, it was widely known, spent much time in the haunts of the worldly.'

There was a hint of irony in his voice. 'Finally, I had to ask him to cease his activities and I am afraid he lost his temper. A very headstrong young man. Pride will be a great disadvantage to him until he conquers it.'

'The deadly sin,' said Rollison, smiling.

'No sin is deadly in the young,' murmured Anstruther.

'A generous concession,' said Rollison. 'Who lodged the complaints against him in the first place?'

The old eyes grew sober and gazed at him steadily. Very little passed Anstruther by, thought Rollison, wondering if Anstruther was going to ask him why he wanted to know.

Instead:

'Is Kemp in serious trouble?' he asked.

'Very serious indeed.'

'And you hope I can help him.'

'I do, very much,' said Rollison.

Anstruther seemed to go into a brown study and then said:

'Several people told me that he was getting into bad company and, finally, Mr Straker advised me that the feeling against him was so strong that he would either have to cease his activities or else resign. Mr Straker's judgment is rarely at fault. I am quite at a loss to see how the information will help you, Mr Rollison.'

'It might,' Rollison said and stood up.

'Sit down, please,' said Anstruther, his gaze so compelling that Rollison obeyed. 'I have been frank with you. I hope you will be as frank with me. How can such information help you?'

Rollison pondered and then said quietly:

'I understood from Mr Straker that you, not he, had insisted on Kemp's resignation. A slip of the tongue, perhaps—or I may have misunderstood him.'

'Yes, you might have done. Look after the young man, Mr Rollison. If there is any other way I can help, please do not hesitate to let me know.'

'I won't,' Rollison promised and shook hands.

He felt the influence of Anstruther's words and manner as he walked from the house but was not so absorbed that he failed to notice that he was being followed. He gave no indication that he knew but went by a roundabout way to the flat.

The man following him was small and wiry, flashily dressed and at great pains to pretend that he was interested in everyone but Rollison. He had not been at hand when Rollison had left the flat, nor had he followed him to Anstruther's house, so probably the house had been watched.

It could only be because Straker had wanted to find out whether he pursued his inquiries.

Even then, he did not think that any bare-faced attempt at harming him would be made in Gresham Terrace although he was wary as he approached his flat and put his hand to his pocket, gripping a small automatic pistol. A taxi turned into the street and came at a rattling pace towards him. He saw the flashily dressed man motion towards its driver.

The taxi slowed down and a man in the back fired at Rollison through the open window.

CHAPTER NINETEEN

MORE OF MR STRAKER

Rollison fired back, dodging to one side as he did so. His aim was wide but so was that of the man in the taxi. As it drew level, two more shots were aimed at Rollison who aimed more carefully. As the taxi reached the corner, one of the rear tyres burst. The taxi swerved across the road. The flashy man took to his heels. The driver and his passenger jumped from the taxi as it was moving and raced towards Piccadilly. A dozen people saw the taxi crash against the curb.

Rollison turned towards the flat as Jolly came hurrying from it.

'Keep the police away, if you can,' said Rollison, 'stall them for ten minutes, anyhow.'

'I'll do my best, sir.' Jolly hurried towards the scene of the crash where a man was already pointing towards Rollison while talking to a policeman. Rollison hurried upstairs and telephoned Grice.

'I've been wanting—' began Grice.

'Never mind what you've been wanting,' said Rollison, urgently. 'A Mr Arthur Straker lives in South Audley Street. Have him watched closely and don't let him get away, whatever you do. When you've fixed that, you might send a man to Gresham Terrace to convince the constable who is shortly coming to see me that I only fired at the taxi in self-defence!'

'Fired? What taxi?' cried Grice. Rollison heard him lift another telephone and say into it: 'Come in at once, Bray.'

'I think it was the one in which I was taken for a ride the other night,' said Rollison. 'The driver has escaped. It was a daring attempt to stop me,' he went on, 'but there isn't time to discuss that now. Do find out what you can about Straker.'

'I know quite a lot about Straker already,' said Grice, unexpectedly. 'He is a director of a firm of cartage and transport contractors and some of his vans have been used for delivering—'

'Whisky!' cried Rollison, exultantly. 'what a pity we can't be entirely frank with each other! Anything on Straker himself?'

'No. We've been looking for one of his men.'

'Your man is Straker himself,' said Rollison confidently. 'Ah, here come the coppers. Hustle your sergeant over here, won't you.'

'He won't be long,' promised Grice.

Rollison replaced the receiver then looked up into the face of a youthful policeman who had entered with Jolly.

By the time Rollison had made a statement, the sergeant from the Yard had arrived—a clean-cut individual who reassured the constable and even congratulated him on using shorthand.

When they had gone, Rollison said to Jolly:

'That's Bray, the man who arrested Craik. Grice is fair.'

'Bray is having a chance to rehabilitate himself, presumably,' said Jolly who was obviously thinking of something else. 'Do you know what made the men attack you?'

'Yes. A worried Arthur Straker!'

'I thought perhaps that was the case, sir—I have been able to find out that his firm not only serves the East Wharf but many others nearby and also has contracts for two firms of whisky distillers. It wouldn't be surprising if we have found the distributors.'

'We certainly have,' said Rollison, beaming. 'Things should move fast now. Grice will have evidence against Straker but Straker won't know it yet, I shall still be his enemy Number 1. There isn't much to do but watch Kemp. They might still try to make him the scapegoat. I should have asked Grice—'

He broke off at a ring at the front door. It was Grice who came in by himself.

'Enter the bird of ill-omen,' greeted Rollison, promptly. 'Have you released Kemp, yet? If not, it's time you did.'

'We have not,' said Grice.

'Have you charged him?' demanded Rollison.

'Not yet,' answered Grice.

'You can't hold him much longer in detention, can you? Will you act in defiance of all known laws of the country and commonsense and hold on to him until he has a good chance of making you look a fool—which, usually, you're not.'

'Aren't you being a bit severe?' demanded Grice. 'You first put us on to him.'

'Yes, I know,' said Rollison. 'I thought, and think, that the young man is in great danger. And on second thoughts—' he gave Grice so charming a smile that the Yard man looked taken aback '—you're a wise old bird, William! A spark of genius makes all Yard men kin! Yes, hold Kemp. If needs be, even charge him—but keep him with you. He'll at least be safe.'

'Would you mind talking like a sane man?' demanded Grice.

'*I'm* sane,' said Rollison. 'Straker knows it which is his reason for having men in taxis and with firearms. Much evil, much hypocrisy but some radiance shining through. The power for good is greater than that for evil—but, being a policeman, you probably don't think so!'

'Why have you suddenly swung over to Kemp?' demanded Grice.

Rollison told Grice all he had learned and when he had finished Grice—picking at a piece of peeling skin—spoke thoughtfully.

'You think that Straker first had Kemp sent away from Mayfair, in order to—'

'Not sent away, driven away. He made clever use of Kemp's own chief failing, pride in himself. The same thing that made you jump to the conclusion that he was stalling. Yes, Straker discovered that Kemp was nosing about the clubs and, undoubtedly, Kemp came near to finding out something. So, what happened? Kemp was driven to the East End. Why? Because Straker, his one friend in the West End, put it to him. Early in this affair he told me that a friend had suggested that he went to see Cartwright—I think we'll find that Straker was that friend. Straker wanted him watched and also where he could do no harm. Kemp, probably not knowing that he had discovered anything that might be hurtful to Straker & Company, set about his work of reform. His passion for putting the world right got him into trouble again. He came close to making another discovery, although we don't know what. There must be something which he would find in the ordinary course of his parish work.

'Straker must have seen his mistake and tried to have him driven out, as he felt sure that there would be no danger. Just a fighting parson without a friend, a failure in society circles, a failure with the lowly. But Kemp has a basic commonsense. He made inquiries, discovered that I had a reputation for knowing his district and came to see me.'

Grice laughed. 'You aren't without vanity yourself, are you?'

'Who, me?' exclaimed Rollison, in amazement. 'Great Scott, *I'm* not proud. Very humble, in fact. As I should be; I was once half-convinced Kemp might be the rogue. However, even if you catch Straker, even if you close up the distribution of the stuff, you haven't found the source of supply. And a lot of problems will remain. For instance, in Whitechapel—someone did *kill* O'Hara, not to mention Cobbett.'

'I was wondering how long it would be before you got to that,' said Grice, sarcastically. 'Your case for Kemp is very plausible but there seems to be something you don't know.'

'Yes? What?'

'Kemp saw Cobbett at the Jupe Street hall. He appears to have been the last man to have seen him alive,' said Grice, quietly. 'The back door of the hall near East Wharf was opened with a key—your own observation, I gather from Chumley. Kemp was seen in the vicinity, a short while before you discovered Cobbett. The two men who were watching the hall for you, the boxer and his second, saw Kemp but

211

didn't think that you would be interested in him. Even without the evidence of my own ears and eyes, I should have to question Kemp. I may even have to charge him and the charge would be the murder of Cobbett. I came here because I wanted to find out if you had any real evidence that I'm wrong.'

CHAPTER TWENTY

DISAPPOINTMENT FOR A PARTY

'No,' said Rollison, after a long pause, 'I've nothing tangible. All the same, I hope you won't charge him yet. I think he's been cleverly framed, they've worked faster than I realised. You can at least hold your hand until Straker has been interrogated. Is Kemp restive?'

'Very!'

'I'll see him,' said Rollison. 'I think I can keep him quiet. Don't act too soon, Bill.'

'I can see the day out,' said Grice, slowly.

'I'm sure you won't regret it. Jolly, ring up Miss Crayne, find out if she's still at home and ask her to come here at once. If she isn't in, find out where she is. Have you traced Gregson and the man who might be Keller yet?' he asked Grice.

'No.'

'Thinking back a little, the man whom we've

never been able to find is the shadowy individual who first called himself Keller, the doer of evil deeds with a praiseworthy motive, the man who committed crimes for the sake of goodness. But he killed O'Hara and killed Cobbett. You've still got the man Harris under charge, haven't you?'

'Yes.'

'Go hard at him. He might know who Keller is. Have his friend, Spike Adams, questioned on the same lines. Trail the foreman, Owen. Get hold of the drivers of Straker's lorries and have a go at them. The presumption is that the whisky is brought to East Wharf and other wharves and a little at a time is distributed from there, probably to a lot of warehouses. It's obviously distributed to clubs and pubs quickly so there is never a hoard in any one place at any one time. That's an essential part of the whole scheme, you know. The police wouldn't be likely to worry about a few dozen bottles at a time. Will you get busy?' He spoke appealingly.

'When I've decided what's worth doing,' Grice promised. 'I'm not convinced that you're right.'

Grice left in a subdued mood.

Jolly had hardly reported to Rollison that Isobel was on the way before she arrived. She was in uniform and hatless.

'Kemp is safe for the time being,' Rollison told her. 'He'll stay safe only if you and I can persuade him to stay at Cannon Row police station for the rest of the day.'

'Are you going to let him down *again*?' demanded Isobel. 'Oh, my sainted aunt!' moaned Rollison. 'Isobel, love, I'm on his side. I tell you the only safe place for him is in the police station.'

He convinced her at length and soon they were in the little room at Cannon Row where detained persons were held. Any solicitor could get them out, unless they were held under charge. Kemp was not sullen but he was bitter and he appeared to have little time for Rollison, until Isobel persuaded him that Rollison was working for his best interests.

Rollison said: 'You could go free but more likely the police would charge you with some offence, so as to hold you. If they let you go, you'll be in greater danger than ever. And this is no time for saying that you can stand on your own two feet. You might get a satisfying sop to your vanity and a fillip to your physical courage but you're the key to the problem. We can't solve it without you, so we need you alive.'

Reluctantly, Kemp agreed.

'I'm sure you won't regret it,' enthused Rollison. 'Now, think as you have never thought before. What do you know of Arthur Straker, at your first church?'

'He was the only man who ever gave me the slightest support,' said Kemp. 'What do you

214

know about him?'

'Nothing,' said Rollison, promptly. 'I'm just checking that you think he's reliable.'

'I am *quite* sure,' insisted Kemp.

'Good. Do you know who telephoned asking you to go to the club this morning?'

'It was the man who calls himself Gregson,' said Kemp. 'I had been there before—I once tried to get the club closed down but I couldn't convince the police that it was necessary. While I was there I saw a number of people taken ill after drinking whisky. Gregson used to tell me that he did his best to make sure he got hold of quality stuff only and he rang up this morning and said he thought I would be interested to know that he had discovered how the poison reached him. So I went.

'When I got there, he asked me whether I made a profit out of helping to distribute it and then, when the police arrived—I think he *knew* you were outside—he made the conversation sound pretty incriminating. If the police hadn't been so arbitrary—'

Rollison smiled.

'You aren't the world's most tactful suspect, you know! Unbend now. Unbend as far as you know how. The police don't want to see an innocent man convicted.' Without waiting for Kemp to respond, he went on: 'One other thing. Did young Cobbett—the crane-driver—come to see you an hour or so before he was killed?'

'Yes.'

'Why?'

'He seemed badly upset,' said Kemp. 'Very remorseful about the accident. I told him not to worry. As a matter of fact, Rollison, I think you were wrong about him.'

'Make sure you tell the police that. Even if you appear to be incriminating yourself, tell them everything. After all,' he added, 'you don't want to break Isobel's heart!'

Then he left Kemp and Isobel together.

He did not think it would be long before he knew the whole truth and, at the back of his mind, there was an exasperating suspicion that he had missed something so obvious that when eventually he discovered what it was, he would be annoyed with his own blindness.

He was most concerned with Cobbett's murder. That had been a clever trick which could still put Kemp in the dock on a capital charge. Doubtless Cobbett had been sent to apologise, to allay the curate's suspicions; then had been killed near a place where Kemp would be the obvious suspect.

'And who told Cobbett?' Rollison asked himself. 'Owen?' Owen had made no move during the day to suggest that he was involved. The East End was like a city of the dead. There was a furtive, hang-dog look about most of the people whom he did see and there were more policemen in plainclothes about than was usual.

216

Passing Craik's shop, he saw the little man through the open doorway—the broken panel of the door had been replaced. Craik called after him timidly and he turned to see the shopkeeper standing on the doorstep rubbing his hands.

'I don't like worrying you, sir,' said Craik, his lips quivering. 'But—but *is* it true that Mr Kemp has been arrested?'

'No,' said Rollison, emphatically.

'Oh, it isn't! Oh, I *am* glad!' exclaimed Craik. 'I was afraid it was true, this is such a wicked affair, sir. It—it seems to affect all the best-meaning people. He hasn't been seen since this morning.'

'He doesn't have to stay here all the time,' observed Rollison, annoyed by this leakage of information. 'who told you anything about it?'

'One of my customers,' said Craik.

'Which one?' demanded Rollison.

Craik could not be sure. The shop had been crowded in the morning and the subject had cropped up in general conversation. He would not name any individual, for fear of doing injustice. Pressed, he admitted that he had been so rushed that he had not really noticed who had been in the shop. He remembered old Mrs Whiting because she had appeared to think that Kemp might be guilty of some crime.

'I soon put her in *her* place,' said Craik, virtuously.

'And so you should,' said Rollison. 'Has the story of Kemp's arrest got around much do you know?'

'I'm sure I couldn't say,' Craik answered. 'I know I haven't said anything!'

Rollison, feeling sceptical of these protestations, went to 49, Little Lane. Whiting was out but his wife was there and two of Ebbutt's men were on the other side of the street. Mrs Whiting looked troubled, asked Rollison in and then turned on her mother who came tottering into the front parlour.

'There's no need for you, Ma!'

'I got my rights, ain't I?' demanded the old woman. 'What's worrying you, now,' she shot a venomous glance at Rollison.

The younger woman looked on edge but made no further attempt to send her mother about her business.

'I've heard a rumour about Mr Kemp—' Rollison began.

'There you are,' put in the old crone. 'I knew it wasn't a lie, just because you said it was. I don't care what you say, *I'm* going to tell Mrs Parsons and—'

'If you say a word to her or any other mealy-mouthed old gossip, out of this house you go!' cried Mrs Whiting and her tone so startled her mother that the old woman sat down abruptly, gaping. 'It's wicked, it is really, Mr Rollison,' went on Mrs Whiting, nearly in tears. 'Someone has been saying that Mr Kemp is

218

under arrest.'

'It isn't true,' Rollison assured her.

The little woman's face became positively radiant.

'Oh, I *am* glad! You see?' She shot a triumphant glance at her mother.

'Where did you hear it, Mrs Whiting?' Rollison asked. 'Joe Craik told me and *he* ought to know,' declared the old crone.

'Did it come from him personally?' asked Rollison.

'From his own lips. I was the only one in the shop and he made me promise not to breathe a word,' the old woman said. 'But he didn't mean I wasn't to tell my best *friends*!'

Rollison said, slowly:

'It's much better that no one should know— you were quite right, Mrs Whiting. You're sure no one has been told?'

The younger woman said feelingly:

'I haven't let Mother go out since she told me. I didn't mean to let a scandal like that get around because I knew the minute she told Mrs Parsons—'

'You leave your mother's friends alone,' complained the older woman.

'Mrs Parsons and I are old friends,' said Rollison.

'P'raps she is and p'raps she ain't!' snorted the old woman and flounced out.

'You're so good with the old people, sir,' Mrs Whiting said. 'I do wish she wouldn't talk so much. Sometimes I think she's as bad as Mrs Parsons. Why, only this afternoon ...'

For the first time, Rollison heard of the conversation between Craik and Cobbett the crane-driver and the fact that Cobbett had appeared sincerely anxious to make amends. He wondered whether Grice or Chumley had heard the story.

After leaving Mrs Whiting he telephoned four people to find out whether any of them knew of the rumour about Kemp's arrest. They did not.

He stepped out of the kiosk, walked past Craik's shop and returned to Gresham Terrace by bus and tram, hoping that his movements were watched. He was on the look-out for further assaults but none came. It looked as if Straker had shot his bolt.

Smiling to himself, he reached the flat and rang the bell.

He was rubbing his hands, not unlike Joe Craik, when Jolly admitted him.

'Now, we won't be long!' said Rollison.

But his mood changed for Jolly looked troubled and Grice appeared from behind him, looking very grim. Then Isobel appeared from the drawing-room. She looked angry, hair dishevelled and face shiny. 'When *are* you going to make the police see sense?' she demanded.

'What's wrong now?' asked Rollison.

'Everything's wrong,' exclaimed Isobel.

'What is it?' Rollison asked Grice. 'And let's sit down and have a drink. Jolly!'

They relaxed a little as they sat down.

'At least we've got Straker,' reported Grice. 'The first crack came from the man Harris but we also caught the taxi-driver and the flashy man who followed you. He had received his orders from Straker personally.'

Rollison began to smile.

'So, they were panicking, I hoped they were when the taxi turned into the street. One grain of truth from Anstruther completely upset the applecart. Have you held Gregson and the others?'

'No,' said Grice. 'I

'Tell him!' Isobel almost shouted.

'Now what *is* all this?' demanded Rollison as Jolly came forward with a laden tray.

Grice said: 'We've questioned every man we've caught. Gregson isn't among them, nor is Keller, nor is the unknown man in Whitechapel—if one exists. They all say the same thing—that Kemp is involved down there.'

'Do they, b'God,' said Rollison.

'They must be lying!' exclaimed Isobel.

'The fact remains that we have a detailed story about practically everything,' said Grice. 'We know how the whisky was stored, how it was distributed and where it was made. Straker is in it up to the hilt and so are the others whom we've caught—and all of them implicate

221

Kemp. What is more, Straker says that Cobbett discovered that Kemp was involved and went to blackmail him.'

'Oh,' said Rollison, again. 'Cunning on the part of Cobbett—a public conversation with Craik, so as to put himself in a good light, then a little gentle blackmail. There's one obvious reason for all accusing fingers pointing at Kemp,' he went on. 'They're still covering someone else. There can't be any other explanation. What are you going to do?'

'What *can* I do but act on the evidence?' asked Grice.

'Rolly, I just don't believe that Ronald's concerned in this,' said Isobel, passionately. 'Can't you do *any*thing?'

CHAPTER TWENTY-ONE

THE MALICE OF MAN

'I'm certainly going to do something,' said Rollison after a long pause. 'Does Kemp know the latest facts?'

'Not yet.'

'When he's told, keep him away from Straker! The malice of men is an ugly thing. Straker is going down and wants to pull everyone else with him, especially Kemp who blundered in with his crusade. When you come to think of it, that's not been a failure.'

'Why are you standing there talking?' demanded Isobel, sharply. 'How can you disprove what Straker says?'

'By finding the truth,' said Rollison. 'I think we can. Don't look so down in the mouth, my love!' He turned to Grice. 'Bill, can you have a strong cordon of police flung round the Jupe Street area including East Wharf? Not one man here and there but a really large party so that, if there's a concerted rush to break away, your chaps can stop it. By now, whoever is working down there will have heard of the trouble and won't want to stay for long. I mean Gregson and Might-be-Keller, of course.'

'If you can give me—'

'More tangible evidence? I can't but it stands to reason that both men will be in that neighbourhood. All the trouble has been centred round there. You've had the whole district combed out; it isn't asking much, surely, to do this.'

'Can't you be more explicit?' asked Grice.

'No,' said Rollison. 'Chumley warned them of the danger, so they're in hiding. Now they're shouting 'Kemp' to sidetrack us. If we tell them where we are concentrating the next attack, they'll get out of the area. So neither you nor anyone else should know where the next attack will be concentrated—yet.'

'Do you mean *you* know?' asked Grice.

'I think so. And so should you, you've had

access to the evidence! And of course I might be wrong and I'd hate to spoil my reputation! *Am* I asking so much?' he added, appealingly. 'You went for Straker and lo! you were rewarded.'

'All right,' said Grice and stepped to the telephone.

'Rolly . . . ' began Isobel.

'Hush!' said Rollison. 'It's time for action. Talking's over.'

'Do you really think there's a chance?'

'We shall have your Ronald out of this spot before very long and Straker Brothers in a very much deeper one. Perhaps even the proprietors of East Wharf, too. I suppose it's no use asking you to go and see your friends at Caterham?' he added, hopefully. 'You owe them a visit and an apology.'

'I'm coming with you,' said Isobel, firmly.

'I was afraid you were. But for Kemp's sake, do as I ask. He won't want you a corpse and there *is* deep malice, not only in Straker but in the others. Kemp has completely upset their plans. He started them on the downward path and, by George, he's seeing them drop into the River Styx itself! They hate him, as they've already proved, but why should they have a chance to wreak vengeance on you? Take out your mobile canteen. Go down there to the East Wharf area where you'll get a grandstand view.

Isobel still hesitated.

'Go with Miss Crayne, Jolly,' ordered Rollison and smiled in approval when his man said: 'Of course, sir,' without even looking disappointed.

Isobel and Jolly went off. Rollison looked at his watch: it was just after five o'clock.

Grice returned from the telephone.

'That's done, he said. 'I hope you know what you're talking about.'

'So do I,' said Rollison, as they started downstairs. 'I don't think there's much doubt, Bill. The original Keller, the good old original director of operations on the Whitechapel front—that's the man we're after. The imaginary Keller, doer of good deeds.'

'What do you mean?' demanded Grice.

'Obviously, sooner or later you were going to wonder whether Kemp *was* taking the law into his own hands,' went on Rollison. 'That's why they had him lured down to Whitechapel. It wasn't my fault only that you suspected Kemp—they've been leading up to it for a long time. And their case against him will probably be pretty strong.'

'It is,' said Grice. 'Straker has crossed the *t's* and dotted the *i's*.'

'Yet he didn't convince you?'

Grice did not answer until he was at the wheel of his car and driving away from the kerb. Then he said:

'I'm open to conviction. You've done pretty well in a few days—and we'd been after

225

Straker for weeks. If you're right about one thing, why not another?'

'Oh, what a generous heart!' beamed Rollison. 'We really should work together more. By the way, do you know who the real Keller is? The man who killed O'Hara? The man who sent Cobbett to apologise to Kemp and afterwards murdered him?'

'No. Do you?'

'Yes. But you haven't heard all the evidence. The rumour that Kemp was under arrest got round. I denied it but didn't explain that he had been detained for questioning. It could only have reached Whitechapel *vide* police— who can be ruled out—or the crooks themselves. But the rumour wasn't widespread. Few people knew of it when Joe Craik told me. I went along to see the Whitings, the old hag of which family was sizzling with impatience to go round and spread the news but her daughter had stopped her. Craik told me that he had heard it from one of his customers but the only one who appears to have known of it was the Whitings' *grandmère* who said that Craik told her. She has a garrulous friend, a Mrs Parsons, who has a reputation for spreading news quicker than anyone else. Had Mrs Parsons heard about it, then it would have got everywhere. The gallant Mrs Whiting prevented that, and so gave me the answer.'

'*Craik*?' exclaimed Grice.

'Craik himself, yes. He made one mistake—he relied on the Whitings' mother to tell Mrs Parsons. He thought it safe to say he had heard from the neighbours but, thanks to Mrs Whiting, no one else knew.'

Grice said, slowly:

'Apart from the fact that we first arrested him and let him go, what real grounds have you for saying this, Rolly? He did try to kill himself, didn't he?'

'I thought so and I said so. Very clever fellow, Craik. But although I actually saw him in bed, holding the gas tube, there was one piece of evidence that I missed. Behind the bed was a hole in the wainscotting. When I found that I thought it was used to store his poison, assuming he was a secret drinker. Actually, it would have been easy for him to have staged a suicide attempt while holding the end of the tube to the wainscotting, so that the gas went out into the street. There was a smell of gas above the shop but none inside it, the point I missed at the time. Craik told one or more of his customers he would be open, then closed up. He knew that anything unusual would quickly reach Kemp's ears and wanted to be 'seen' in the middle of a suicide attempt. Pretty smart, wasn't it?'

'If you're right, he's capable of anything.'

'Of all that's happened, yes. Of course, O'Hara knew that he was a party to the crime, that's why Craik killed O'Hara with his own knife. Then he had to make it look as if he were being framed. First, the threats against the Whitings, to stop Whiting from talking. Then a message through Harris, who admitted having stolen the knife—you can bet he was handsomely paid for that 'confession'! Next, information leaked to Chumley through the unknown Keller, a man who doesn't exist but who has been built up to create the right impression.'

'What about the man who calls himself Keller?' demanded Grice.

The rest of the journey to Whitechapel passed in silence.

At the far end of Jupe Street stood the WVS mobile canteen with a view of the street and of the wharf. The wharf appeared very busy and Grice drove past Craik's shop and to the wharf where a tight-lipped Chumley appeared.

'Is everything set?' asked Grice.

'Yes, sir,' said Chumley, sending a resentful look at Rollison. 'When do you want the men to close in?'

'We won't necessarily want them to close in,' said Rollison. 'We want to make sure that no one can get out. Isn't that right, Superintendent?'

'Yes,' said Grice.

'Perhaps you wouldn't mind telling me who I ought to be looking for,' said Chumley, sarcastically.

'Gregson and Keller, of whom you have

228

descriptions,' said Grice. 'And the man who let himself be talked of as Keller.'

'*I* think that was Kemp,' declared Chumley.

'That's what you were intended to think,' said Grice. 'Mr Rollison and I are going to Craik's shop. Have two or three of your men keeping an eye open there.'

'Craik!' gasped Chumley.

'The man Sergeant Bray arrested and whom you later released,' murmured Rollison.

Grice turned the car and drove to Craik's shop. He and Rollison hurried into the shop, catching Craik by surprise as he stood behind the counter with a thin knife in his hand; it was poised over some tinned pork, for two waiting customers.

'Why, good afternoon!' said Craik, round-eyed. 'I hope—'

'It's no use, Keller,' said Rollison. 'We know who you are.' He was almost taken by surprise by the other's speed. Craik swung his right arm, slicing the air with the knife. Rollison backed swiftly, picked up a tin from the counter and flung it. The customers screamed. The tin caught Craik on the side of the head and made him stagger against the shelves. Rollison darted through the gap in the counter and to the stairs. By the time two of Chumley's men were holding Craik and Grice was coming after Rollison, there were footsteps above their heads. Rollison put his shoulder to the door of the back bedroom and broke it down.

As he stood aside, a bullet came from the window.

'Look out!' he shouted.

He could not see into the room as he stood against the door, taking his automatic from his pocket. Then the door swung back a little and he saw two men by the window, one climbing out, and the other—Keller—standing still, his gun pointing towards the door.

Rollison fired through the crack.

The shot went wide but distracted Keller's attention. Rollison pushed the door open wider and fired as the other tried to reach the window. Keller lost his grip on his gun and Grice leapt at him but by then Gregson was out of sight.

Rollison looked out of the window down into the narrow yard.

Gregson was standing in the middle of it, not certain what to do. Two plainclothes men were approaching rapidly. Gregson turned and made as if to enter the shop by the kitchen door but two more policemen entered the yard from there. Gregson looked right and left desperately but there was nothing he could do. Rollison called down to him.

'Make up your mind, Gregson!'

The vicious expression on Gregson's face was made absurdly meaningless as the police closed on him from both sides.

Rollison turned back to the room.

Keller, who was not badly wounded, was

glaring at him. His fine brown eyes were filled with malignance but he no longer looked impressive.

'Now all we need to know is why they were so anxious to frame Kemp,' Rollison said.

'Surely because he could lead to Straker,' Grice suggested. 'Much more likely that Kemp actually knew something without realising its significance,' said Rollison.

He broke off outside the door of the bedroom where he had seen Craik apparently on the point of killing himself. On the bed were several books which looked like ordinary ledgers. He went closer. One was marked:

St Guy's Poor People's Relief
Fund

Another was marked: '*Church Reconstruction*', a third: '*Church Accounts*'.

'Now what have you found?' demanded Grice.

'The thing we wanted, I think,' said Rollison, opening one of the pages. 'Yes—end of fiscal year for St Guy's—July 31st. In about a week, the accounts would have had to be shown. *Honorary Treasurer*—Joseph Craik, Esq.' He turned over some of the pages, smiling oddly. 'Many, many entries,' he went on. 'Almost certainly the records of the whisky transactions. As the old Vicar was so ill, Craik had everything under his own control. This looked quite safe until Kemp came along. The day was fast approaching when Kemp would want to see the accounts. Falsified accounts—not smaller but infinitely larger than they had any right to be. Obviously it was essential that Kemp should not come across them until dummy accounts had been made up. You certainly find him everywhere,' Rollison added, heavily.

'Find who?' asked Grice.

'The Devil,' said Rollison. 'Ever heard of him?'

'You're an unpredictable fellow,' remarked Grice. 'I wish—'

What he wished was not voiced for there were hurried footsteps outside and a man burst through the shop. As he did so there were sounds from further away, shouting, crashing, banging noises, as if Bedlam had been let loose.

'What is it?' called Grice.

'There's trouble at the wharf, sir!' gasped the man. 'Some of the dockers have started a riot there's hell-let-loose, sir!'

'Nothing unpredictable about me,' said Rollison, as they rushed downstairs. 'You can guess what's happened?'

Grice did not answer but ran through the shop where Craik was standing with his lips quivering, already handcuffed. Grice flung himself into his car and Rollison scrambled in as it moved off. As they approached the end of

Jupe Street and the wharf, he saw that the mobile canteen was in the middle of a heaving mass of people. Standing inside it, with Isobel, Jolly was lashing out with what looked like a tea-urn.

The loudest of the voices had an Irish brogue.

'Someone spread the rumour that the canteen attendants were demanding the sack for the Irish,' a nearby policeman said. 'If they get hold of Miss Crayne—'

Rollison's face was bleak.

CHAPTER TWENTY-TWO

'LET'S BLAME THE IRISH'

The police among the seething mass were heavily outnumbered. Bricks and stones and staves of wood were being used, heads were being cracked and now and again a part of the crowd surged forward as people fell with arms and legs waving, voices screeching in fear and terror. Nearer the wharf, a horse and cart was standing and the horse was squealing with terror and rearing up.

Grice drove as near as he could.

'We'll have to walk,' he said.

'Walk if you want to,' said Rollison, white-faced. He was more than a hundred yards from

233

the canteen and he knew that Jolly would not be able to stand out much longer. The main attack was undoubtedly directed towards the canteen. Buns and sandwiches were being flung in all directions and cups and saucers were hurtling through the air.

Grice got out.

Rollison slid into his place and raced the engine, startling the people nearest him. They scrambled out of his way. He edged the car forward and Grice appeared at the other door, suddenly, and climbed in again. A man cuffed his head, another caught his finger in the door as it slammed and howled with pain. Grice opened the door and caught a glimpse of a man's thumb, dripping blood, and a face which had gone white. The face dropped away. Rollison drove the car faster, bumping three people out of the way. He wound up his window as someone smashed a stave against it. Grice locked his door. The surging crowd surrounded the car but Rollison would not let them stop him. When half a dozen people put their weight against the radiator and the bumper he raced the engine and forced them aside. Men clung to the running-board, one sitting on the bonnet, battering at the windscreen with his fists. Rollison ignored him, craned his neck and managed to keep the canteen in view.

A giant with a crop of red hair was leaning over the counter and had caught Jolly's wrist.

He was trying to pull Jolly into the crowd. Isobel was battering at his head with an enamel jug. A second man clutched her wrist and she snatched up a knife from behind the counter.

The man let go.

'Good for Isobel!' said Rollison.

The canteen was still twenty-five yards away and the crush around it seemed to be too great even for the car to get through. Tight-lipped, he sent two men down; they were dragged aside. The crowd swayed away and he was able to make another ten yards; then another ten.

The red-haired man had disappeared but two others were tugging at Jolly and now one man had his fingers buried in Isobel's hair. Not far away, someone was swinging a stick but he was a short fellow whom Rollison could not see properly. He seemed to be battering his way towards the canteen. Two uniformed policemen were battling towards it.

The car reached the canteen, drawing up only two yards away from it. A dozen people were battering at the doors. Tight-lipped and pale, Rollison drew his automatic.

'Be careful!' Grice snapped.

'Careful be damned!' Rollison brandished the gun and it was enough to make the nearer men back away. He opened the door and leapt towards the canteen counter. Using the gun as a club, he cracked it on the heads of the men tugging at Jolly, forcing them to relinquish

235

their grip. He struck the man who was pulling Isobel's hair and heard the crack of the blow. The man dropped back and Isobel drew away, brushing the hair out of her eyes.

Rollison vaulted over the counter, nearly knocking Jolly over, and swung round, pointing the gun at the crowd. Grice joined in, the four of them a tight fit inside the canteen.

There were hundreds of men in front of them, roaring, swearing, cursing.

Above the din, Rollison could hear the stentorian voice of Foreman Owen. It was he who was brandishing the stick and forcing his way up. He burst through, and turned to face the crowd.

'Get back to work, you . . .' he roared. 'Get back, if a mother's son of you stays another minute, I'll—'

What he was going to add was drowned in another roar but it was caused by a different crowd, coming down Jupe Street—and, in the van, Rollison saw Billy the Bull and Bill Ebbutt. The members of the gymnasium club were coming in a solid phalanx, pushing everyone before them. Soon, the malice of the crowd was turned towards them.

By now the police had been reinforced and were appearing along side streets and from the wharf. Rollison, gasping for breath, watched the riot subside as the men began to slip away, many returning to the wharf. Owen chased after them, yelling his head off.

Rollison turned to Isobel.

'There's your mild little man,' he remarked.

Isobel laughed, in spite of herself. Her face was scratched and a few strands of hair had been torn out but she was not seriously hurt. Jolly had an ugly gash in his right cheek and his wrists were swollen but he was smiling as he watched the crowd moving away.

'I was getting a little perturbed, sir,' he admitted.

'I was scared stiff!' said Rollison. 'I bet Kemp will be sorry he missed this one. He's in the clear, by the way.'

Isobel stared.

'By the way!' she echoed.

'Well, in a manner of speaking,' smiled Rollison. 'He'll be out within an hour, I should think. Eh, Bill?'

'Yes,' said Grice. 'Why on earth did *this* begin?'

'As I understand it, sir,' said Jolly, 'there was a sudden outburst of trouble at the wharf. A party of Irish were abused by some of the others and that started a free fight. It spread very quickly—the Irish have a reputation for being bellicose, as you probably know.'

Grice frowned. 'The Irish—'

'Oh, let's blame the Irish, by all means!' said Rollison, taking out cigarettes and proffering them. 'But let's be serious, Bill. The fact that a police cordon had been flung round a wide area leaked out—as it was bound to. Craik and the others tried a diversion. There's bad blood between some Irish dockers and some English and it never takes much to start a fight, as Isobel and I saw the other evening,' he added.

'There *are* often scuffles,' admitted Isobel.

'Yes. The easiest way to start a row is for an Englishman to call an Irishman in England a neutral,' went on Rollison. 'Our pretty bunch had always tried to draw attention to the wharf and the Irish workers. Today, they had a new idea and tried to cause trouble for Isobel. However, the distraction didn't work, we went to Craik too quickly.

'Craik!' exclaimed Isobel.

Rollison smiled but Grice did the explaining for Rollison was suddenly besieged by members of the club who wanted to know what it was all about.

*   *   *

The whole story, checked and cross-checked, was not known for the better part of a week but the essentials were known before the following day was out.

Every effort had been made to make it appear that the illicit whisky came in at East Wharf, whereas it was actually made at several depots of Straker Brothers Cartage and Transport Company. The depots were also distribution points throughout the country. Crates of the illicit whisky were delivered with the genuine cases but since the buyers knew where to look for it, there had been no danger of that fact leaking out.

From the beginning, Craik had been in charge of the Whitechapel district. Gregson's companion *was* named Keller but the name had also been used by Craik to cover an imaginary character behind which he could hide and, which had been planned, would help to frame Kemp. Gregson and the real "Keller" had been the managers for the whole of the East End, going further afield in some cases, and also handling the West End sales from the Daisy Club. Craik had used the St Guy's records to cover his own, thinking that he would not have to show them until Cartwright was better and always putting off making dummy church accounts. The arrival of Kemp had put Craik in danger but Kemp had first been a threat in the West End.

Straker had believed him to be working on it because he suspected who was behind it—a suggestion which Kemp dismissed airily, on the following morning.

'I had no idea he was in any kind of racket. He had always impressed me as being a very sound fellow.'

'As did Craik,' said Rollison.

Kemp frowned. 'Ye-es. Oh, I know they hoodwinked me but Craik always seemed such a sincere little man, timid as they come.'

'Moral—don't confuse timidity with

humility,' advised Rollison, sitting back in his favourite chair. 'The truth was that you prod-nosed to such good effect that you had them badly worried. As you were likely to be much easier to handle in the East End, Straker did a little sales-talk and there you went. The question is—are you sorry you went to St Guy's?'

'Great Scott, no!' cried Kemp. 'I wouldn't be anywhere else for the world!'

'You mean that?'

'I do,' said Kemp, fervently. 'I don't mind admitting that I decided to go down there feeling something of a martyr and with a great spirit of self-sacrifice but—' he shrugged, 'give me people like Billy the Bull, Bill Ebbutt, the Whitings—oh, there are hundreds of them. D'you know, Rolly, since I've been down there and seen the conditions under which they live, the marvel is that they *are* such a decent bunch.'

'My way of thinking for a long time,' said Rollison.

'The trouble is, there's such a gulf between them and the rest of London. I mean—'

'No gulf that can't be crossed,' said Rollison. 'Our job is to help 'em bridge it. It'll be nice to have some help, eh, Isobel?'

'*You* don't need much help,' declared Isobel Crayne.

'Oh, come! Without Jolly I'd be lost—wouldn't I, Jolly?'

'I very much doubt it, sir,' said Jolly coming in with a tea-trolley, 'but it is always a great pleasure to work with you on these little excursions—or, one might say, these aberrations from the normal.'

'Yes, mightn't one?' murmured Rollison.

'Oh, did I tell you?' asked Kemp, shortly afterwards, munching a muffin with a great show of nonchalance and carefully avoiding Isobel's eye, 'Isobel and I have decided that as we're both rather fond of the district and the people, and two together can probably do much more than one—I mean—well, we've decided—'

'Fast workers, both of you,' smiled Rollison. 'I'm delighted. The others will be, too.'

'Others?' asked Isobel.

'All your little brothers and sisters East of Aldgate Pump!' said Rollison, grandly.

On the Sunday morning following the riot, he went to St Guy's with Jolly and took up a stand at a point of vantage near the entrance to the churchyard. Keeping out of sight behind some shrubs, he watched the cavalcade approaching. Rarely had the narrow streets been so crowded at that hour.

Children with red and shining faces and shoes newly-cleaned, women heavily made-up and wearing all their finery, men with carefully brushed hats, newly-pressed suits and highly polished shoes, all followed on. Many of them had a self-conscious air but not the Whitings, who were glowing with happiness, nor Owen, who was never likely to feel out of place.

Jolly nudged Rollison.

Striding along with his diminutive second was Billy the Bull, wearing an old-fashioned bowler hat with a curly brim, light brown shoes and a bright blue suit. Now and again, he looked over his shoulder, almost furtively. Nearby was Bill Ebbutt, his face now almost normal, with his wife, in 'Army' uniform, striding out beside her—she looked as if she would soon burst into huzzahs. Red-haired Irishmen, puny-looking Cockneys, dark-skinned Lascars and almond-eyed Chinese mixed freely with the others.

Rollison nudged Jolly.

Walking alone and certainly self-conscious, but putting a bold face on it, was Inspector Chumley.

Soon afterwards, a taxi drew up and from it alighted the venerable figure of the Rev Martin Anstruther. After him, hurrying with the stragglers, came Isobel in her WVS uniform. She went inside, breathlessly.

'A good show,' murmured Rollison. 'We'll be lucky to find a pew.'

They did not find one but chairs from one of the halls had been brought in. The sidesmen were busy, bustling and perspiring, and one hoped Rollison and Jolly would not mind sharing a hymnal. Soon the Rev Ronald Kemp began to take the service. His powerful voice was pitched low, as if he were also self-conscious. His damaged eye was no longer badly swollen but was of many colours. When at last he went into the pulpit and began his sermon, he chose to preach on pride—the deadliest of sins; and he did not pull his punches. As he talked, his voice grew more powerful and he completely lost himself.

Afterwards, Anstruther caught a glimpse of Rollison and smiled and cocked a thumb, a surprising gesture from the old man. Isobel was beaming. The *grande dame* of the Whiting family declared audibly, and with a sniff, that he *could* preach—and she supposed that was something.

Chumley hung back until he saw Rollison.

'I'm sorry we didn't see eye-to-eye, Mr Rollison,' he began.

'Bygones are really bygones,' declared the Toff. 'You and Kemp ought to swap ideas.'

'He'll probably force his on me!' said Chumley, wryly. 'And so,' said Rollison to Jolly, as they made their way homewards, 'everything in the garden is lovely until Old Nick pops his head up again.'

Jolly smiled, benignly.

'If I may use the expression, sir, I think that when he does, Kemp will dot him one vigorously. Don't you agree sir?'

We hope you have enjoyed this Large Print book. Other Chivers Press or Thorndike Press Large Print books are available at your library or directly from the publishers.

For more information about current and forthcoming titles, please call or write, without obligation, to:

Chivers Large Print
published by BBC Audiobooks Ltd
St James House, The Square
Lower Bristol Road
Bath BA2 3BH
UK
email: bbcaudiobooks@bbc.co.uk
www.bbcaudiobooks.co.uk

OR

Thorndike Press
295 Kennedy Memorial Drive
Waterville
Maine 04901
USA
www.gale.com/thorndike
www.gale.com/wheeler

All our Large Print titles are designed for easy reading, and all our books are made to last.